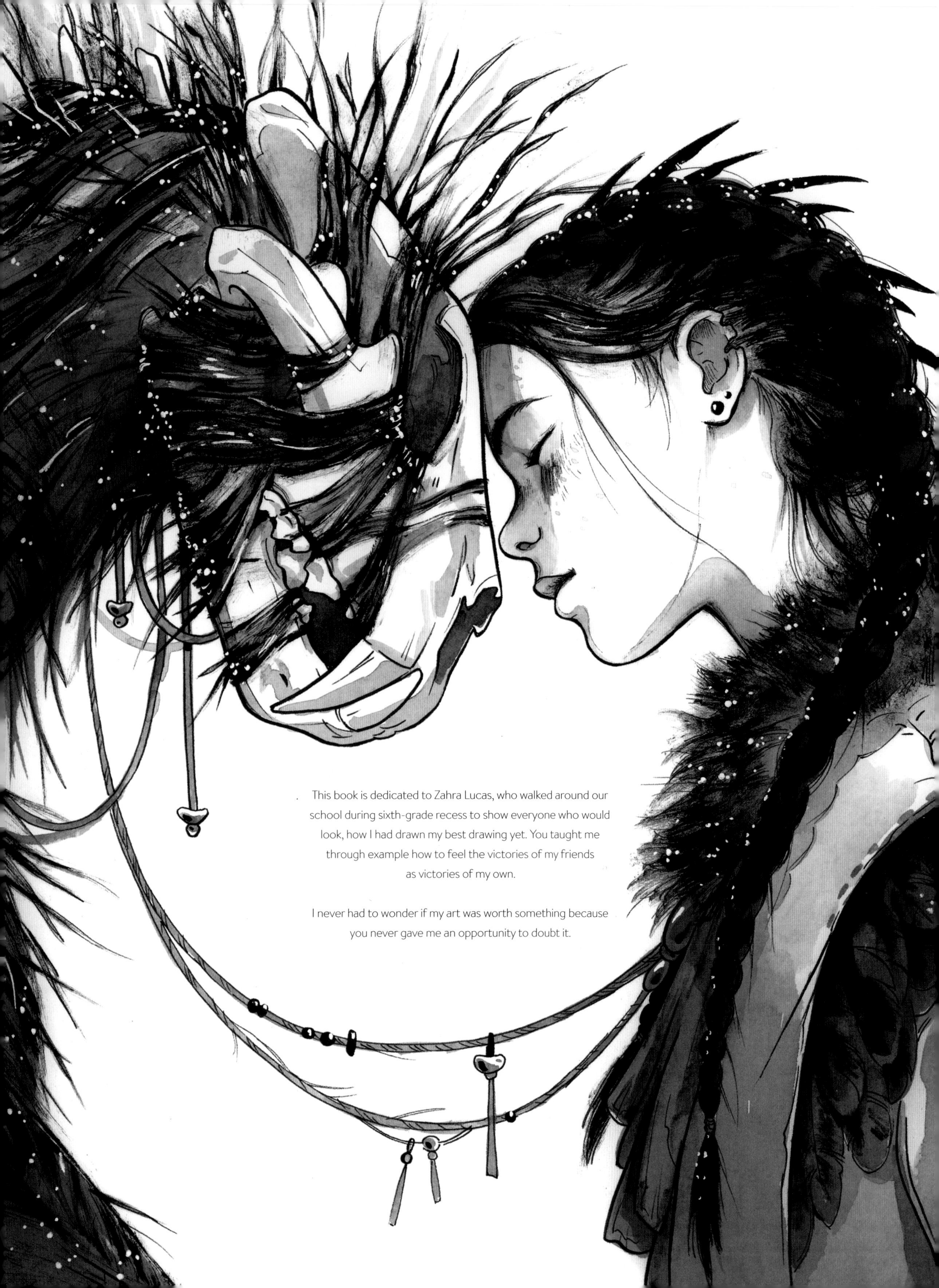

This book is dedicated to Zahra Lucas, who walked around our school during sixth-grade recess to show everyone who would look, how I had drawn my best drawing yet. You taught me through example how to feel the victories of my friends as victories of my own.

I never had to wonder if my art was worth something because you never gave me an opportunity to doubt it.

3dtotal Publishing

Website: www.3dtotal.com
Correspondence: publishing@3dtotal.com

First published in the United Kingdom, 2021, by 3dtotal Publishing.

Address: 3dtotal.com Ltd, 29 Foregate Street, Worcester, WR1 1DS, United Kingdom.

Hard cover ISBN: 978-1-912843-46-6
Printing and binding: Leo Paper Products Ltd. www.leo.com.hk

Visit www.3dtotalpublishing.com for a complete list of available book titles.

Managing Director: Tom Greenway
Studio Manager: Simon Morse
Lead Editor: Samantha Rigby
Lead Designer: Fiona Tarbet
Editorial Project Manager: Sophie Symes

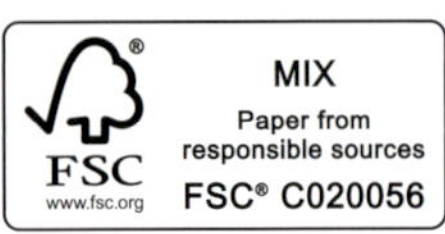

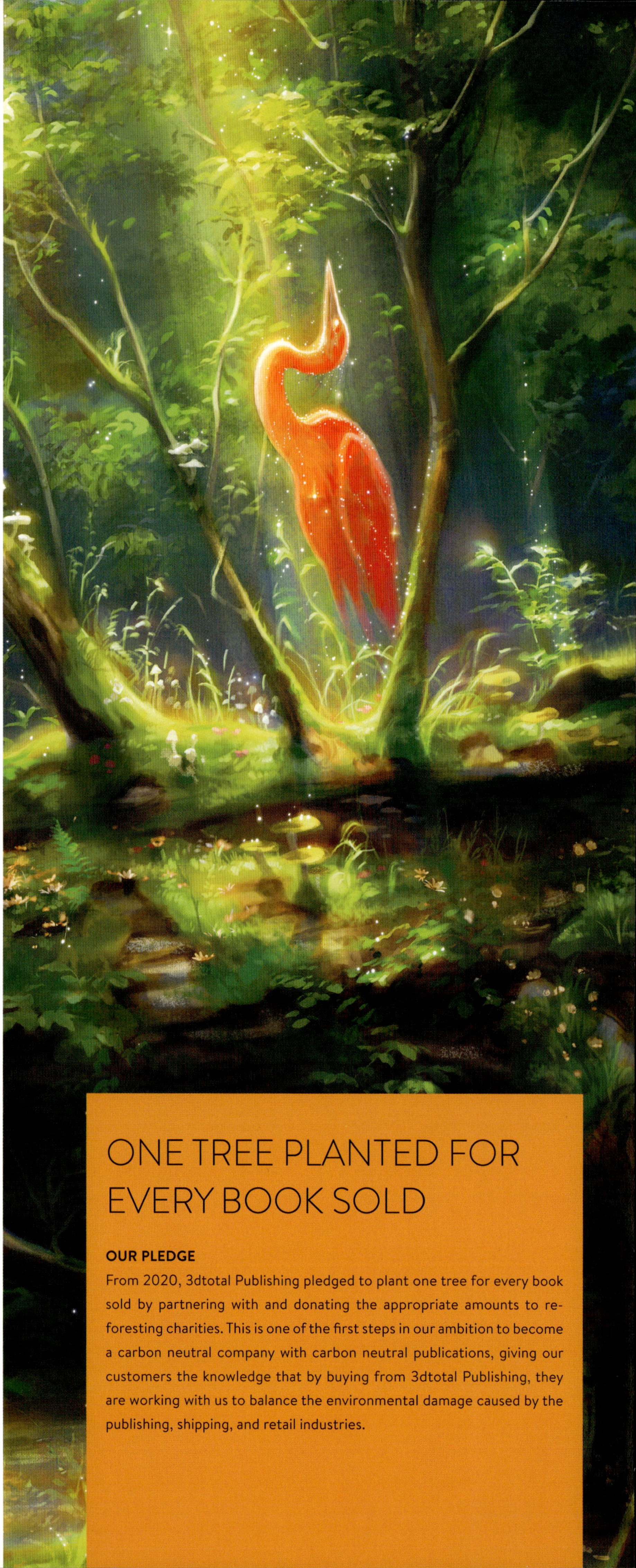

ONE TREE PLANTED FOR EVERY BOOK SOLD

OUR PLEDGE

From 2020, 3dtotal Publishing pledged to plant one tree for every book sold by partnering with and donating the appropriate amounts to re-foresting charities. This is one of the first steps in our ambition to become a carbon neutral company with carbon neutral publications, giving our customers the knowledge that by buying from 3dtotal Publishing, they are working with us to balance the environmental damage caused by the publishing, shipping, and retail industries.

CONTENTS

FOREWORD

As a teacher, I can't help but be thrilled to watch a former student rise above and beyond what I have to offer. Devin Elle Kurtz studied with me several years ago and has returned with this volume of brilliant images.

It's in my nature to get deeply excited about the technical distinction of the works here, but it's the effectiveness of how they're used that means the most. The draftsmanship is not just correct, it's effective. The contrasts are not just glittery and decorative, they're used to create meaning. The temperatures aren't just warm and cool because they look good together, rather they stage and give meaning to the subject. And the local colors of the objects and characters aren't random; they're designed with purpose. The words "design" and "purpose" are so important. Design means to visually communicate, to speak in a language that every human being can understand. To make sure that every line, shape, edge, and color is designed in support of the greater purpose of the image. The art teacher in me is thrilled to see images designed effectively and with purpose.

At the same time, when I look at the images in this book, it's through the eyes of my professional career. I'm someone who did not understand visual communication and storytelling well enough when I began my career twenty-five years ago as an animation artist. I learned very painfully that my work had to drastically improve to emotionally connect with the greater audience. Those lessons were hard-learned, and I admit I'm a bit envious of Devin so quickly grasping the importance of the emotional connection to the audience.

The special place of artists and storytellers is that they have the ability to create experiences we don't get in our everyday lives; we have to go to someone like Devin, who has sharpened her skills to the point where she is actively able to engage our imagination. We can never go to or see a place in real life like the visions portrayed here, and so we have this book!

And as to the subject of windows, there are few subjects more literally and symbolically compelling. We all spent a portion of our childhood staring out of the window, dreaming of being somewhere else and doing something more exciting. Windows have always been a canvas for our imagination – where we are is the ordinary, but outside the window lies endless possibilities.

For all of these reasons, I love this book! I hope you enjoy it as much as I have.

NATHAN FOWKES
INSTRUCTOR & CONCEPT ARTIST AT DISNEY, DREAMWORKS, BLUE SKY STUDIOS & PARAMOUNT

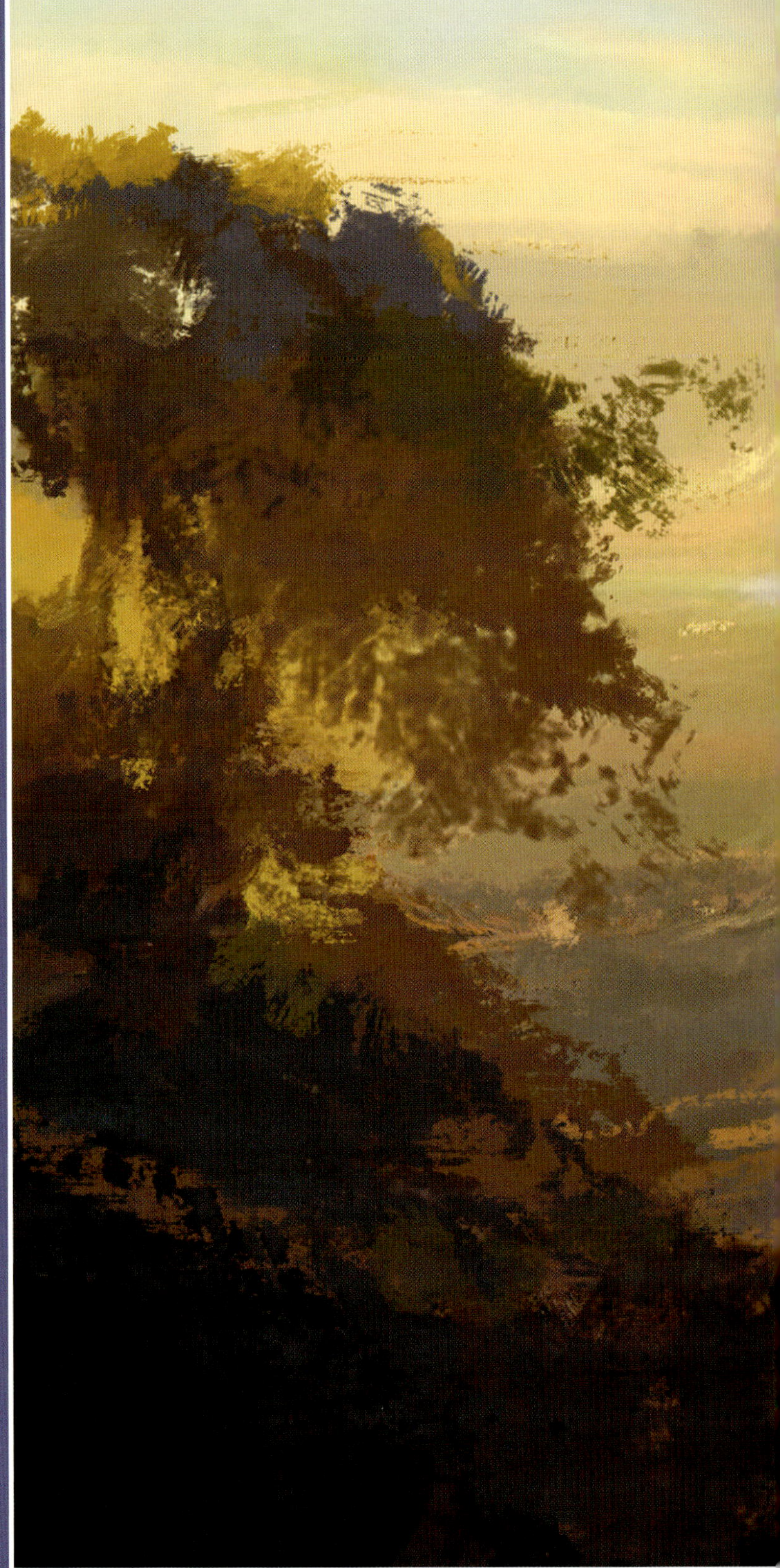

DUSK CASTLE / NATHAN FOWKES, DIGITAL, 2016

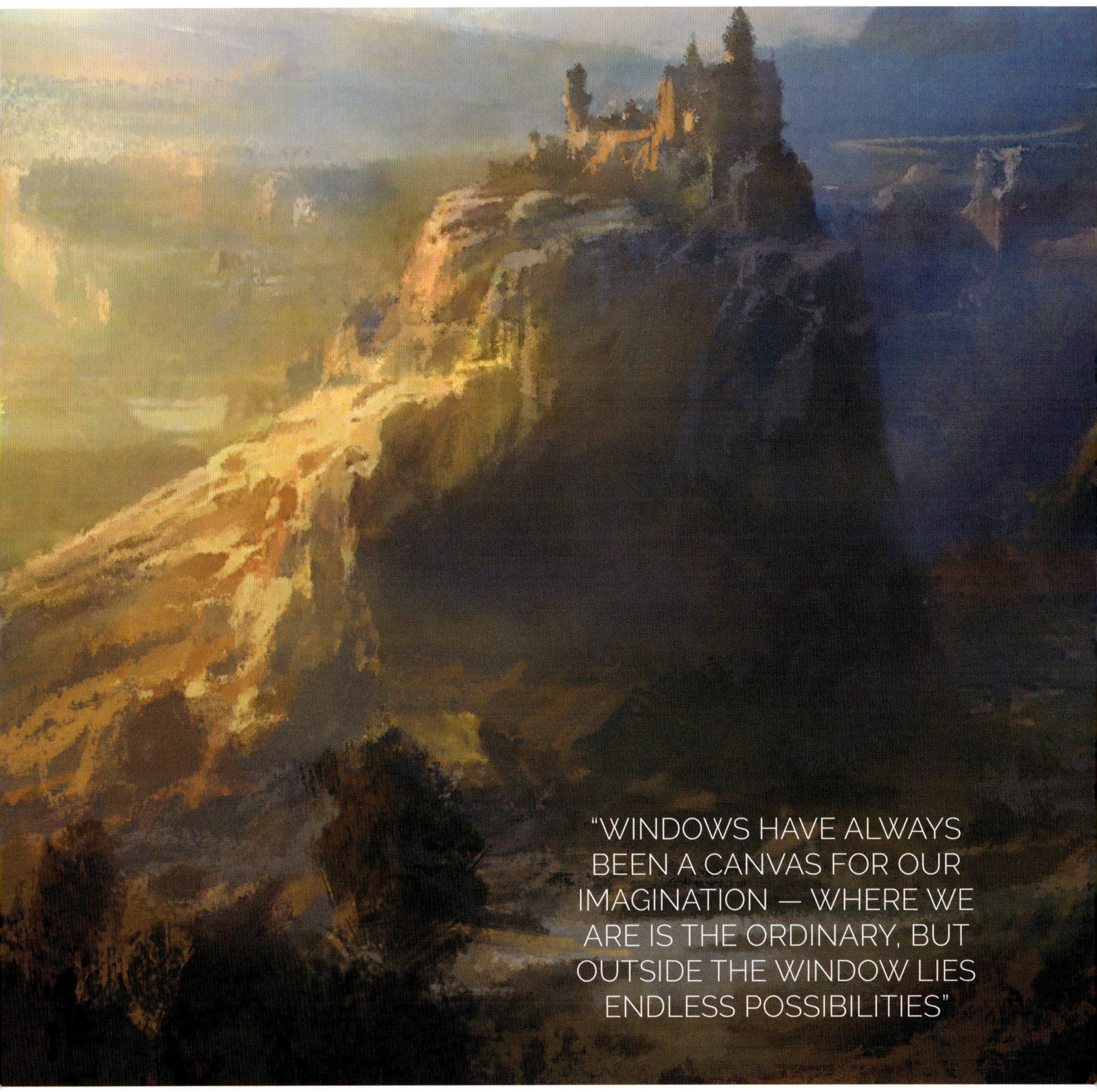

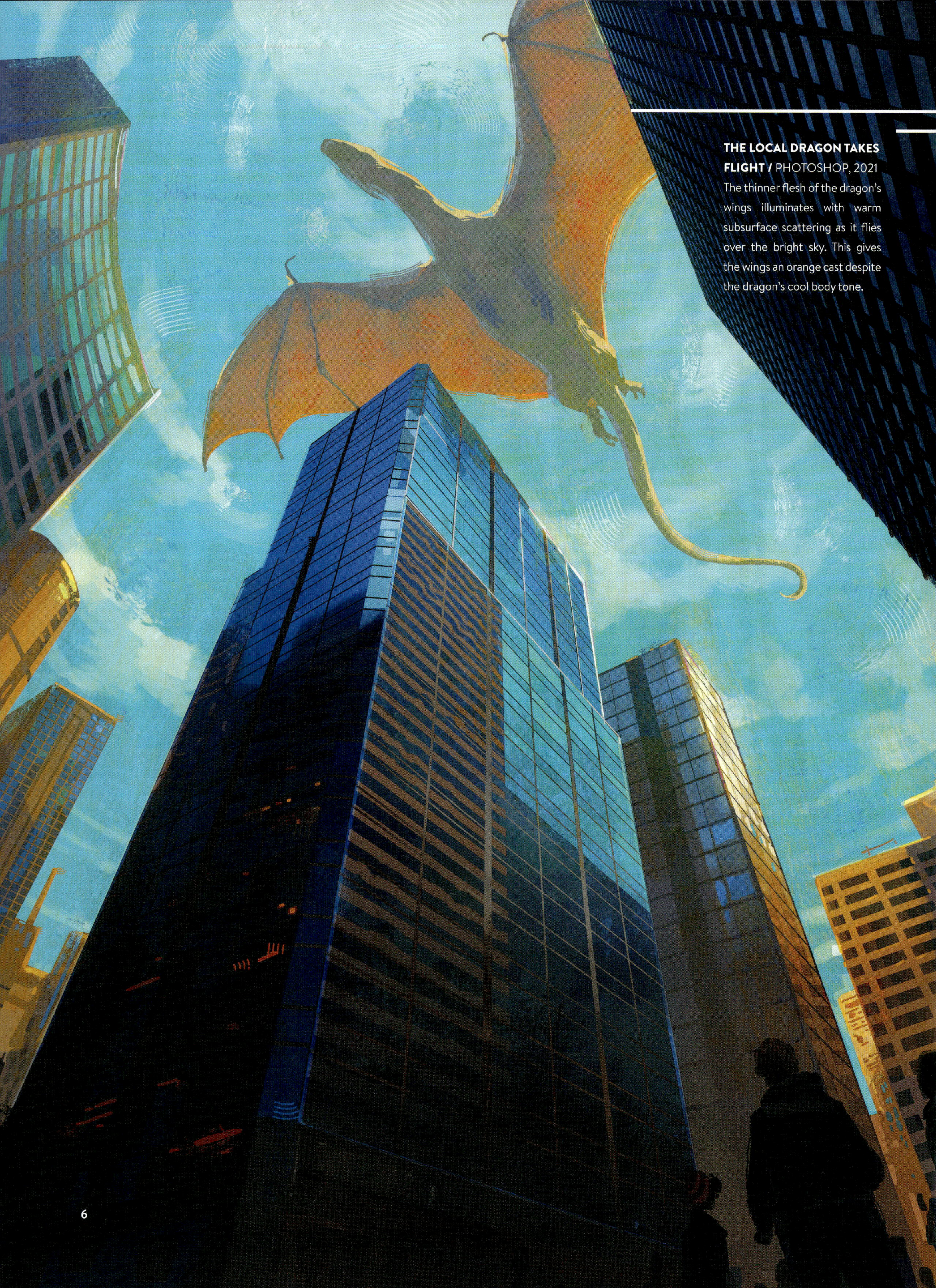

THE LOCAL DRAGON TAKES FLIGHT / PHOTOSHOP, 2021
The thinner flesh of the dragon's wings illuminates with warm subsurface scattering as it flies over the bright sky. This gives the wings an orange cast despite the dragon's cool body tone.

INTRODUCTION

When I was eight years old, my mom took me to see an animated movie called *Howl's Moving Castle* by Studio Ghibli. There's a moment in the movie when the titular character Howl shows Sophie, the hero, a new destination on his magical door that transports them from location to location with just the flick of a dial. Something about this scene enchanted me in a deep and reverent way. The door that is a portal to a haunting warzone of otherworldly airships and rippling fire is also an entryway to a field of wildflowers, and a stream so serene it can only be described by the orchestral score that plays during the scene. This movie enchanted me not only through what it told me, but also what it didn't tell me. There was no omniscient narrator who explained either the bomb-rattled warzone or the serene mountain meadow. The viewer isn't told why there's a war, nor what's taking place during the dream-like battle scenes; there is no exposition through narration nor dialog. We are a ghostly visitor in a tumultuous and magical world, and it feels much more real as a result. It's presented without explanation, without indication that there might be a person who lives anywhere other than in this ethereal world. *We* don't exist there. We're just watching these people live their lives through the glowing window of the theater screen. It didn't feel like a story to me; it felt like a real, genuine peek into a rich fantasy world that couldn't be anything other than truly alive.

I rapidly devoured everything Studio Ghibli created in the months following that trip to see *Howl's Moving Castle* at the Del Mar Theater. The films left me feeling a type of awe that was difficult to describe. They encapsulated glimpses into the lives of people who felt so real in worlds so unlike anything I'd ever known. In 2007, when I was eleven, I stumbled upon a Manga (Japanese comic) by author Daisuke Igarashi in the Kinokuniya bookstore of Japantown, San Francisco. The cover had three wide-eyed children, about my age at the time, tumbling through a sparkling ocean. It was called *Children of the Sea*. This manga fulfilled my precise desire for the mysterious adventures of children like me in a magical world. Igarashi vividly characterizes the ocean as the womb of the universe, where human lives and galaxies are born and re-absorbed in a haunting and joyous cosmic festival reminiscent of the movie *2001: A Space Odyssey*. There's a type of existential grandeur portrayed in *Children of the Sea* that I connected with on a very deep level – a dichotomous portrayal of birth and death as both callously casual and simultaneously sacred, and a portrayal of humanity itself as something magical and wonderful.

I knew I wanted to tell stories like this too. I wanted to tell the people of our world about the universes that lived inside my head, and show them moments in the lives of the real people in these imaginary worlds. I wanted to make people wonder if magic was real, the way we do when we're six years old and don't yet understand how the world works. I wanted to capture the emotion felt upon waking from an epic and exhausting dream. My memories of being a very young child feel like this too – when the world is strange, and bright, and new, and sometimes overwhelming.

Stories such as *Howl's Moving Castle* bring me back to the sensation that there are countless strange, new experiences to be had, beyond my comprehension or imagination. I want to evoke that feeling too. I feel that as long as there are people dreaming of these worlds, they do indeed exist. More worlds exist than could ever be explored in a lifetime, more strange and bright and new experiences inside my mind and inside yours, too. I hope you'll enjoy this window into the world of my imagination, and into the stories of the people who live there.

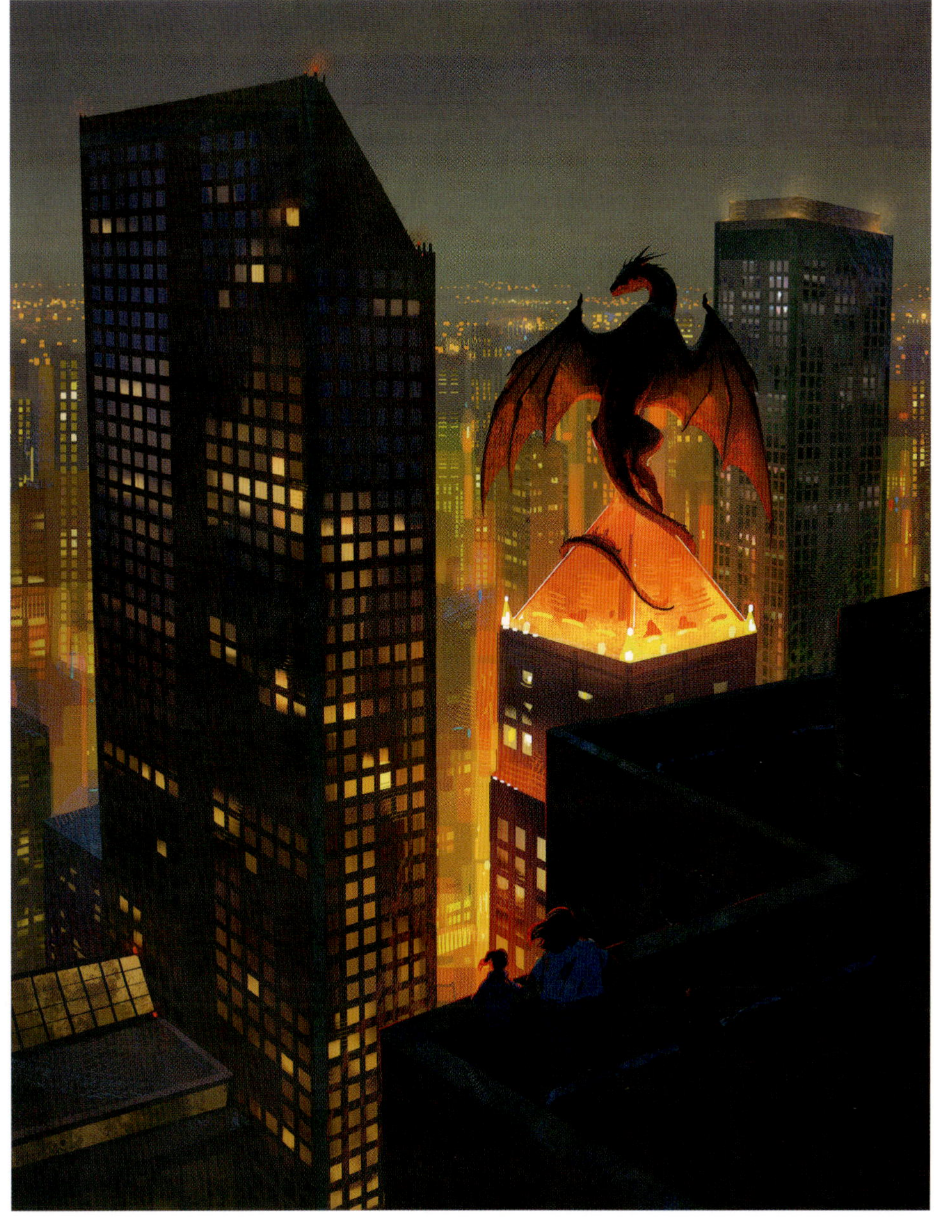

OBSERVING THE LOCAL DRAGON / PHOTOSHOP, 2021

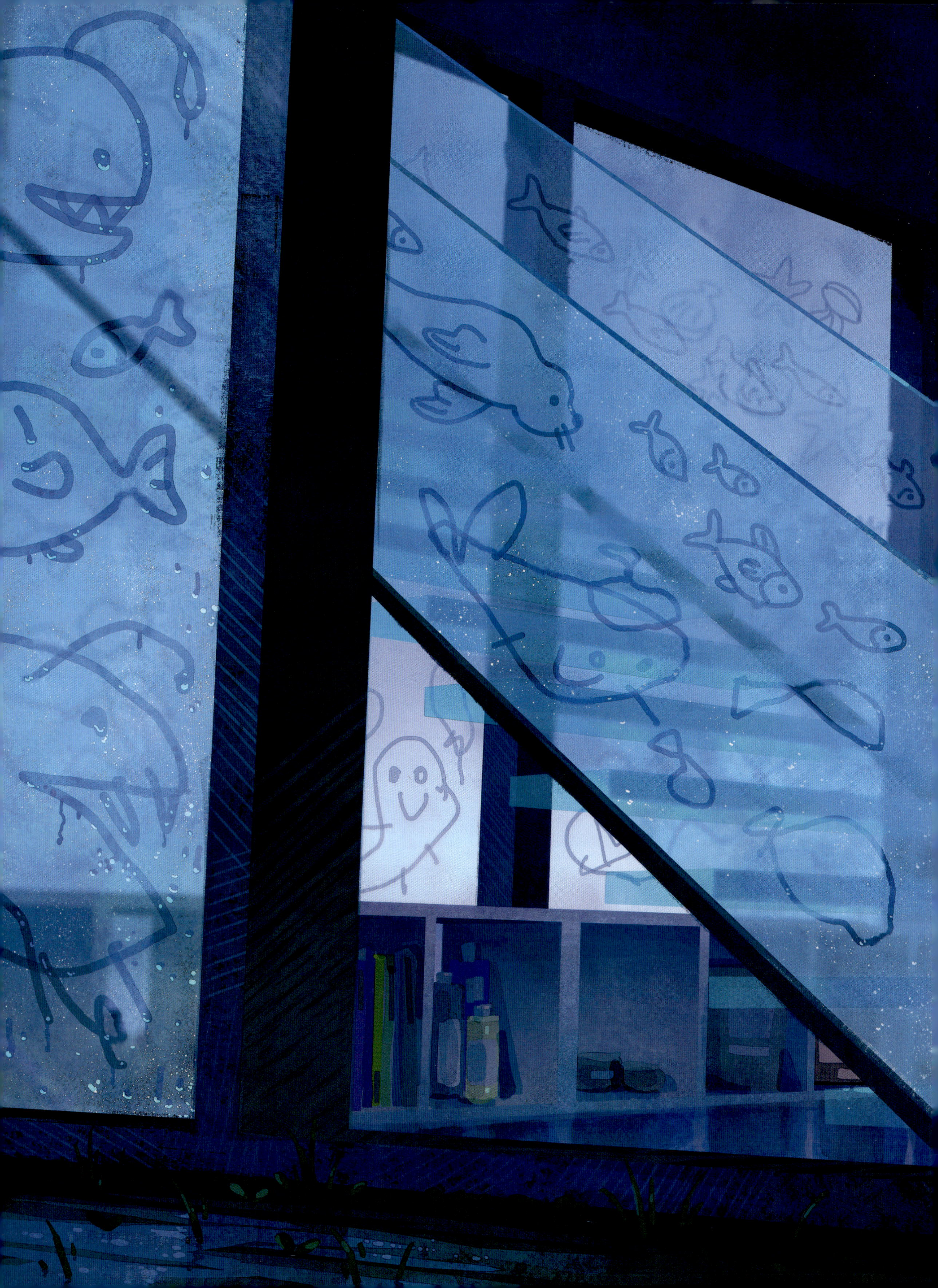

CREATIVE JOURNEY

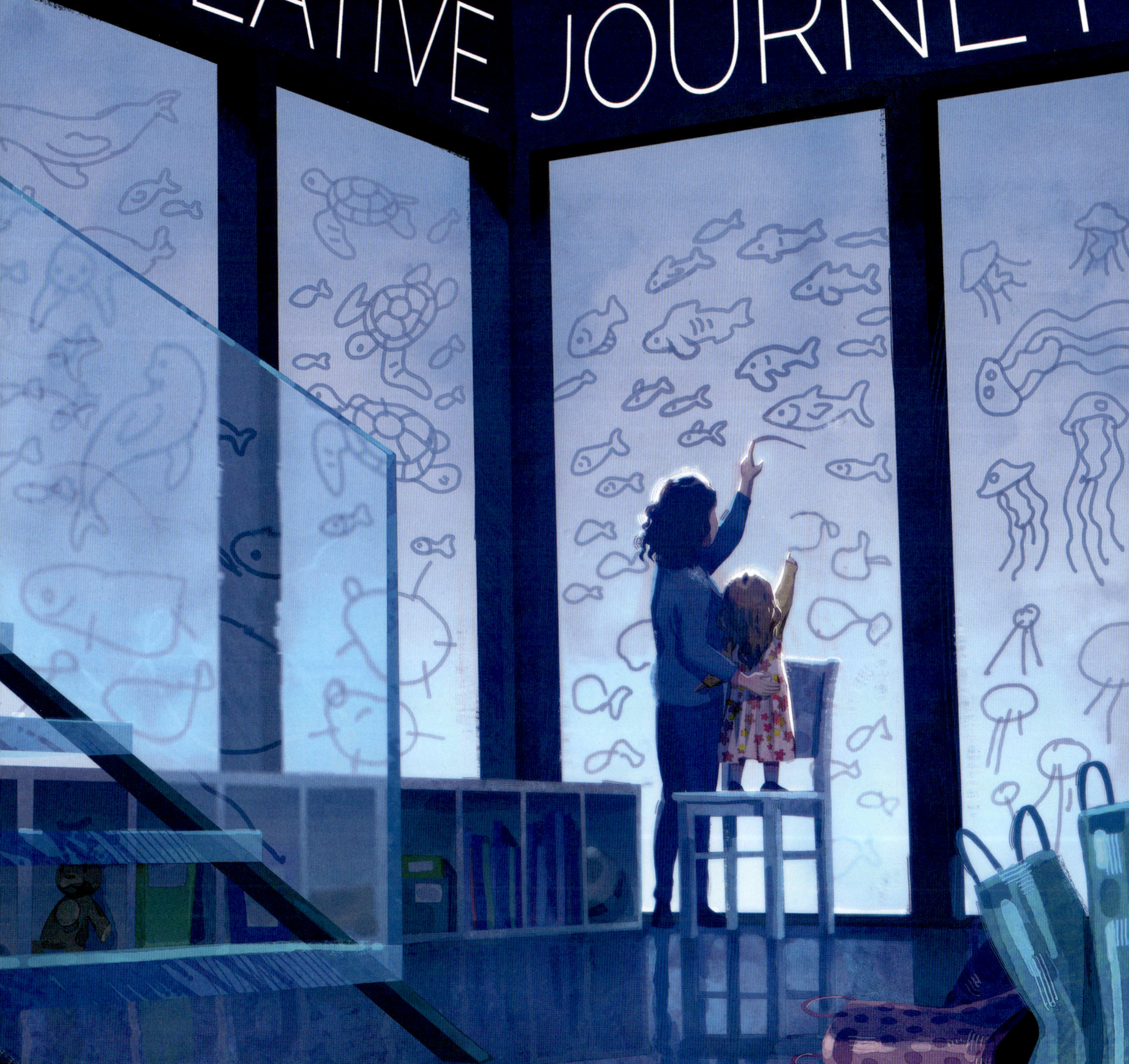

I WANTED TO PAINT

REPLENISH / PHOTOSHOP, 2021

On a warm June morning in 2017, my mom checked me out of the emergency room at the Kaiser Permanente medical center in Pasadena, California. From there, she drove me thirty minutes across town so that I could take my first art test for a job as a background painter on the TV show *Disenchantment*. I was twenty years old, and midway through an aggressive antibiotic treatment for a secondary stomach infection. We had ten minutes to spare before I was scheduled to arrive, and we spent it sitting mostly in relieved silence, the laughable absurdity of the situation not lost on us. We were not strangers to running directly from the hospital to an appointment, but this was the most impressive turnaround to date.

While I readied myself to enter the studio by tying up my hair and removing my hospital bracelet, my mom turned to me and fixed me in a firm but gentle stare:

> *"Just making it here is enough, no matter how it turns out. If you decide you want to quit halfway through, you just call me, okay? You have to give yourself permission to do that, if you need to."*

She echoed out loud a sentiment I already knew as a fundamental truth. Raising a child with a chronic illness, my parents did everything they could to instill moral neutrality into anything I achieved or failed at in a world built for able-bodied, healthy people. Thankfully, for that reason alone, I didn't walk into the studio that day because I felt like I needed to prove anything. I did it because I wanted to paint.

As far back as I can remember, making art has been a source of calm and peace. This was the case on the day of that art test. After a night of restlessness and fever, beeping hospital machinery, and fast walks through cold hallways, my heart and mind raced as I climbed the concrete stairs to Rough Draft Studios for the first time. But the moment I sat down in that black computer chair to paint, it was like the prickling nerves washed down through my body, from the top of my head and down through the soles of my feet. Painting, for me, has always been a meditative practice. From the first moment I read through their prompts and opened up my Photoshop canvas, I knew I would make it through the day. I didn't yet know if I would pass the test, and I almost didn't care; almost, but not quite. The potential financial stability that this job offered was impossible to put entirely out of mind. I understood though, in that moment, that what I really wanted to do was just to make art. Where I made it, what I made it for, and who I shared it with – these things were secondary. What I wanted most was to spend my time in the state of calm that fell over me during the test that day, where it feels like the world falls away, and all that matters is my steady breath and the marks I'm making on the canvas in front of me.

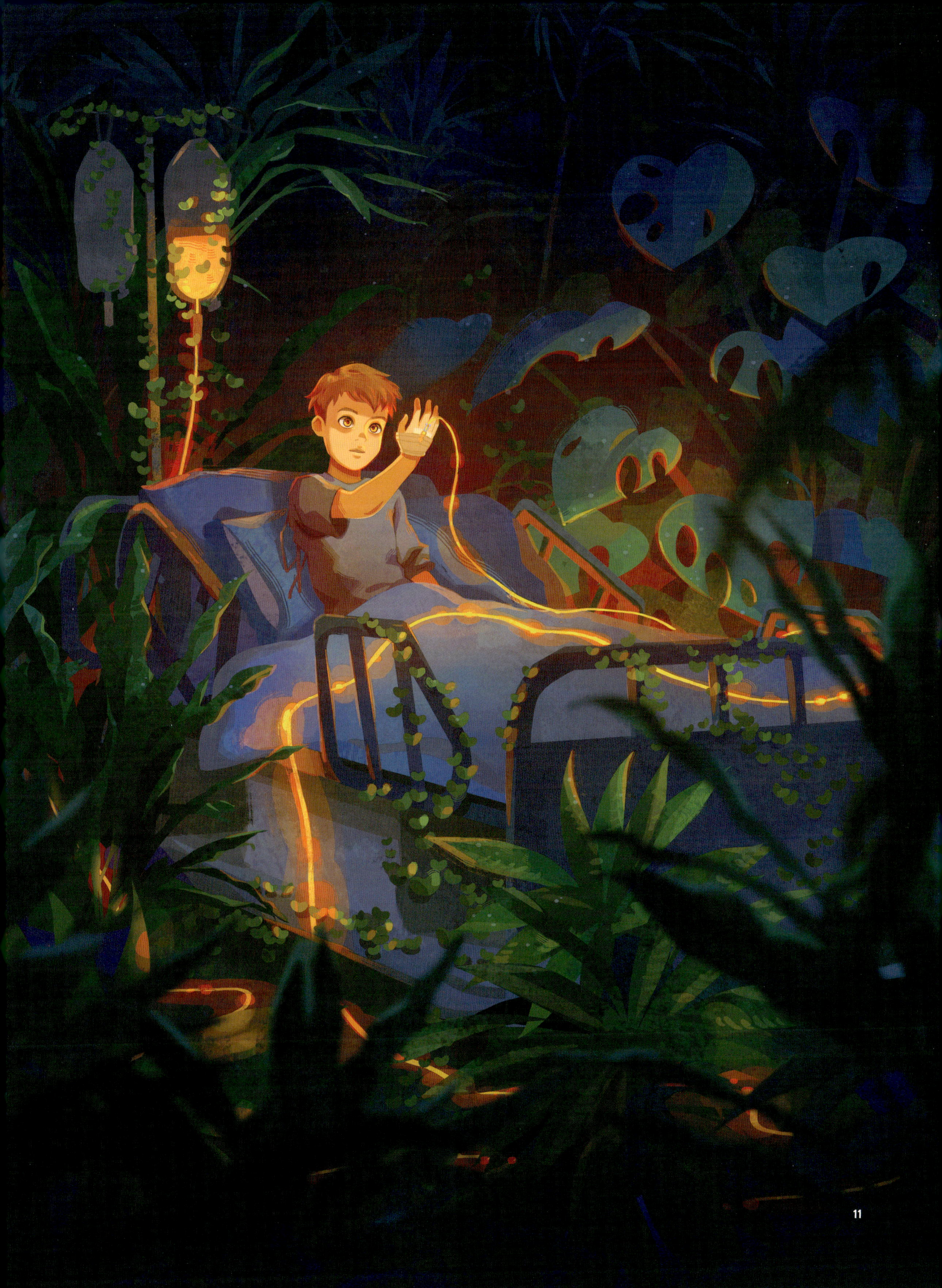

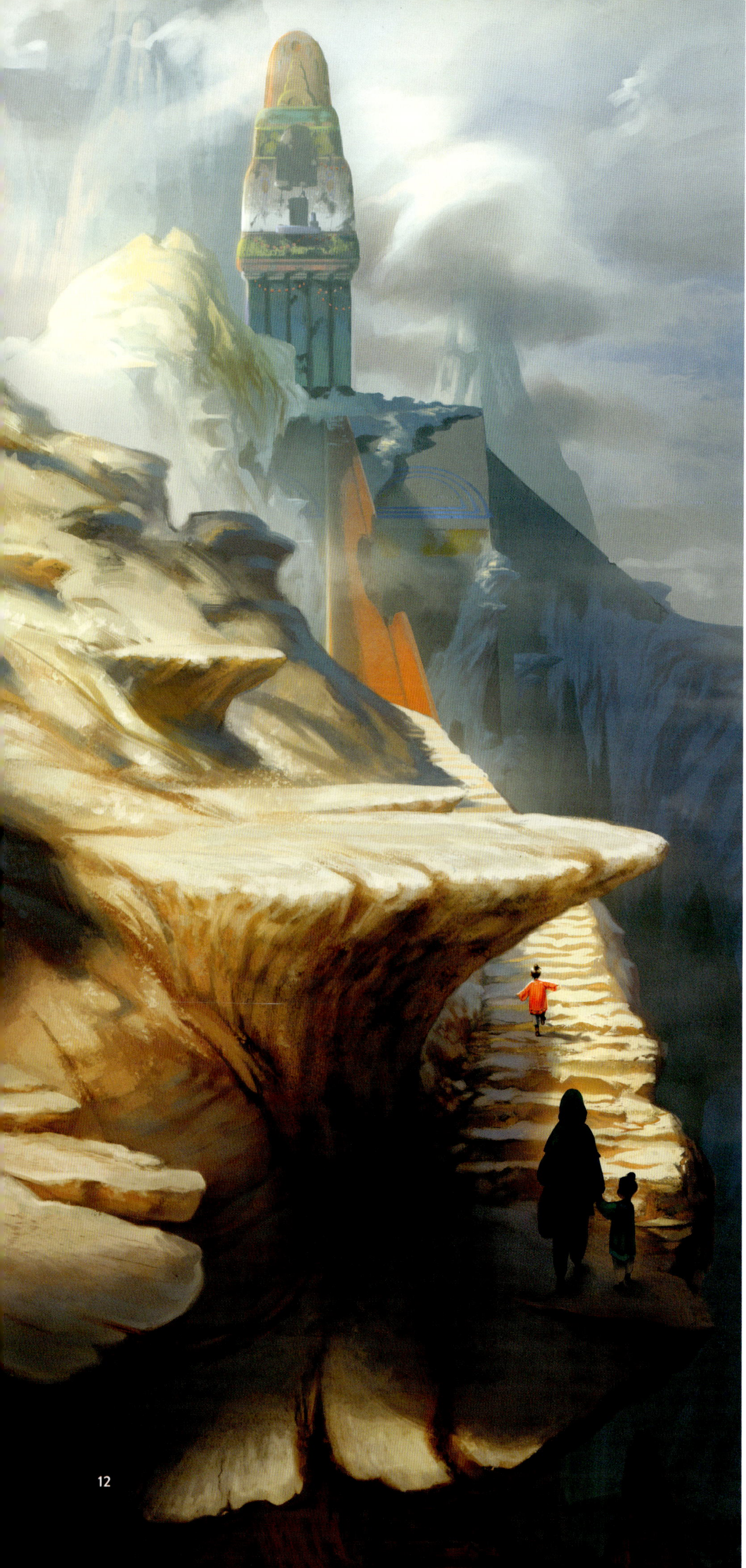

PILGRIMAGE / PAINTED FOR AN ENVIRONMENT DESIGN HOMEWORK ASSIGNMENT, 2016

I remember a summer when I was in middle school, aged twelve, during which I spent nearly all day, every day, painting. It consisted of, not coincidentally, some of the worst months of my life. My chronic illness, a condition called cyclic vomiting syndrome or CVS, had worsened dramatically as it often does around the onset of puberty, and we hadn't yet found a treatment that was effective. Despite this, I remember that summer very fondly. I spent it constructing a fantasy world that was deep underground, in winding tunnels through selenite crystal and expansive caverns filled with wrinkled, eerie creatures. That summer, I think I lived in that underground world more so than in the world we're familiar with. I have always felt that we really do coexist in both the real world as well as the tiny universes we construct, whether in books and games, or just inside our heads. To me, these worlds felt real; the paintings I made were just a window I created for people outside my mind to peer through and explore.

Miraculously, I did get the job I tested for at Rough Draft Studios in June 2017. In all honesty it could have easily gone the other way. I was operating on about two hours of sleep and, regardless of any peaceful mental state, the actual quality of work I produce when I'm feeling unwell is varied. Once, in the midst of a bad episode of CVS during high school, I submitted an essay so dubiously constructed that the sympathetic teacher called me in during lunch and spent thirty minutes trying to decode it. Execution aside though, the show I tested for that day was looking for artists who were interested in crafting unique, immersive worlds. I think they saw that I was someone looking to do the same.

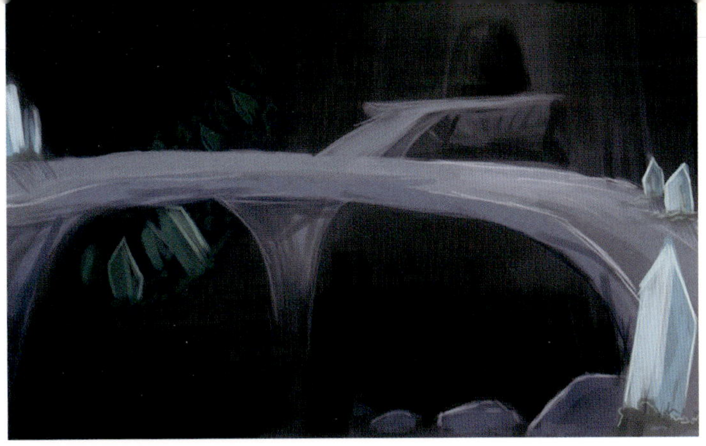

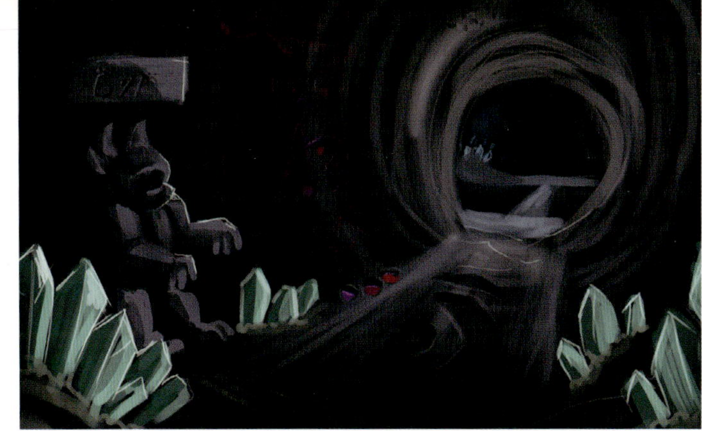

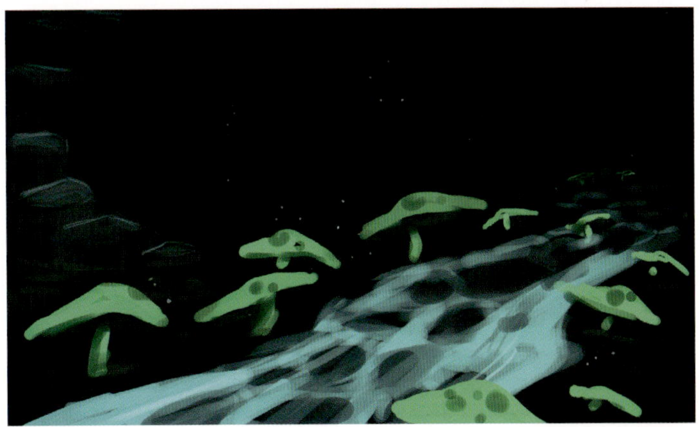

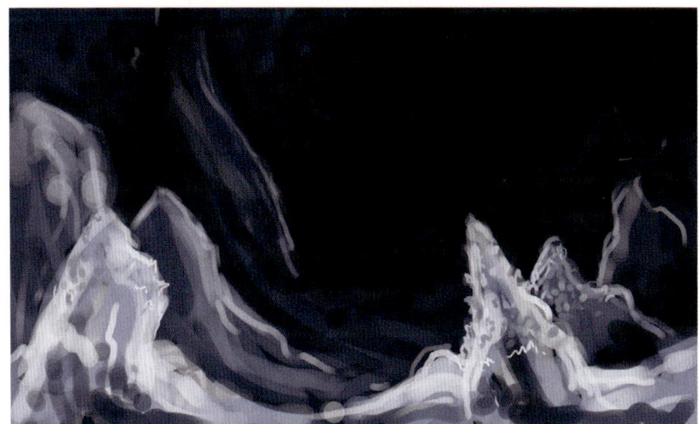

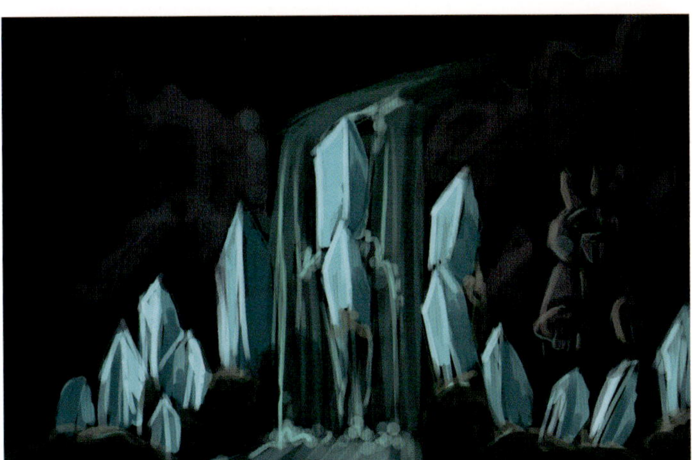

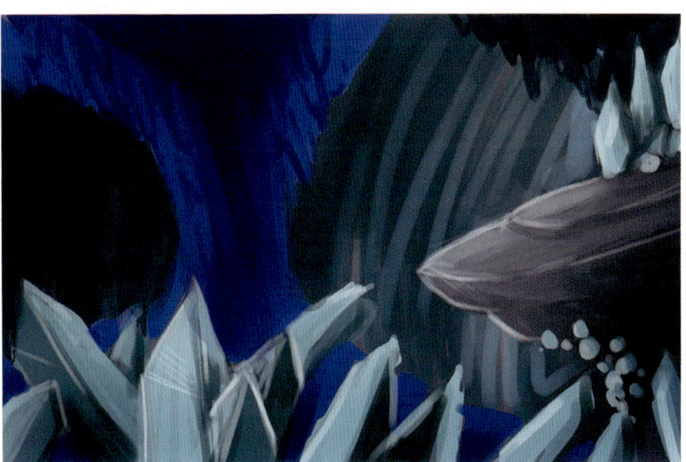

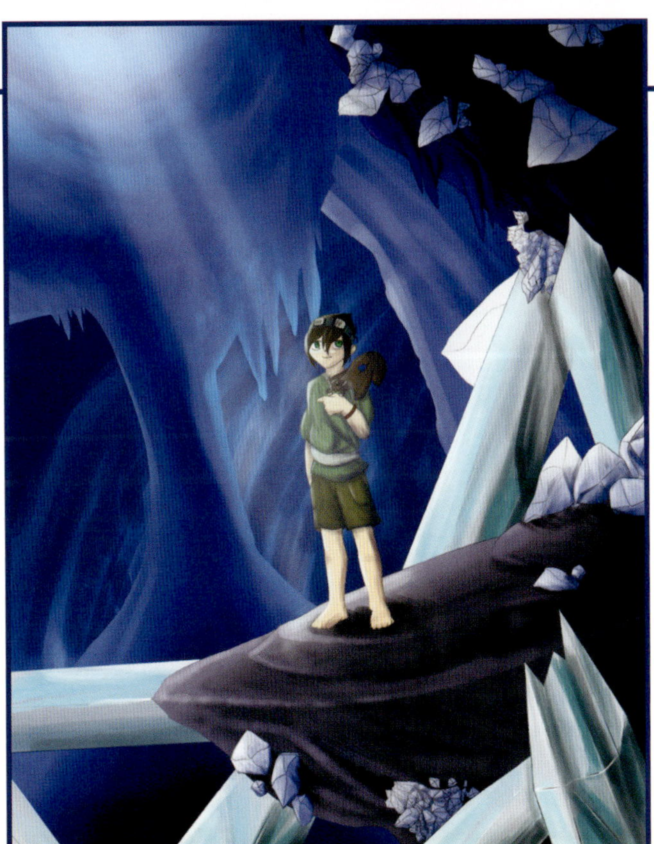

WORLDBUILDING FOR ZAKANI AND THE CAVES /

PHOTOSHOP, 2009, AGE 12

My first real, long-term worldbuilding project was the story of a boy named Zakani who lived underground in crystal caves. I remember sitting at the computer for hours, poring over articles and videos about caves and crystals. This was when I learned the value of thorough research for believable environmental storytelling.

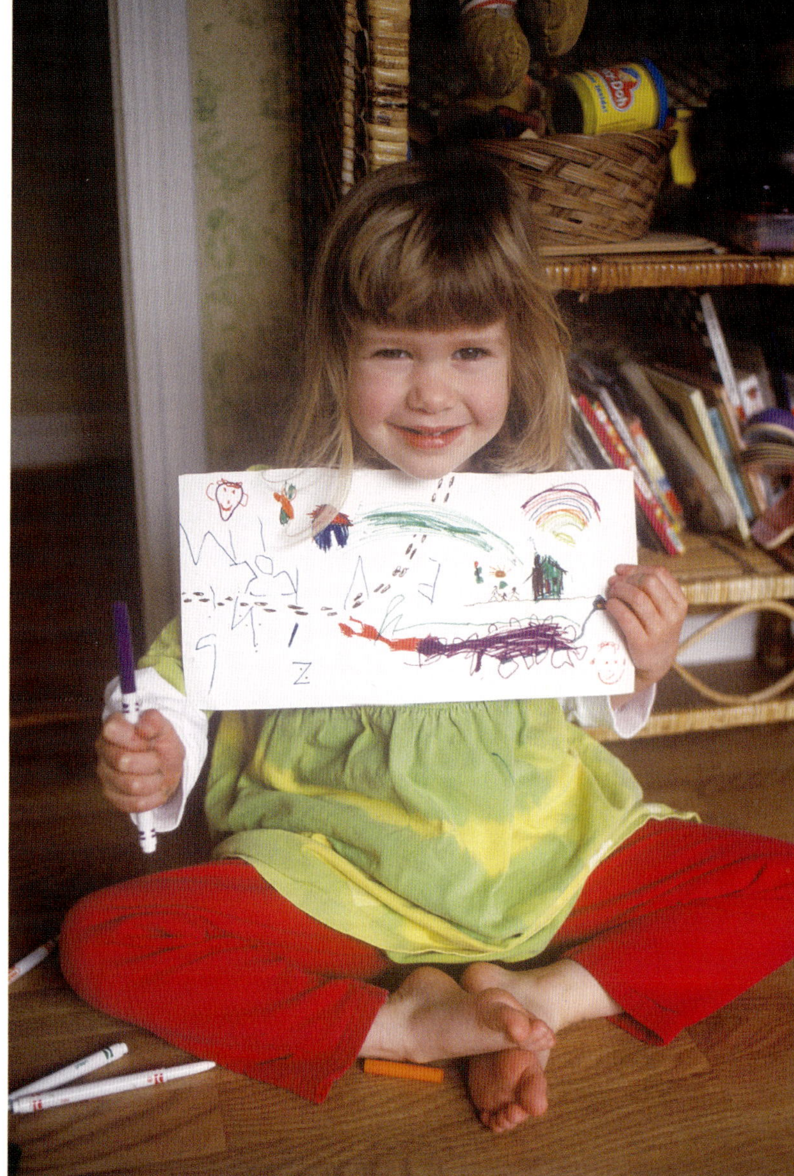

ARTISTIC DEVELOPMENT

My first digital painting that I have a record of is from 1999. I was two years old, and it consists entirely of scribbles. My early forays into digital painting can be attributed entirely to my mom, Susan Opilo Kurtz. For me, she exemplified breaking from the traditional life path in my early years by going back to college at age forty-three for a complete career shift. I have vivid memories from my early childhood of tagging along with her to night classes at Cabrillo, the community college she attended as she slowly but surely completed an associate degree in graphic and web design. During this time, she was also working and raising me alongside my dad.

Many of my early childhood memories take place in her makeshift garage-turned-office: spinning in computer chairs, watching her cycle through fonts in Illustrator, lounging on our futon couch while shuffling through Pantone color cards. As my mom learned how to embed images with HTML, kern text, and use the Photoshop Pen tool, she taught me these skills too. We shared a blue 1998 Wacom tablet, so old that the clear film in the center lifted so you could insert papers underneath and trace them. She used to draw gardens for me in Photoshop, just like a digital coloring book, and I'd fill them in on the same layer with the Paint Bucket tool, leaving behind a white pixelated rim I didn't yet know how to eliminate.

At around seven years old, I graduated to drawing things myself, usually with markers on paper, then scanning them to be colored in Photoshop. It took me until I was ten or eleven to finally feel as comfortable drawing digitally as I did on paper, but from that point on, painting in Photoshop consumed my life. Around that age, I inherited my mom's old tablet when she upgraded hers, and my hippie-adjacent parents thankfully let go of their anti- "screen time" agenda to allow my digital art-making to proceed uninterrupted. And I certainly took advantage of this, sometimes drawing or painting entire days away fervently.

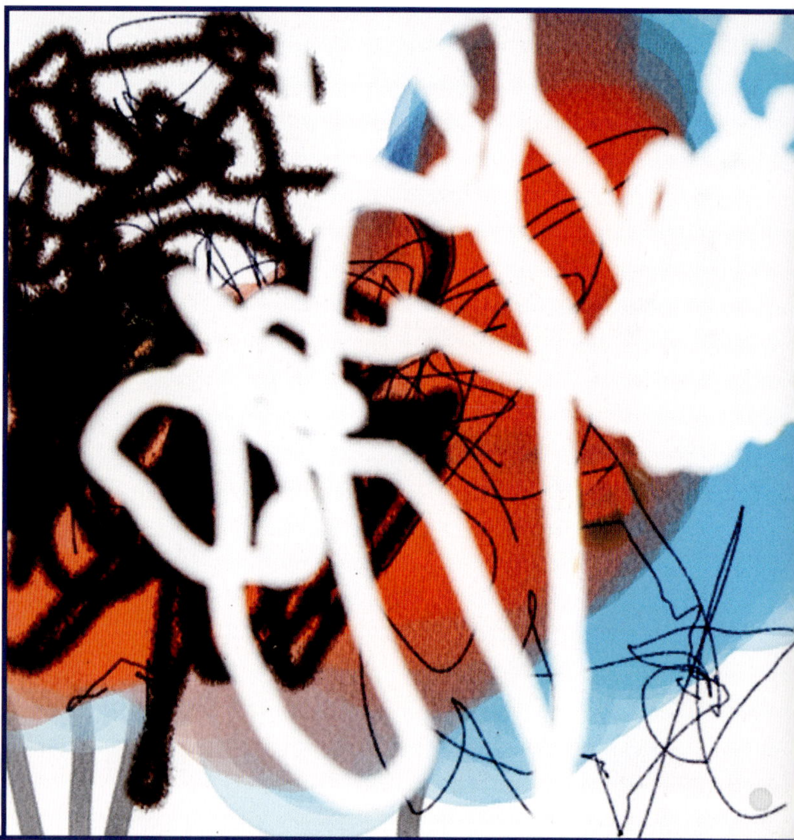

MY VERY FIRST DIGITAL PAINTING /

PHOTOSHOP, 1999, AGE 2

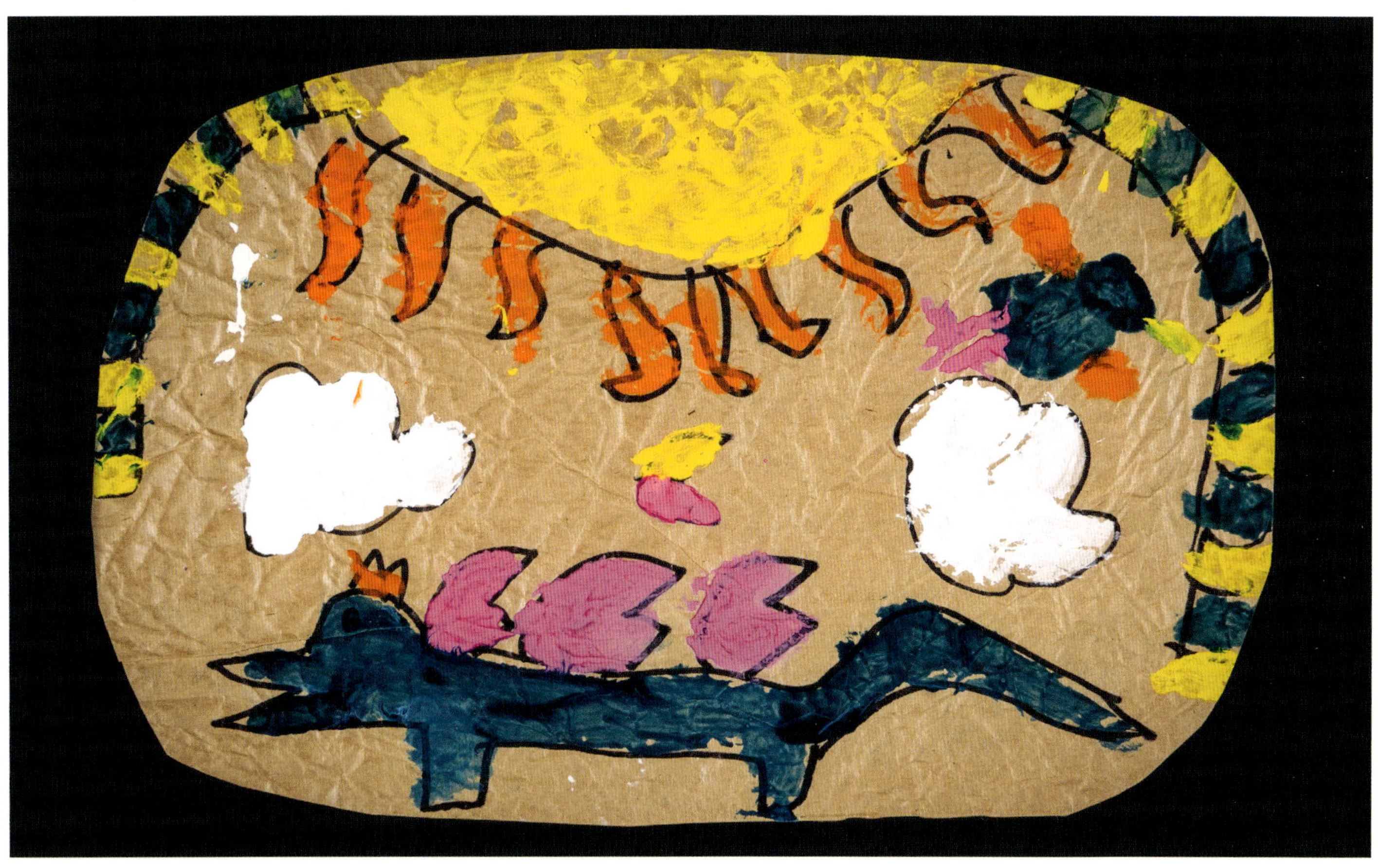

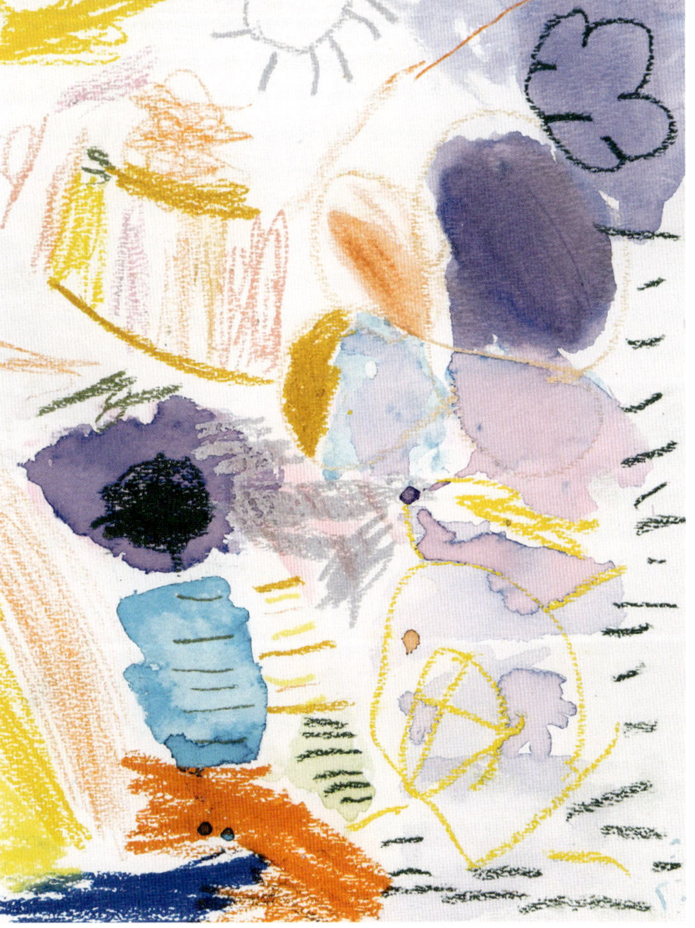

CHILDHOOD ART / TRADITIONAL MEDIA

The freedom I was permitted likely had more than a little to do with the fact that both of my parents are full-time professional artists. My mom completed her degree and has been a graphic designer ever since, first as a freelancer and then later as the in-house designer for a non-profit organization. While she introduced me to shape language and font choices, my dad, Steve Kurtz, a professional photographer, introduced me to lighting, composition, and digital retouching. Hiking out in nature and stopping so my dad could photograph while I sat and sketched became a regular occurrence. Having access to these tools and my parents' knowledge was truly a blessing.

I grew up on the internet. My art education consisted of watching livestreams and reading DeviantArt tutorials. I asked for the "art of" book to every Disney movie for every Christmas and birthday. As a child I had difficulty focusing in school, and "can't sit still" regularly appeared on my student evaluations. But miraculously, when it came to drawing and painting, you couldn't tear me away. I would draw entire days away, sitting cross-legged on my bedroom floor until my legs went numb and my eyes stung. During that time, I would painstakingly copy screenshot after screenshot of Disney movies, trying to understand how the shapes came together to form the characters I loved.

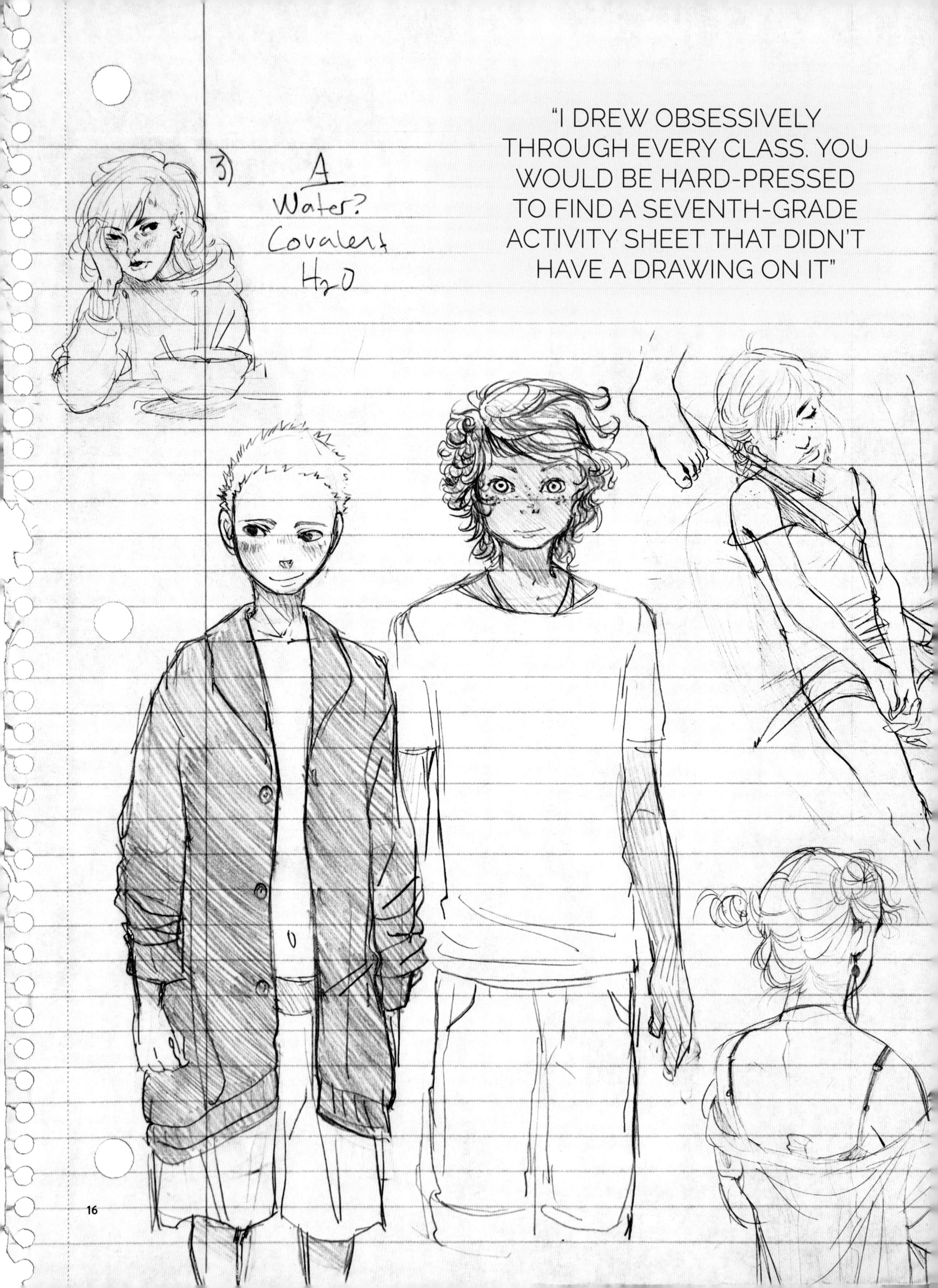

"I DREW OBSESSIVELY THROUGH EVERY CLASS. YOU WOULD BE HARD-PRESSED TO FIND A SEVENTH-GRADE ACTIVITY SHEET THAT DIDN'T HAVE A DRAWING ON IT"

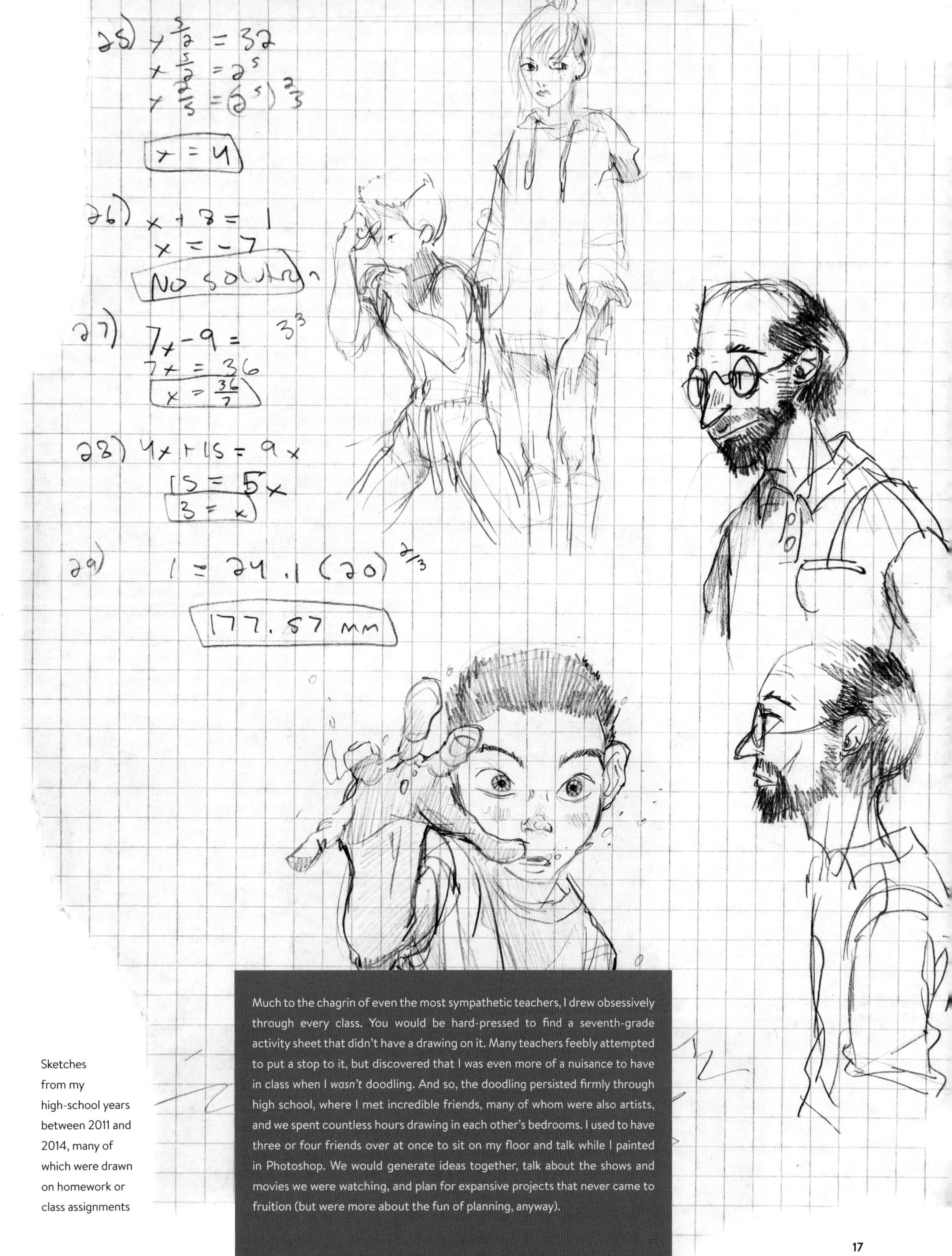

Sketches from my high-school years between 2011 and 2014, many of which were drawn on homework or class assignments

Much to the chagrin of even the most sympathetic teachers, I drew obsessively through every class. You would be hard-pressed to find a seventh-grade activity sheet that didn't have a drawing on it. Many teachers feebly attempted to put a stop to it, but discovered that I was even more of a nuisance to have in class when I *wasn't* doodling. And so, the doodling persisted firmly through high school, where I met incredible friends, many of whom were also artists, and we spent countless hours drawing in each other's bedrooms. I used to have three or four friends over at once to sit on my floor and talk while I painted in Photoshop. We would generate ideas together, talk about the shows and movies we were watching, and plan for expansive projects that never came to fruition (but were more about the fun of planning, anyway).

"I SPENT MANY LUNCHTIMES DAYDREAMING ABOUT THE FREEDOM SUMMER WOULD BRING"

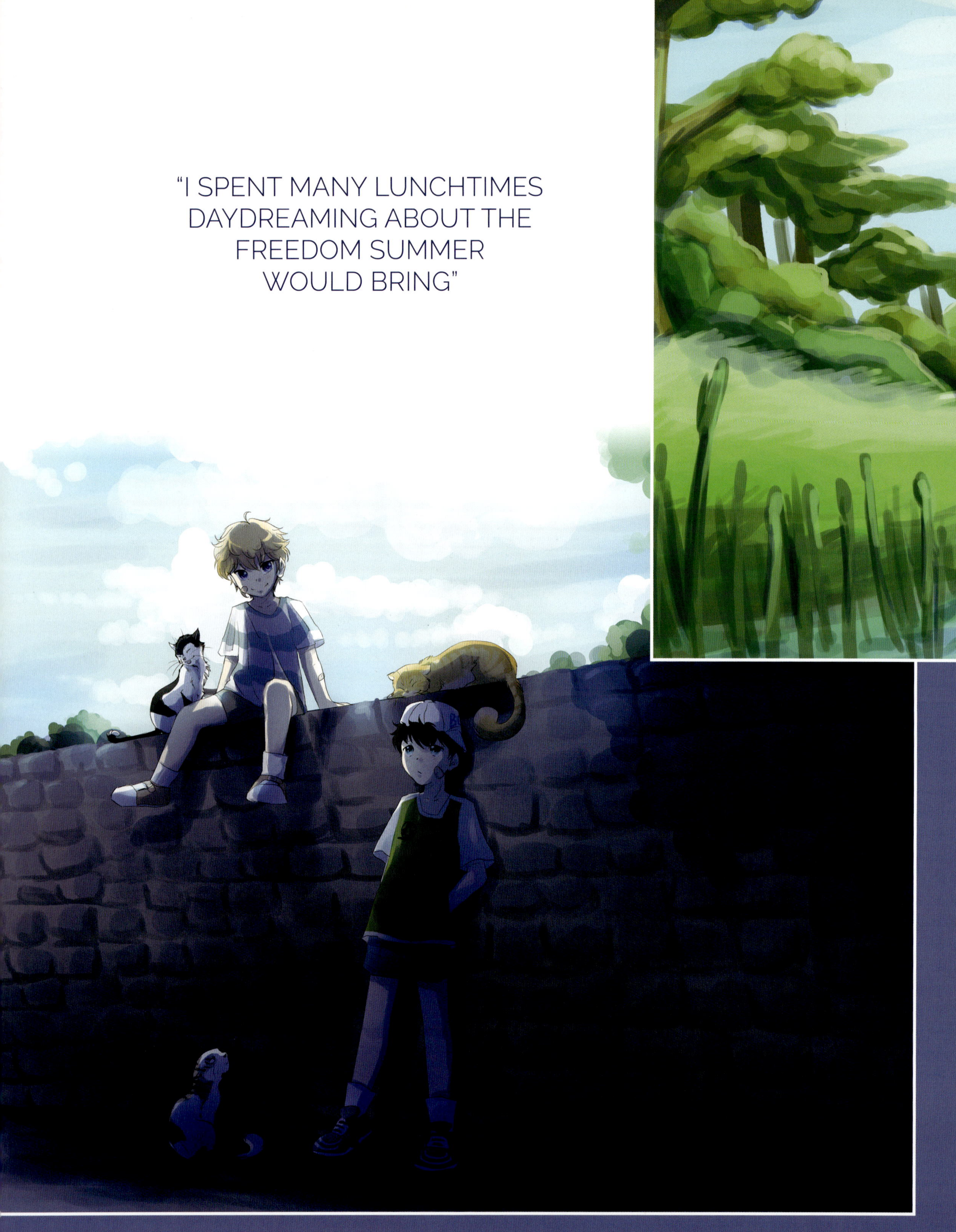

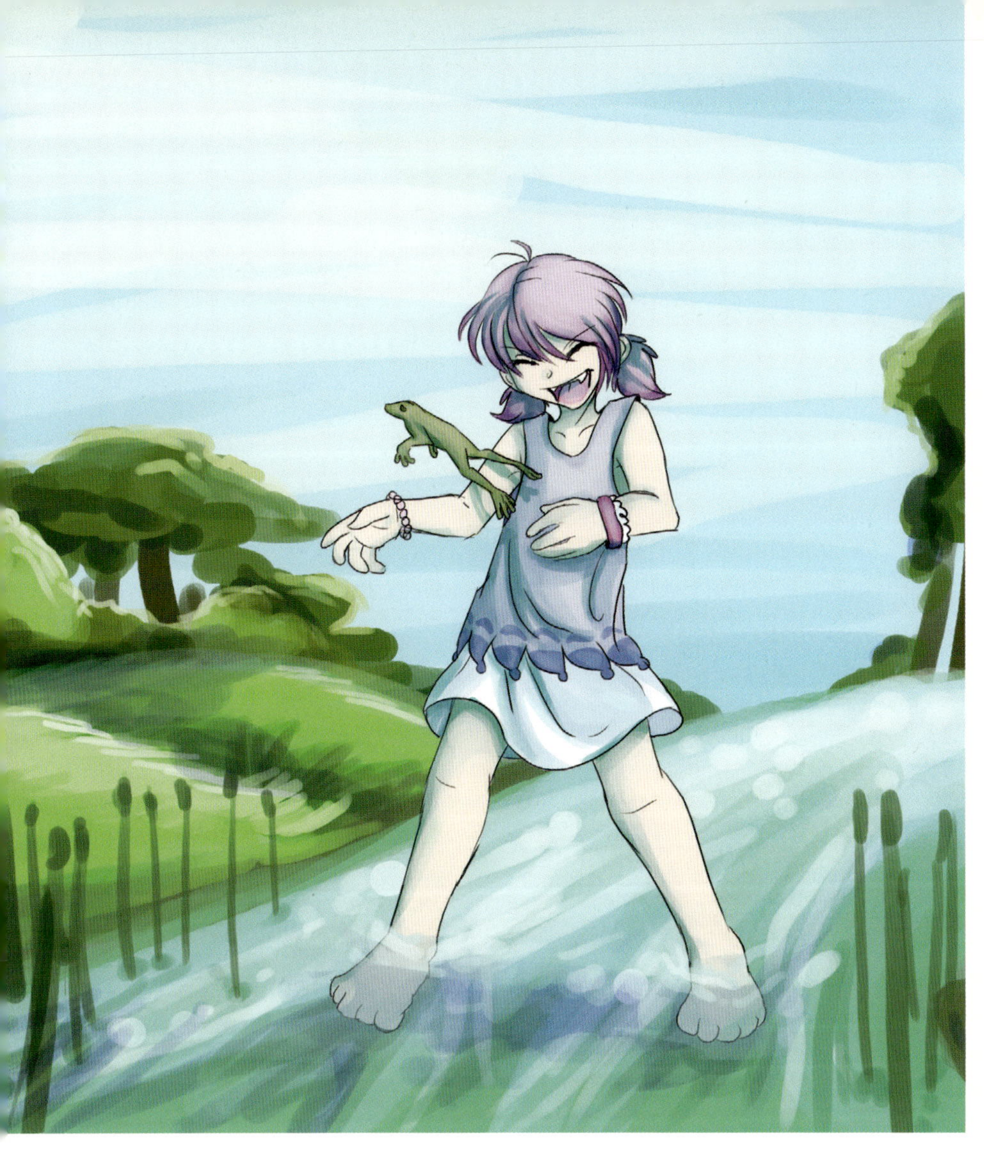

A SERIES OF SUMMER-THEMED ILLUSTRATIONS /
PHOTOSHOP, 2010, AGE 13

In eighth grade, my friend Zahra Lucas and I spent many lunchtimes daydreaming about the freedom summer would bring. I painted this series over the course of that year, trying to encapsulate the way we felt about summer through the adventures of a group of friends. Developing this project taught me about building mood and character through color and design.

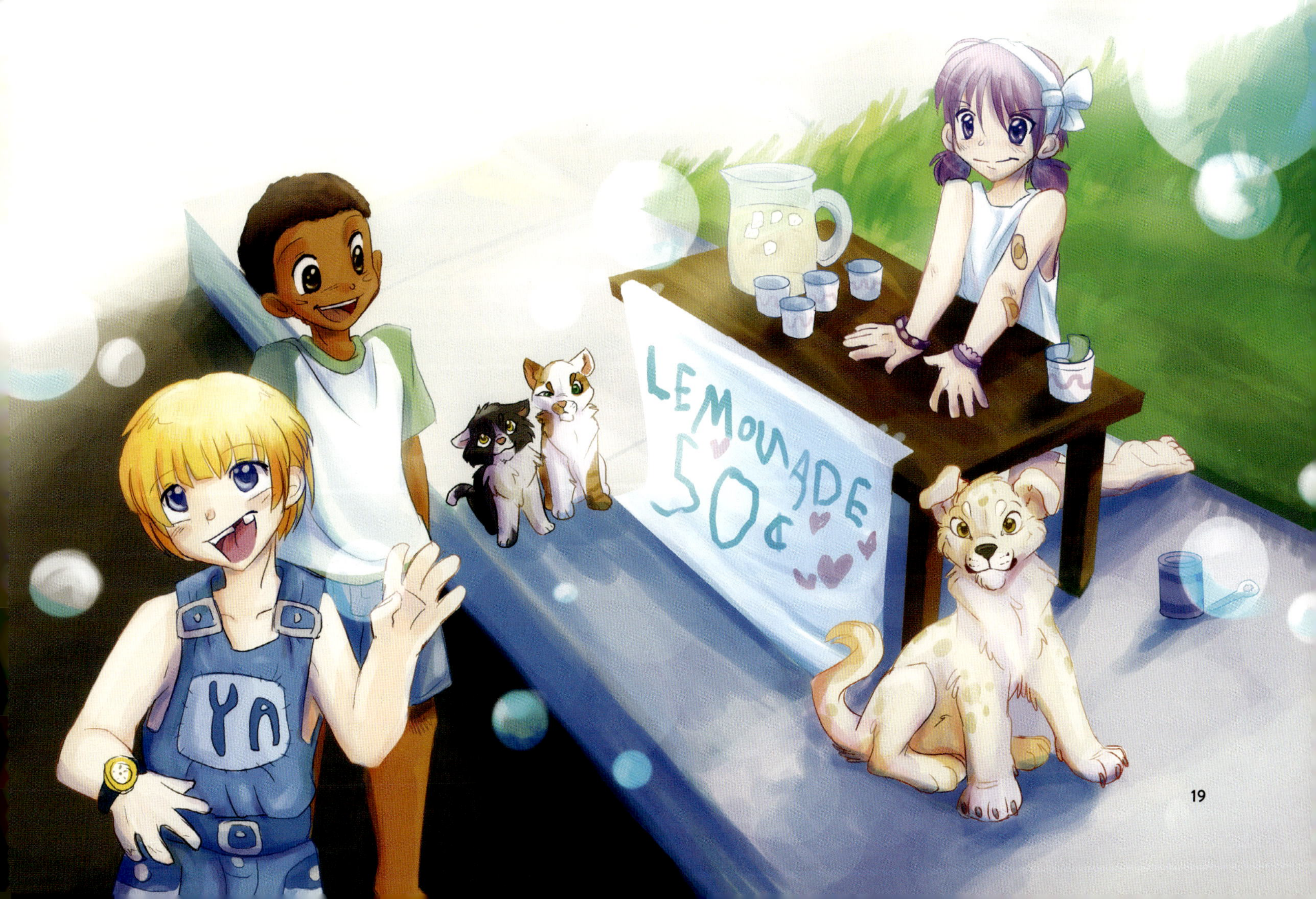

STRUGGLES WITH CHRONIC ILLNESS

Even when I was surrounded by support and loving friends, having a chronic illness as a teenager took a toll on me mentally. Episodes would sometimes last for days, forcing me to miss events and leaving me sprinting on the endless hamster wheel of catching up with the school curriculum. CVS episodes are unpredictable and can strike at random. The fear of being caught off-guard with an embarrassing medical situation always plagued me. I want to share these struggles now because when I was young, I didn't see anyone I could look up to who was dealing with chronic illness. The constant warnings of how fast-paced and competitive the professional world is can be panic-inducing for anyone with a chronic illness or disability. As I approached graduation, I spent more and more time second-guessing. Unhealthy "grind culture" messaging (the notion that artists should be constantly pushing well beyond their comfortable limits for improvement) peaked in a lot of online art communities in the mid-2010s, and that scared me. Over-exerting myself led to excruciating recoil that often set me back for days. Pushing myself in the way that "grind culture" asked of artists was a true impossibility, and I feared this meant a career in the arts may be an impossibility too.

I won't lie and say it's been easy. But I will record it here, in this book, so that you know it's possible – or at least it was for me. We are all different people, and the world is not built for people with chronic illnesses or disabilities. The world is still full of things made completely inaccessible for many people who belong to marginalized communities, through design and through lack of motivation to fix it from those in power. I put great importance into staying aware of the ways the privileges I have facilitate my ability to exist in this industry as a person with a chronic illness. I believe it is vital that I use the power and platform I have to help break as many barriers as I can for those following this path in the future. It would have meant a lot to me, as a teenager, to know that there were people in the field I wanted to work in, fighting to make it a more hospitable place. That part I can guarantee; we're out there, and in succession we will each leave the industry a better place than we found it.

NEW GROWTH /
PHOTOSHOP, 2019

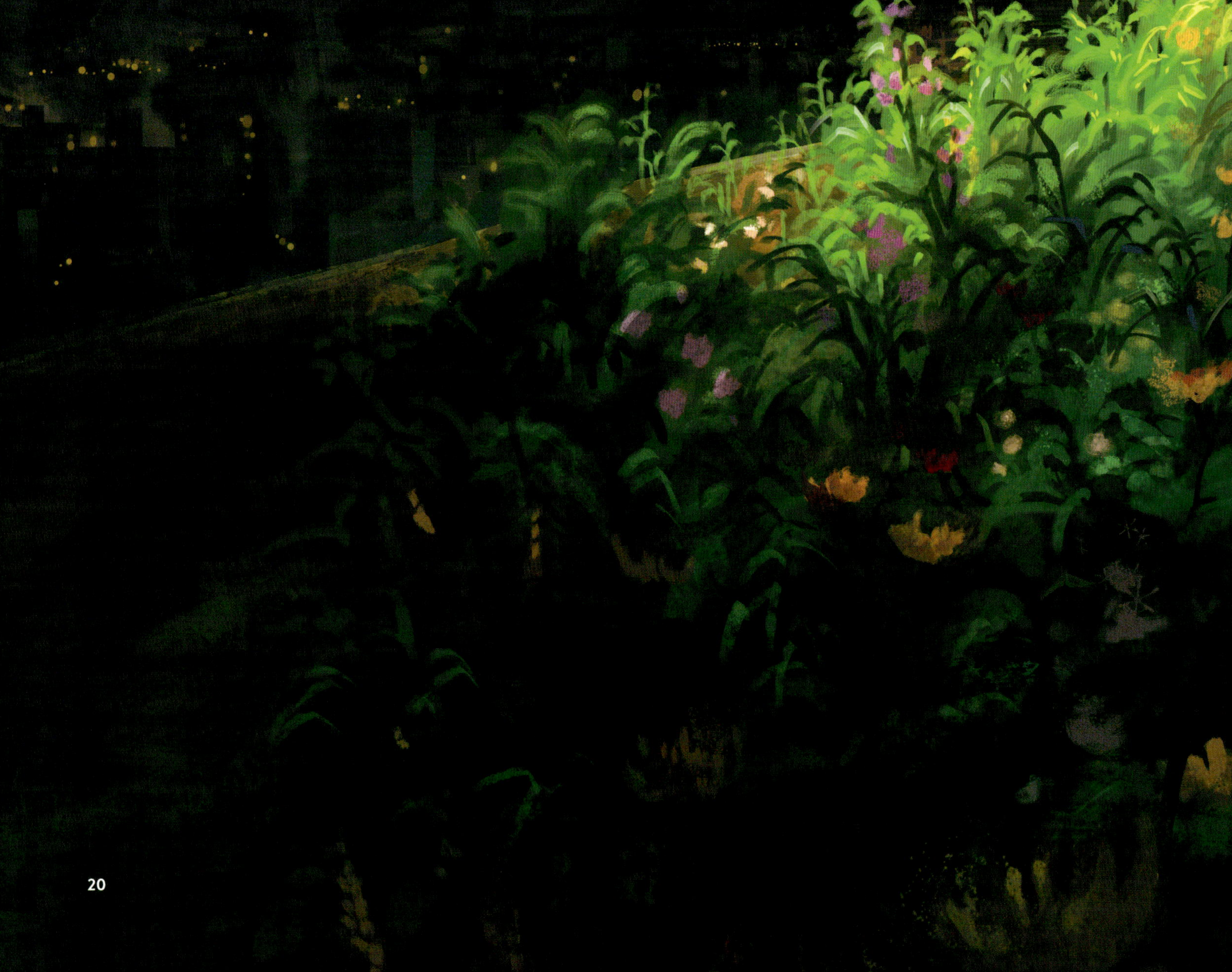

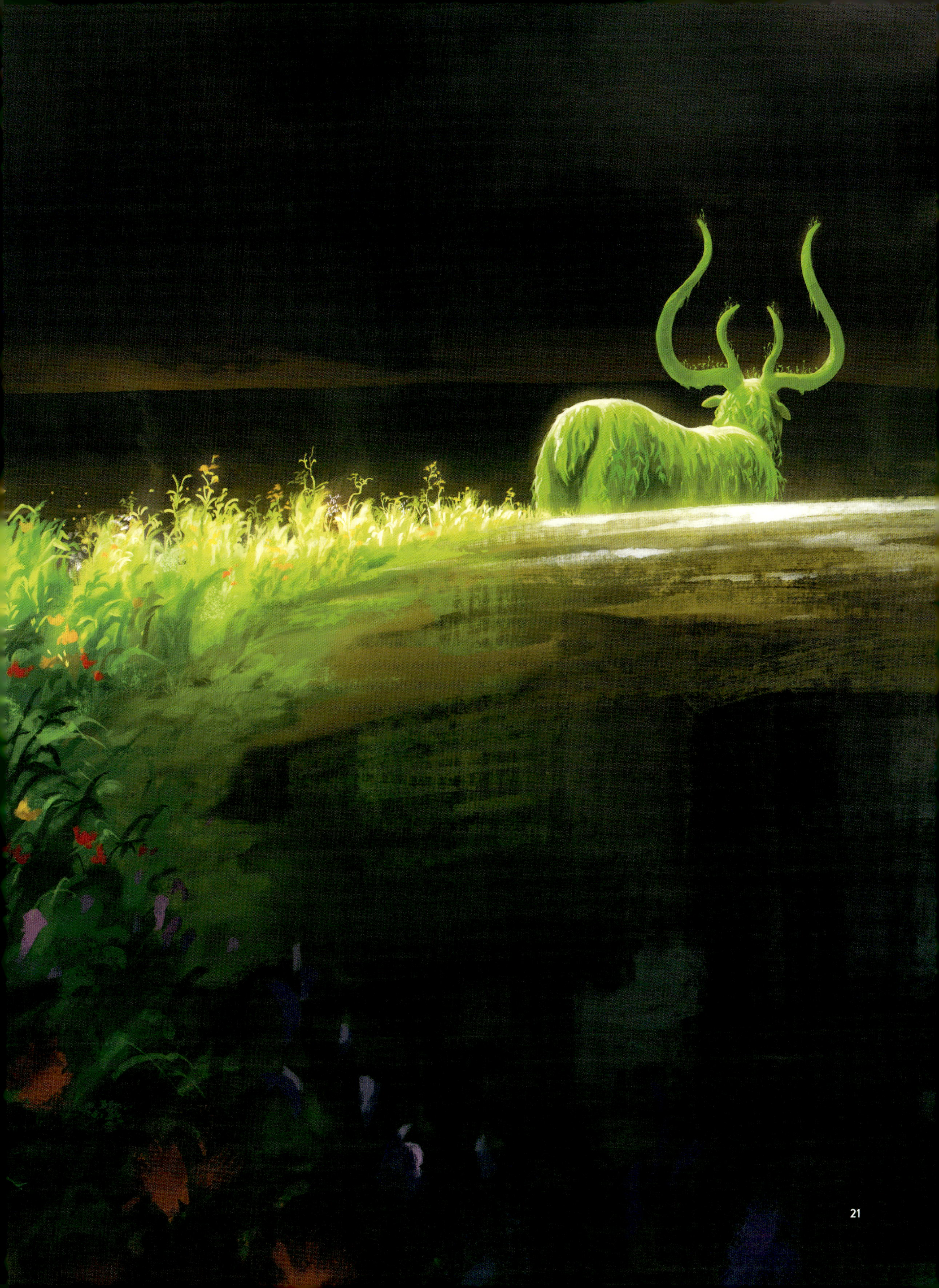

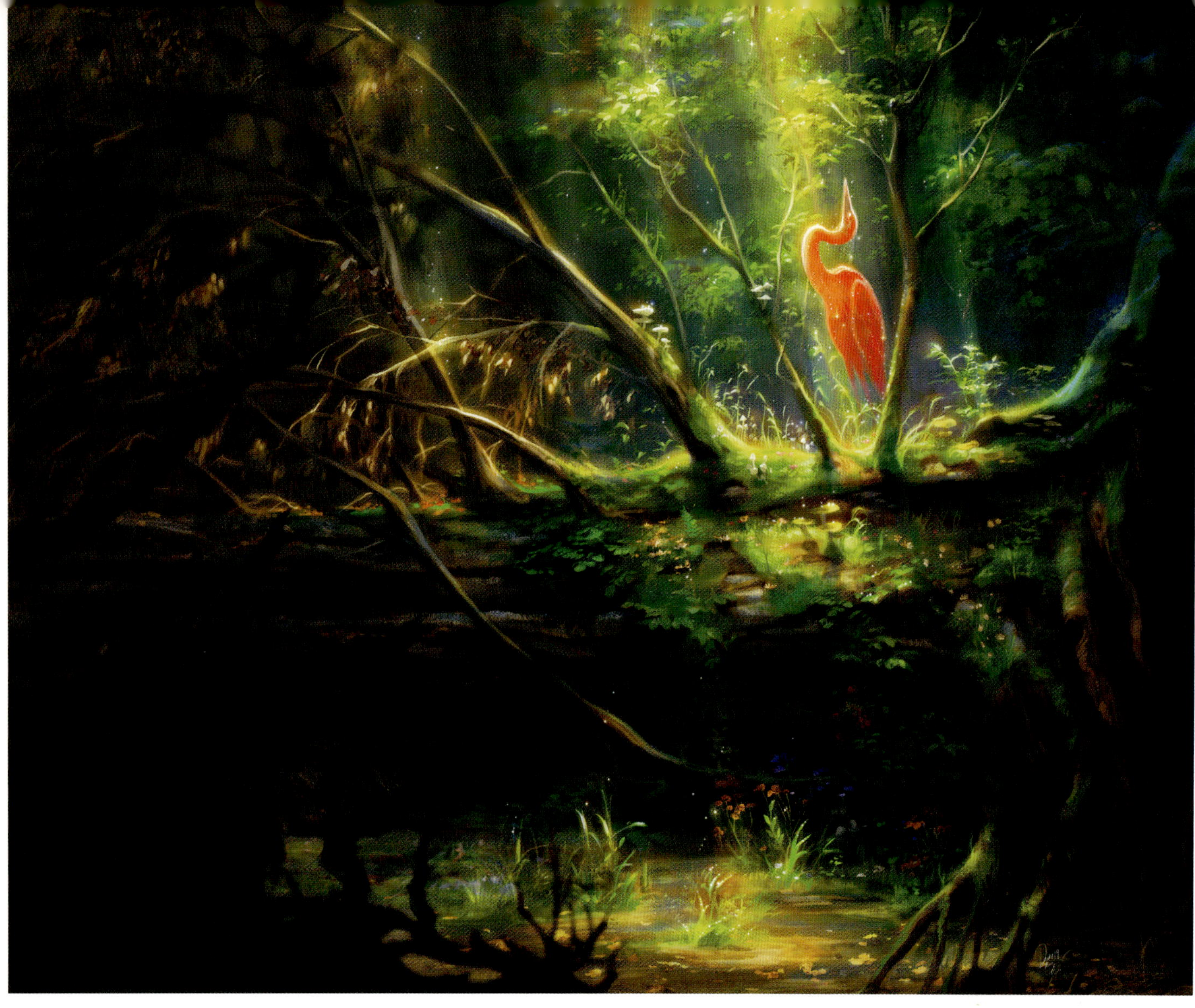

RESTORATION / PHOTOSHOP, 2019

AN EDUCATION

I left Santa Cruz for Laguna College of Art and Design when I was seventeen years old. But not even a year later, I had to make the very difficult decision to drop out. During my first semester at the school, I had a week-long CVS episode that left me spending time in the hospital and playing catch-up in every class during the months following. The experience drained me profoundly, and both the mental and physical weight of it ultimately became too much. I lasted until the end of my second semester, but did so only by working long hours and late nights. It became a vicious cycle of exhaustion triggering further CVS episodes, and those episodes leaving me little time to accomplish everything without exhausting myself once again. The year after I left college was really difficult. I was living in a water-logged apartment full of cockroaches and black mold, and struggled to figure out my direction in life. I constantly questioned my decision to leave behind a massive scholarship and the only path I'd seen lead artists into the animation industry. I was really cruel to myself at times during this period, and pushed myself brutally toward improvement I didn't yet know how to achieve.

When I was eighteen, I began taking classes at Concept Design Academy and online with Schoolism. Through positive reinforcement from instructors and my growing community of friends in the area, I managed to slowly crawl out of the hole I'd unwittingly sunken into. I realized, even more slowly, that none of the internal criticism I was constantly leveraging against myself had actually worked. Accepting kindness from the people around me and treating myself with that same care did more for my own growth than being ruthless to myself ever had. I realized that my behavior needed to change. I started prioritizing sleep and nourishment above everything else. I stopped allowing myself to berate my own work and actions internally. I put an end to the lie that slowing down and taking breaks were indications that I was lazy.

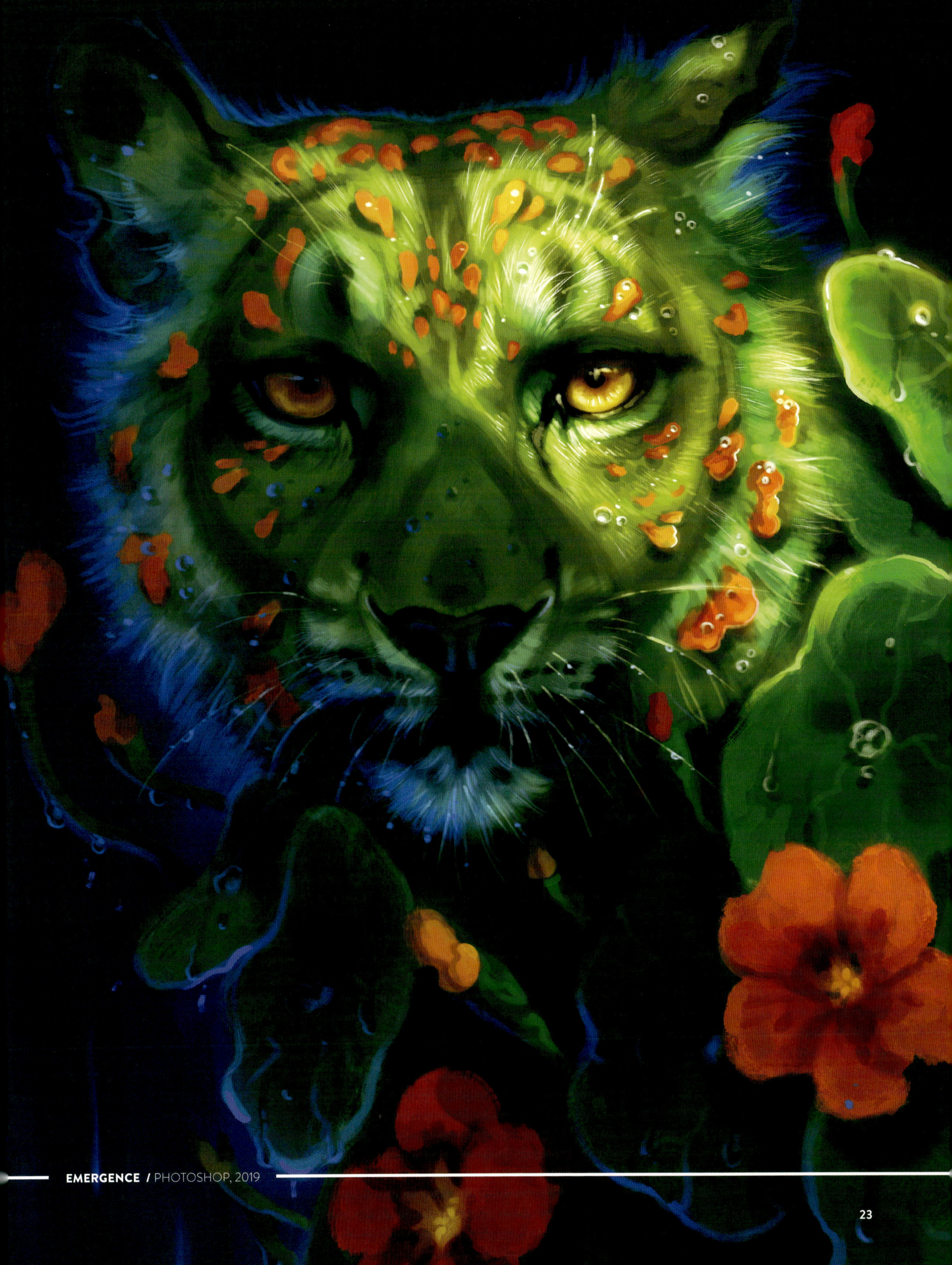

EMERGENCE / PHOTOSHOP, 2019

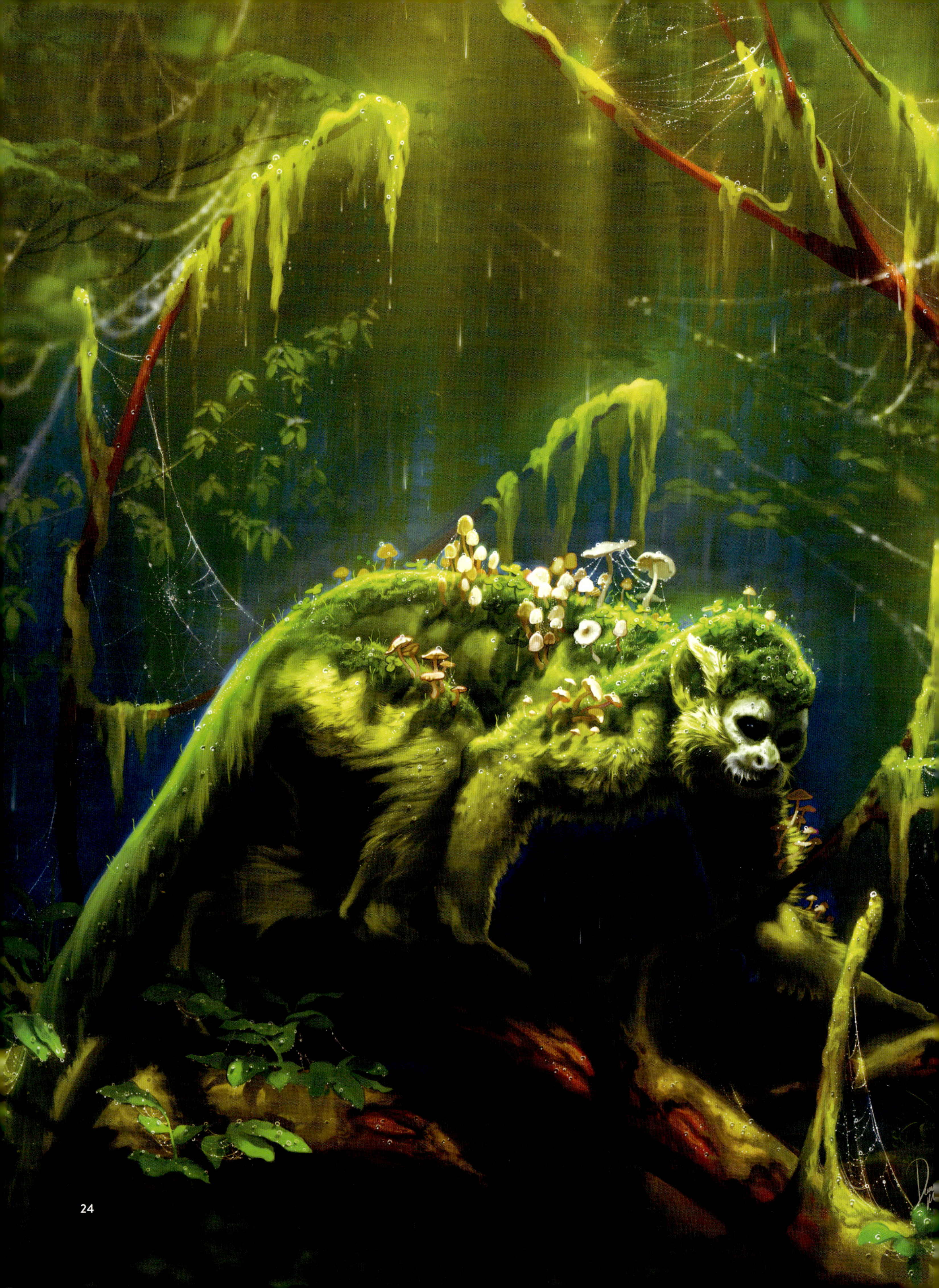

Changing these patterns of behavior is difficult, and it's an ongoing battle for me still, six years later. But challenging the damaging narratives I'd built around rest and accomplishment proved to be vital. I was running myself ragged trying to chase an idea of success that wasn't even fully formed.

As I spent the next few years working my way through my patchwork art education, I solidified ground rules for myself:

> ***I was never allowed to call myself lazy.*** *If the thought invaded my brain, as it often does, I was to always argue back against it: "No, I'm not lazy; I'm exhausted. I'm distracted. I'm in pain. I'm overwhelmed." I found that reframing downtime as purposeful rest and rejuvenation allowed me to actually regain energy in my off-time rather than spending it worrying about what I "should" be doing. I realized that taking time for rest is a gift not only to the "me" that exists now but also to the "me" of the future, who would much prefer not to be in chronic pain from exhaustion.*
>
> *I determined that* ***nurturing my love for my craft had to take precedence*** *above all else. That doesn't mean that I never have a bad day where art is a struggle; in fact, I have many of those. It means the opposite, actually; it means being gentle with myself on those difficult days and asking myself why I'm struggling. It means continually striving to be kinder to myself during the most challenging moments.*
>
> *Finally, I learned that* ***no one would ever know exactly what the right path was for me except myself.*** *Teachers and mentors could point me in the direction they thought was best, and often their years of knowledge resulted in great guesses. But at the end of the day, it was up to me, and me alone, to decide whether each piece of advice applied to me or not.*

In 2017 I started my job at Rough Draft Studios and have been working in the animation industry ever since. As with any fast-paced media industry career, there are always ups and downs, but I've made incredible friends and worked on amazing projects. Through it all, I've always firmly set aside time for personal work. Working on paintings for myself is one of my greatest joys in life. I am lucky to now be in a place in my career where I can make that personal work a priority. I look forward to sitting down to re-read this book, maybe ten years in the future. I wonder where I'll be on that day, and what kind of art I'll be making. I look forward to seeing it one day.

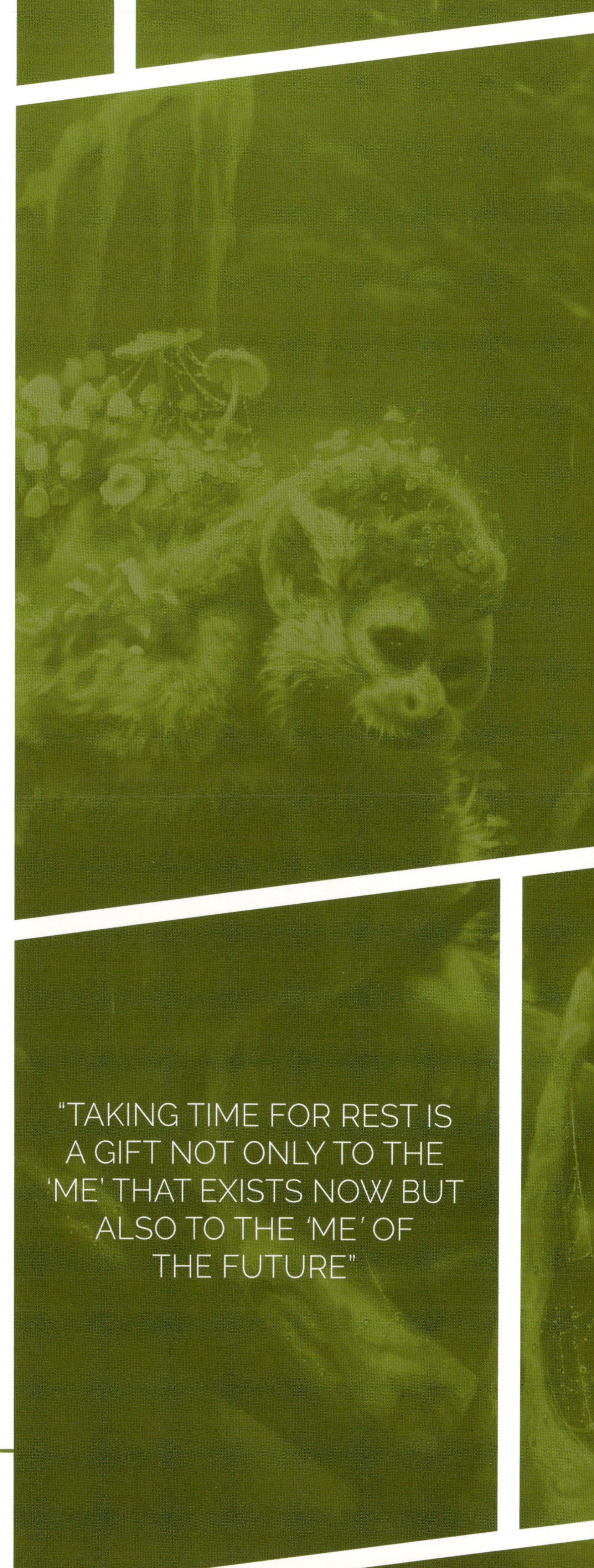

"TAKING TIME FOR REST IS A GIFT NOT ONLY TO THE 'ME' THAT EXISTS NOW BUT ALSO TO THE 'ME' OF THE FUTURE"

TRAVELER / PHOTOSHOP, 2018

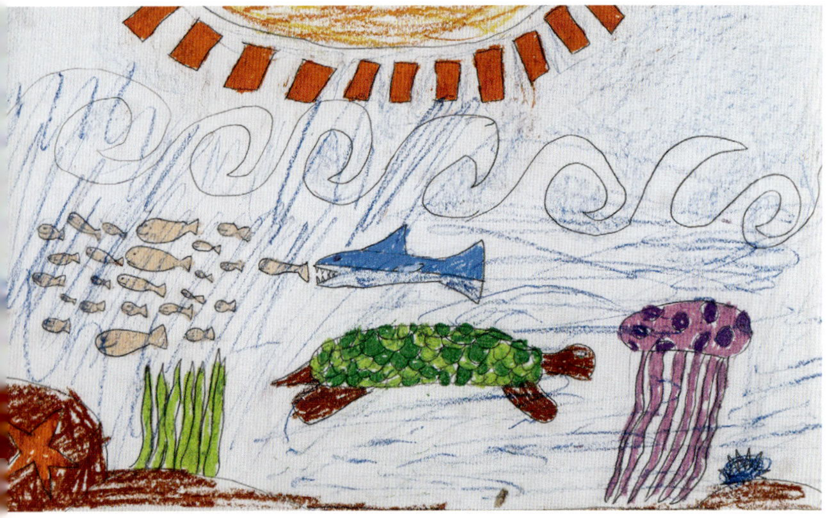

A DRAWING OF THE OCEAN FROM AROUND AGE 7

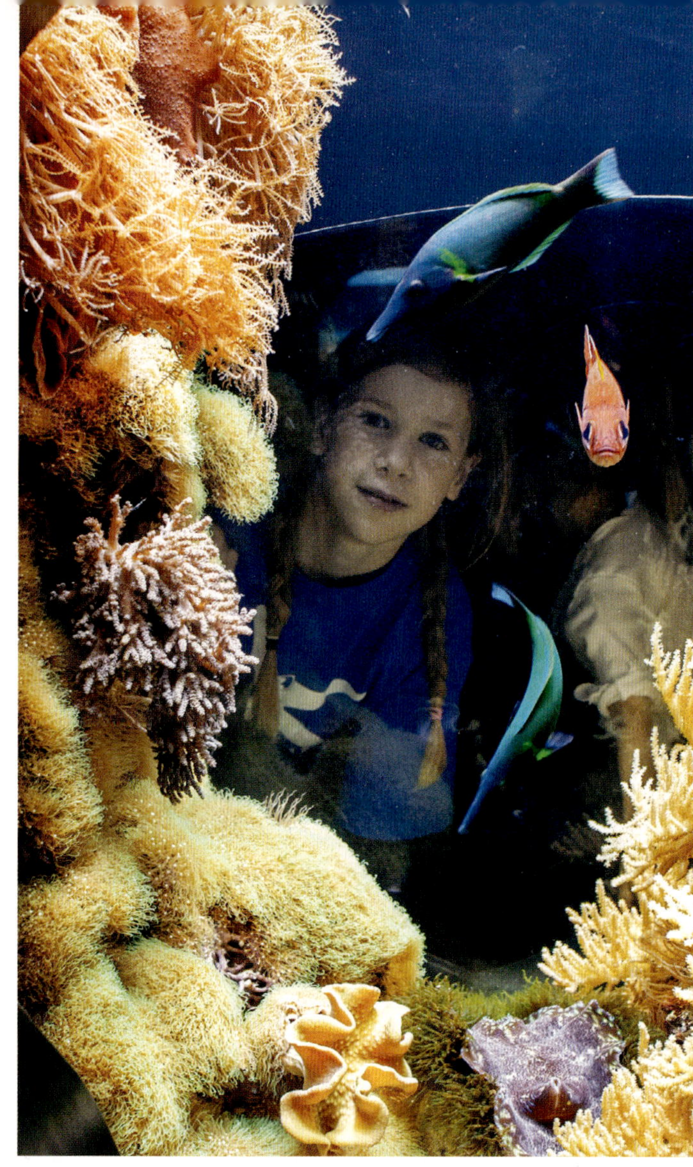

INSPIRATIONS AND RECURRING THEMES

NATURE

I grew up about an hour away from Monterey Bay Aquarium and it has long been one of my favorite places to spend a day. I remember spending hours in front of the big tanks watching the sharks swim. The ocean has always been a huge source of inspiration for me. When I was fifteen, I swam out around the Santa Cruz wharf and came face-to-face with a sea lion. It came up next to me while I was treading water and we stared at each other for a moment before it disappeared beneath the surface again. Its eyes held so much more intelligence than I had anticipated. I was struck by the majesty of sea creatures, and that feeling of wonder has never left me.

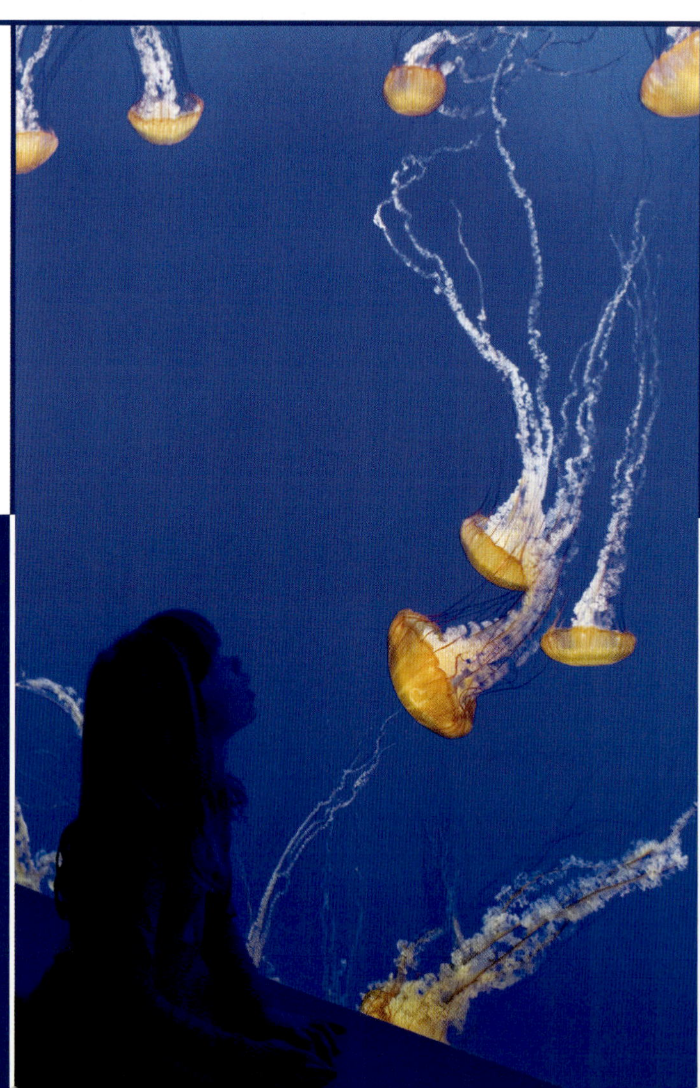

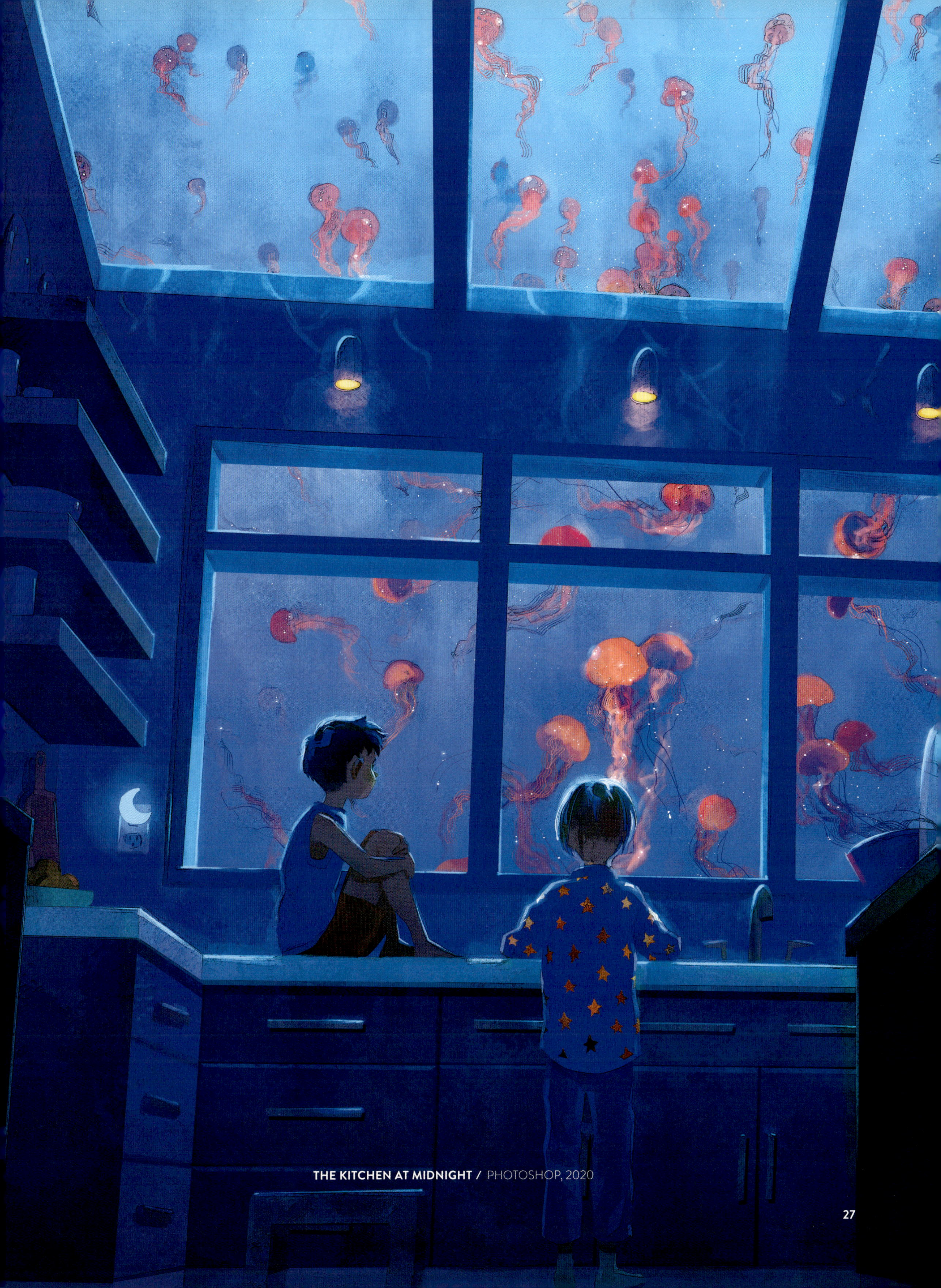

THE KITCHEN AT MIDNIGHT / PHOTOSHOP, 2020

The piece on this page is taken from the summer-themed series mentioned previously. It depicts a girl in her greenhouse impossibly high among the clouds. I decided to repaint it for this book, at almost twice the age I was when I originally painted it! I thought that between then and now, her plants would have grown a bit!

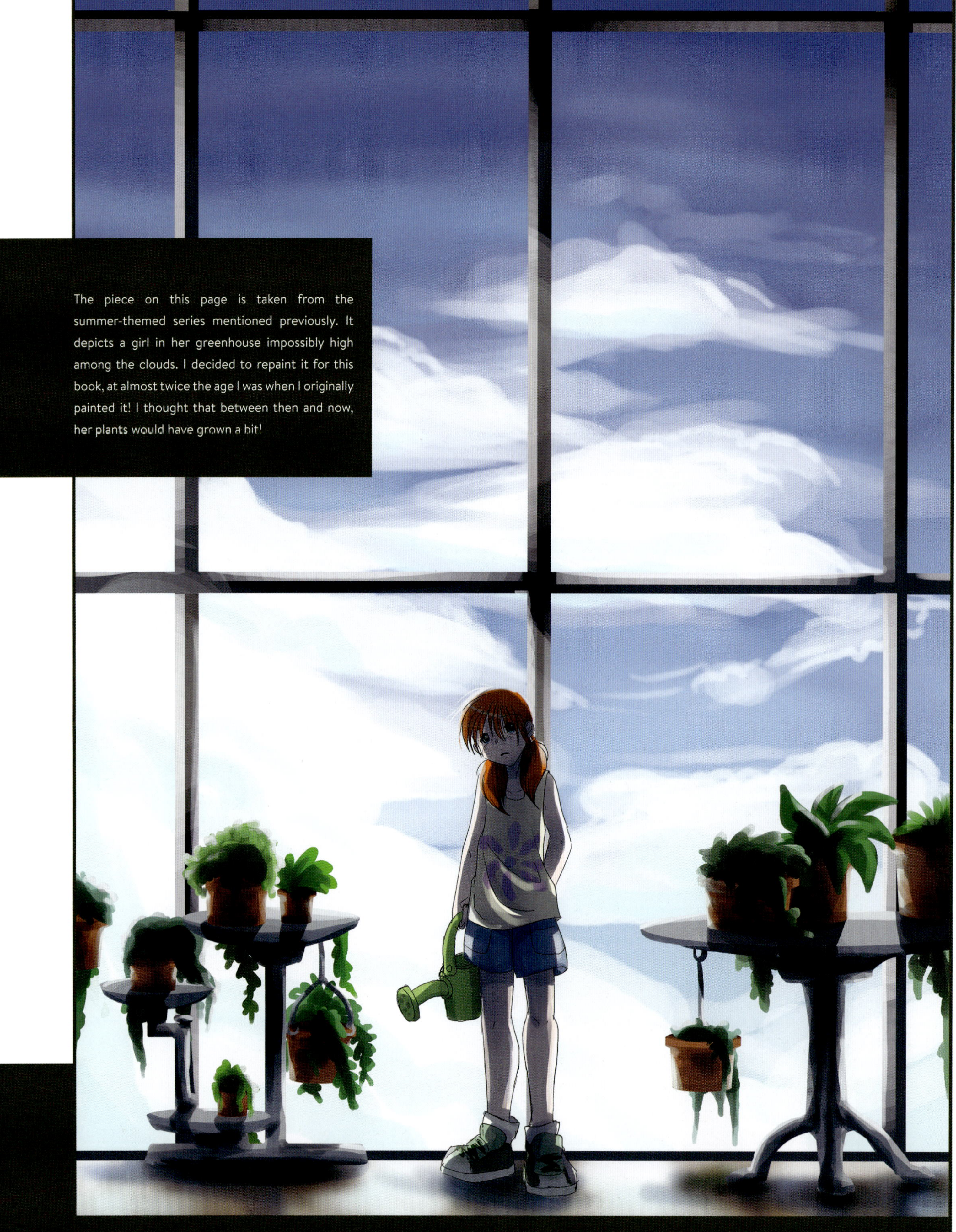

The original greenhouse painting is from 2010, when I was about 13 years of age. I repainted it in 2021, at 24!

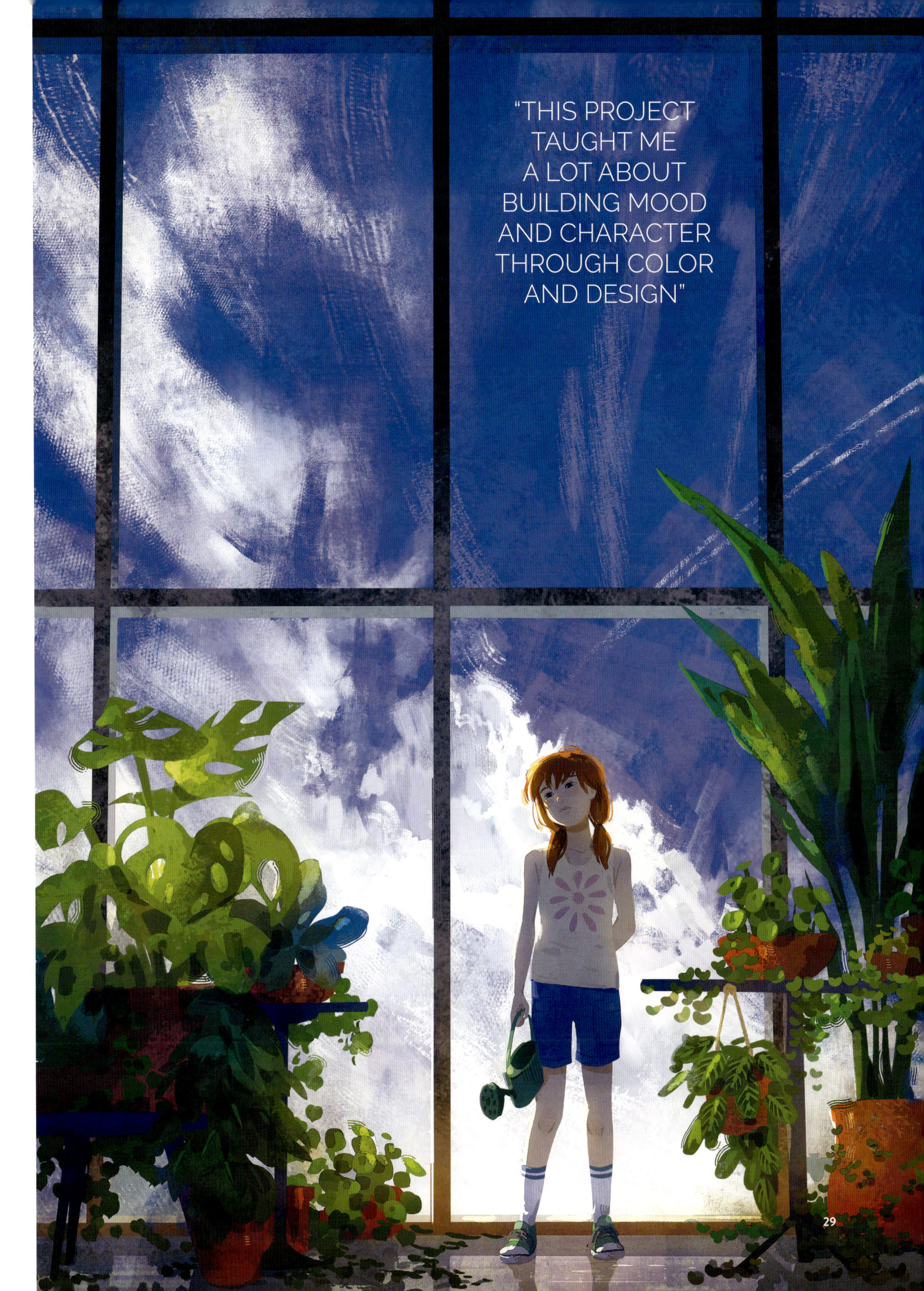

"THIS PROJECT TAUGHT ME A LOT ABOUT BUILDING MOOD AND CHARACTER THROUGH COLOR AND DESIGN"

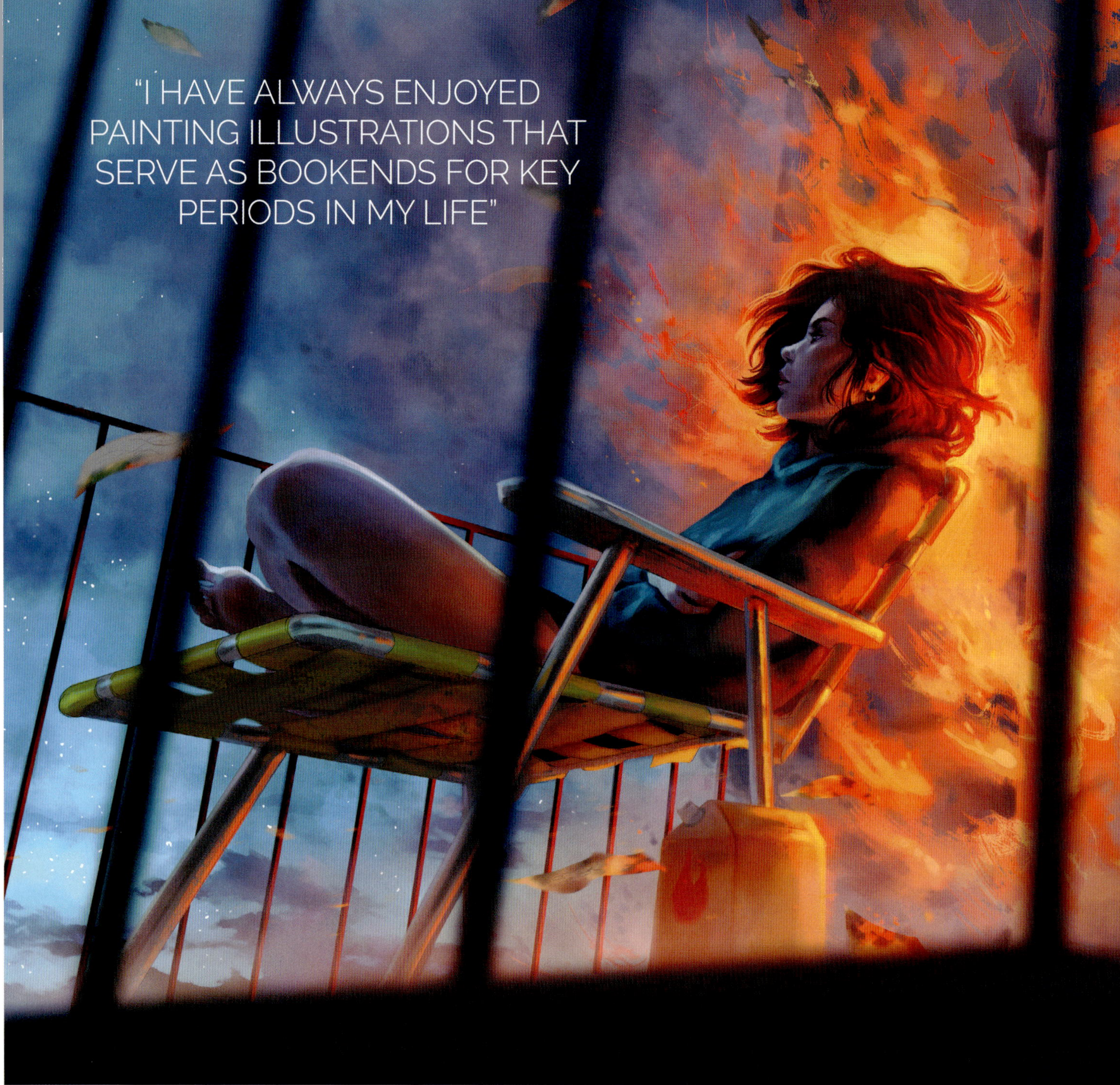

CONTROLLED BURN / PHOTOSHOP, 2016

CAPTURING A MOMENT

A recurring theme of my work is the encapsulation of an emotionally charged moment. In particular, I have always enjoyed painting illustrations that serve as bookends for key periods in my life. In creating these pieces, I immortalize the experience, like a visual diary. I painted *Dying Sun* in the last month of my senior year of high school, as I prepared to leave the seaside town I loved dearly. I painted *Controlled Burn* the summer after I dropped out of college, as I metaphorically scorched the path I believed was meant for me, and looked forward to hopefully find bluer skies on the horizon. My friend, Chloe, left college at exactly the same time I did, and facing the unknown together made the fear a little bit easier to wade through. That said, I think the character's expression is a touch more resolute than mine was at that time.

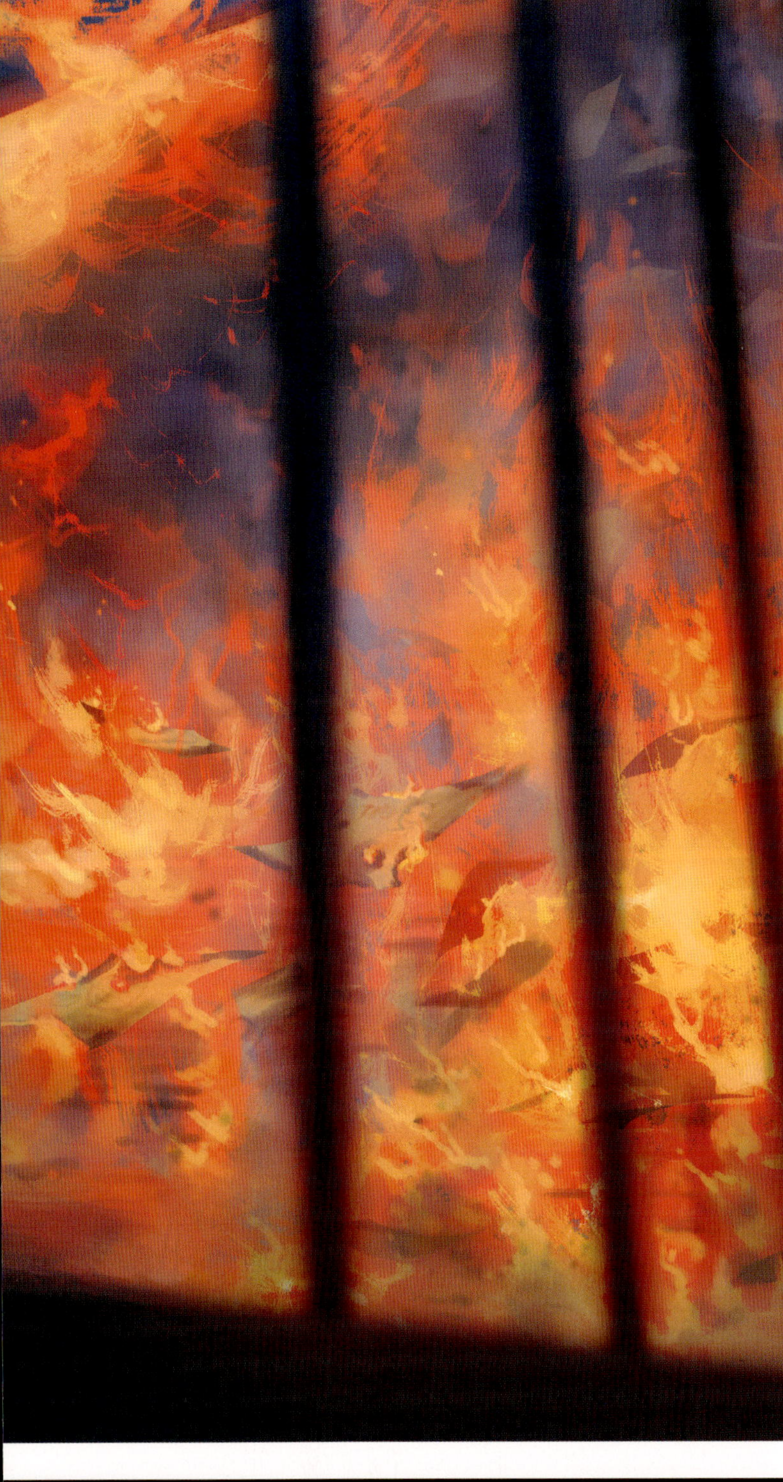

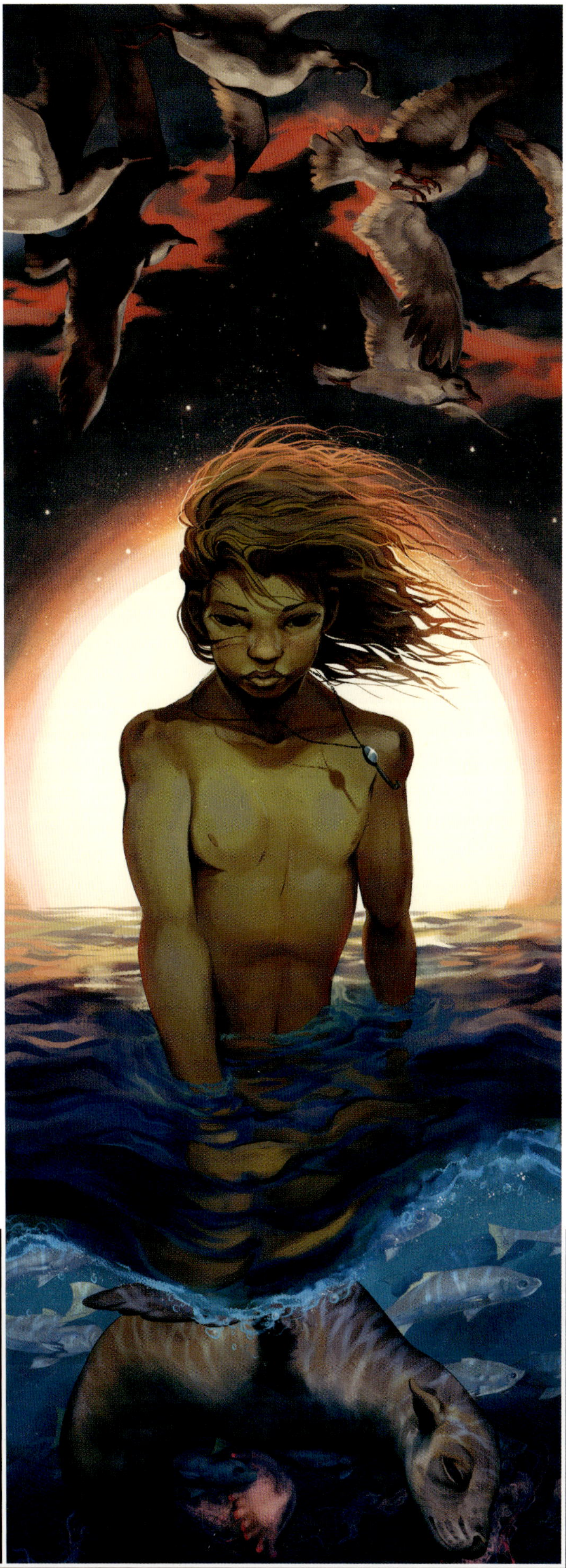

DYING SUN / PHOTOSHOP, 2014

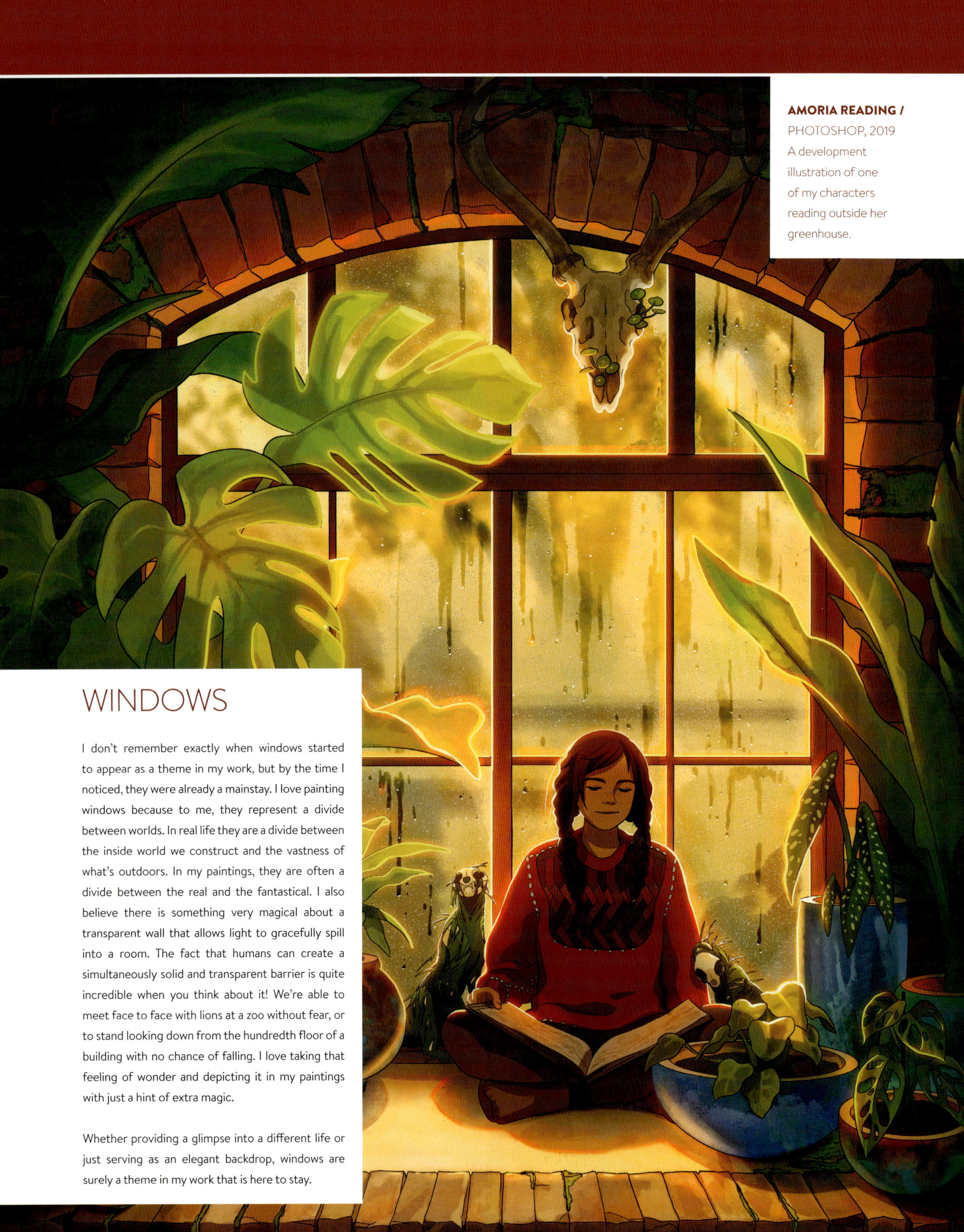

AMORIA READING /
PHOTOSHOP, 2019
A development illustration of one of my characters reading outside her greenhouse.

WINDOWS

I don't remember exactly when windows started to appear as a theme in my work, but by the time I noticed, they were already a mainstay. I love painting windows because to me, they represent a divide between worlds. In real life they are a divide between the inside world we construct and the vastness of what's outdoors. In my paintings, they are often a divide between the real and the fantastical. I also believe there is something very magical about a transparent wall that allows light to gracefully spill into a room. The fact that humans can create a simultaneously solid and transparent barrier is quite incredible when you think about it! We're able to meet face to face with lions at a zoo without fear, or to stand looking down from the hundredth floor of a building with no chance of falling. I love taking that feeling of wonder and depicting it in my paintings with just a hint of extra magic.

Whether providing a glimpse into a different life or just serving as an elegant backdrop, windows are surely a theme in my work that is here to stay.

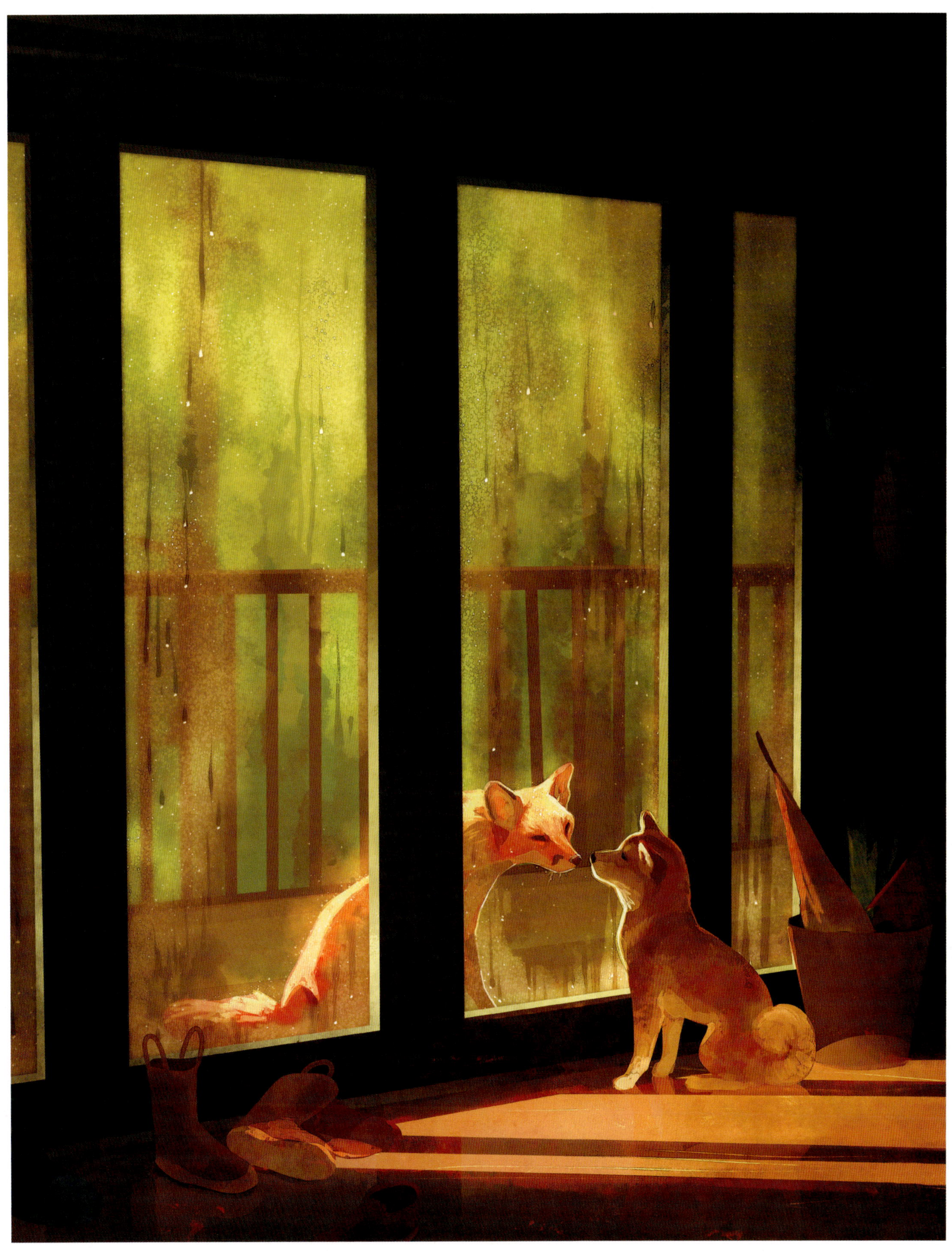

A NEW FRIEND WHO LOOKS LIKE ME / PHOTOSHOP, 2020

VISIT FROM AN OLD FRIEND / PHOTOSHOP, 2017

I painted *Visit from an Old Friend* in 2018, about a year after my dear cat Luka passed away from a genetic heart condition at only eight years old. Our other cat, Shinji, sometimes sat and stared endlessly out the window. I like to imagine that Luka's spirit comes to see him sometimes.

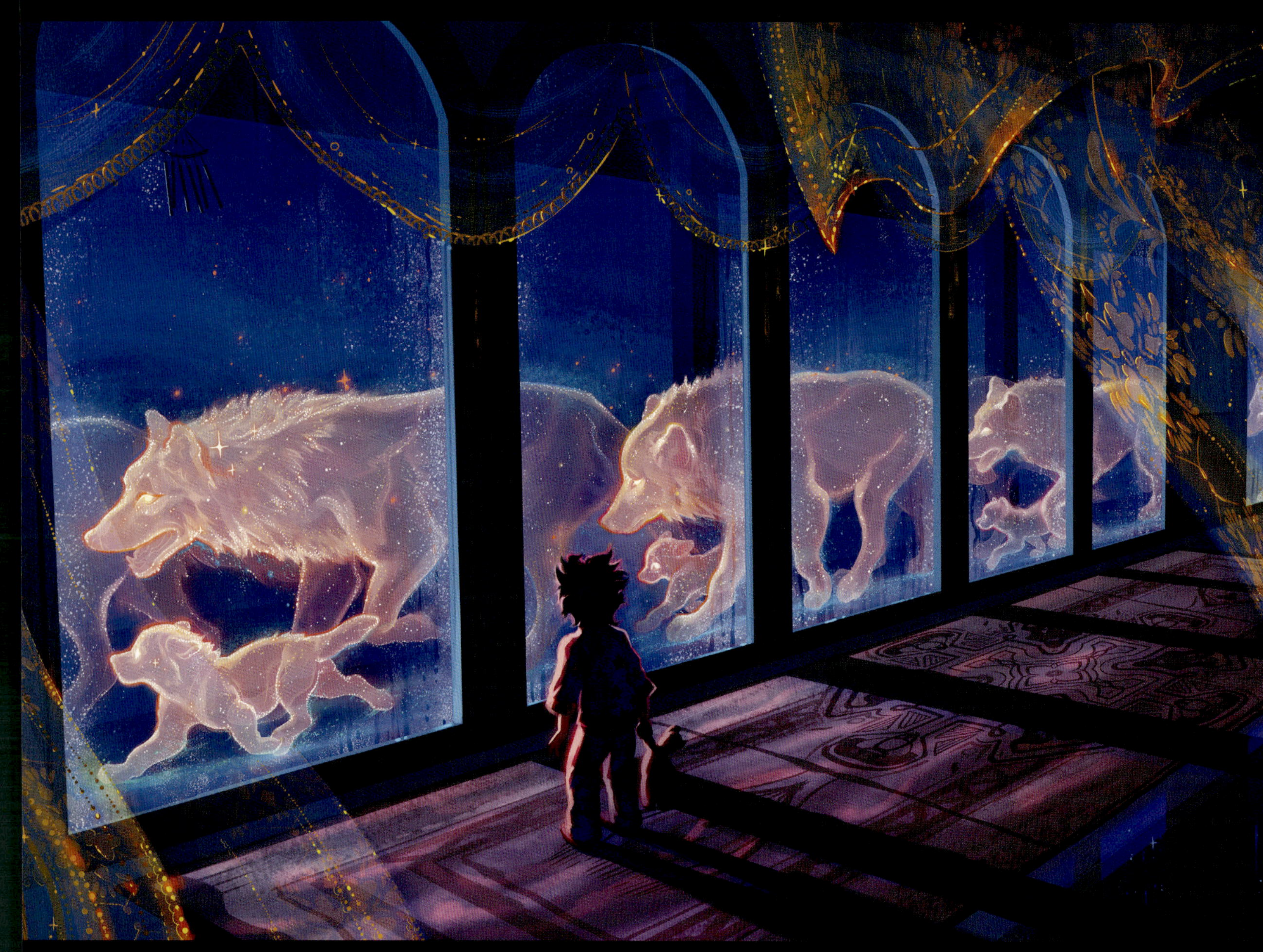

CHANCE ENCOUNTER / PHOTOSHOP, 2018

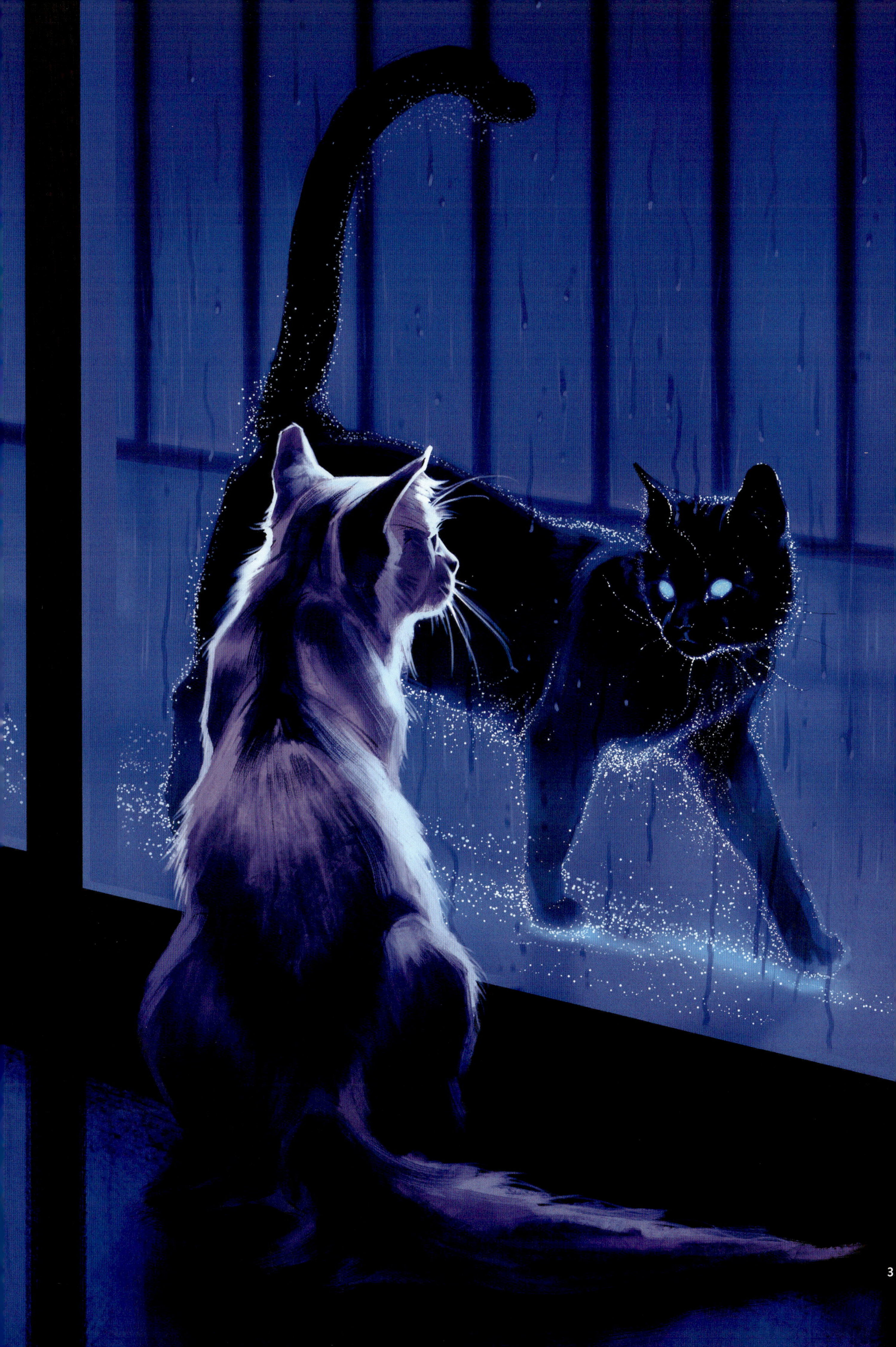

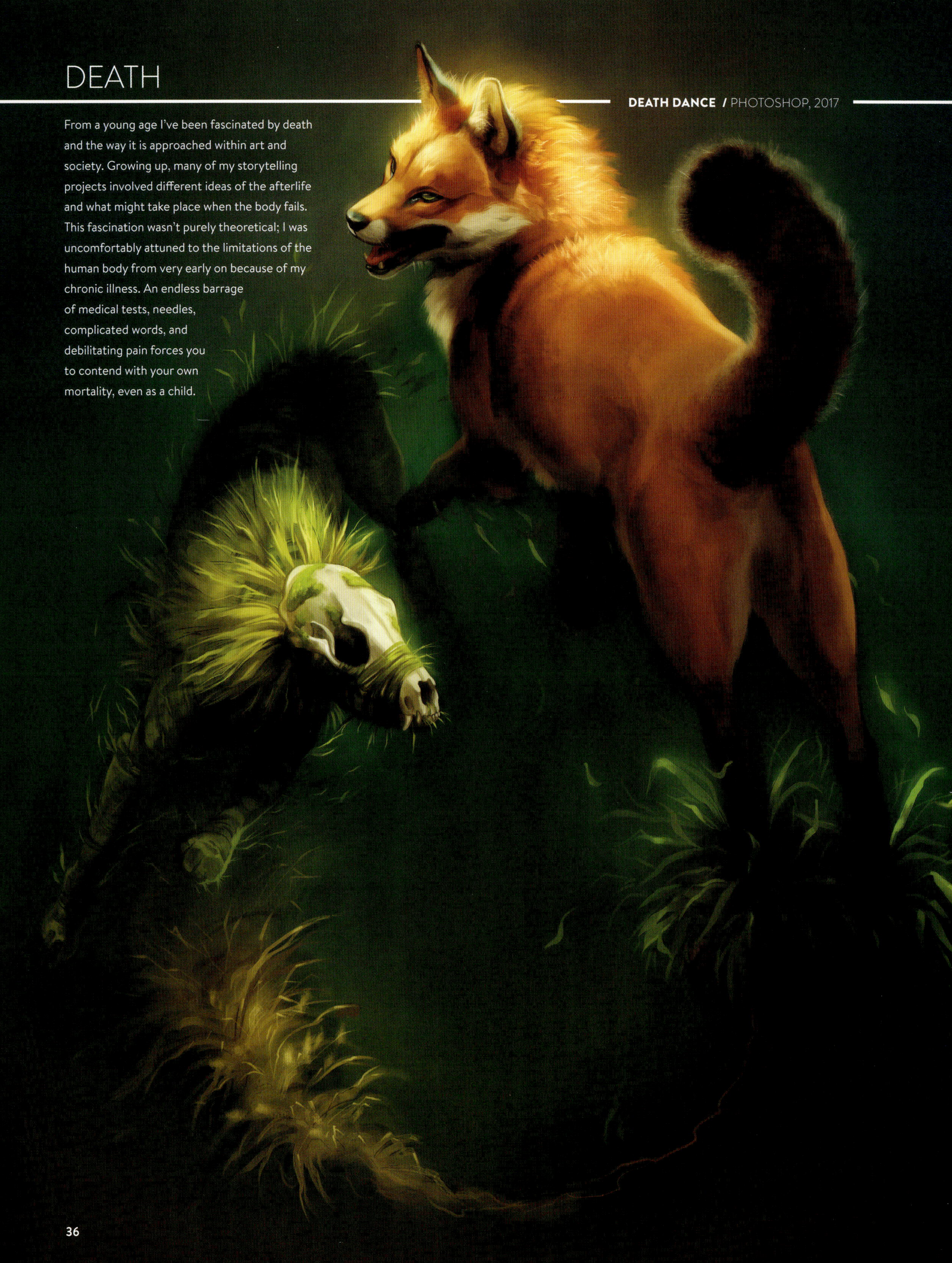

DEATH

DEATH DANCE / PHOTOSHOP, 2017

From a young age I've been fascinated by death and the way it is approached within art and society. Growing up, many of my storytelling projects involved different ideas of the afterlife and what might take place when the body fails. This fascination wasn't purely theoretical; I was uncomfortably attuned to the limitations of the human body from very early on because of my chronic illness. An endless barrage of medical tests, needles, complicated words, and debilitating pain forces you to contend with your own mortality, even as a child.

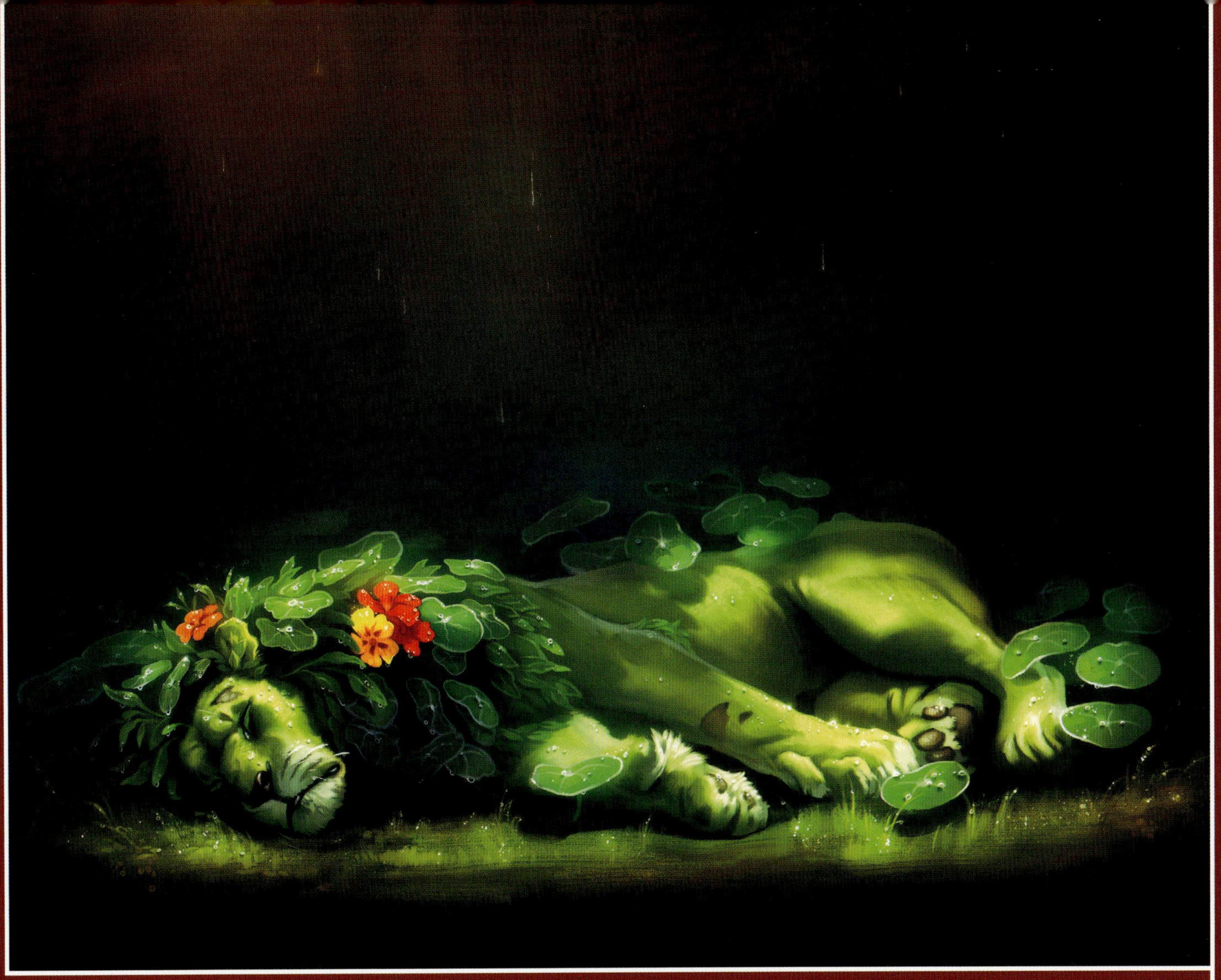

RECLAMATION / PHOTOSHOP, 2017

I felt a lot of solace when death was depicted in a natural, cyclical way. The idea of being overtaken by nature and returned to the earth was deeply comforting. I painted *Reclamation* in an attempt to bring beauty and peace to the concept of death.

REUNION / PHOTOSHOP, 2017

I painted *Reunion* when my uncle Philip passed away. I've continued to explore death imagery throughout my work, often as a physical companion to humanity, living among us in a natural and peaceful way.

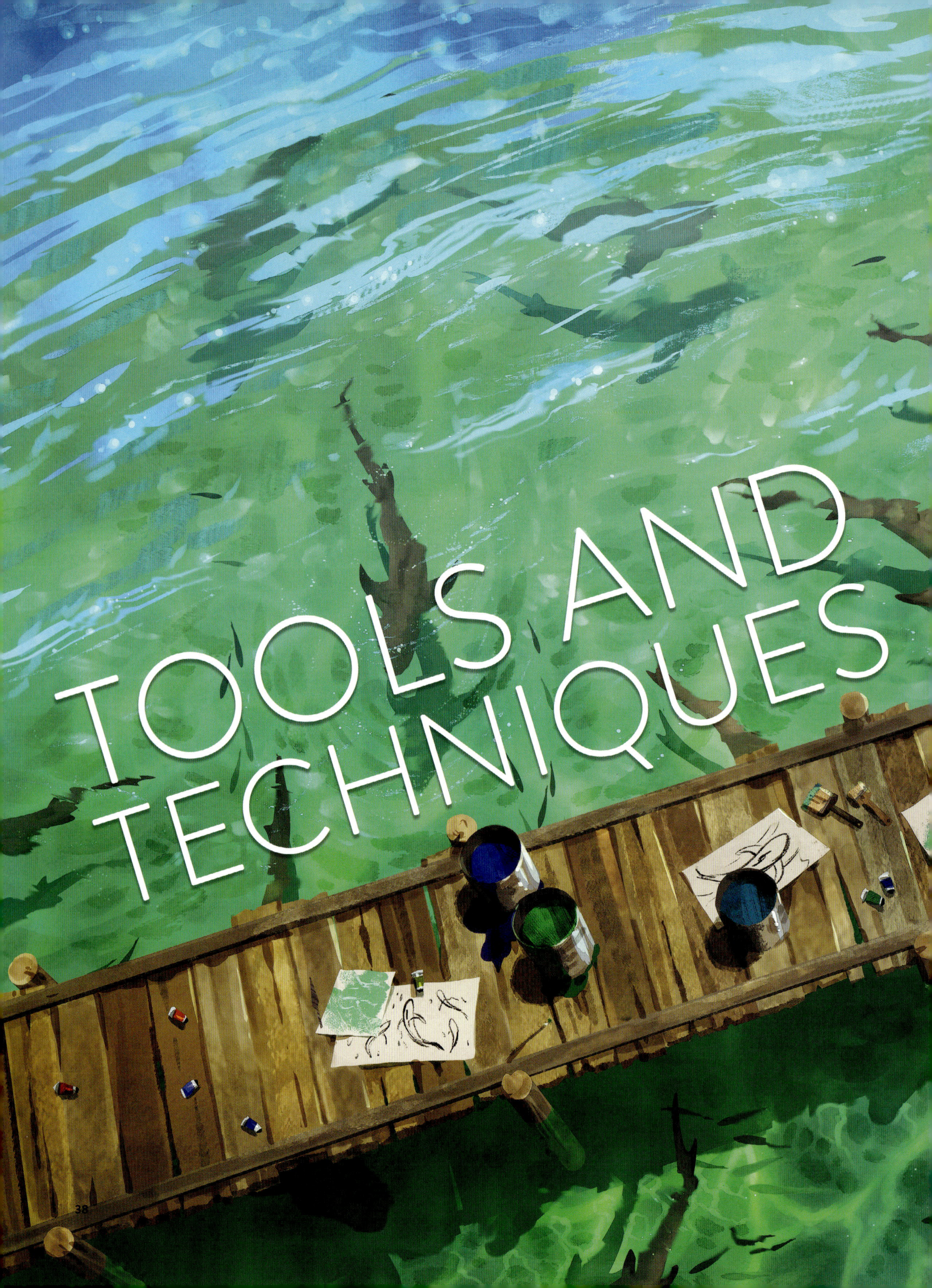

TOOLS AND TECHNIQUES

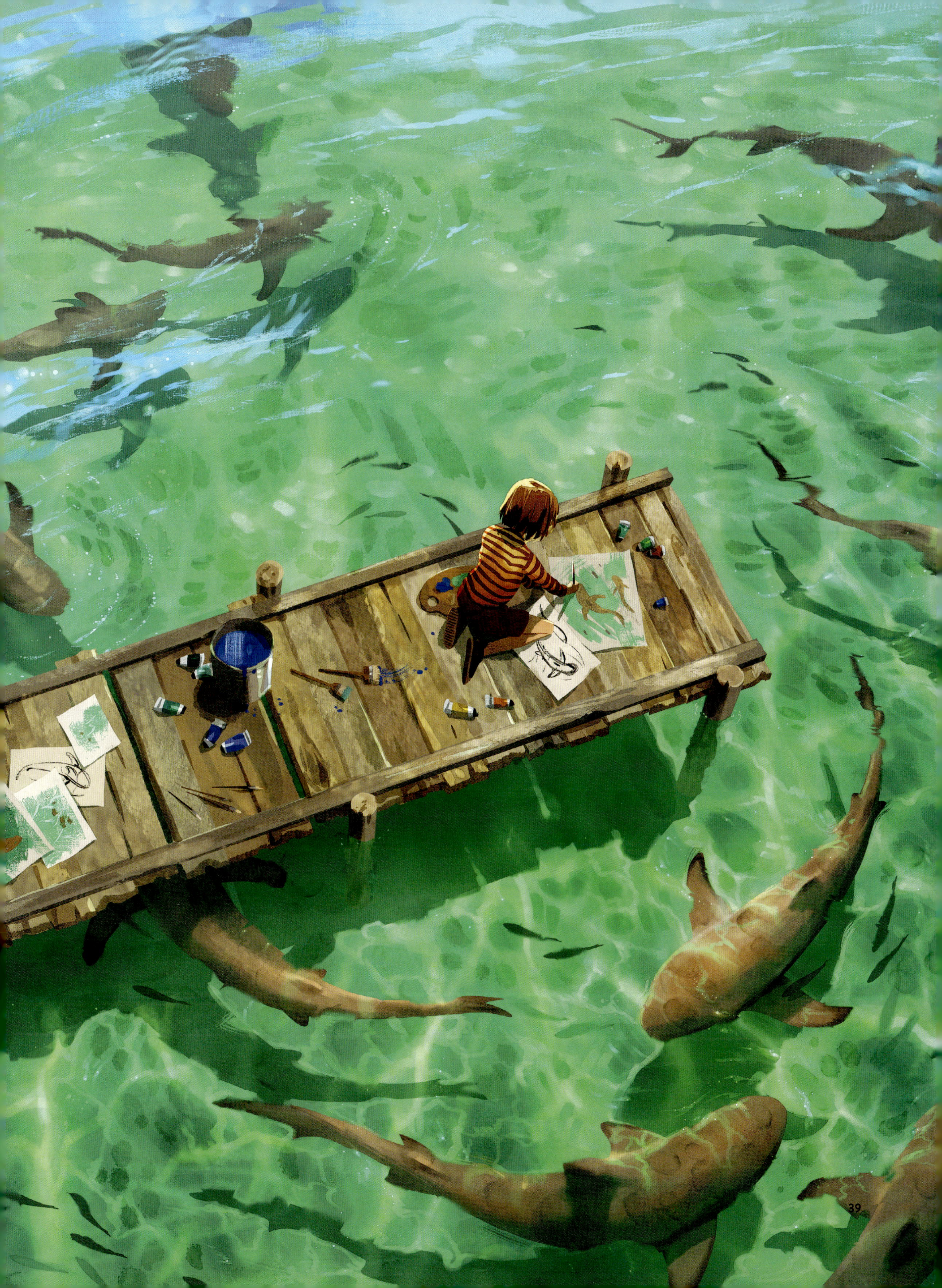

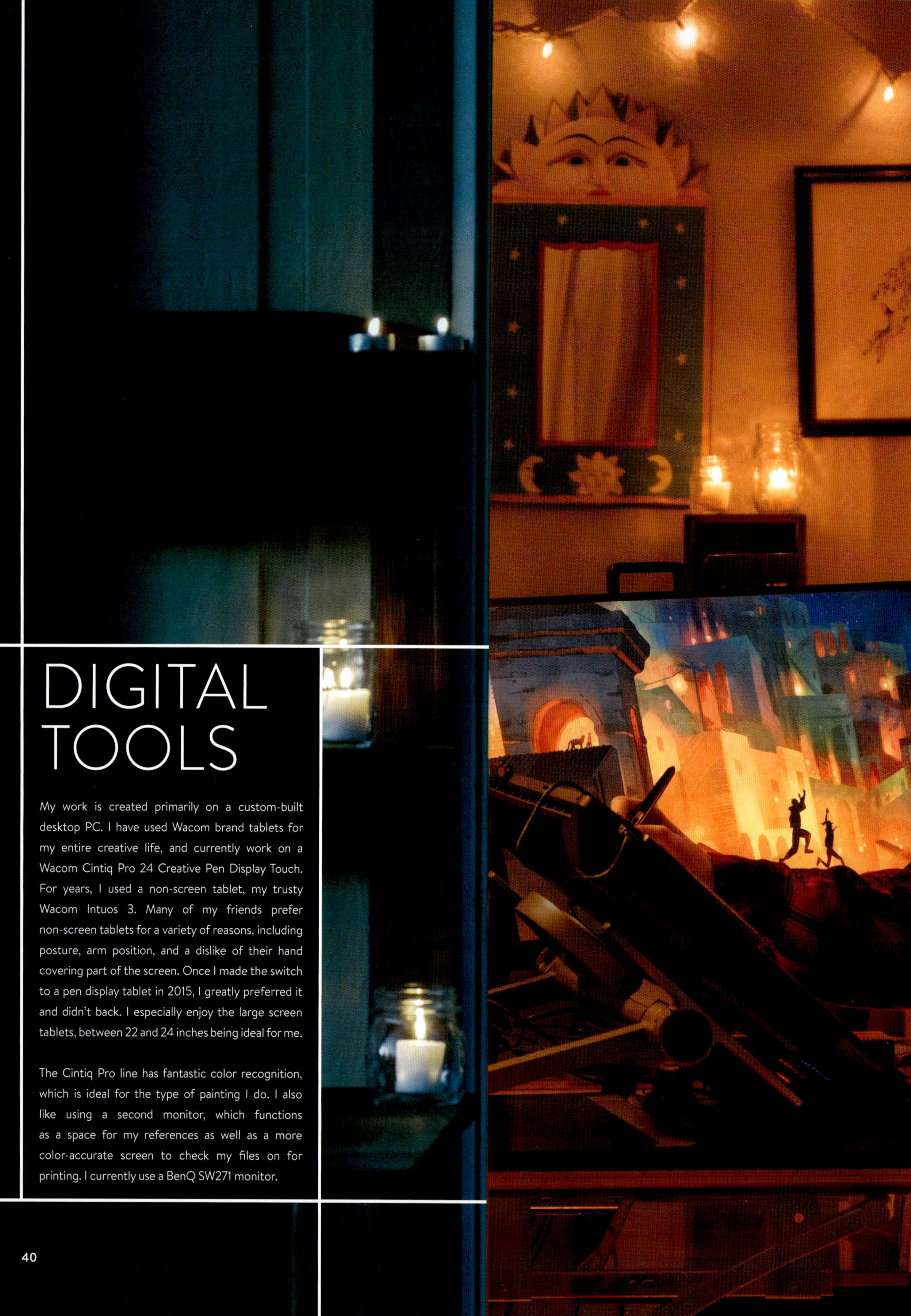

DIGITAL TOOLS

My work is created primarily on a custom-built desktop PC. I have used Wacom brand tablets for my entire creative life, and currently work on a Wacom Cintiq Pro 24 Creative Pen Display Touch. For years, I used a non-screen tablet, my trusty Wacom Intuos 3. Many of my friends prefer non-screen tablets for a variety of reasons, including posture, arm position, and a dislike of their hand covering part of the screen. Once I made the switch to a pen display tablet in 2015, I greatly preferred it and didn't back. I especially enjoy the large screen tablets, between 22 and 24 inches being ideal for me.

The Cintiq Pro line has fantastic color recognition, which is ideal for the type of painting I do. I also like using a second monitor, which functions as a space for my references as well as a more color-accurate screen to check my files on for printing. I currently use a BenQ SW271 monitor.

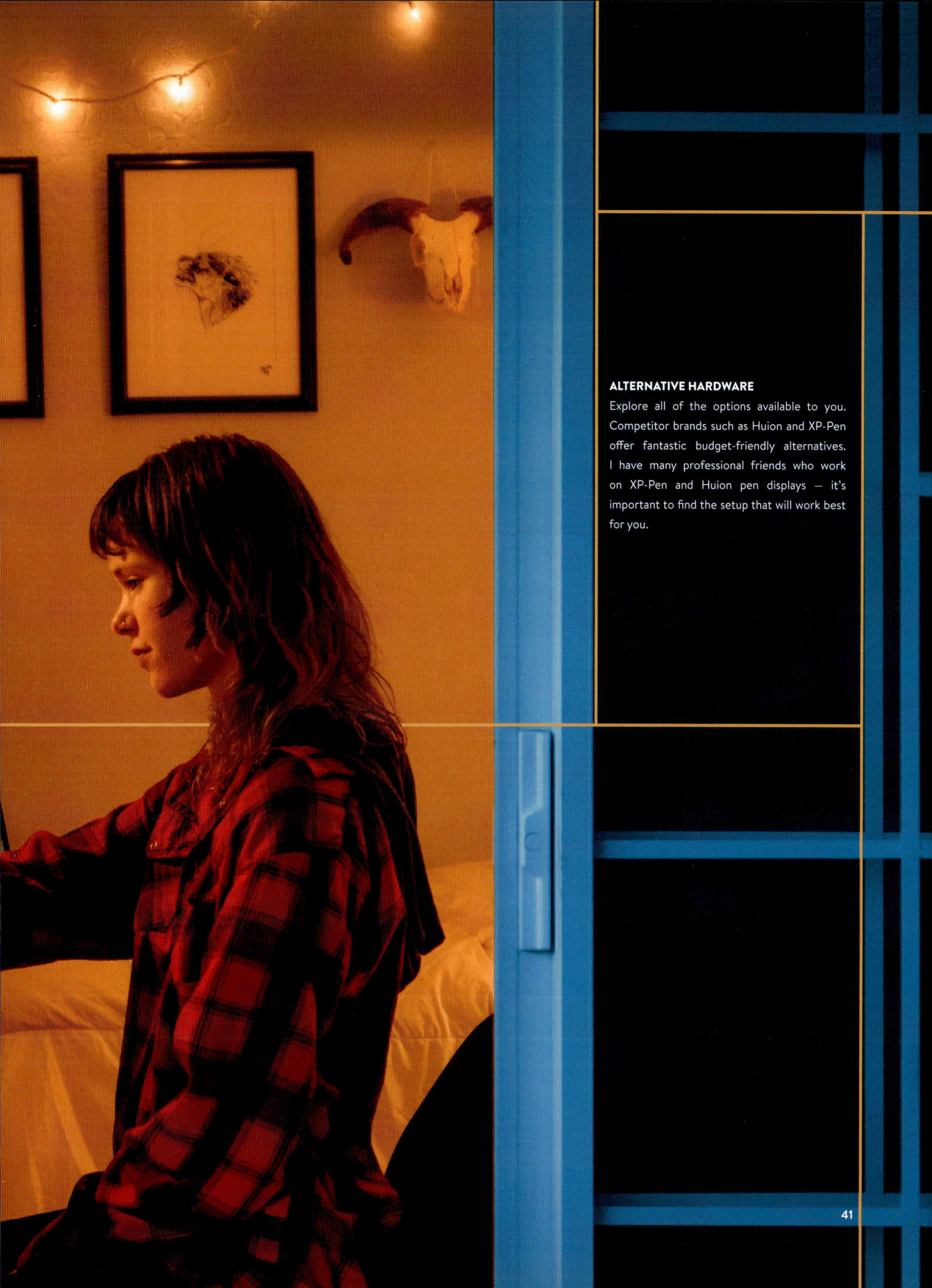

ALTERNATIVE HARDWARE

Explore all of the options available to you. Competitor brands such as Huion and XP-Pen offer fantastic budget-friendly alternatives. I have many professional friends who work on XP-Pen and Huion pen displays – it's important to find the setup that will work best for you.

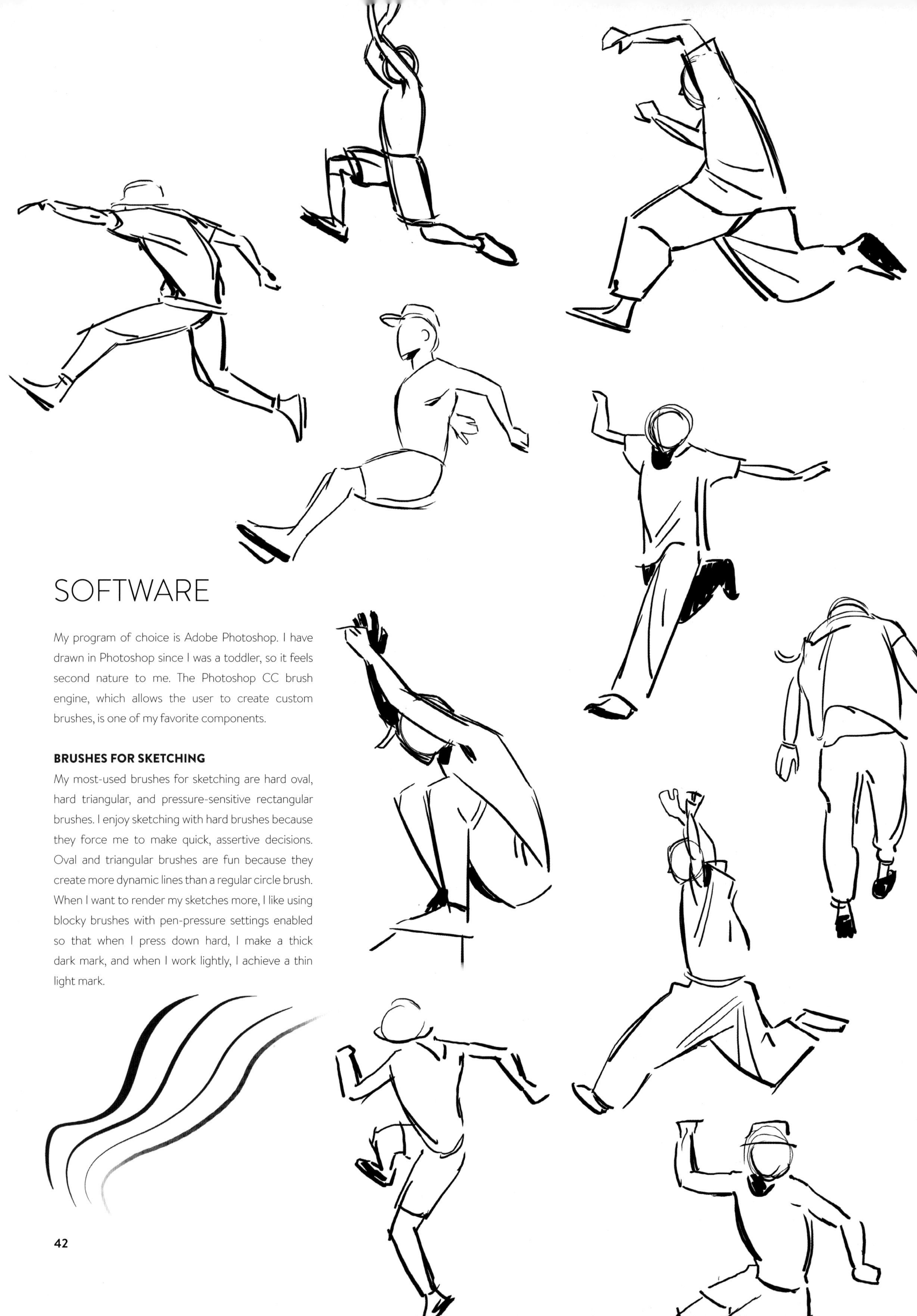

SOFTWARE

My program of choice is Adobe Photoshop. I have drawn in Photoshop since I was a toddler, so it feels second nature to me. The Photoshop CC brush engine, which allows the user to create custom brushes, is one of my favorite components.

BRUSHES FOR SKETCHING

My most-used brushes for sketching are hard oval, hard triangular, and pressure-sensitive rectangular brushes. I enjoy sketching with hard brushes because they force me to make quick, assertive decisions. Oval and triangular brushes are fun because they create more dynamic lines than a regular circle brush. When I want to render my sketches more, I like using blocky brushes with pen-pressure settings enabled so that when I press down hard, I make a thick dark mark, and when I work lightly, I achieve a thin light mark.

"I USE TEXTURED BRUSHES IN CREATIVE WAYS TO IMPLY A LOT OF DETAIL QUICKLY"

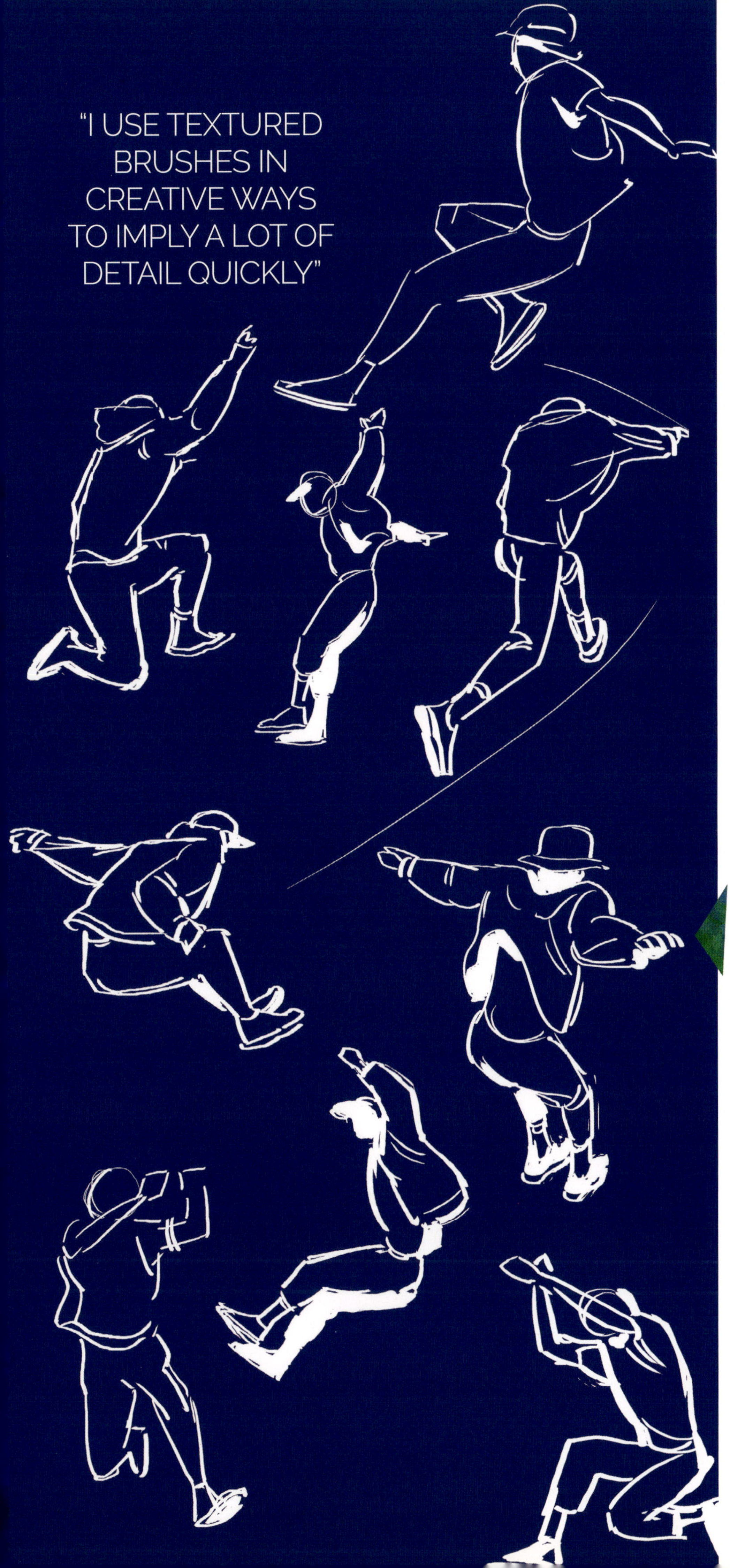

FILLING BASE COLORS

After sketching, I decrease the opacity of the sketch layer to 20–30% and fill in key shapes using the Lasso tool (more about this tool next!) and a grainy or textured brush with Color Dynamics enabled, which introduces a randomness to the application. My favorite brush for filling in base colors is the splotchy brush from the Kyle T. Webster Impressionist pack that comes with a Photoshop CC subscription. I've been using Kyle's brush packs for nearly a decade, and they're some of the best Photoshop brushes available.

THE LASSO TOOL

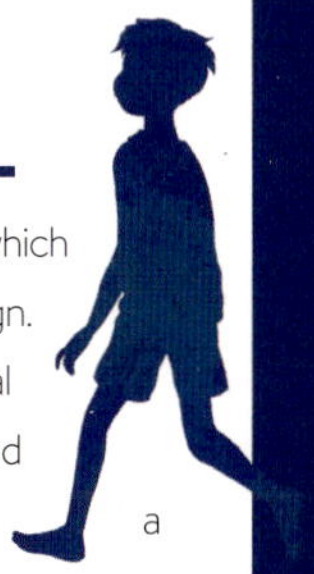

One of my favorite tools is the Lasso, which allows for free-form selection within a design. I toggle between the regular and polygonal Lasso tools in a single selection by holding and releasing the Alt key. The ability to do this is a huge asset because it allows me to easily select shapes that have a combination of straight and organic edges. After making my first selection, I can also hold the Shift key to add additional selections – I often select many areas at once.

TEXTURED BRUSHES

I enjoy painting with selections because it allows me to add texture at any stage without fear of painting over areas I want to remain untouched. I use textured brushes in creative ways to imply a lot of detail quickly, such as using rake brushes to represent wood grain or roof slats with a single stroke. Splatter brushes quickly add grit or texture. I also really like the graphic quality the Lasso tool lends to my art.

SOFTENING THE EDGES

I start a painting with hard edges, then slowly choose which ones to blend out and soften. Losing and softening edges makes a huge difference to the end result, but working from hard to soft edges is easier for me than working from soft to hard. Early on, I struggled with my environments losing definition, but starting every painting with hard-edged shapes solved this problem. As I determine the important focal areas of a piece, I blend and soften the unimportant edges with painterly brushes that often mimic watercolor or oil-painted textures.

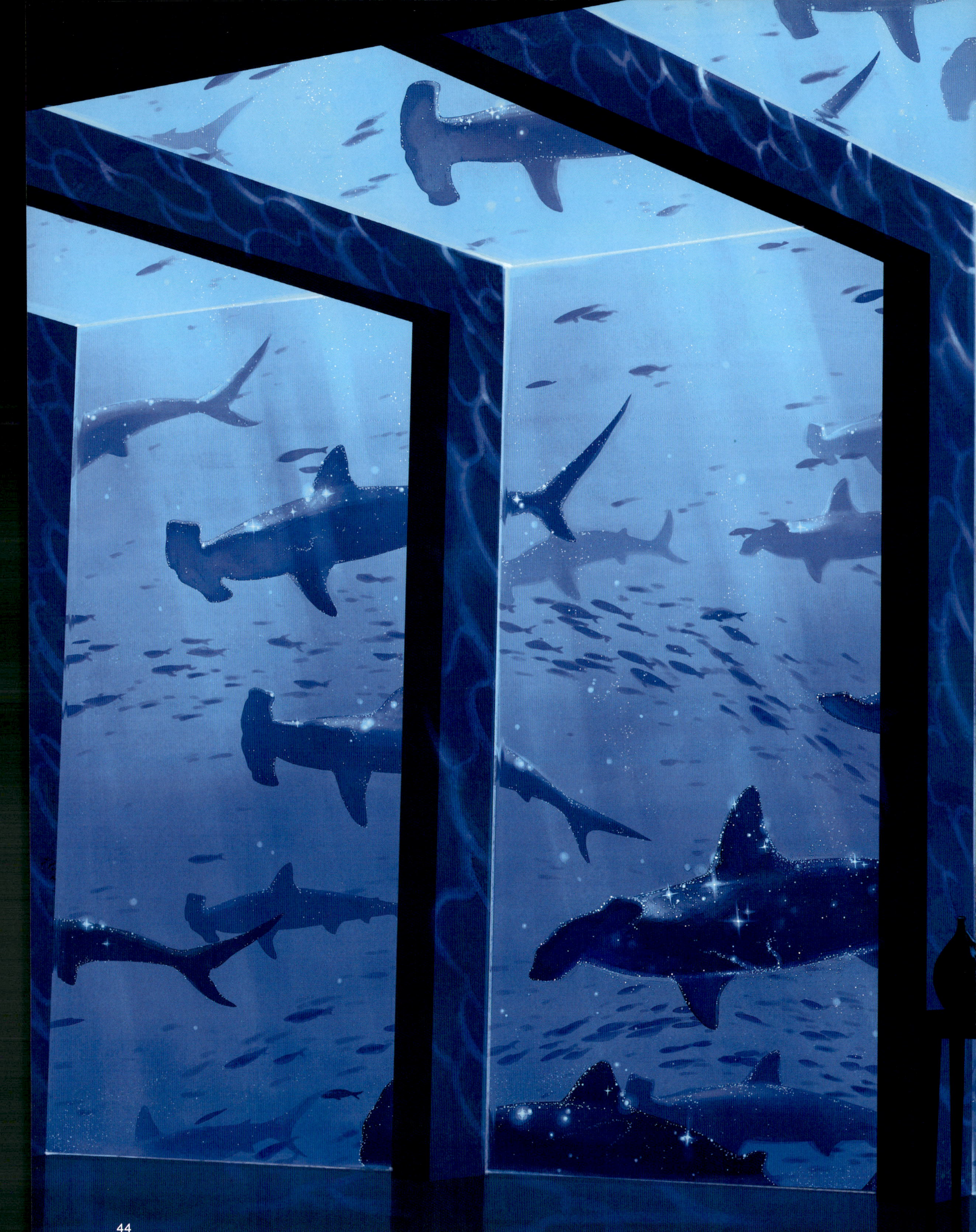

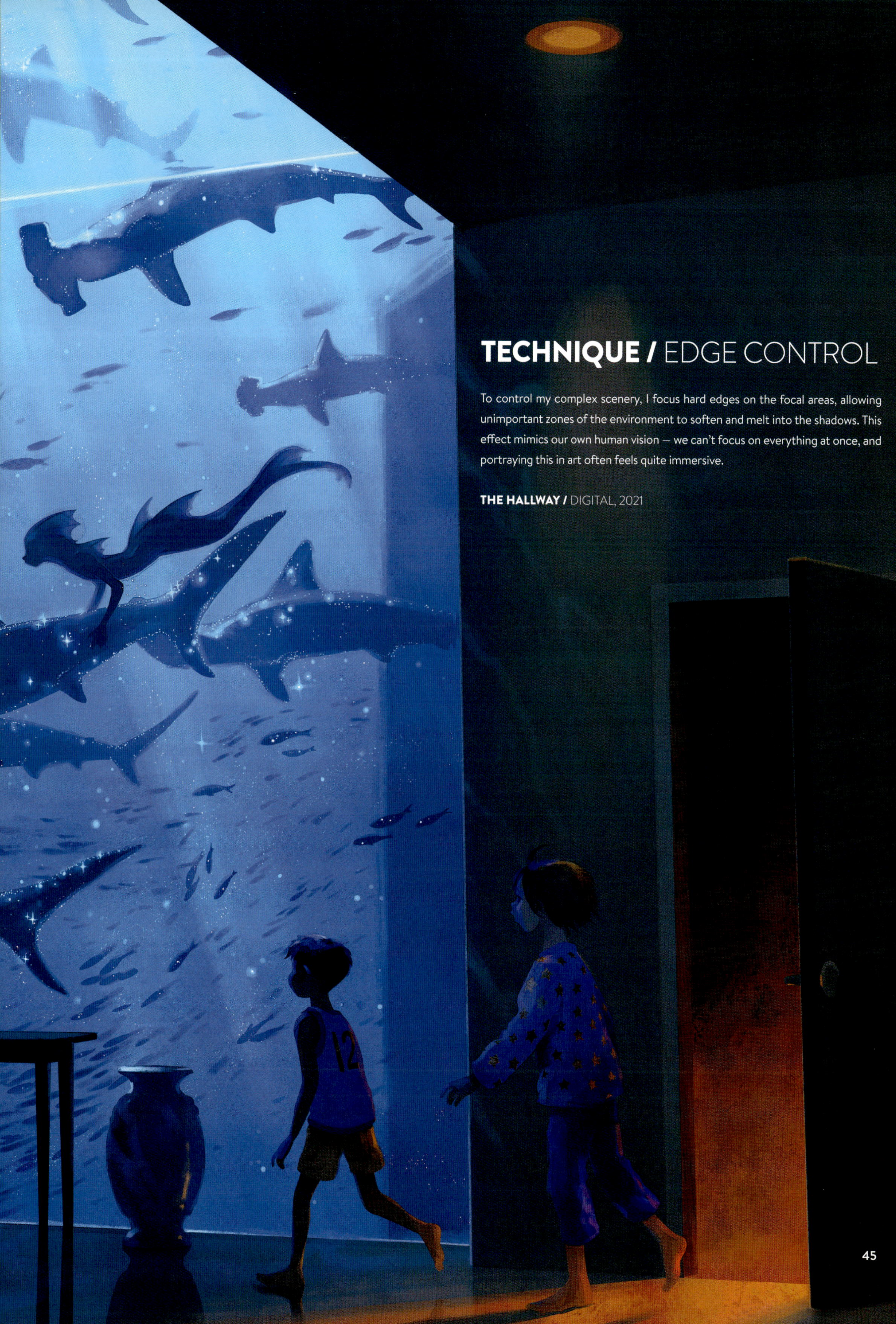

TECHNIQUE / EDGE CONTROL

To control my complex scenery, I focus hard edges on the focal areas, allowing unimportant zones of the environment to soften and melt into the shadows. This effect mimics our own human vision – we can't focus on everything at once, and portraying this in art often feels quite immersive.

THE HALLWAY / DIGITAL, 2021

BRUSHES FOR PAINTING DETAILS

Once the main shapes are filled in, I add little details with hard square or oval brushes. For hard-edged, man-made structures, a square or rectangular brush makes it easier to maintain straight edges while detailing. For organic structures, I prefer an oval brush.

I don't do a lot of rendering in my paintings, but when I do, I like to use brushes with a watercolor or oil-paint texture. The Kyle T. Webster packs work perfectly for this, and in Procreate the Max Ulichney brush packs are a great alternative.

In this piece, *The Hallway*, I have softened many of the edges outside the window to set those forms back in space and allow the foreground to pop forward.

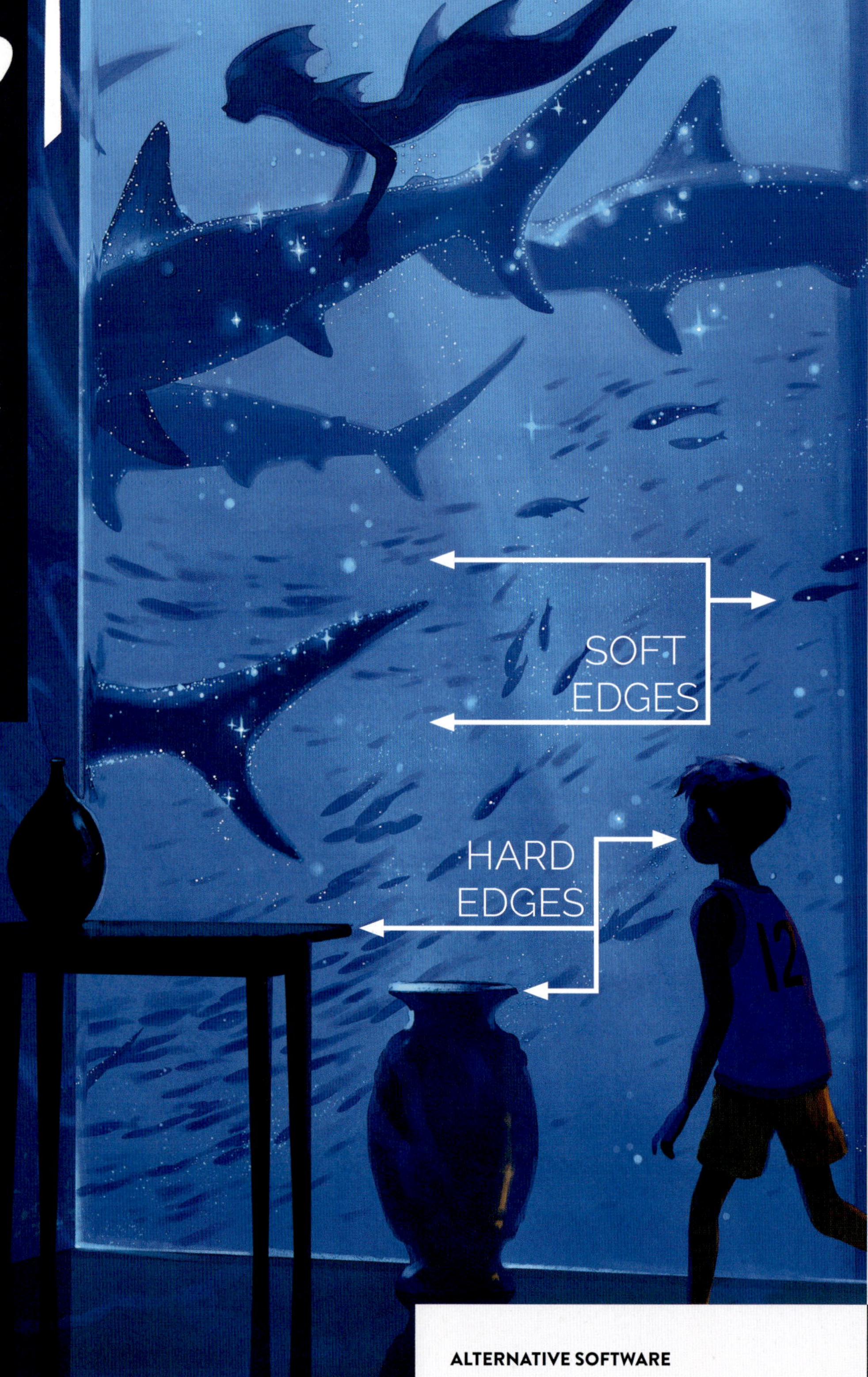

ALTERNATIVE SOFTWARE

Clip Studio Paint and Procreate are excellent program software options; their low one-time purchase costs also make them a potentially superior choice for beginners.

VISITING THE SLEEPING GIANT - NIGHT /
DIGITAL, 2021

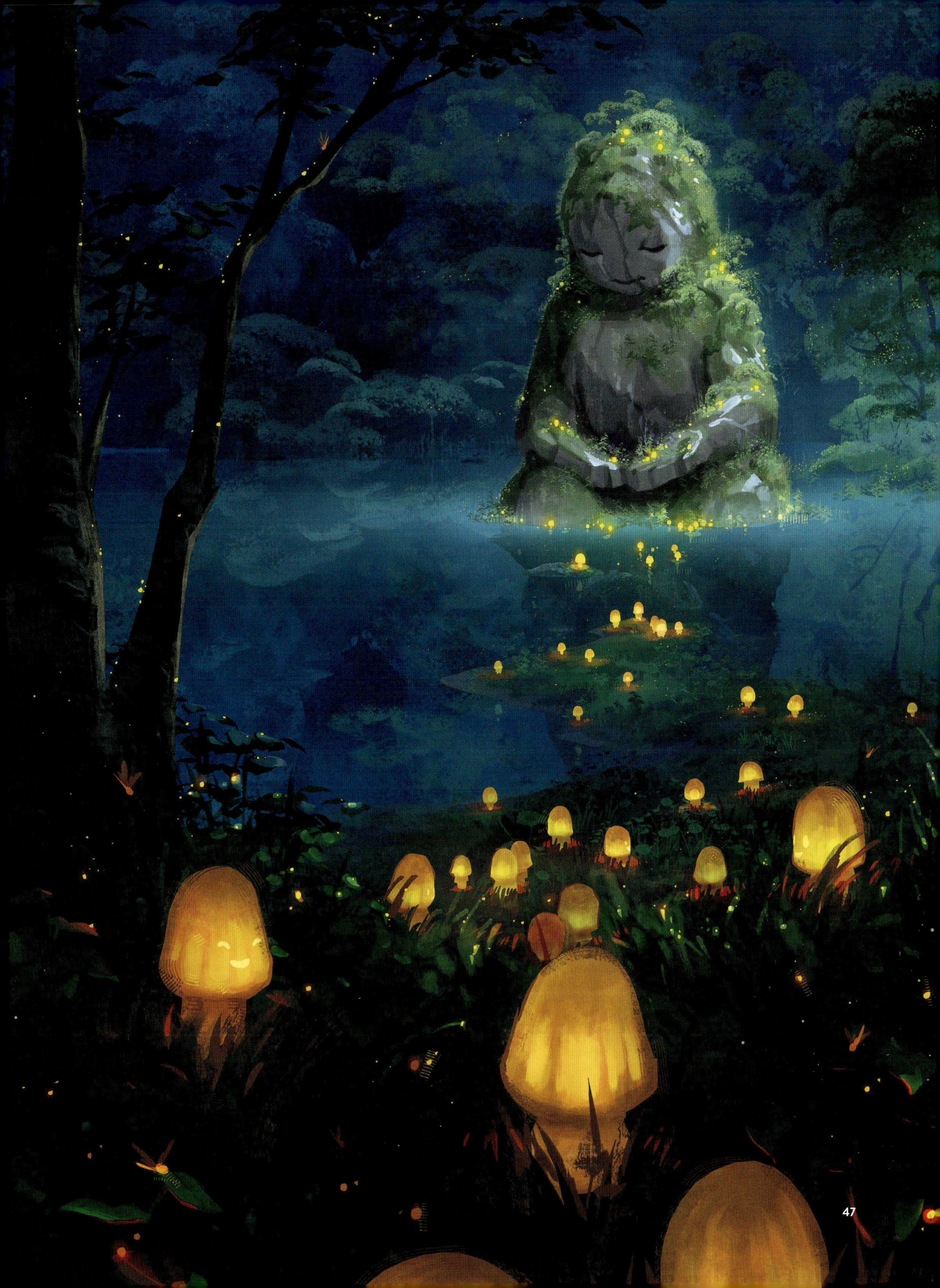

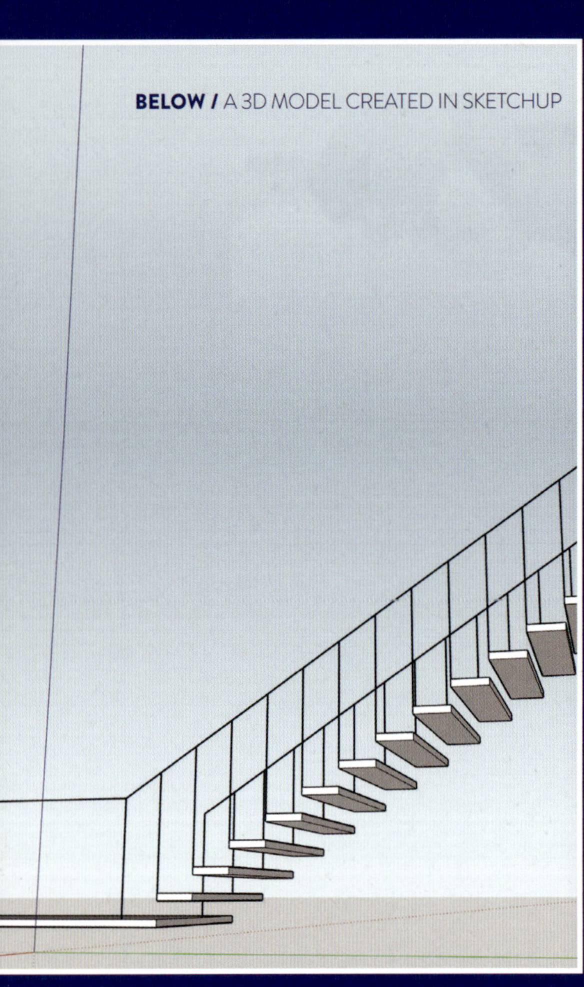

BELOW / A 3D MODEL CREATED IN SKETCHUP

3D SOFTWARE

To further my knowledge of 3D art software, I have recently begun to experiment with SketchUp, an architectural software with a free web version.

Initially, I was drawn to SketchUp due to my dislike of drawing stairs. Drawing stairs in perspective, especially if they curve or wind around, is incredibly challenging, but modeling them in 3D software is simple. This experience convinced me of the value of learning to use 3D software, despite the upfront time investment that sometimes felt frustrating when I was used to drawing what I could see or imagine.

I simply take screenshots of my 3D designs, open the screenshot in Photoshop, and use it as my sketch. I'm very interested in learning more advanced programs such as Blender that would allow me to integrate 3D models into the workflow of my final paintings.

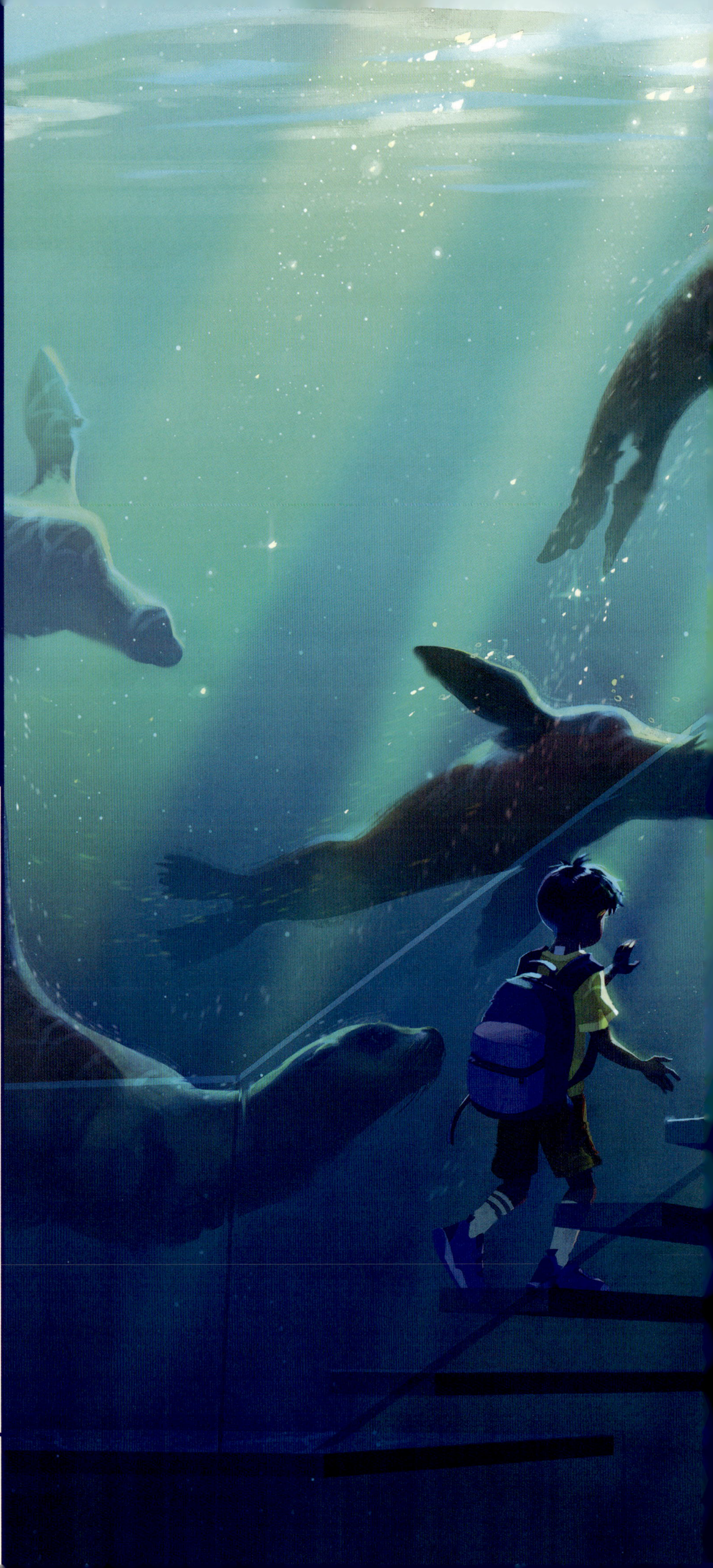

OFF TO SCHOOL / DIGITAL, 2021

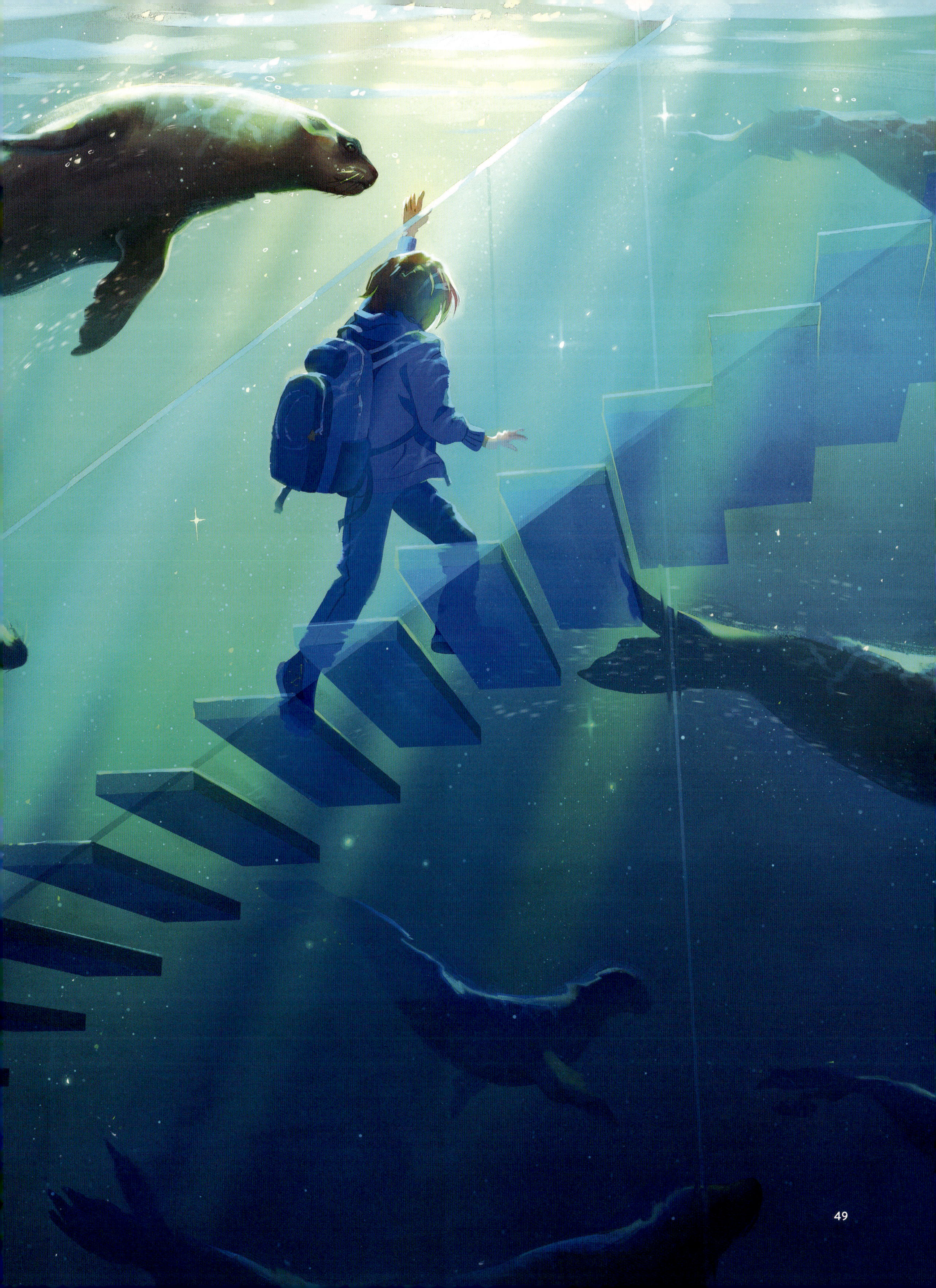

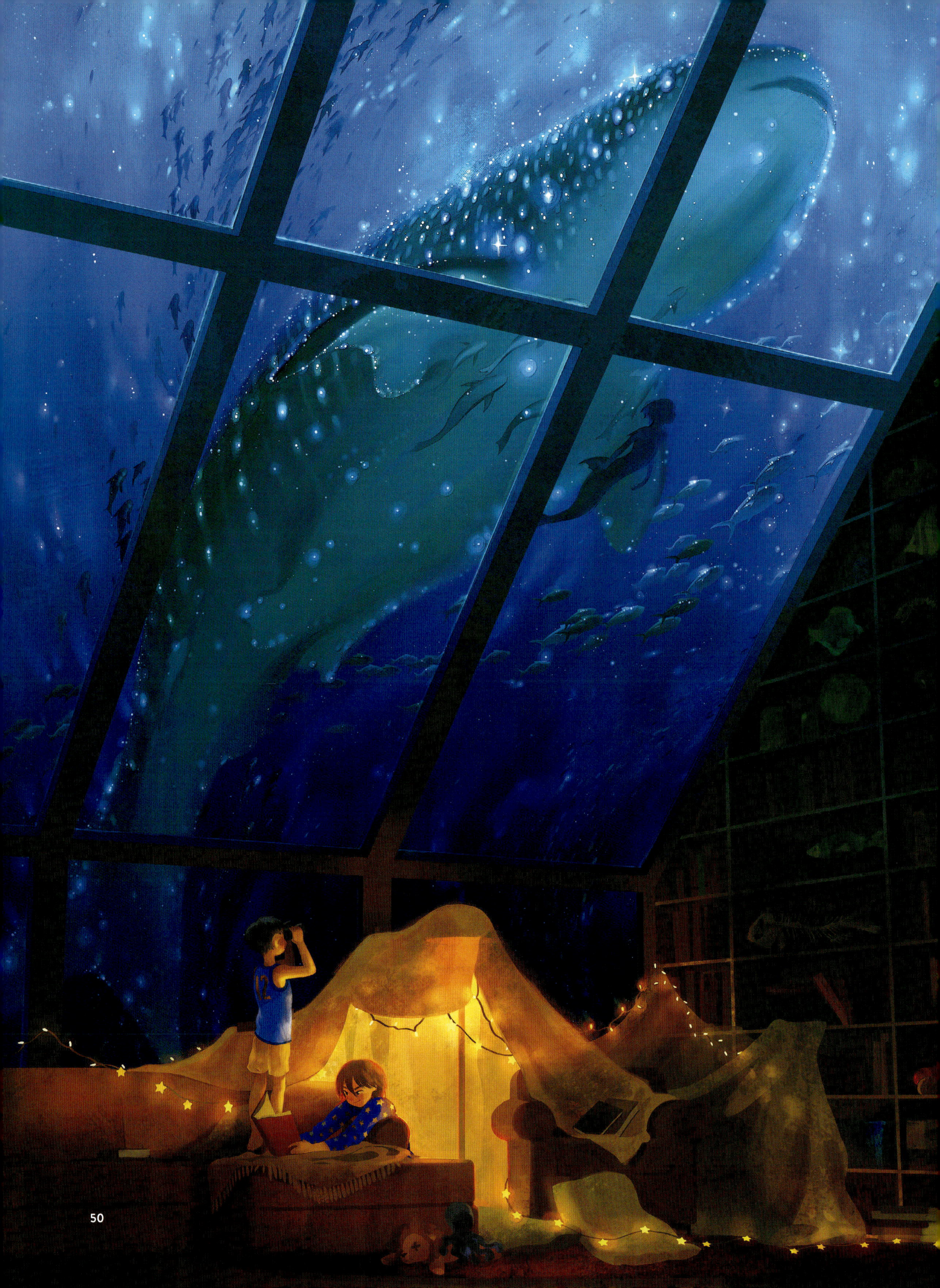

TECHNIQUE / CONTROLLING CONTRAST

I often paint detailed scenes using a lot of complex components. This has consistently been an interest of mine since I was very young, when I would draw detailed fantasy scenes on large sheets of paper. Using colored pencils, I would sketch and draw over the course of weeks or months. As I improved over time, I picked up various techniques, including those to help control the overwhelmingly noisy detail that comes with painting a complex scene. I first picked up these techniques through intuition in my teens, then later put names to those techniques and refined them further through classes at Schoolism and Concept Design Academy.

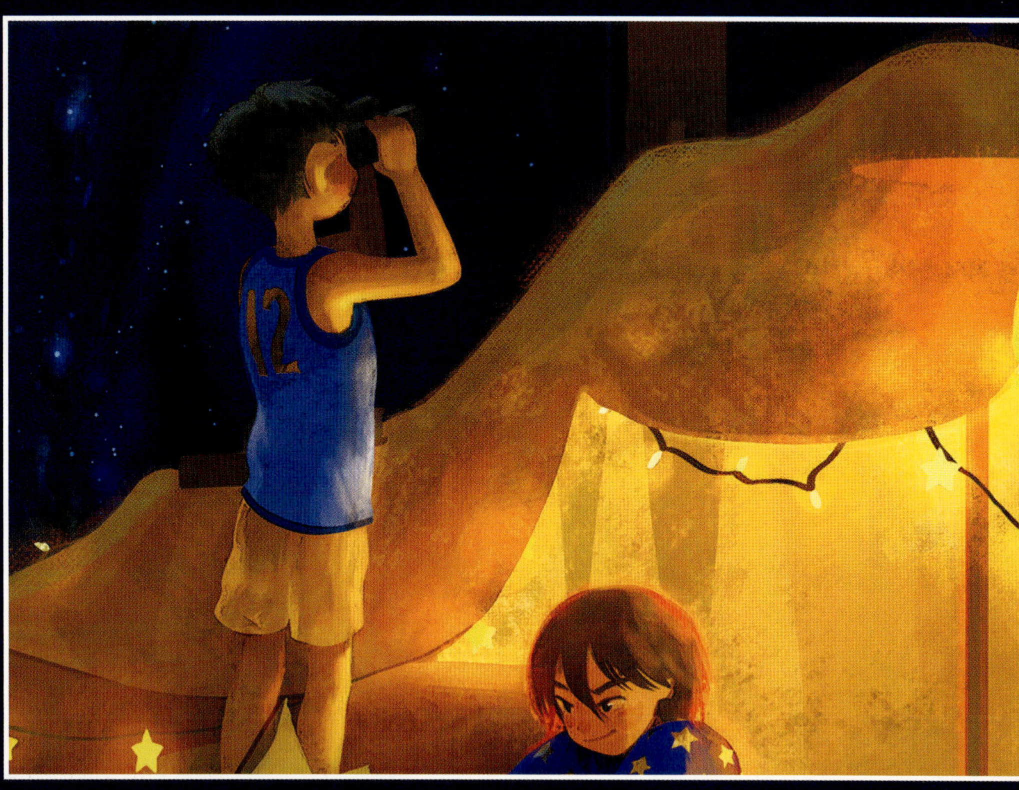

PILLOW FORT RESEARCH OUTPOST /
DIGITAL, 2020

FIVE FORMS OF CONTRAST

Through Schoolism, I undertook Nathan Fowkes' Pictorial Composition course in 2015, which helped me put names and concepts to many of the intuited techniques I'd developed throughout my life. I discovered that being able to control a busy scene often comes down to controlling contrast, and there are many forms of contrast that artists have to balance at once while painting. The key forms that I focus on perfecting are:

> ***Hue contrast***
> ***Saturation contrast***
> ***Value contrast***
> ***Detail or noise contrast***
> ***Edge contrast (hard versus soft edges)***

There are many other forms of contrast, but these five types form the mental checklist I run through when constructing a complex scene. I consider these factors from the moment I conceive an image. I tend to have a strong vision of my painting as I go through the ideation process, when my brain focuses on how to solve the equation of the scene. For example, if I want to paint a girl with a kite, I immediately decide the kite will be bright red against a blue sky and she will be a dark silhouette; I have usually decided how I'm going to direct the focus of the painting before I even start sketching.

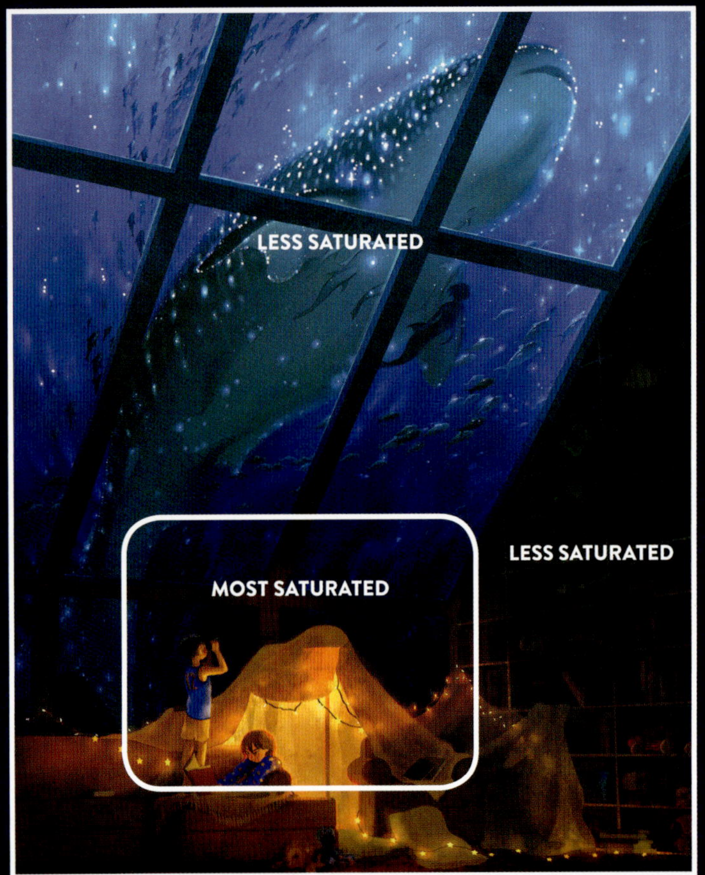

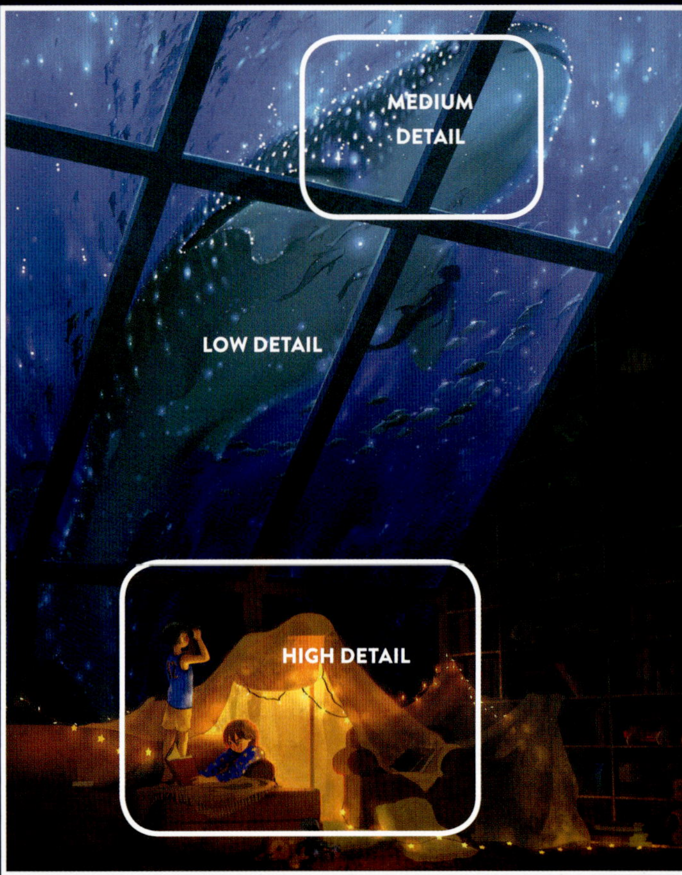

SATURATION CONTRAST / To help solidify the pillow fort as the focus, I made it the most saturated area of the painting. The whale is less saturated and a green-blue color to separate it from the ocean.

DETAIL CONTRAST / The fort and the boys get the most high-contrast, specular details, followed by the whale and then reduced further in the backdrop.

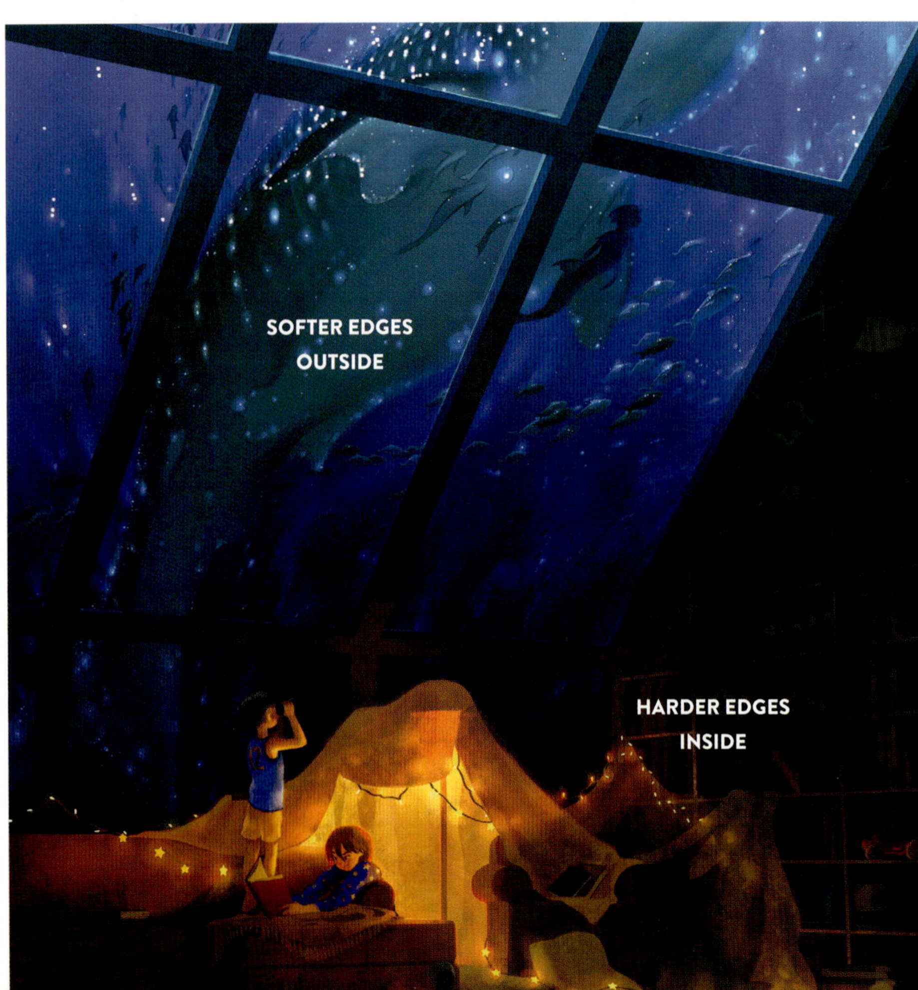

EDGE CONTRAST / The hardest edges are reserved for the interior to bring it forward in space, while the exterior gets softer, more distorted edges through the water.

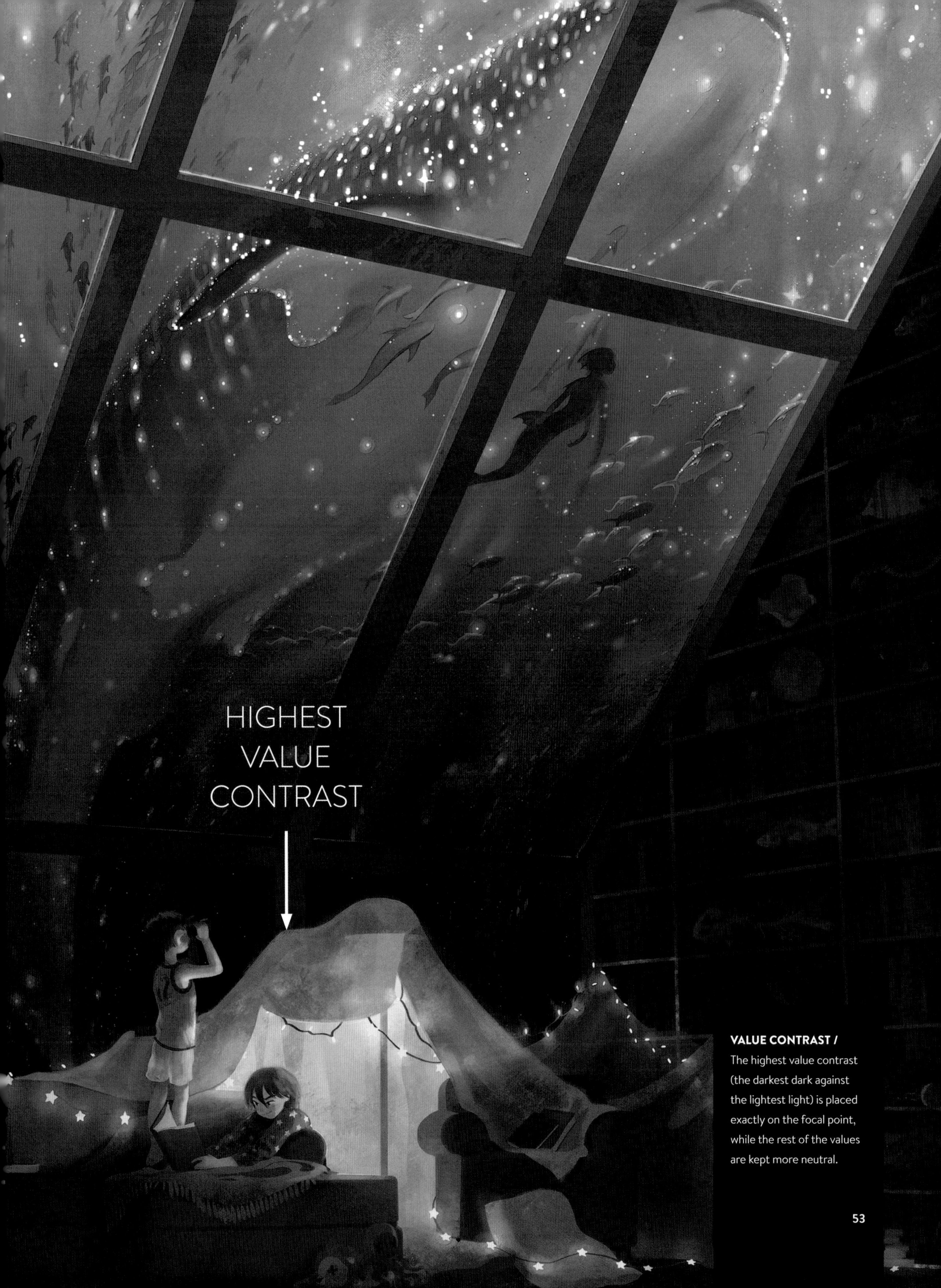

VALUE CONTRAST /
The highest value contrast (the darkest dark against the lightest light) is placed exactly on the focal point, while the rest of the values are kept more neutral.

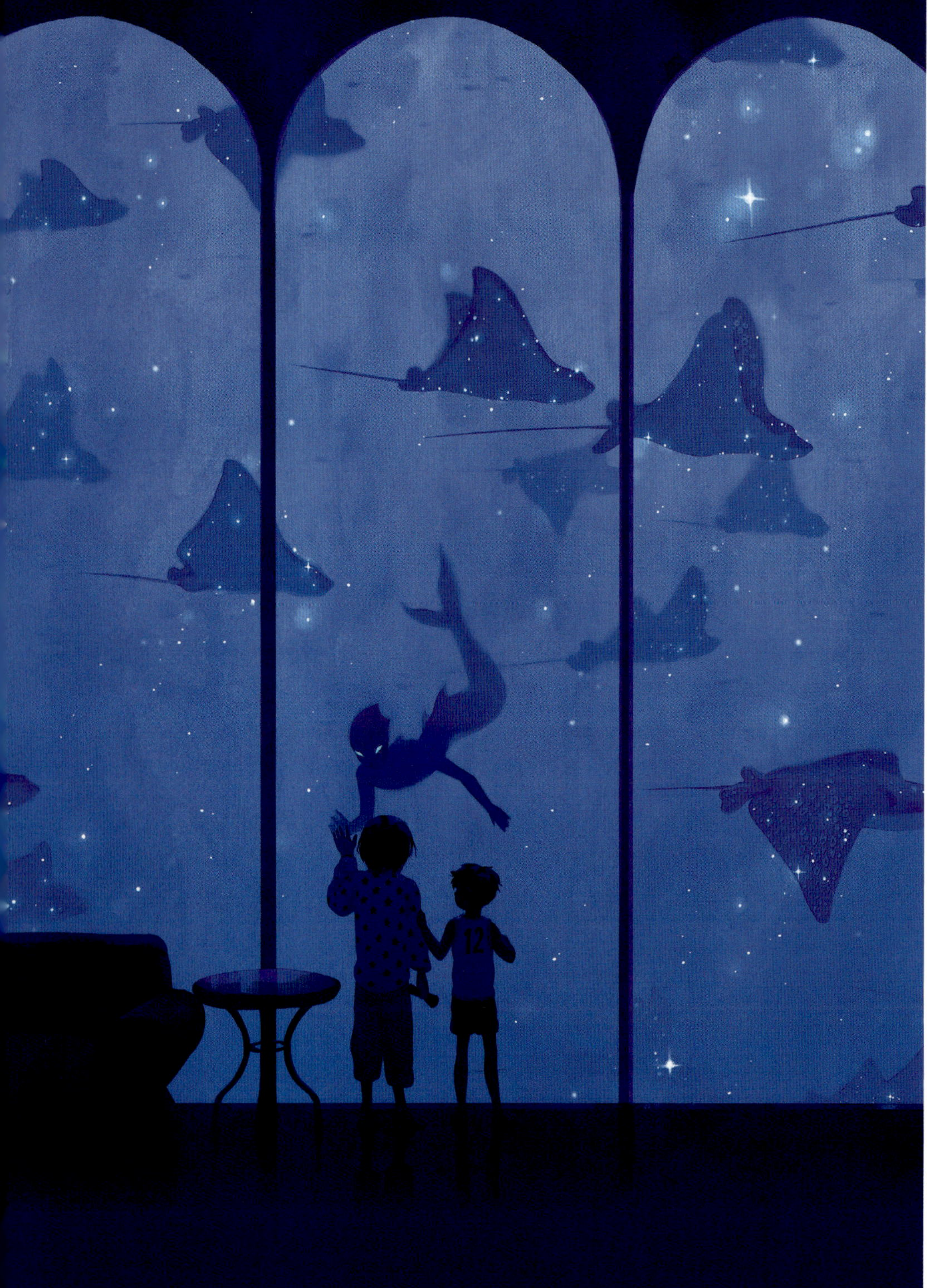

HAND TO HAND / DIGITAL, 2020

THUMBNAIL STUDIES
Creating very tiny studies, often on sticky notes, allows me to immediately check my mental calculations and make sure the idea I have is going to be readable.

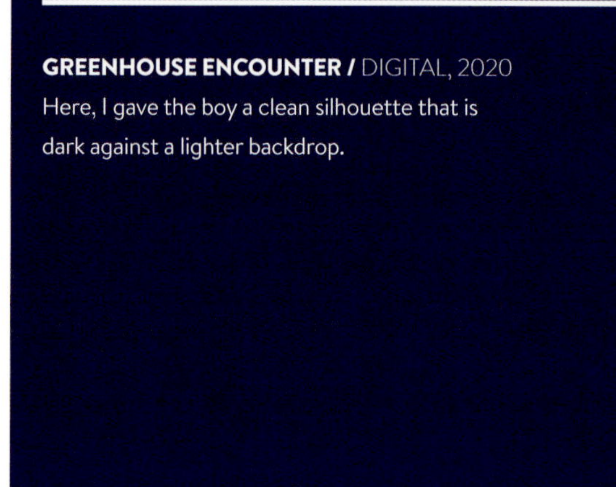

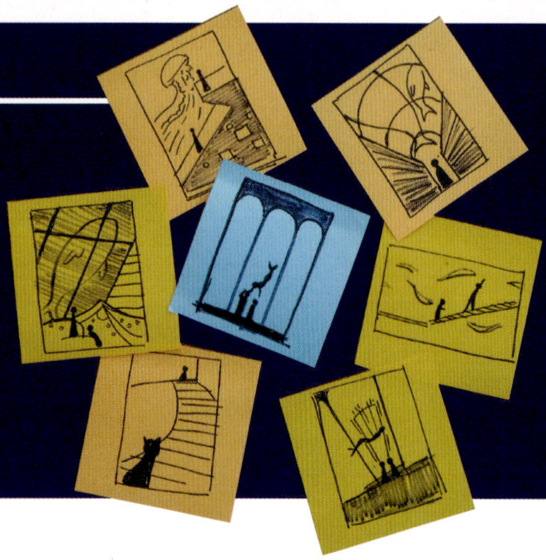

GREENHOUSE ENCOUNTER / DIGITAL, 2020
Here, I gave the boy a clean silhouette that is dark against a lighter backdrop.

TECHNIQUE / PLANNING CONTRAST

Actively working to organize my paintings from the beginning allows me to make better decisions, as I sketch and move very quickly when painting. It also markedly decreases any anxiety I might have; having a solid plan in place for every element of the painting allows me to always know what my next move will be as I go through the painting process.

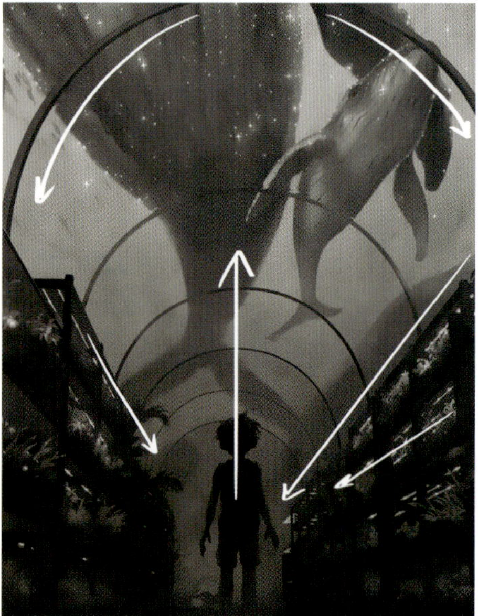

In *Greenhouse Encounter* I wanted the boy to be the focal point, as he is standing in for the viewer in this experience, so I used the grow-lights above the plants to form little runways to lead the viewer's eye to him. The position of the boy then lifts the viewer's gaze, and the archway brings it back around again so that it doesn't leave the page.

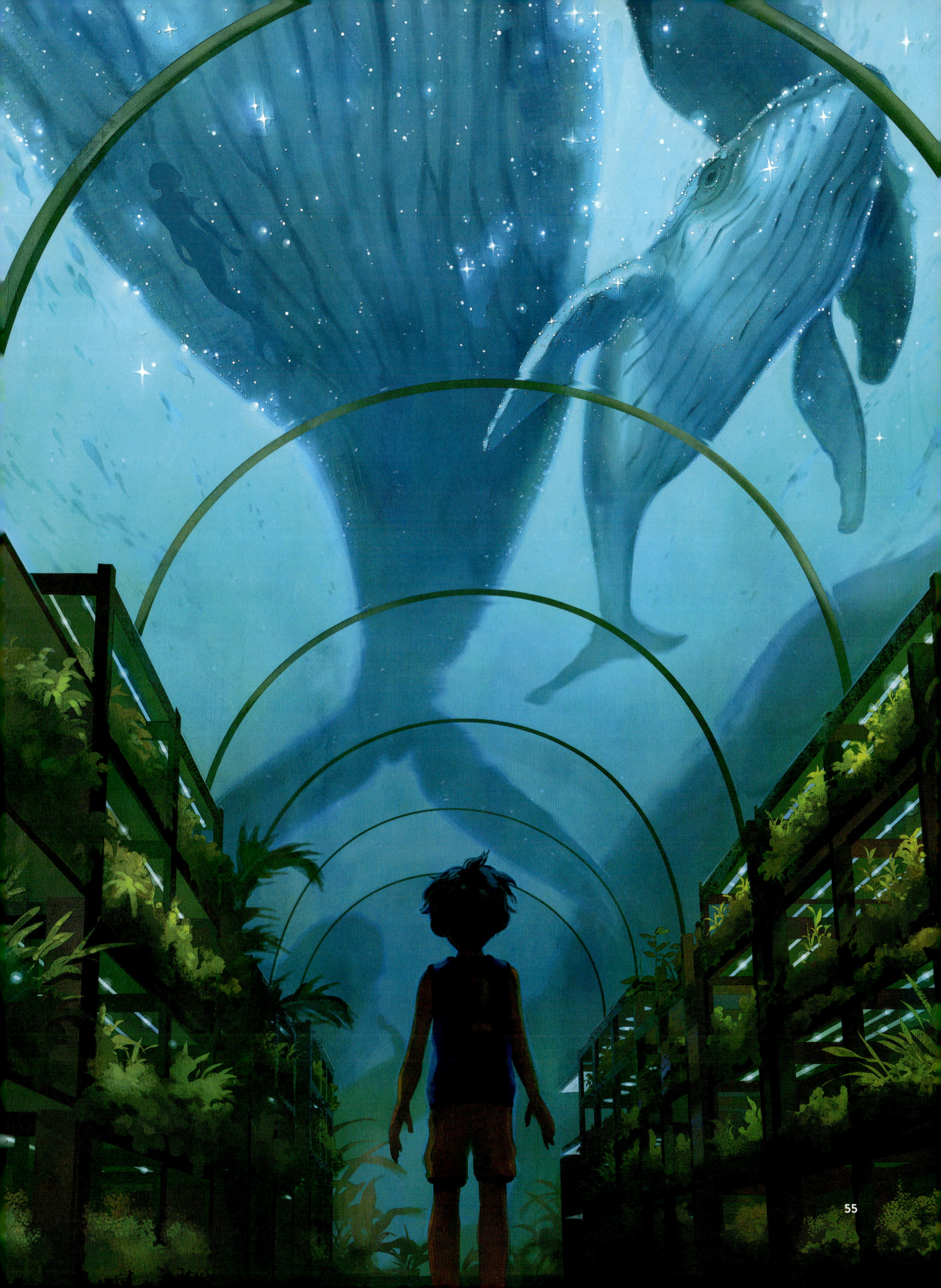

An example of my attempt to create visual cohesion and offer a visual break from overwhelm in the busy halls of Gencon 2019

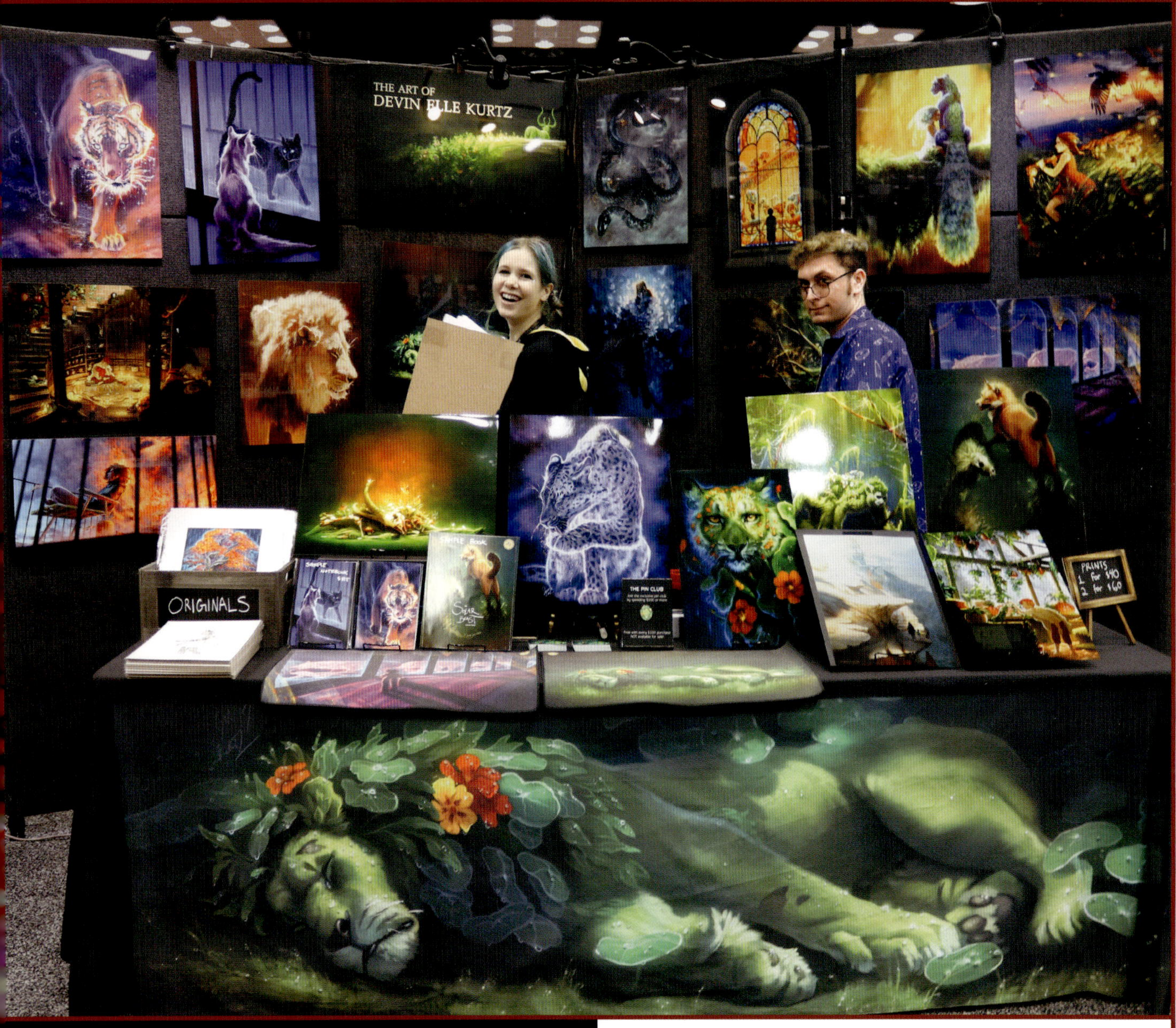

TECHNIQUE / CONTRAST AND CLARITY

When I was eighteen, I exhibited for the first time at the Artists' Alley at WonderCon – the annual film, comic book, and science-fiction convention. I had visited and enjoyed conventions for a decade and was finally able to try selling at one. Figuring out how to make art that would sell well at conventions actually taught me a lot about controlling contrast and creating clarity. A convention hall is an incredibly busy place. Wherever you look as you walk down the aisles of the Artists' Alley, there's an unbelievable amount of information to take in. This area of a convention is often one of the most crowded and visually overwhelming locations in the entire hall, with small tables tightly packed against each other. With such a small space to present an entire body of work, each individual table becomes a busy sea of detail.

CREATING ATTENTION-GRABBING ART

I attempted to counteract the overwhelming effect by painting images with a very clear and immediate visual read. I wanted my paintings to be immediately understandable so that the emotional impact of each piece had the greatest chance of reaching each passerby. As I painted, I started stepping back more, zooming all the way out, and making sure that my images were readable from a distance.

Art that is understandable and reads well from across a convention hall is often also successful on social media. As we scroll down an Instagram feed, we are similarly bombarded by imagery. A painting that can be understood quickly in that context has a higher chance of pausing the scroll. Of course, this isn't the only way to paint, but working from the simplest version of an image and slowly adding detail has worked best for me throughout my career.

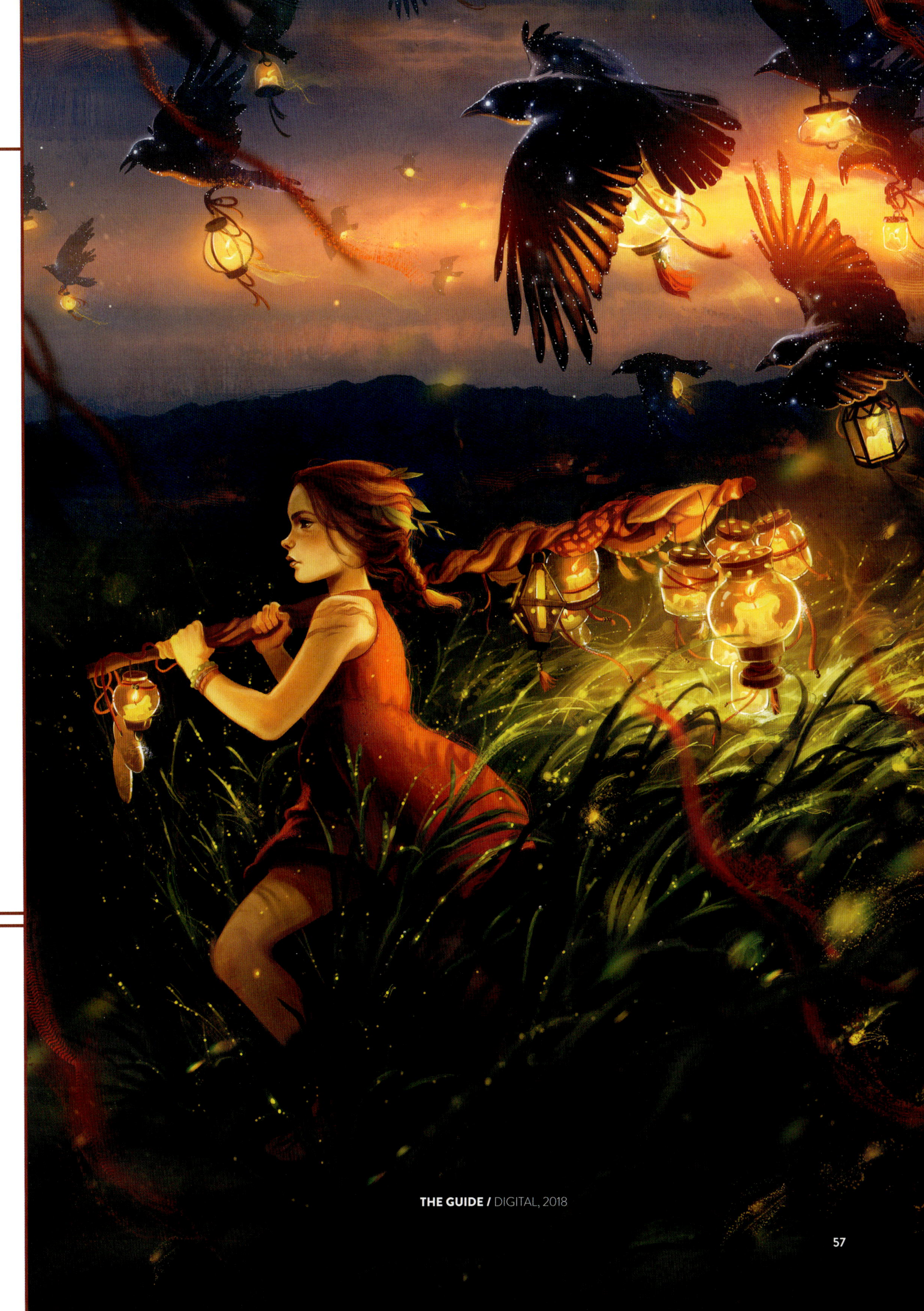

THE GUIDE / DIGITAL, 2018

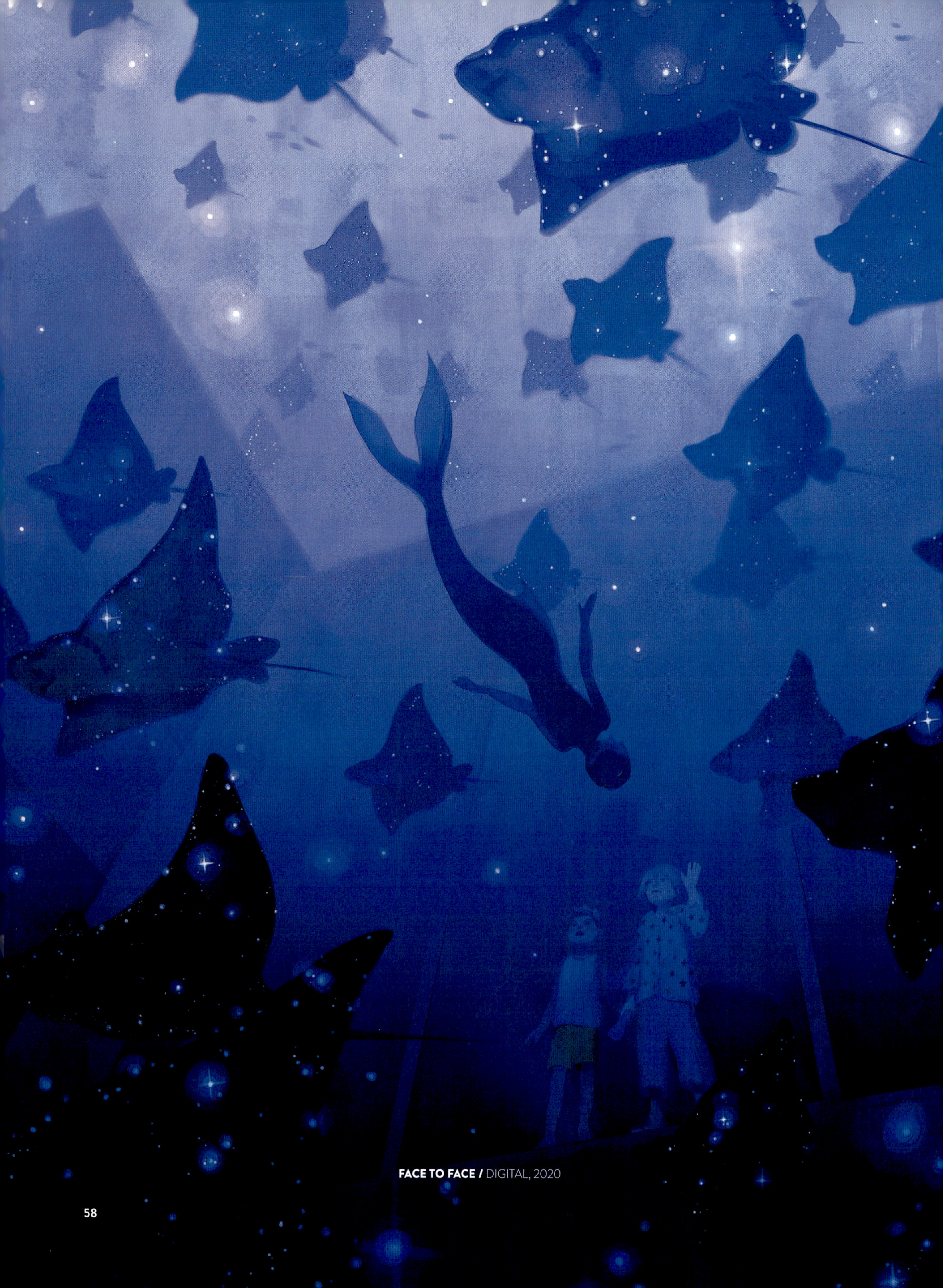

FACE TO FACE / DIGITAL, 2020

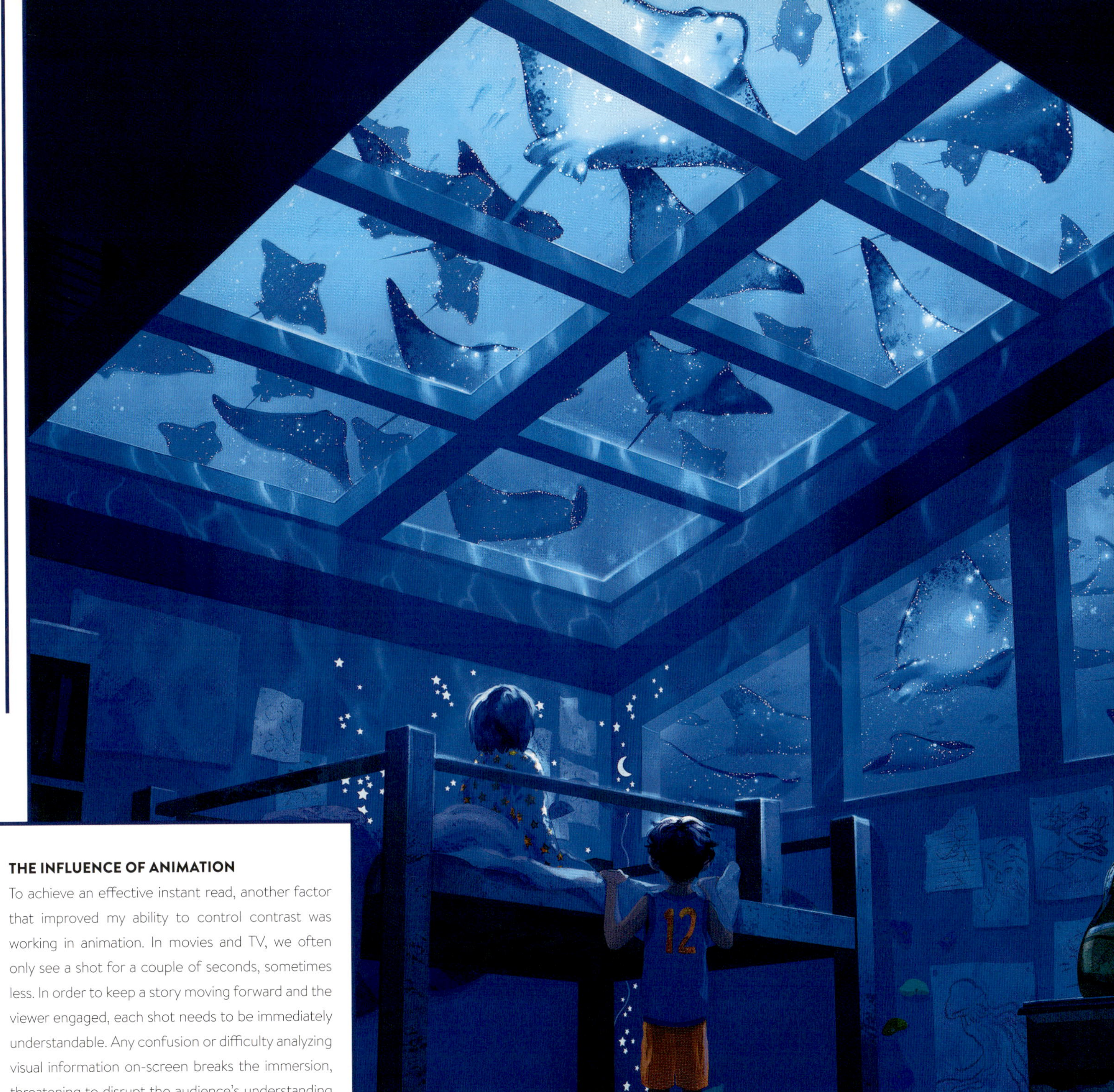

UNUSUAL NIGHT / DIGITAL, 2020

The greatest contrast of value is in the upper-central area of the painting, drawing the viewer's eye up to where the boys are also looking.

THE INFLUENCE OF ANIMATION

To achieve an effective instant read, another factor that improved my ability to control contrast was working in animation. In movies and TV, we often only see a shot for a couple of seconds, sometimes less. In order to keep a story moving forward and the viewer engaged, each shot needs to be immediately understandable. Any confusion or difficulty analyzing visual information on-screen breaks the immersion, threatening to disrupt the audience's understanding of the story. I quickly realized that creating a readable value structure and clear silhouettes should be my number-one concern, even in the busiest scene.

Working on the series *Disenchantment* helped me to overcome my fear of complex environments. They were going to be thrown at me whether I liked it or not, so learning how to control a sometimes immense amount of information in a limited timeframe ended up being a real blessing! With practice, I quickly learned how to turn entire buildings or tree lines into silhouettes and set them back in space with atmospheric perspective in order to get the most effective composition.

TECHNIQUE / VALUE GROUPING

One of the biggest advancements in my ability to paint complex scenes came when I started to understand how to build clear and visually attractive value structures.

Value is how dark or light something is, and value *grouping* is a technique used to bring greater clarity and visual appeal to a piece of art. Sections of a painting can be grouped by value to not only improve readability, but also to direct the viewer's eye to the focal area by controlling the value contrast. I usually use a sliding scale from one to ten to represent value, with number one being white, ten being black, and the shades of gray in between divided into eight.

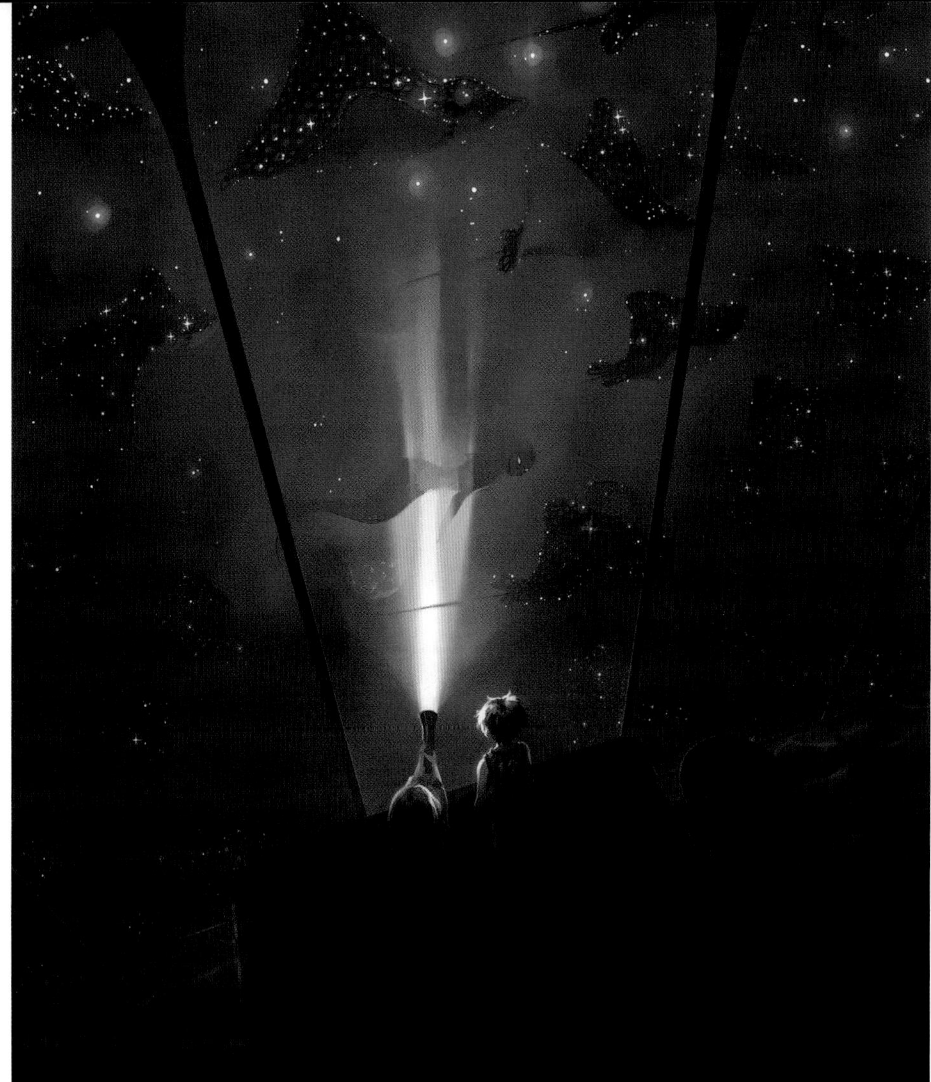

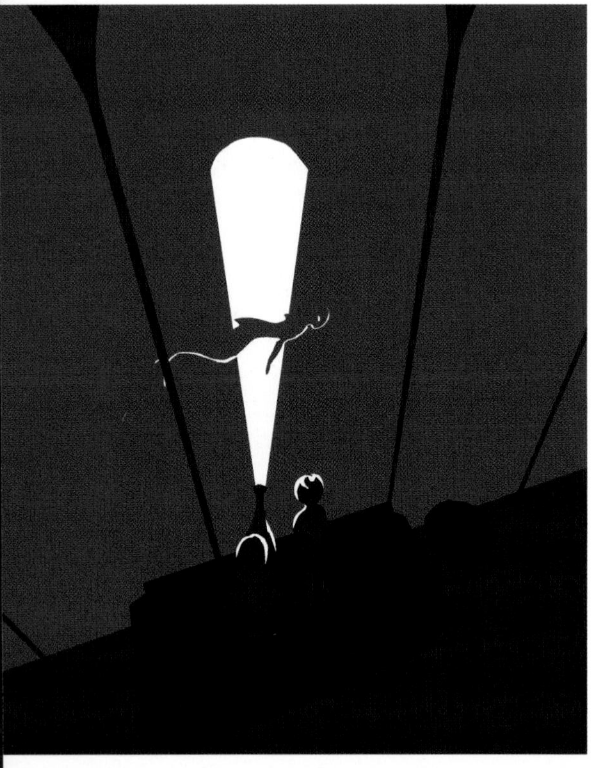

SOLVING THE CONTRAST CHALLENGE

One of the major problems in my work early on was an overabundance of value contrast. I added contrast everywhere because I thought it looked good and would help clarify what was happening in the image. When an area was unclear or difficult to understand, I would zoom in and render the area, often using darker and lighter colors in an attempt to define edges or forms. In the process, I simply added more value contrast to the problem area. Unsurprisingly, this caused more issues when I zoomed out – whatever clarity I gained through rendering was immediately lost in the complex mass of information in front of me. Worse yet, the added contrast in problem areas just drew more attention to them and made the issues abundantly clear to the viewer.

I soon realized that high-value contrast makes an area of a painting feel important. I was adding value contrast everywhere, and when everything is made important, nothing appears important; it all becomes a visually noisy mess. The intended focal point or focal area of a painting quickly became lost in the dense contrast across the entire piece.

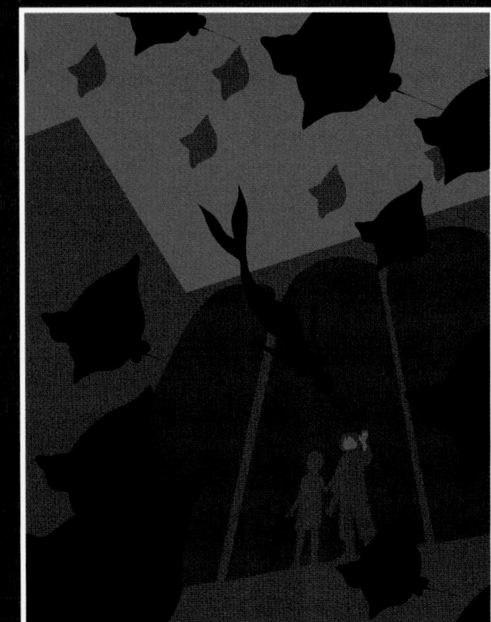

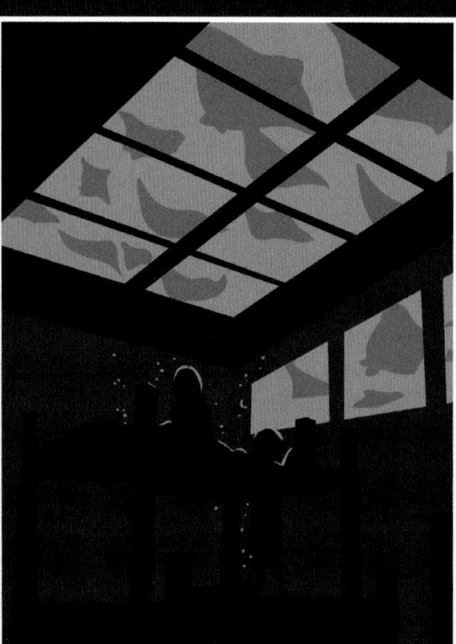

COLLAPSED VALUE STUDIES

One of my absolute favorite techniques for learning to make crystal-clear value structures is to "collapse" images into just three or four values, using only a hard brush (with no blending) to create small value studies. An image that reads clearly with only three or four values is certainly going to read well if that value structure is maintained through to the final result.

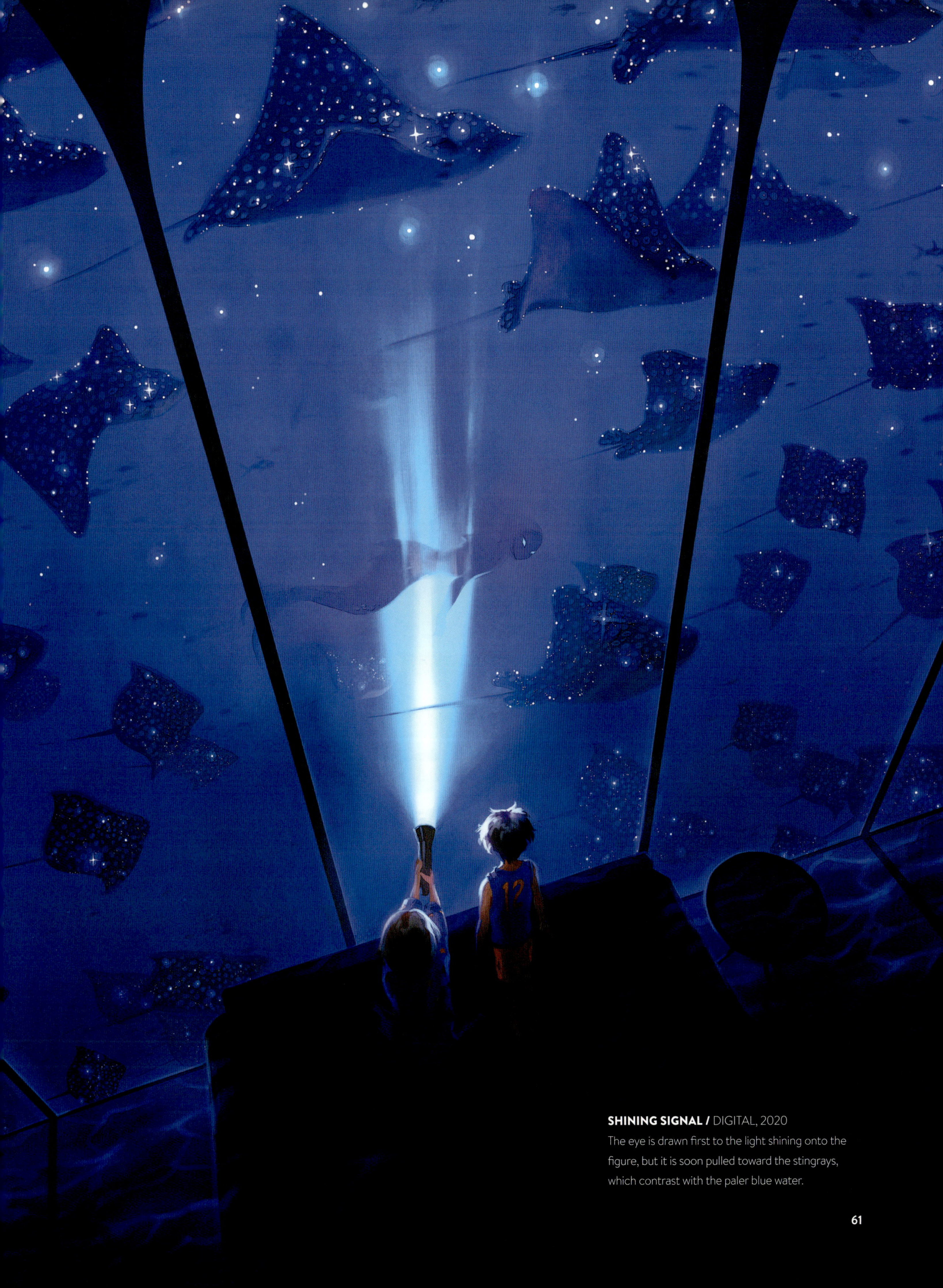

SHINING SIGNAL / DIGITAL, 2020
The eye is drawn first to the light shining onto the figure, but it is soon pulled toward the stingrays, which contrast with the paler blue water.

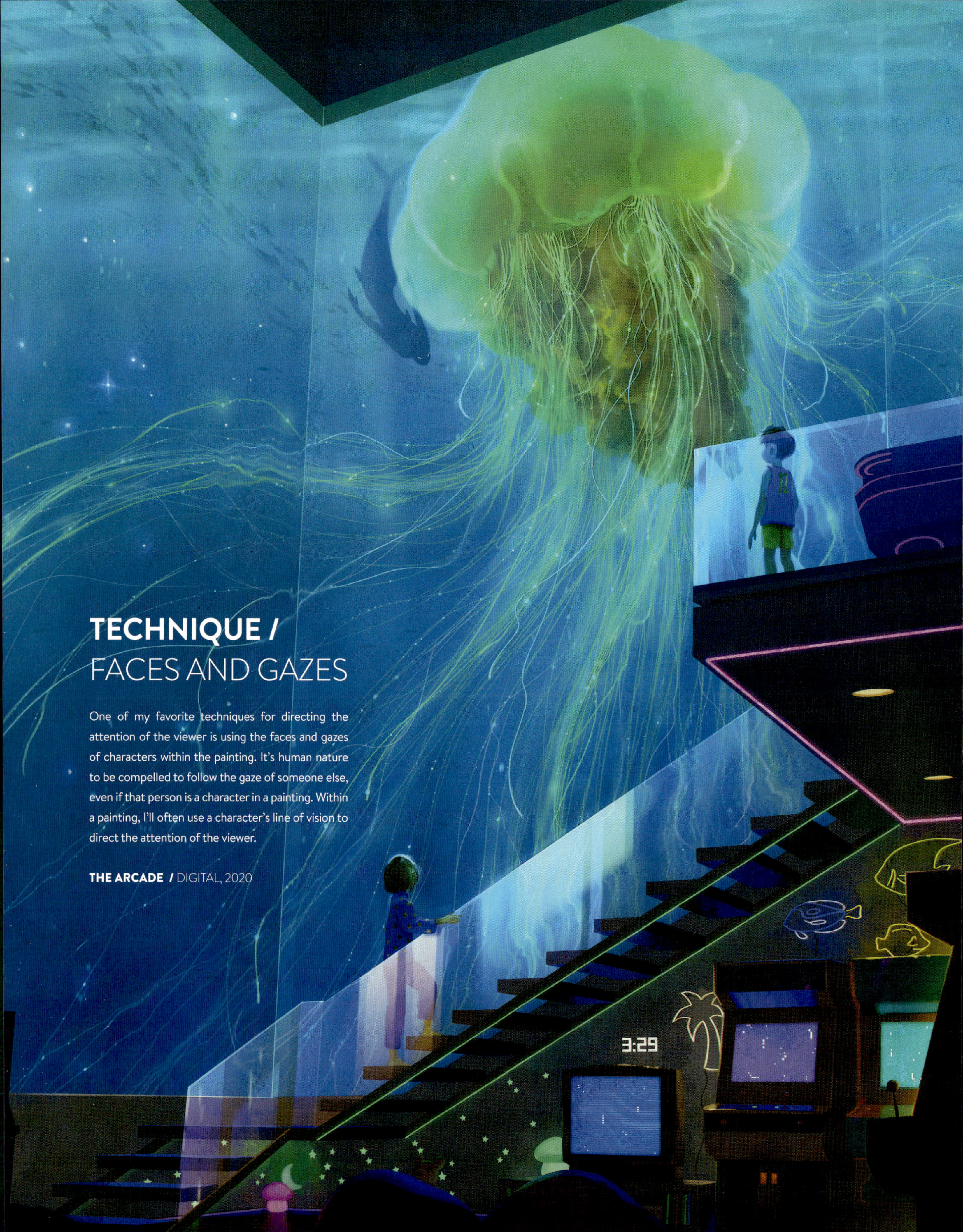

TECHNIQUE / FACES AND GAZES

One of my favorite techniques for directing the attention of the viewer is using the faces and gazes of characters within the painting. It's human nature to be compelled to follow the gaze of someone else, even if that person is a character in a painting. Within a painting, I'll often use a character's line of vision to direct the attention of the viewer.

THE ARCADE / DIGITAL, 2020

TECHNIQUE / FOREGROUND, MIDGROUND, BACKGROUND

Another tool I added to my toolkit from working in animation was imagining scenes as being made up of the foreground (what's closest to us), background (what's furthest away), and midground (what falls between the two).

In animation, these distinctions can often be very literal. Back in the days of painting backgrounds by hand, artists would have to paint on multiple layers of transparent sheets called "celluloid" in order to create panning or parallax effects. The environments would often be literally divided into foreground, midground, and background layers – sometimes even more than that. By the time I started working in animation, the industry was mostly digital, but we still make use of these techniques by grouping backgrounds into digital overlays and underlays (rather than literal sheets of celluloid laying over and under one another). Overlays and underlays are distinctly separated areas of the background that can be turned off and on, moved, or panned. As the names suggest, overlays sit on top of the main area and underlays sit underneath.

By thinking of environments in this way and constructing them with clearly distinguishable planes, I greatly improved the spatial clarity in my work. Interesting foreground shapes that lead the eye in and point it toward the action can be incredibly immersive, whether in a moving animation or still illustration. Learning to set far background elements firmly back in space with atmospheric perspective and low contrast was also an important skill for me to learn.

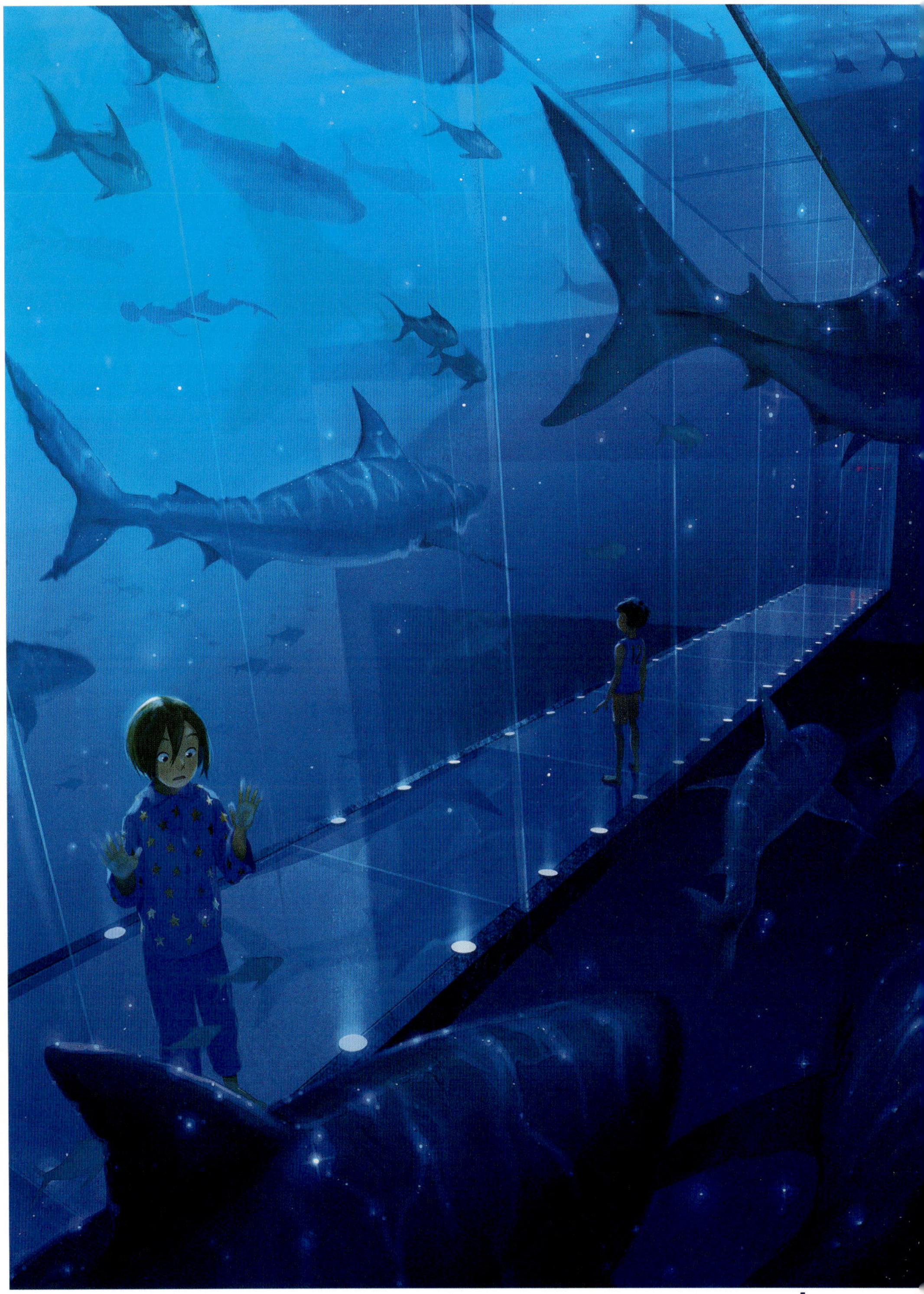

PHOTOSHOP LAYERS

In Photoshop, layer structures provide an excellent visual metaphor. Groups of layers toward the top of the layer menu quite literally sit on top of the layers beneath.

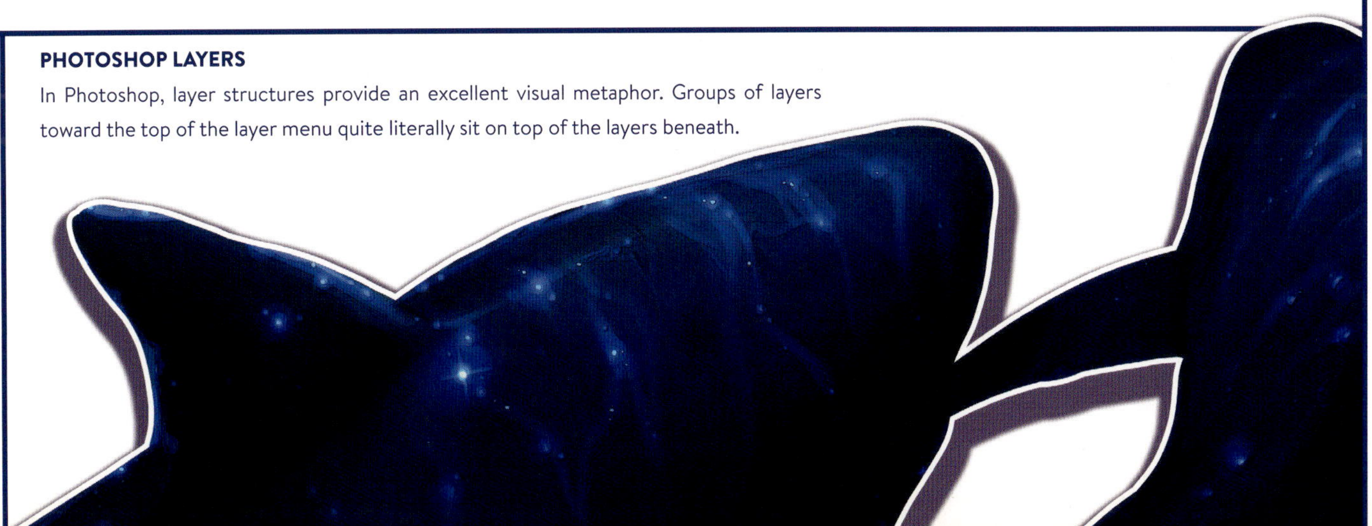

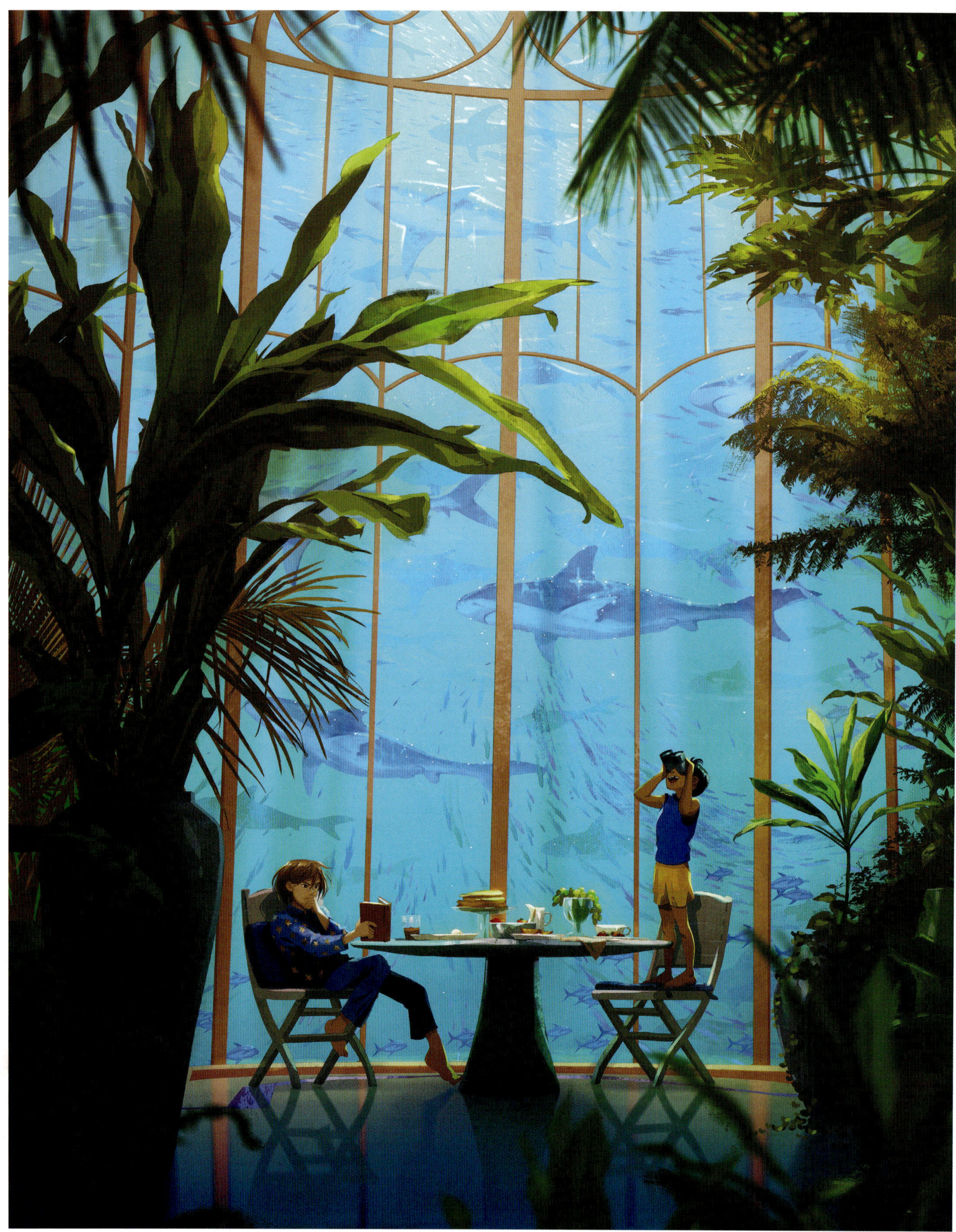

BREAKFAST IN THE KELP GARDEN / DIGITAL, 2020

The blurred foreground leaves provide depth and direct the viewer's eye toward the characters while framing the composition.

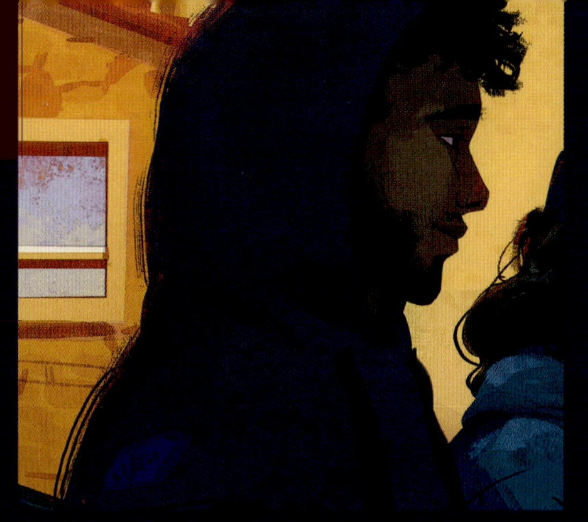

"WHEN LOOKING AT LOOSE SKETCHES, OUR BRAINS ARE GIVEN ROOM TO 'FILL IN THE GAPS' AND MAKE CHOICES ABOUT WHERE WE ASSUME FORMS START AND END"

TECHNIQUE / ENERGY AND LOOSE BRUSHSTROKES

A problem I struggled with a lot is the difficulty of translating the energy and appeal of a sketch into a final painting. Time and time again, I found my sketches would lose their spark by the time I had finished the rendering stage. I spent a long time flipping between my sketches and the final paintings, trying to determine what was taking the life out of my pieces.

What I found was that my sketches often benefited greatly from loosely-placed lines. Instances where I would draw over strokes, or softly sketch estimates of where a final line might fall, conveyed a fluid motion and energy in my sketches. When looking at loose sketches, our brains are given room to "fill in the gaps" and make choices about where we assume forms start and end. When a range is given via a sketchy line doubling back over itself, it can even generate the feeling of movement, as if the sketch has come to life. As I worked through the painting process, I made decisions about where to place lines and create edges of each form. These definitive lines inevitably made the result less appealing than the limitless possibilities offered by loose sketches.

I have since developed a solution by allowing my paint strokes to mimic the same looseness and energy that the sketches carry. Rather than decide on a single solid exterior outline to my forms, I brush over the area multiple times with textured brushes. I use this technique most when a subject is in motion, or when an area of the painting is intended to be hazy or recede into the atmosphere. Our eyes can't focus on everything at once in real life, and we rarely see living creatures in total stillness unless they're sleeping.

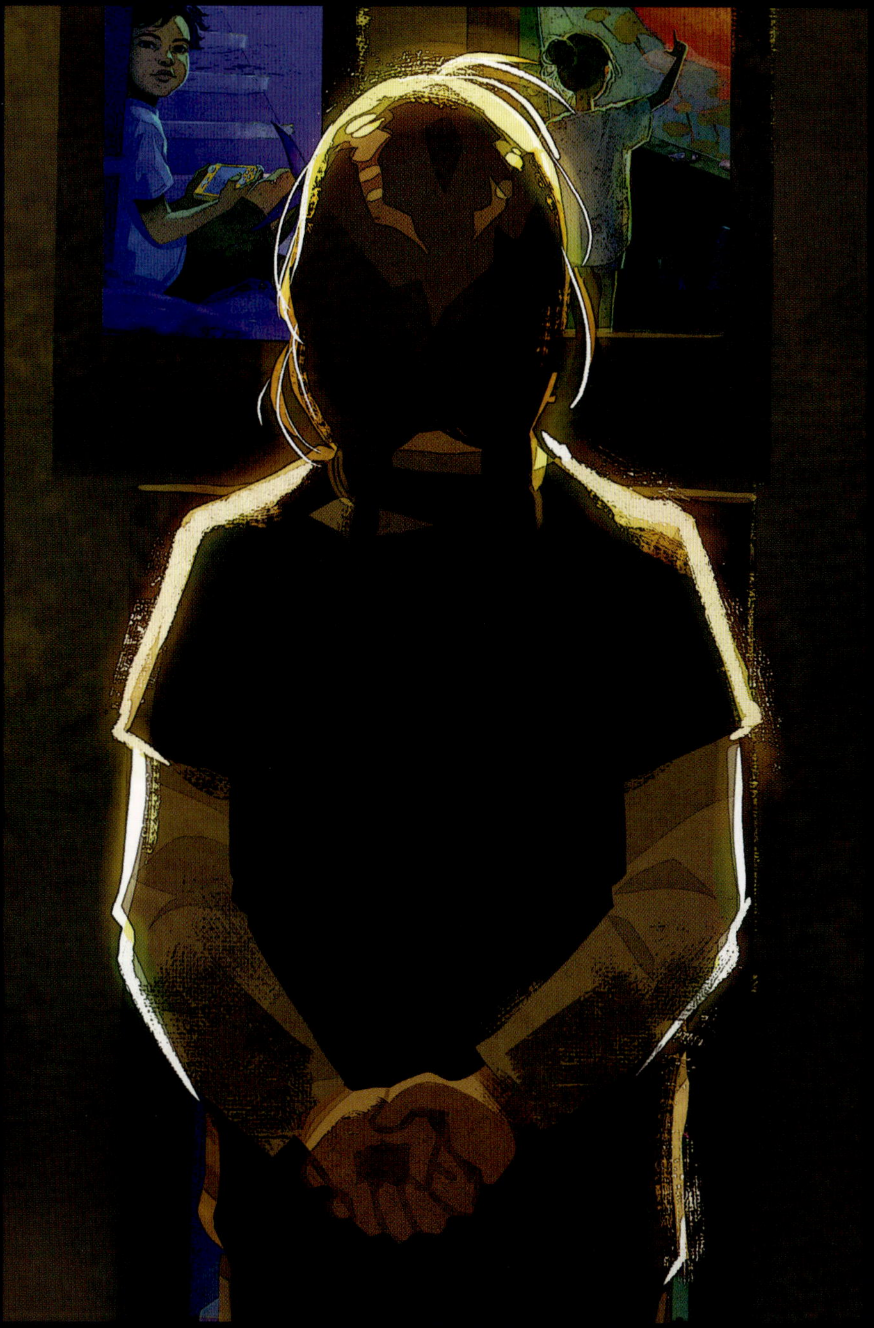

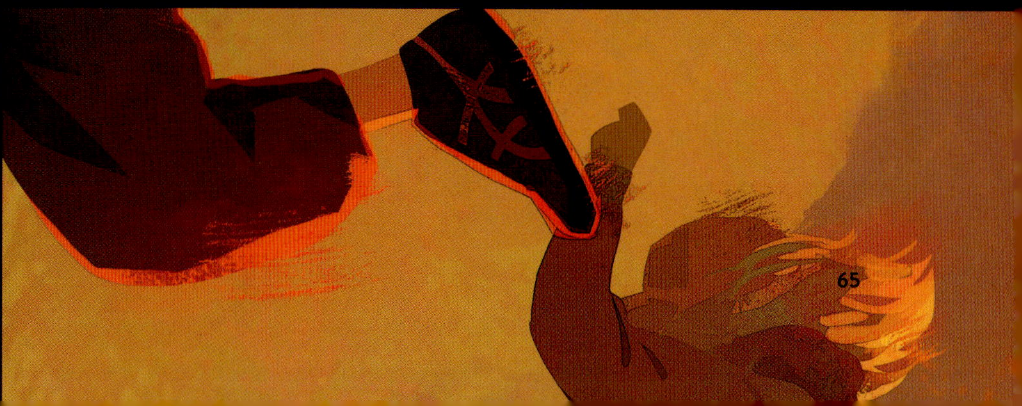

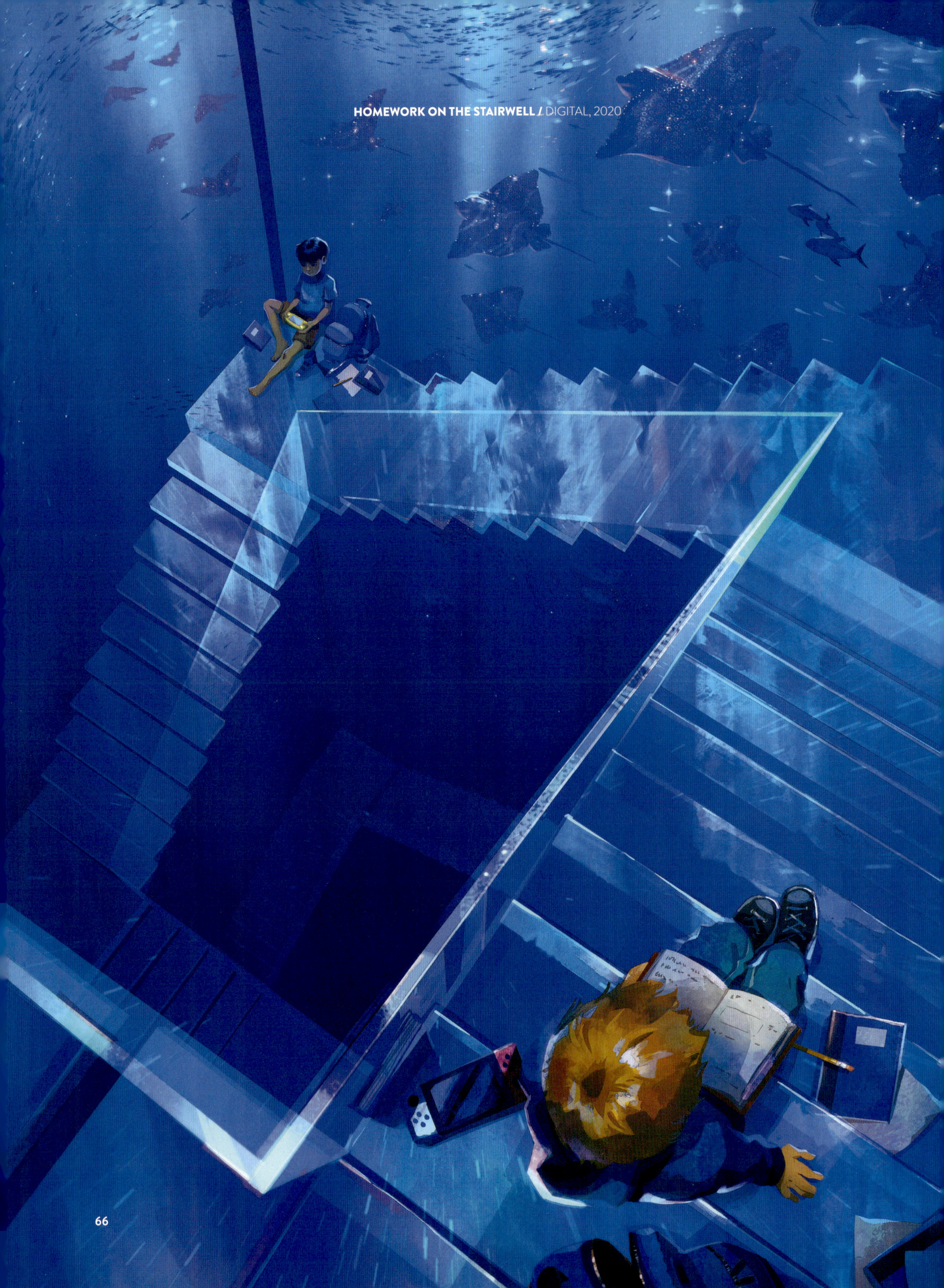

HOMEWORK ON THE STAIRWELL / DIGITAL, 2020

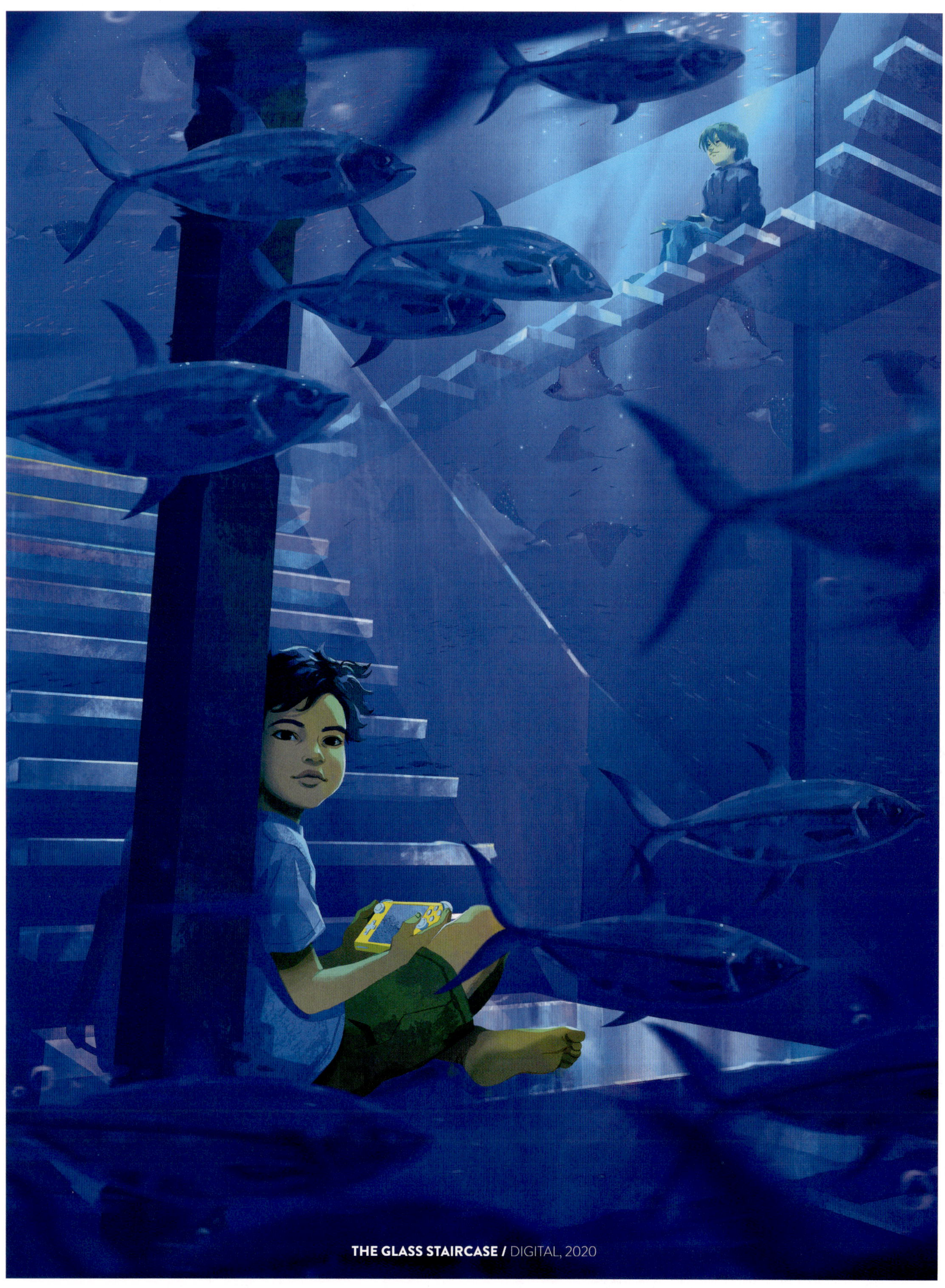

THE GLASS STAIRCASE / DIGITAL, 2020

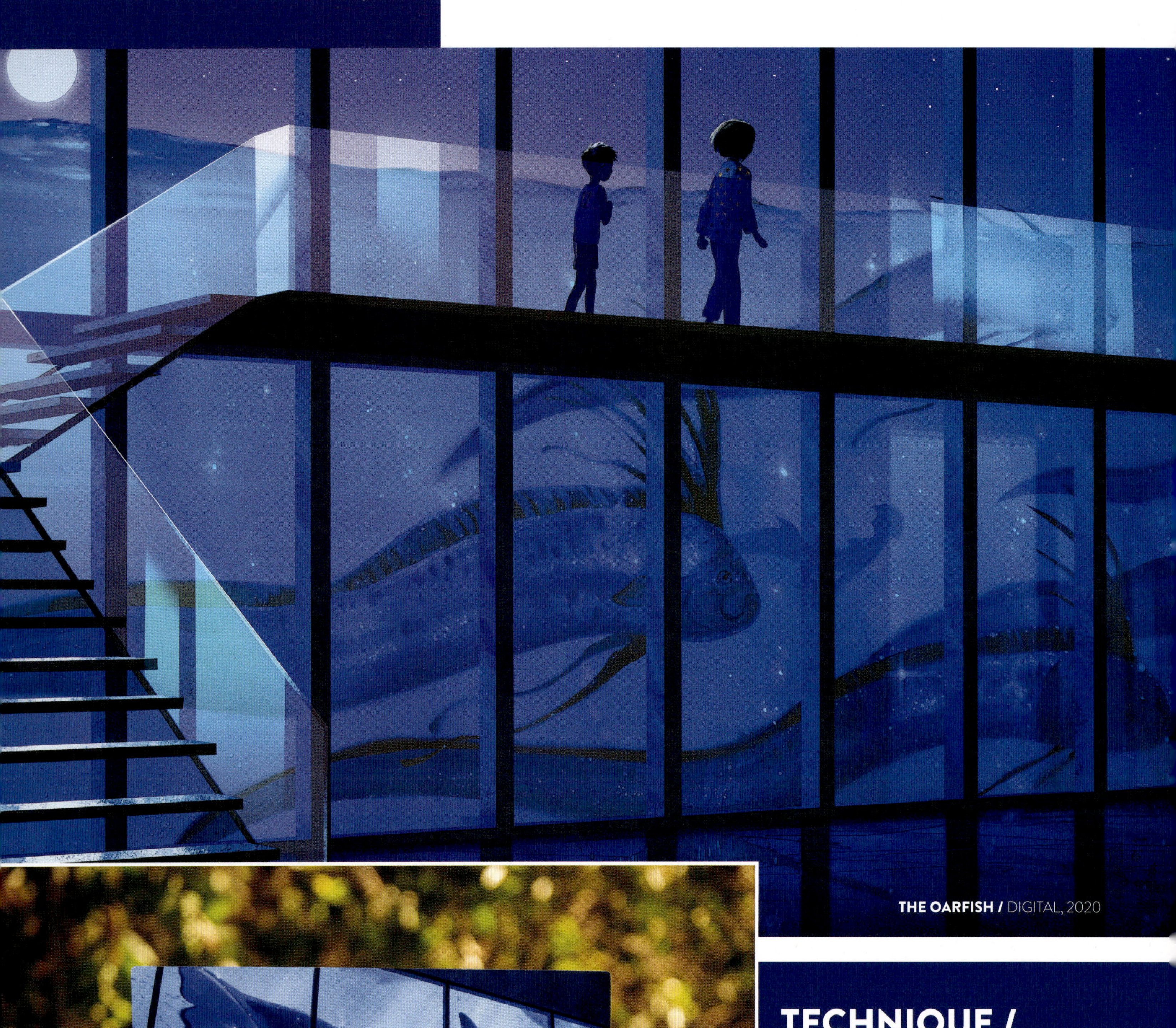

THE OARFISH / DIGITAL, 2020

TECHNIQUE / ADJUSTMENTS FOR PRINT

As I often work with dark, heavily saturated colors, I have to adjust my paintings quite a bit for print, in order for them to resemble how they look on a backlit screen. I mainly use Levels, Curves, and Brightness/Contrast adjustment layers to edit my files. I like to print my work on metal surfaces because when seen under a bright light, it glows!

ORCAS / A METAL PRINT

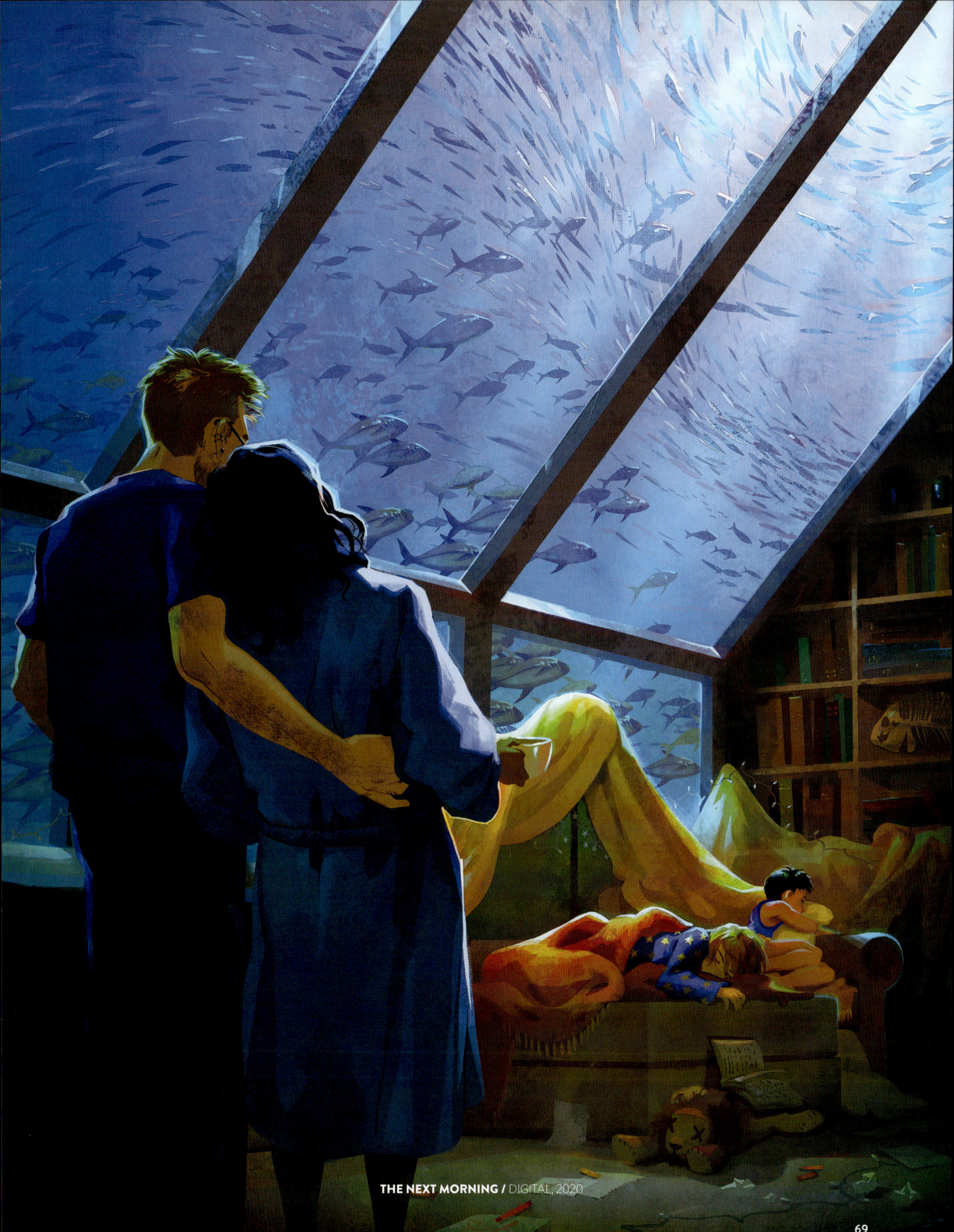

THE NEXT MORNING / DIGITAL, 2020

TUTORIAL / PAINTING SHARKS

I have always loved how sharks look from above in shallow water, and thought it would be fun to explore the theme of "art within art" by featuring the main character painting the sharks as well.

I know I will use this image as a double-page spread chapter opener for this book, so throughout the design process I consider these requirements. To imbue personatility and a sense of narrative into the designs, I took inspiration from various periods of my own life to create the chapter opener illustrations. I used Photoshop CC and my Wacom Cintiq Pro 24 to paint this piece.

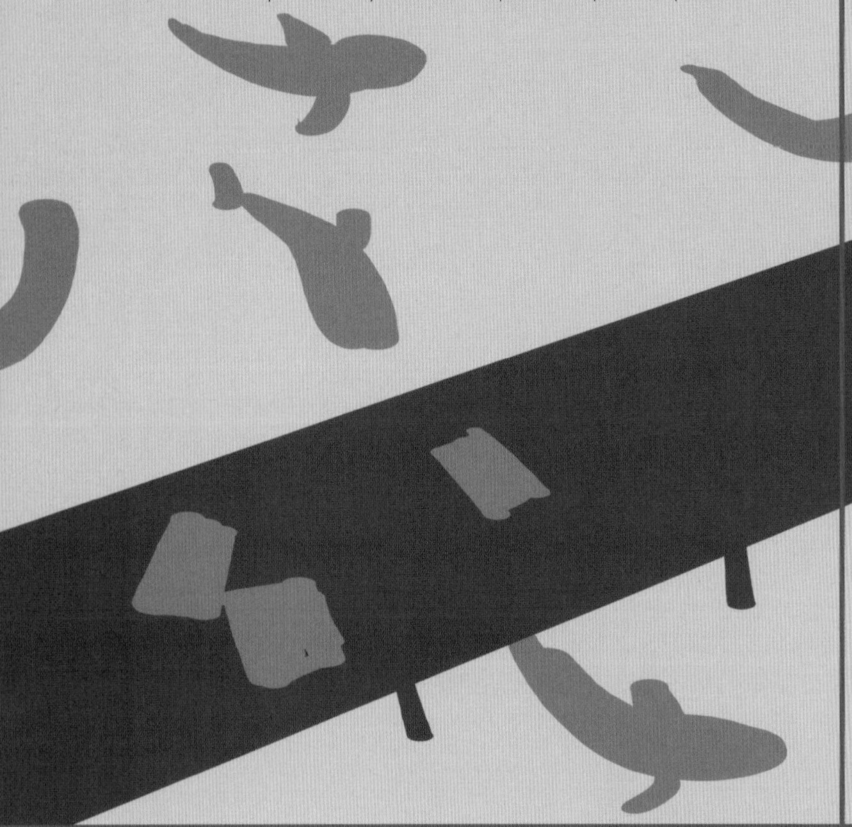

1

1 / ROUGH VALUE THUMBNAIL

Sometimes when I begin a painting, I already have a clear vision in my mind of what I want to create. That was the case with this piece, so my first step is to test my internal vision by depicting it as simply as possible with flat shapes of value. I add the page-spread division because I want to ensure it will read well across two pages of a book.

2 / COMPOSITIONAL CONSIDERATIONS

I want the character to stand out clearly against the background, and I think breaking the silhouette of the deck will be the fastest way to do that, along with concentrating the highest level of value contrast and detail around her body using the art materials. I also use the implied motion of the sharks to swirl around the girl and create a visual flow around the end of the deck. Finally, I can use the implied lines of the deck and her body to create an "X marks the spot" effect right at the focal point, which quickly draws the viewer's attention.

2a

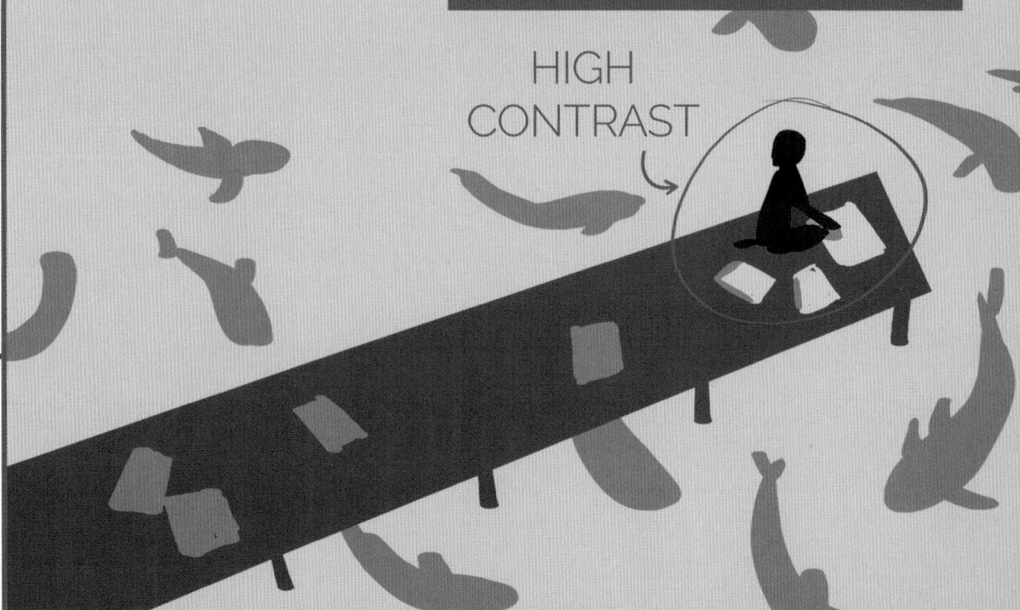

High contrast draws attention to the focal point of the composition.

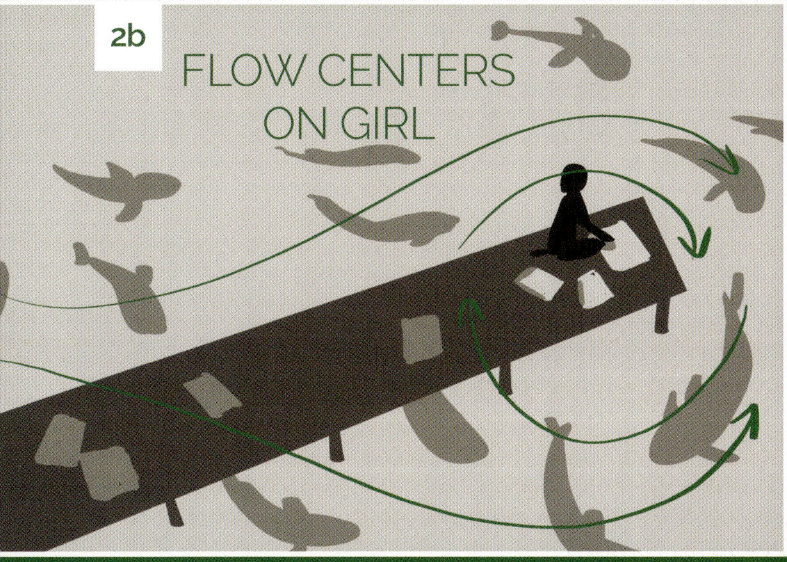

The sharks' movements circle the girl and focus the viewer's eye on her.

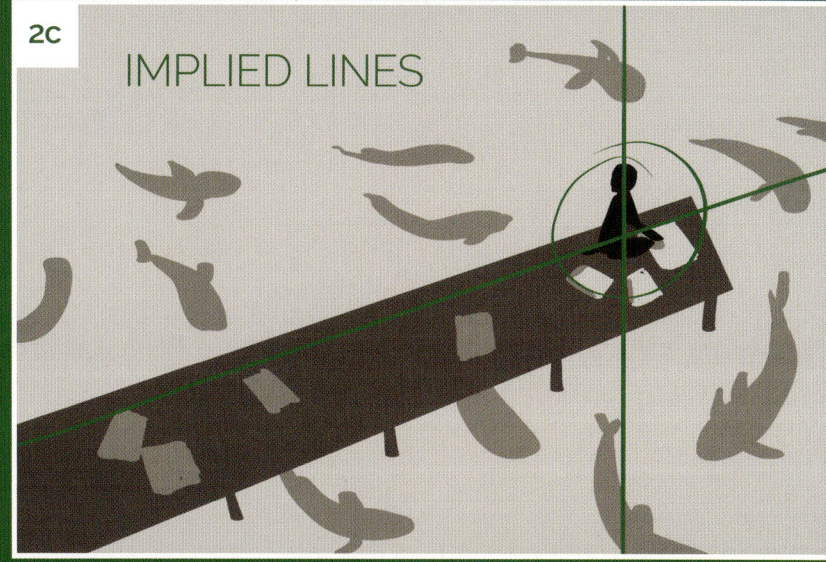

The implied lines also lead the viewer's eye to the girl.

3

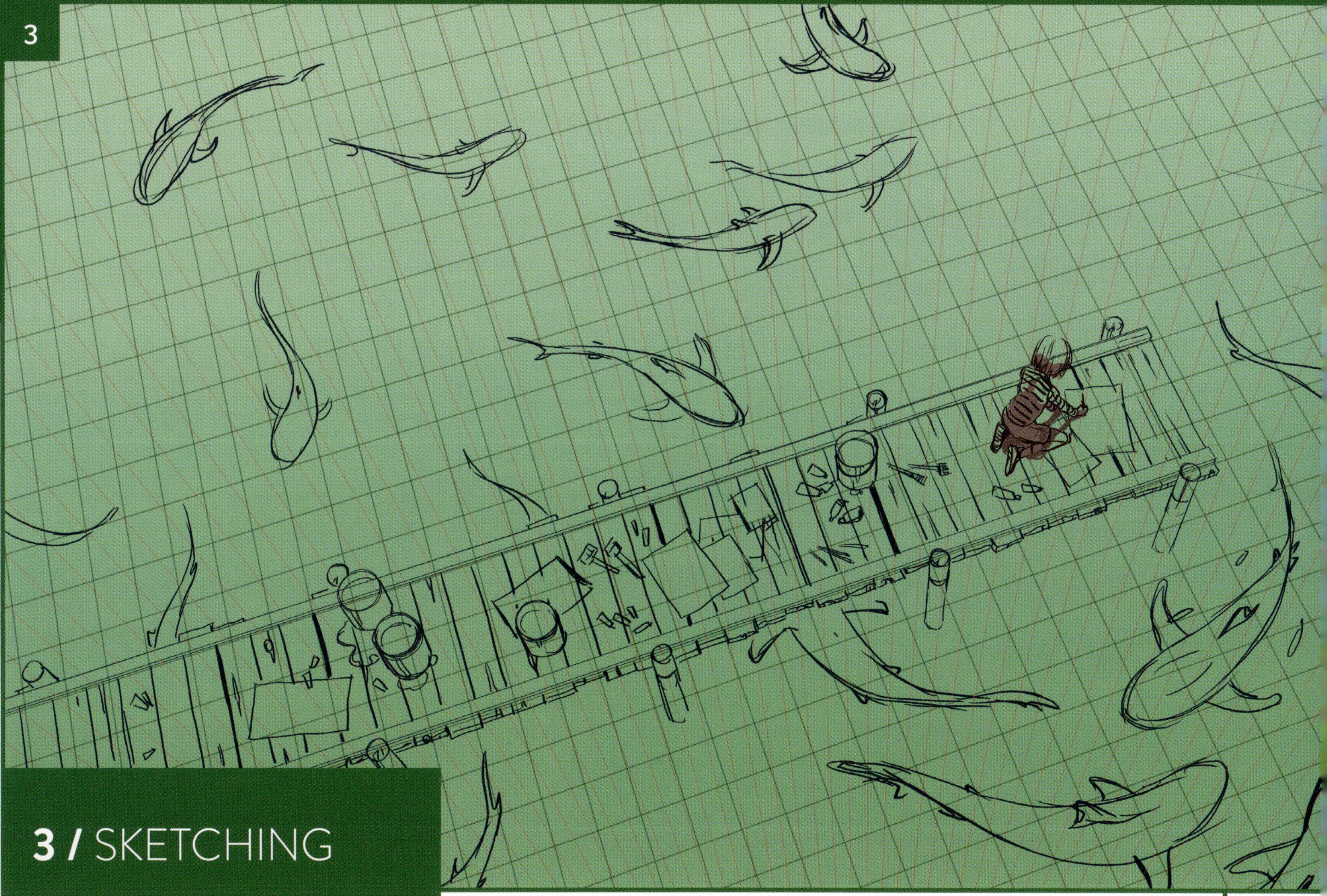

3 / SKETCHING

I decide to spread the art materials out a bit, scattering them almost the full length of the deck. This helps to maintain interest throughout the whole piece rather than having it weighted only on the right side of the composition.

PERSPECTIVE TOOLS

To quickly set up grids, I use the Photoshop CC plug-in Perspective Tools 2 by Sergey Kritskiy. It's a huge timesaver and I wholeheartedly recommend it. Drawing something made up of rectangles in perspective is very easy – just follow the lines of the grid in each direction.

4 / BLOCKING IN THE DECK

I use the Lasso tool to block in the wooden planks of the deck. I try to create a lively pattern of wood colors, all within the same family but with some hue and value variation for interest and contrast. I use brushes with Color Dynamics enabled, mainly Hue and Brightness Jitter, in order to quickly generate even more color variation and interest.

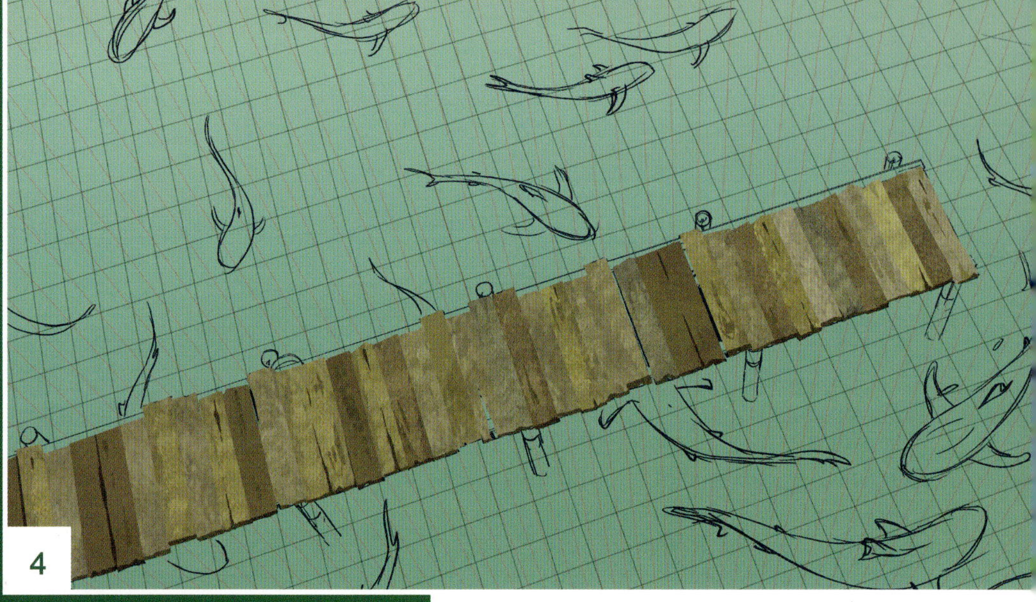

4

PERFECTLY IMPERFECT

As I move across the deck, I keep the perspective lines in mind and follow them as I select my shapes. I follow the perspective lines with about 95% accuracy, skewing them just enough to create gaps and broken-up shapes for interest and believability. We live in an imperfect world, so adding a slight skew can make a design feel more real and lived-in.

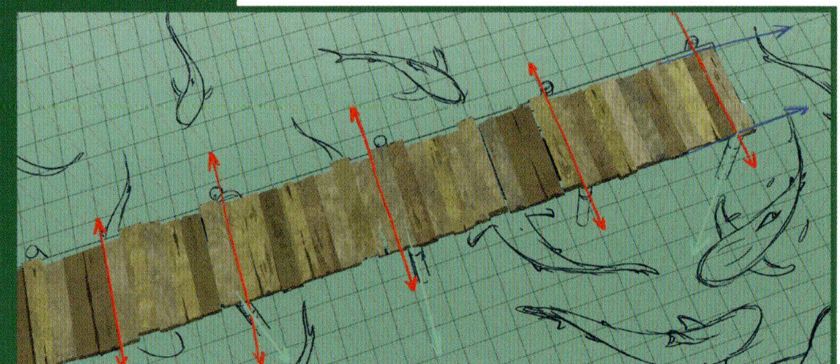

5 / DETAILING THE DECK

I continue using the Lasso tool and textured brushes to block in other items on the deck. I want the elements to feel organically scattered but also balanced and pleasing to the eye. Composing an image is a dance between balance and variation – different elements should feel similar enough to be cohesive, but varied enough that the painting has energy and appeal. Adding little details such as paint spills and splatters creates believability. I create a new layer for each type of object.

5

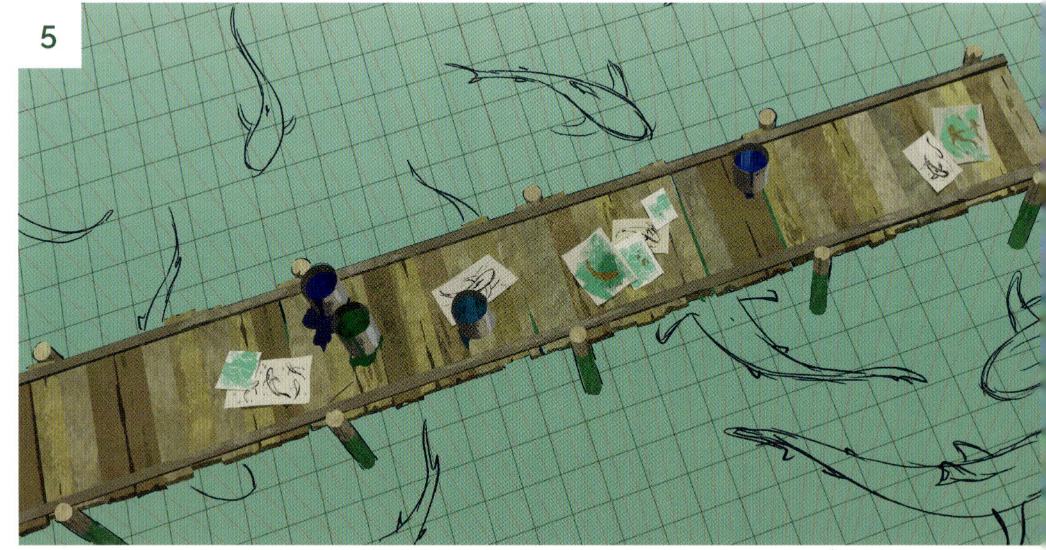

6

6 / PAINTING LIGHT THROUGH WATER

To prepare for this step, I collect references of light patterns on shallow water. Light refracts through water in interesting and beautiful ways. I use soft, painterly brushes to indicate the rippling pattern of lights and darks. I zoom out regularly to conceptualize the image as a whole and ensure the abstract pattern is pleasant in the context of the composition. I use a variety of Overlay and Hard Light layers to paint these light effects. I love to make use of Photoshop blending modes!

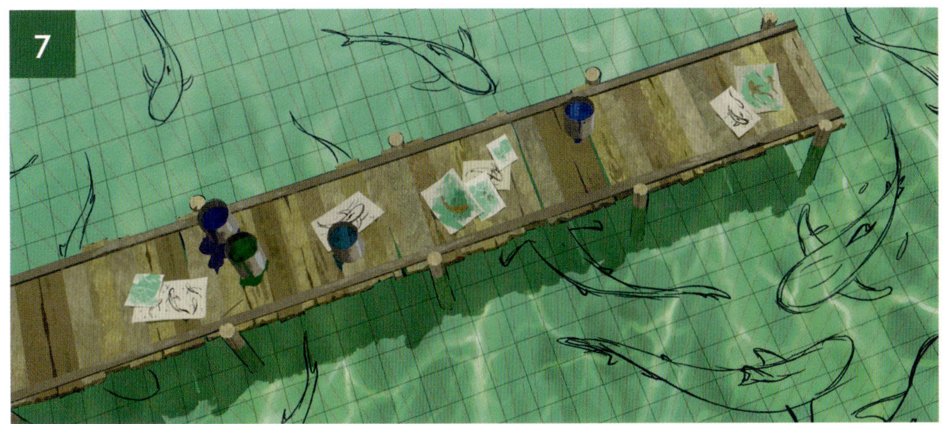

7 / INTRODUCING DECK SHADOWS

I add the shadow of the deck using a Multiply layer. These cast shadows, although very simple, make the biggest difference to the dimension of the painting. I choose a simple overhead light source that casts shadows down onto the surface of the water. I use a clipping mask to fade the light refractions as the image recedes into the distance at the top left of the frame.

8 / PAINTING THE SHARKS

I block in the sharks next, deviating from my sketch slightly in order to make small improvements. After painting the sharks' bodies, I estimate the position of the shadows based on the chosen perspective. I notice in my various references of sea animals in shallow water that the pattern of light distortion diminishes inside the shadows but doesn't vanish completely, so I indicate some soft, light patterns within the shadows.

"DIFFERENT ELEMENTS SHOULD FEEL SIMILAR ENOUGH TO BE COHESIVE, BUT VARIED ENOUGH THAT THE PAINTING HAS ENERGY"

9 / RENDERING THE OCEAN

I use painterly brushes to render the sharks and add other small details, such as the fish. I add shadows and light patterns to try to create a feeling of volume on the sharks. I want them to feel like curved cylinders. I give the greatest level of detail to the sharks in the bottom right, as they are closest to the viewer and would be most visible in the water.

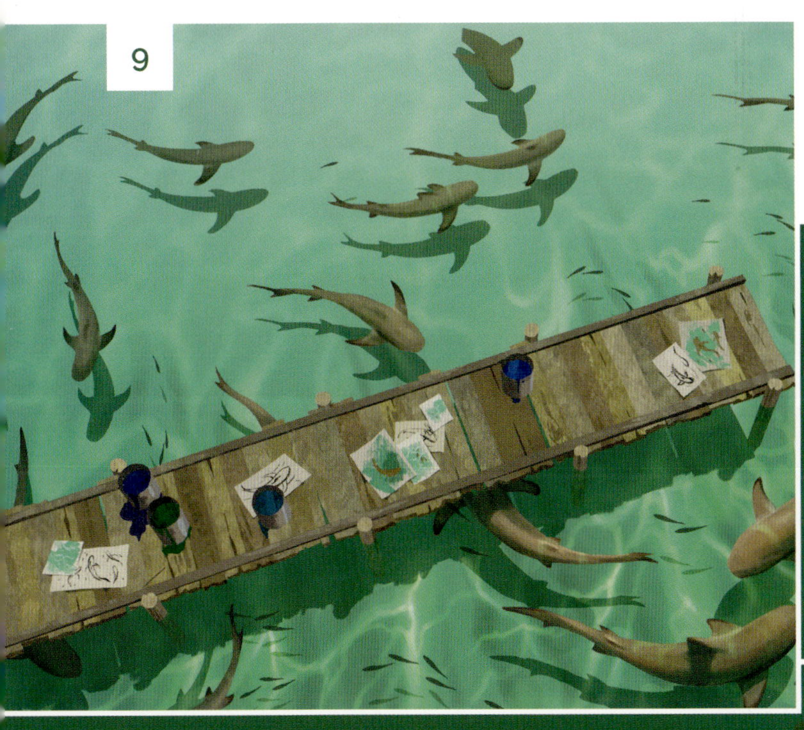

HUE BREAKDOWN

I collapse the image in step 9 into a single mid-tone value, which shows that the structure of the piece is largely built around groupings of green and brown. I find this color combination very summery and pleasant. I dot the ocean with brown sharks, and break up the deck with green art supplies.

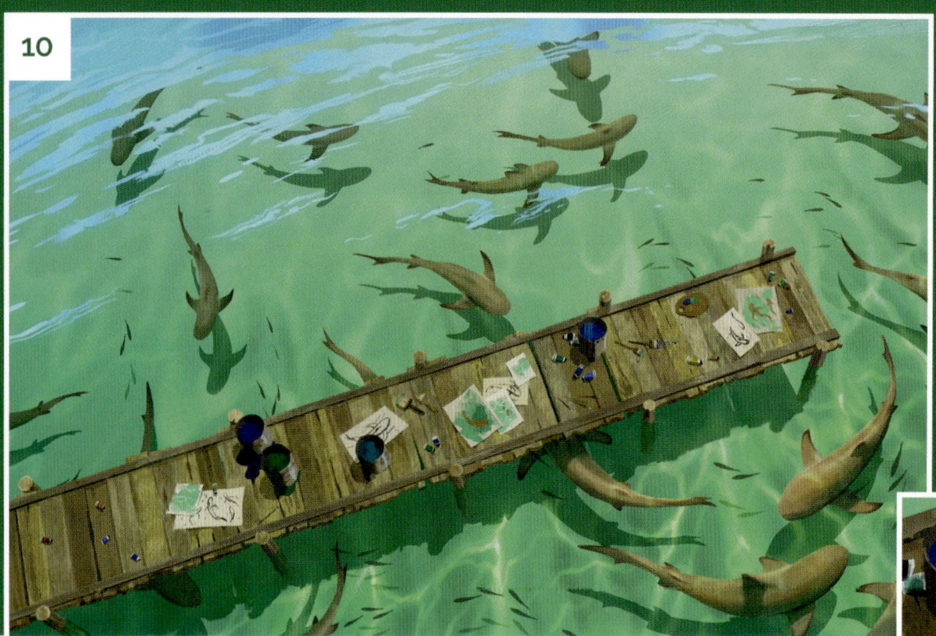

10 / APPLYING LIGHT AND DETAIL

I decide that adding light reflections to the upper left region of the frame will help solidify the surface of the water and concentrate the focus around the lower third of the painting. I also block in various other art supplies. I add more little paint splatters, because I imagine a child painting on a deck would be likely to create a bit of a mess! I also try to give everything at least a hint of a shadow, even the papers, to help create dimension.

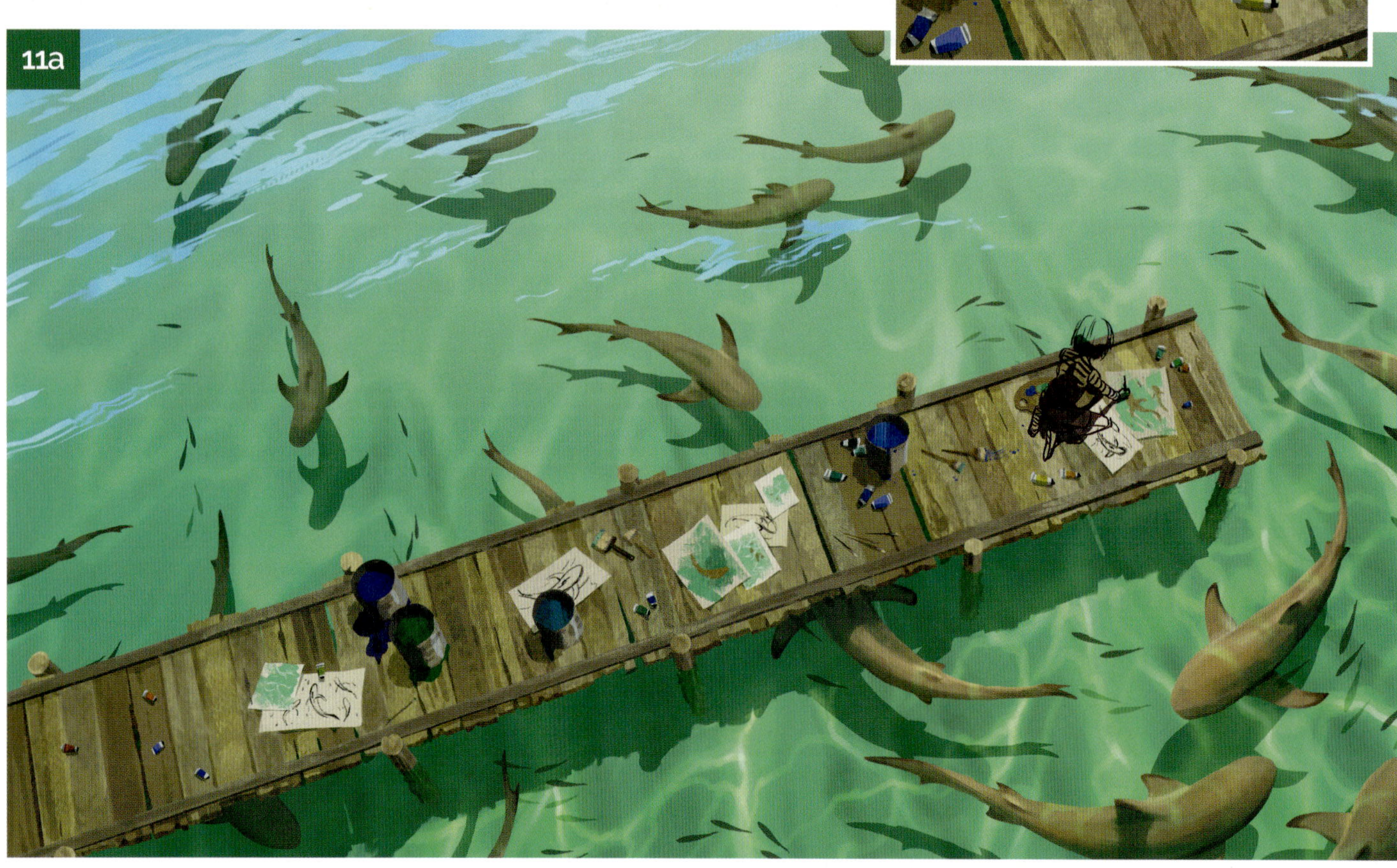

11 / ADDING THE CHARACTER

When I add the character to the dock, I try to use colors and patterns that will draw the eye to her as a focal point. I choose a color scheme that is harmonious enough that it fits with the composition, but also unique enough to attract attention. Adding a busy pattern to a character's clothing is an easy trick for creating additional contrast.

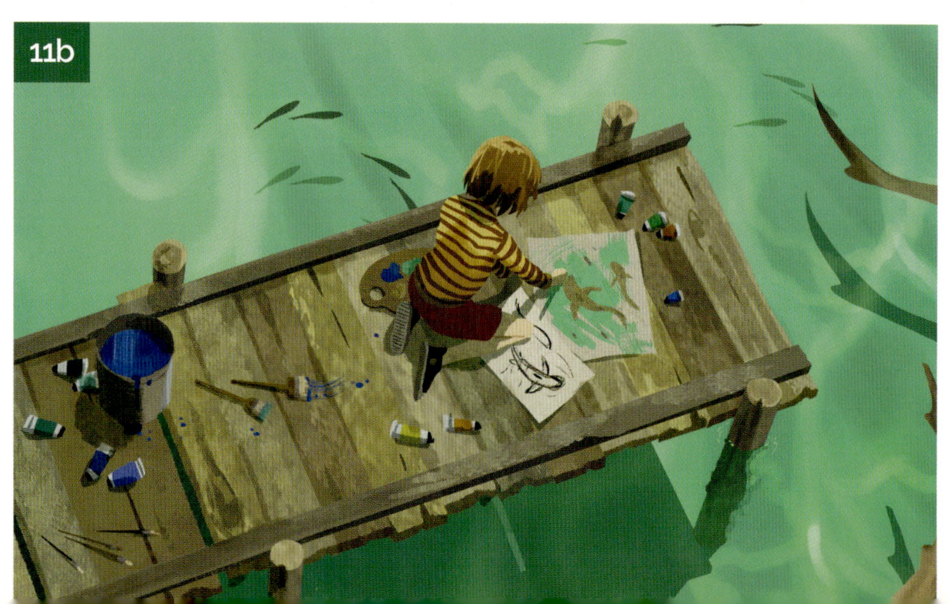

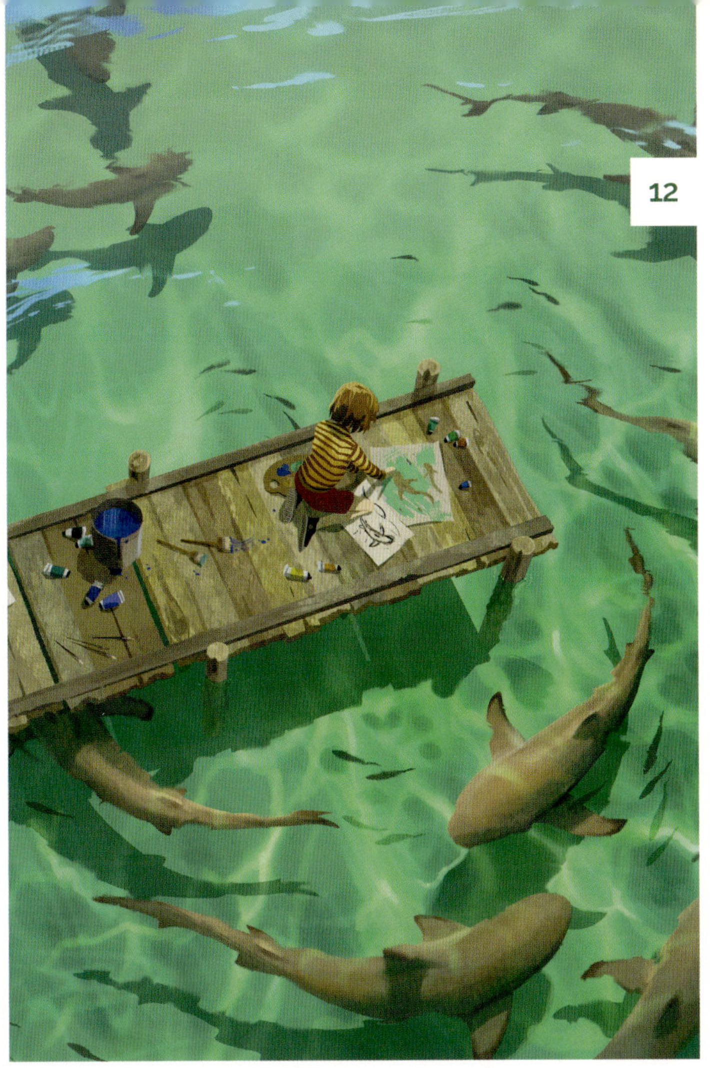

12 / CREATING WATER DISTORTION

At this stage, I Copy-Merged all of the ocean layers to produce a flattened version of my ocean in a single layer. Then, I use the Smudge tool to create patterns of water distortion.

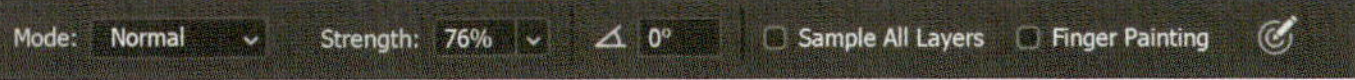

These are the Smudge tool settings I use. I also use an oval brush with Transfer settings enabled.

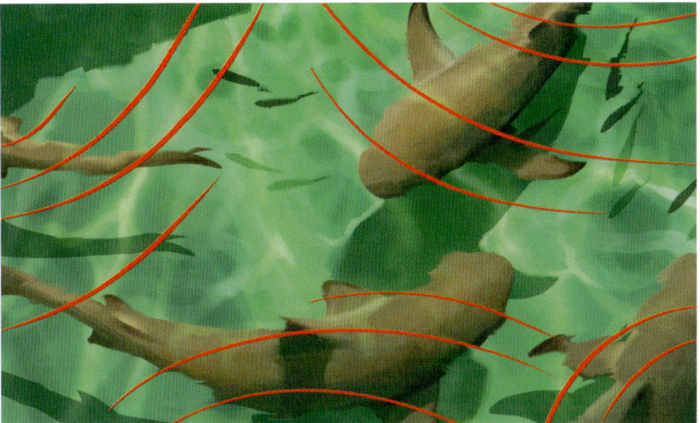

I envision ripple patterns on the water's surface (shown in red) and smudge the layer following those ripple patterns.

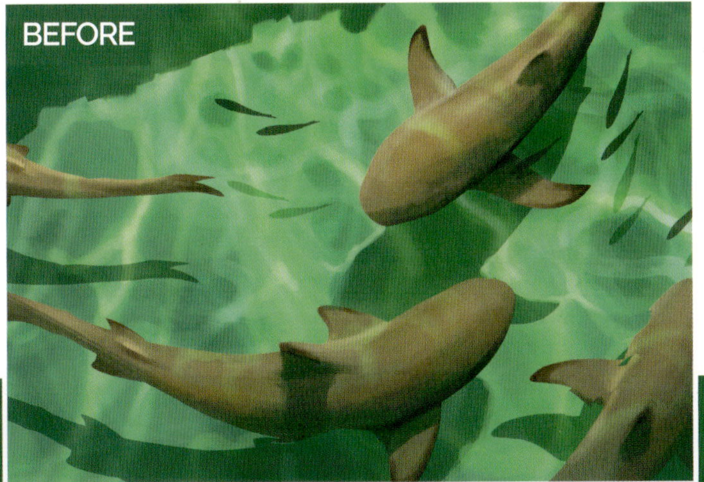

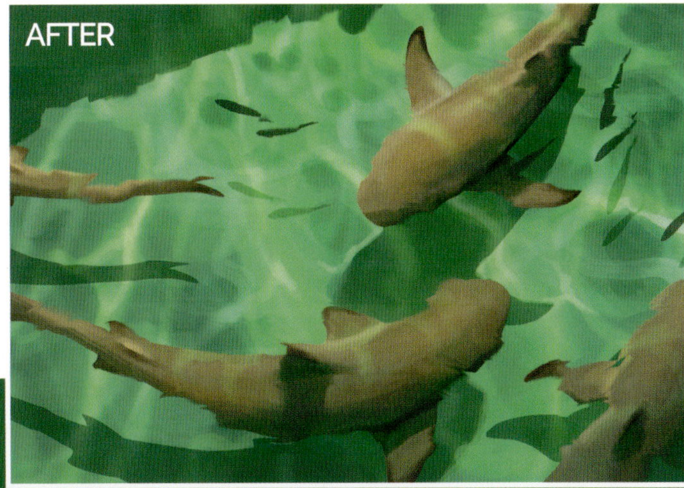

13 / ADDITIONAL RENDERING

I continue to render the water using the Smudge tool, and by painting directly on top. I add small, gleaming highlights. I continue to concentrate the highest level of detail in the bottom right quadrant of the image, and the more distant sharks become heavily distorted by the water. Building a strong visual effect such as water distortion can generate fun and very believable results.

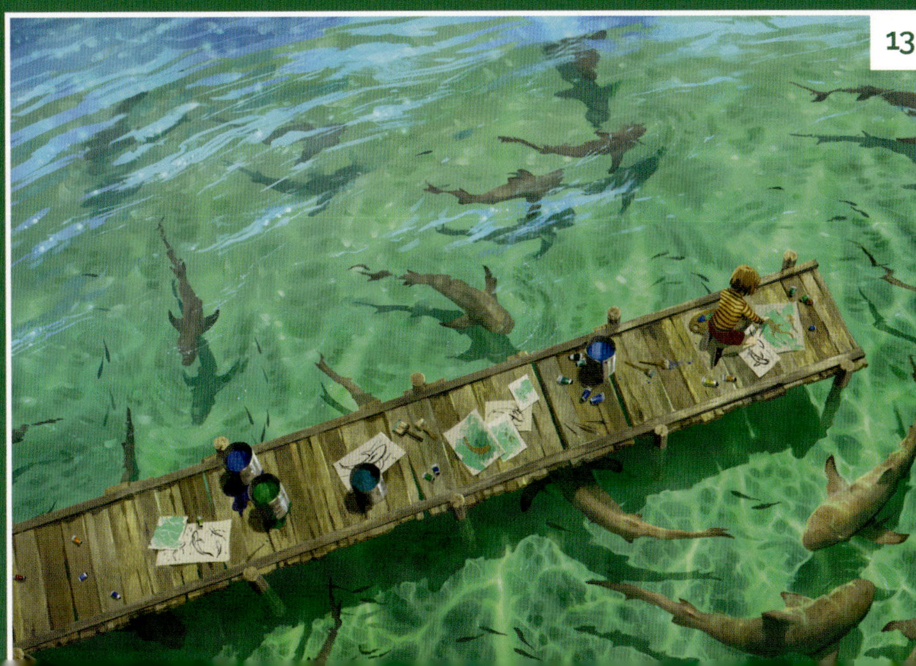

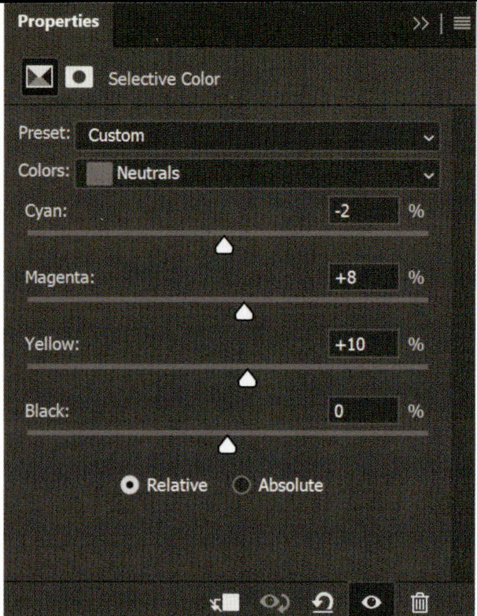

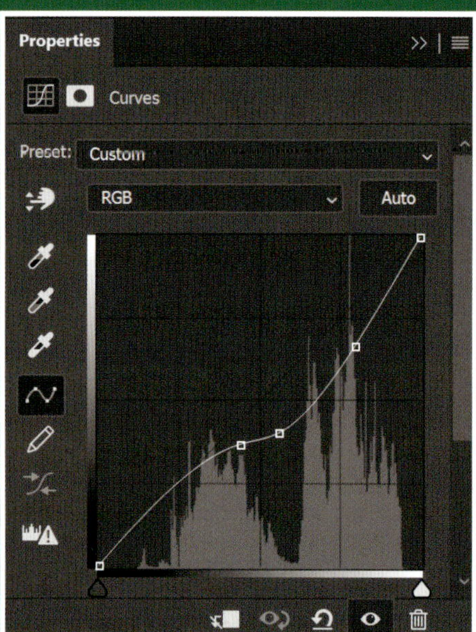

These are the settings I use for Selective Color and Curves adjustment layers in this painiting.

14 / FINAL ADJUSTMENTS

When I reach the end of the painting process, my final steps are always to make small adjustments to the whole image using adjustment layers such as Curves, Selective Color, and Color Balance. Here, I apply warmth and contrast using Curves and Selective Color layers before calling this chapter opener painting complete.

Adjustment layers can be found under the half-light/half-dark circle icon at the bottom of the Photoshop layer menu. I usually spend fifteen to twenty minutes at the end of the painting process playing around with various final tweaks to see how I can enhance my image.

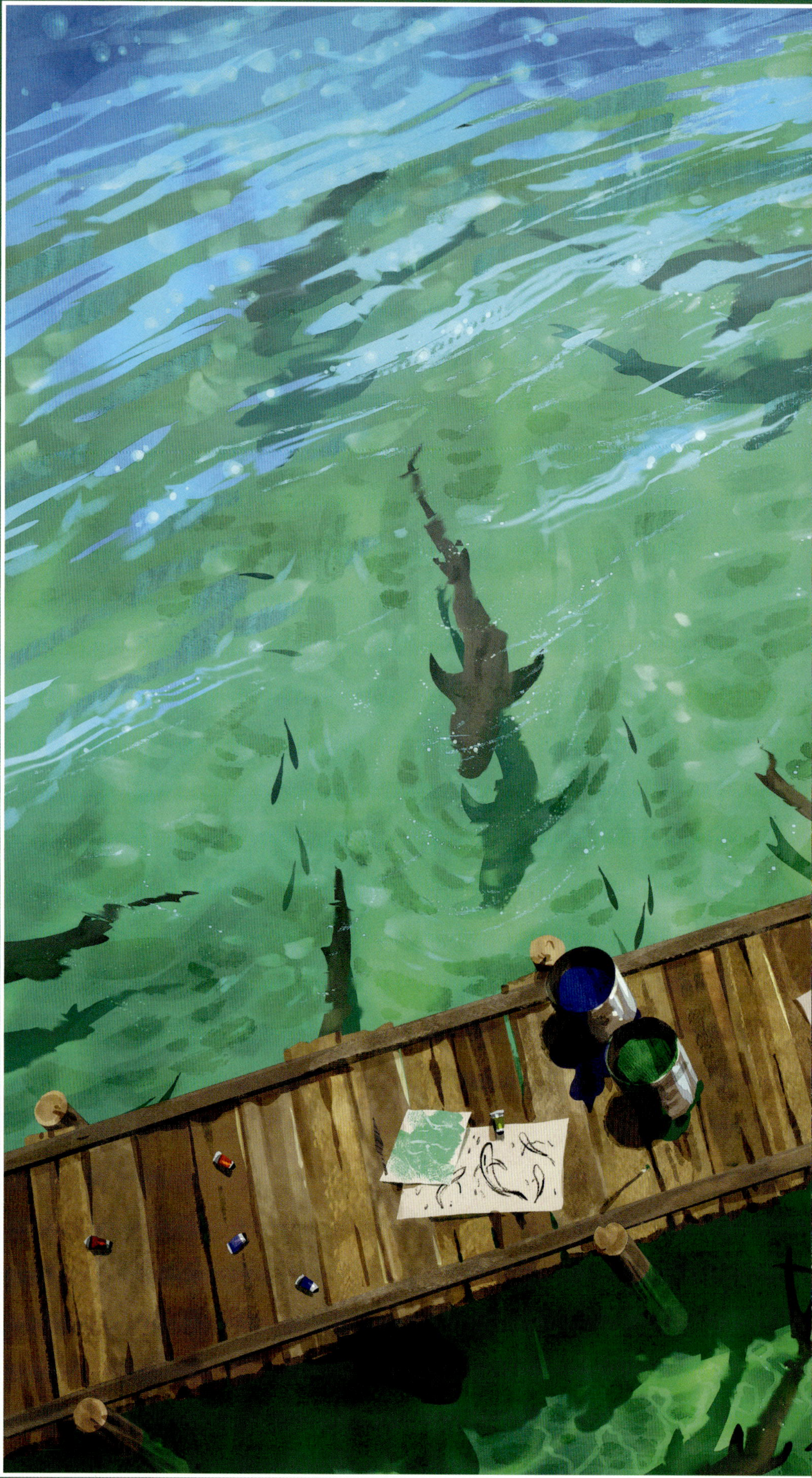

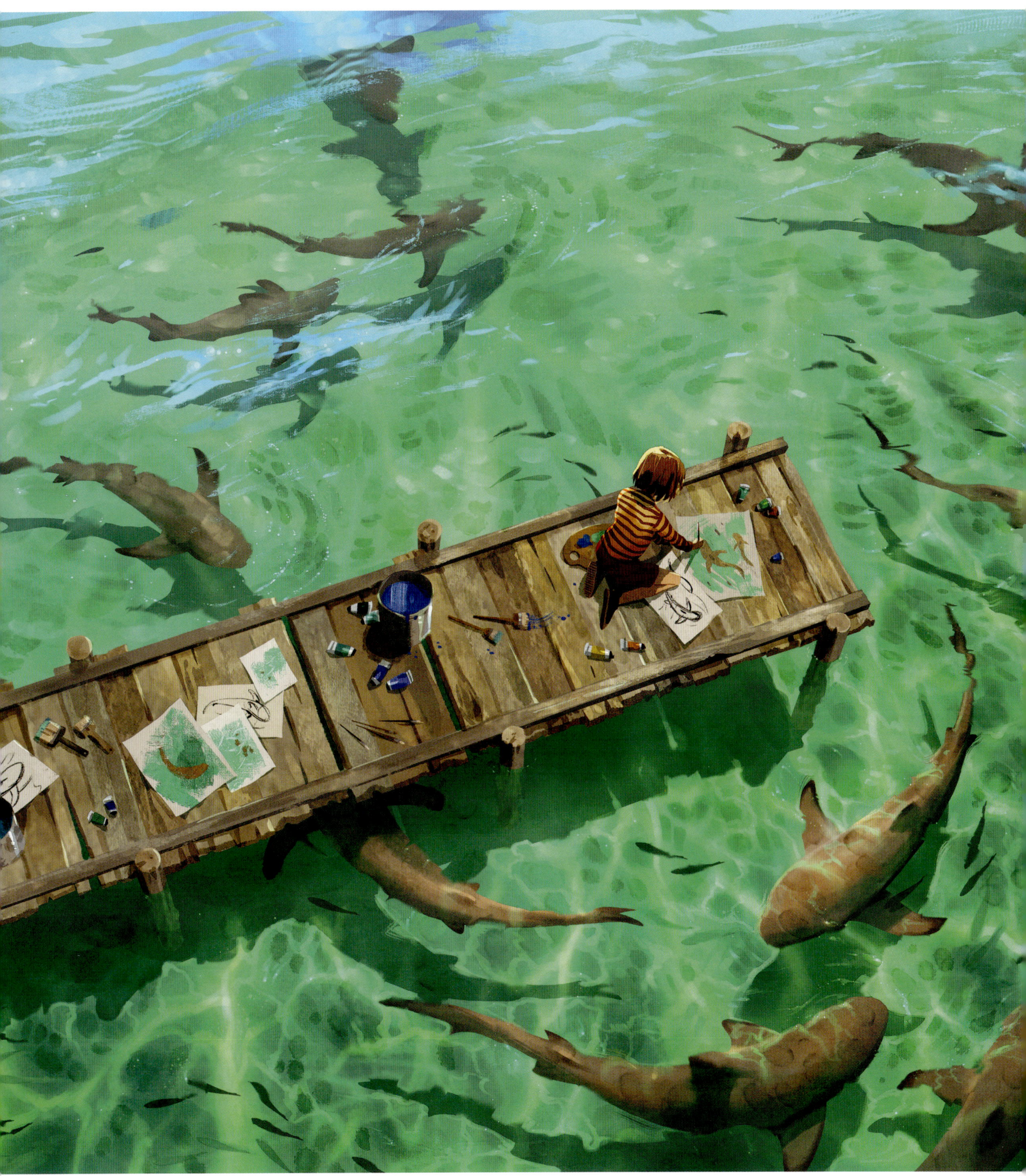

TUTORIAL / DRAWING IN WINDOW FOG

I have always loved drawing in window fog; it's such a charming activity that I remember fondly from my childhood. I would have loved to have a room with such large windows to run around and draw all over!

For this piece, I used SketchUp 3D design software to model the environment, and Photoshop CC to paint the image. I learned to use SketchUp through YouTube alone over just a couple days; it's amazing how easy it can be to learn new skills on the internet. As always, I also used my trusty Wacom Cintiq Pro 24.

1

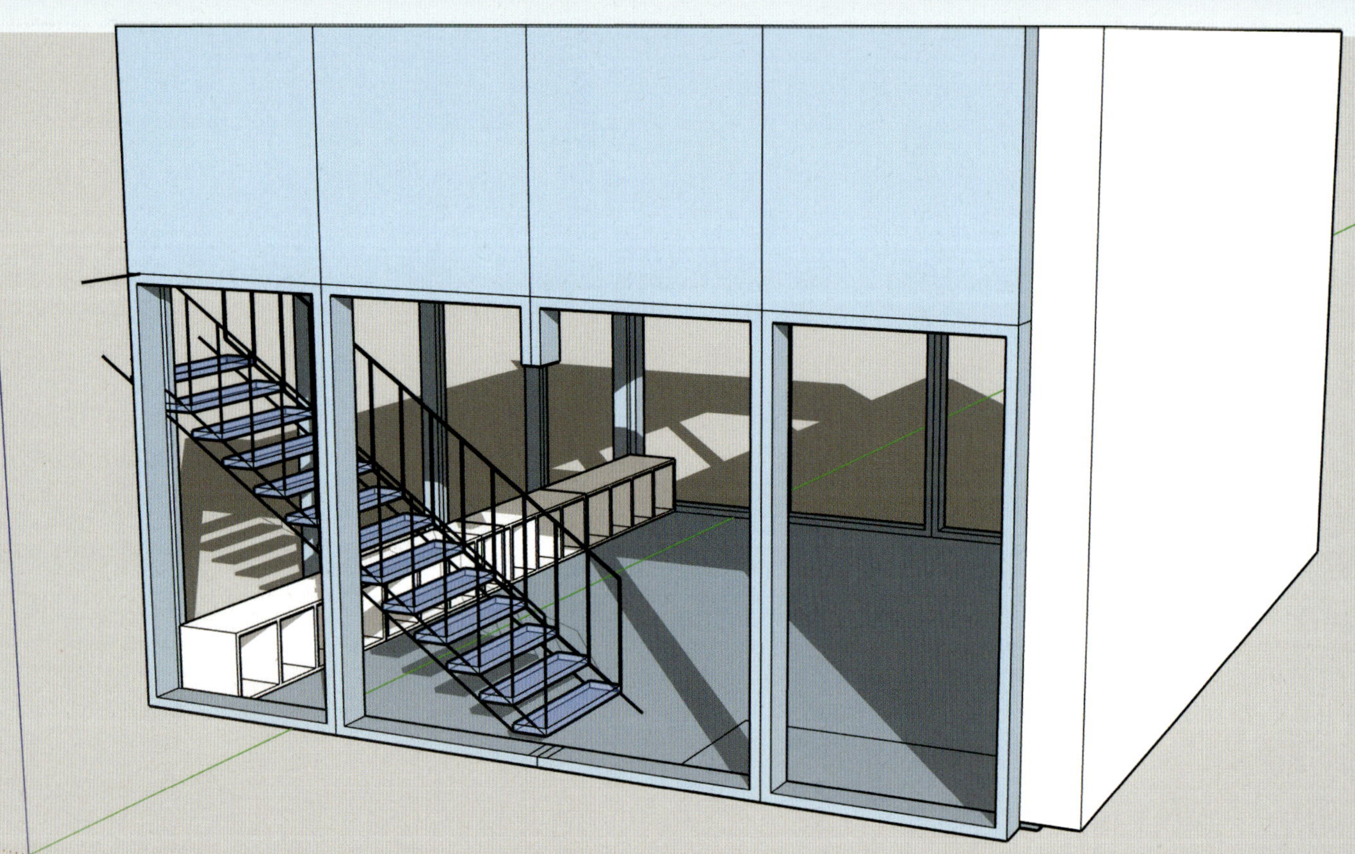

1 / MODELING A ROOM

When I have a clear story idea but no precise mental image of the composition I want to create, I sometimes begin by modeling in SketchUp first. I brainstorm as I model, adding and removing objects as I please. I love the freedom this offers when designing; I can easily rotate an entire staircase if I want to see how it would look from another angle. I often only model exactly what I need in the shot because I am quite single-minded. For example, the staircase here leads to nowhere! I know I want a lot of glass surfaces to populate with window fog drawings – as many as possible – so that's what I focus on!

SIMPLE SILHOUETTES

At this early stage, I create simple "blobs" in place of detailed character sketches because it allows me to iterate quickly and get a good idea of the composition by squinting.

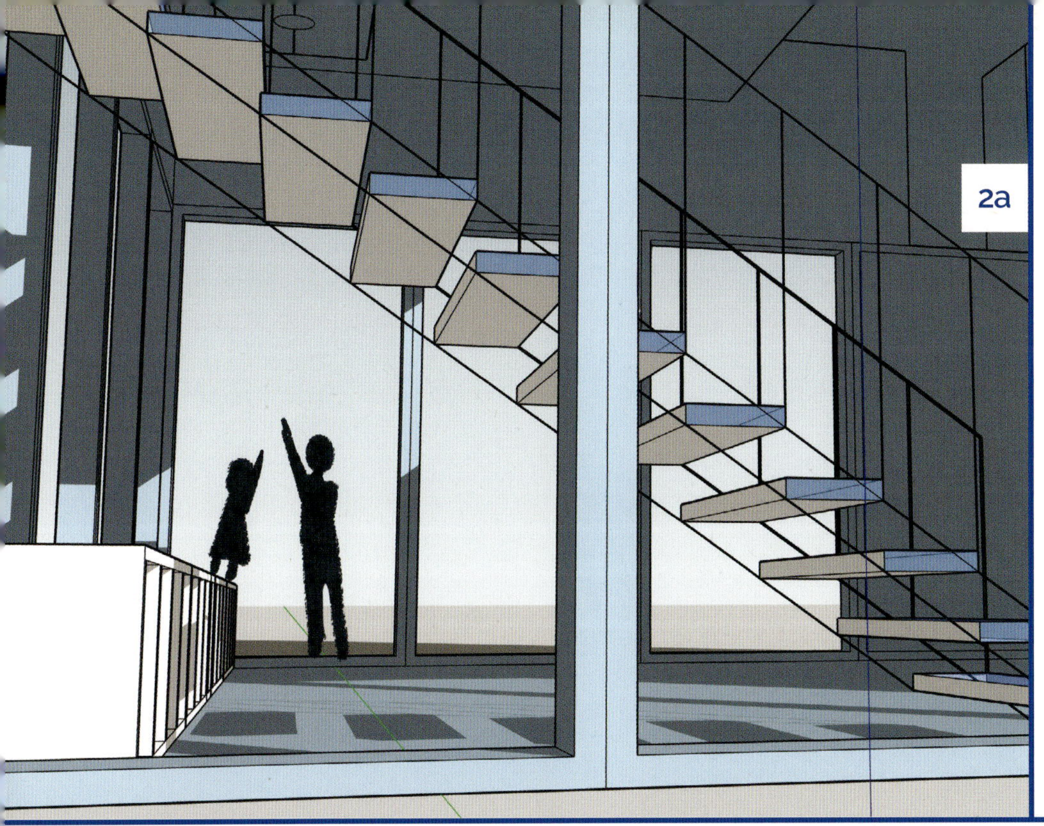

2 / STAGING A SHOT

I begin to create thumbnails, then compare and analyze them to find out which concept works best for both the final design and also the way the drawing might be used later. I create this piece with the intention of it becoming a chapter opener, so consider how this might affect the composition.

2A / THUMBNAIL 1

The first thumbnail contains many elements that I like. The slant of the staircase makes for an interesting compositional element, framing the characters in a fun way. A row of shelves creates a dramatic implied line leading directly toward them. To improve the composition of this thumbnail, I would remove the middle window bar in the foreground to open up the entire wall.

2B / THUMBNAIL 2

The second concept is also fun, but I quickly realize it wouldn't work for a couple of reasons:

> ***(a) If the windows are fogged up, it would be difficult to see inside, and the characters would be obscured.***
>
> ***(b) The characters sit directly along the center of the frame, which doesn't make for a very good double-page spread in a book or magazine!***

At this point I prefer Thumbnail 1 and could just move ahead with it, but I'm not excited about the amount of dead space that would be present on the right page in the spread. I decide to attempt one more design.

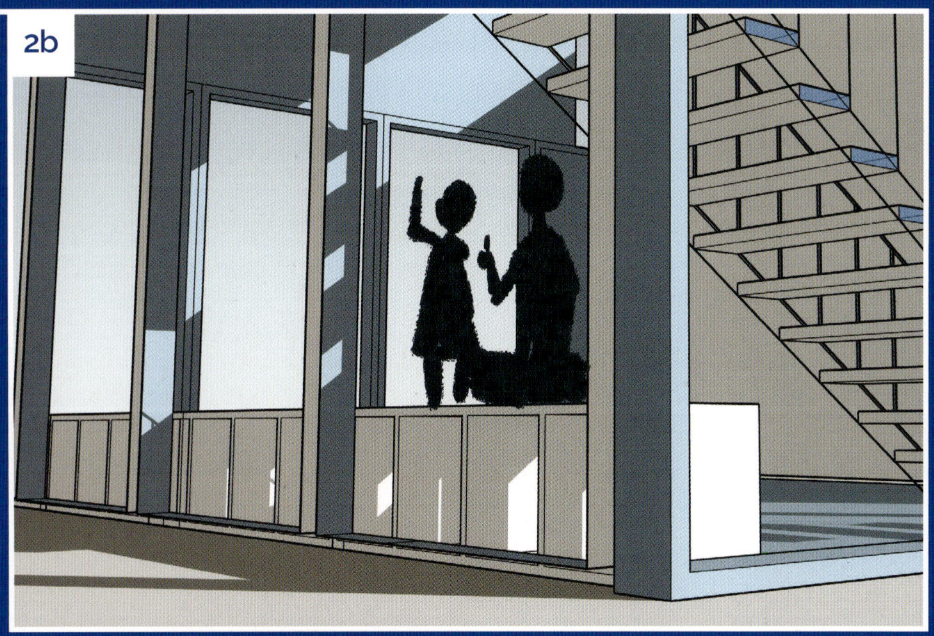

2c

2C / THUMBNAIL 3

For this version, I take elements I enjoy from Thumbnail 1 but reorganize them to fill the space in a more pleasing way. The fun diagonal slant of the stairs is still present, but it now leads the viewer directly to the characters rather than off the page; the side of the image without characters can be full of window-fog drawings rather than empty interior! I decide to move forward with Thumbnail 3.

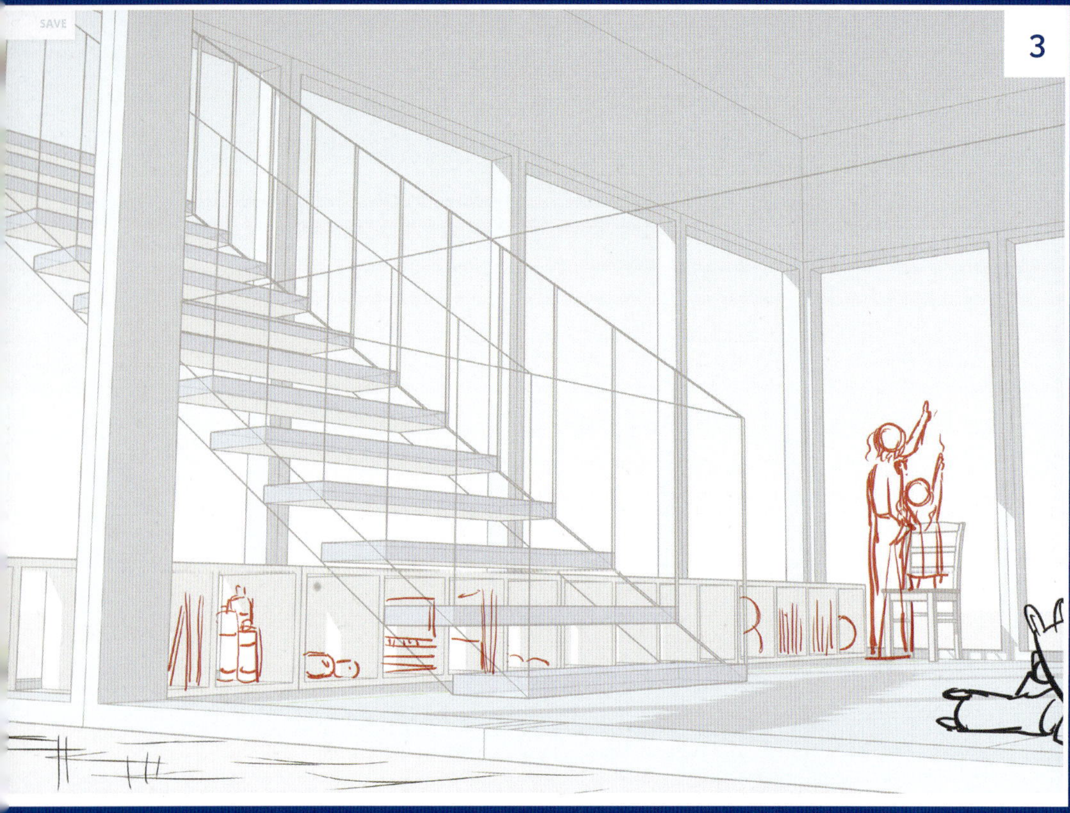

3 / THE SKETCH

For the next step, I move on to working in Photoshop. Depending on the style I'm aiming for, I either create a full sketch over the SketchUp model, or use the model as the base sketch and start blocking in with the Lasso tool. In this case, I decide to keep the architecture very simple and plain, so creating a sketch over it is unnecessary. I sketch slightly more detailed characters and populate the environment with storytelling details such as rain boots, toys, and art supplies. I adjust the character poses slightly to create a warmer, more parental pose, as the characters are meant to represent my mom and me.

COMPOSITIONAL THEORY

I use a Fibonacci-spiral composition often, and aim to create something similar here using the stairs as the major impetus; I use the rain boots to keep the viewer's eye from leaving the page. The smaller implied lines of the windows and shelves also move the momentum toward the characters; I angle one of the boots toward them as well.

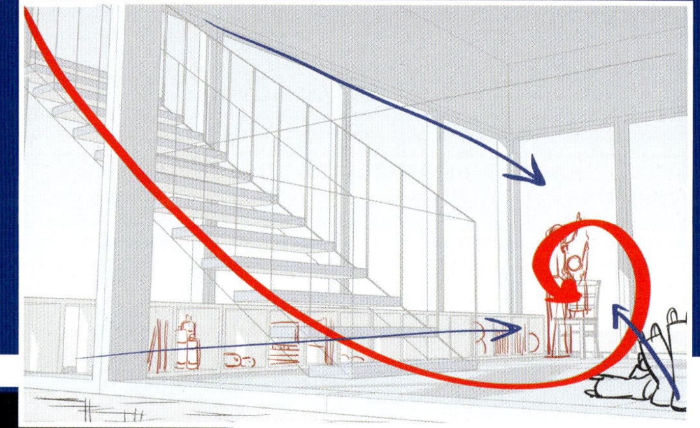

4 / BLOCKING IN LARGE FORMS: *LASSO*

I always begin by blocking in my biggest shapes first. This allows me to conceptualize the composition as a whole more easily. I use the Polygonal Lasso tool to do this, following the SketchUp model the way I would follow a sketch. I don't worry about matching every line perfectly; in fact, I'll skew some lines slightly to create a more animated look.

5 / BLOCKING IN LARGE FORMS: *BRUSHES*

I almost always use brushes with Color Jitter enabled during the blocking-in stage, as I love the variation it gives me within individual objects. I also use rake brushes and other textured brushes from time to time to add additional texture. To begin, I create a new layer for each object in the image and keep them carefully labeled and organized into groups. I use the rain boots as an opportunity for a pop of color. I want the image to stay largely within the blue hue range, but move outside this range for smaller objects to create a more believable environment.

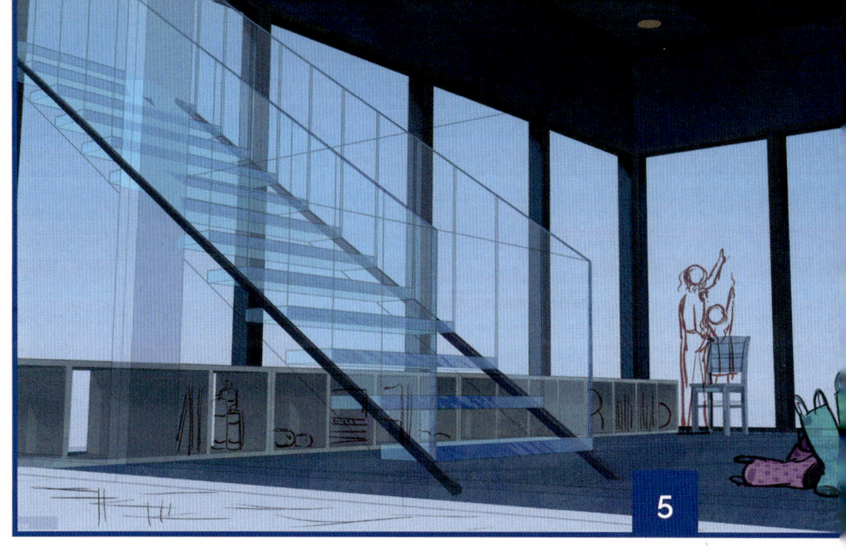

6

6 / BLOCKING IN SMALL FORMS

Once the large shapes have been established, I move on to painting the smaller shapes. I use the Lasso tool to create some objects, but for the majority I paint directly with hard square or oval brushes. By varying the colors in these smaller objects, I create a line of busy detail that leads the eye to where the characters will be.

7 / PAINTING REFLECTIONS

I want the flooring of the room to be highly reflective to add dynamism to the composition. Painting reflections in three-point perspective often means doing a bit more beyond just flipping the objects vertically. I use Transform > Distort to align the reflections with the perspective of the image. I paint the details using a Kyle T. Webster watercolor brush to create a wobbly appearance, which feels more floor-like to me than a perfect reflection.

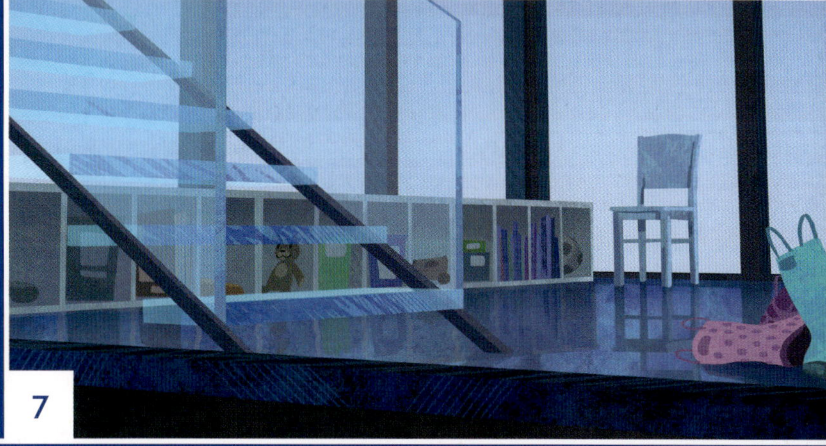

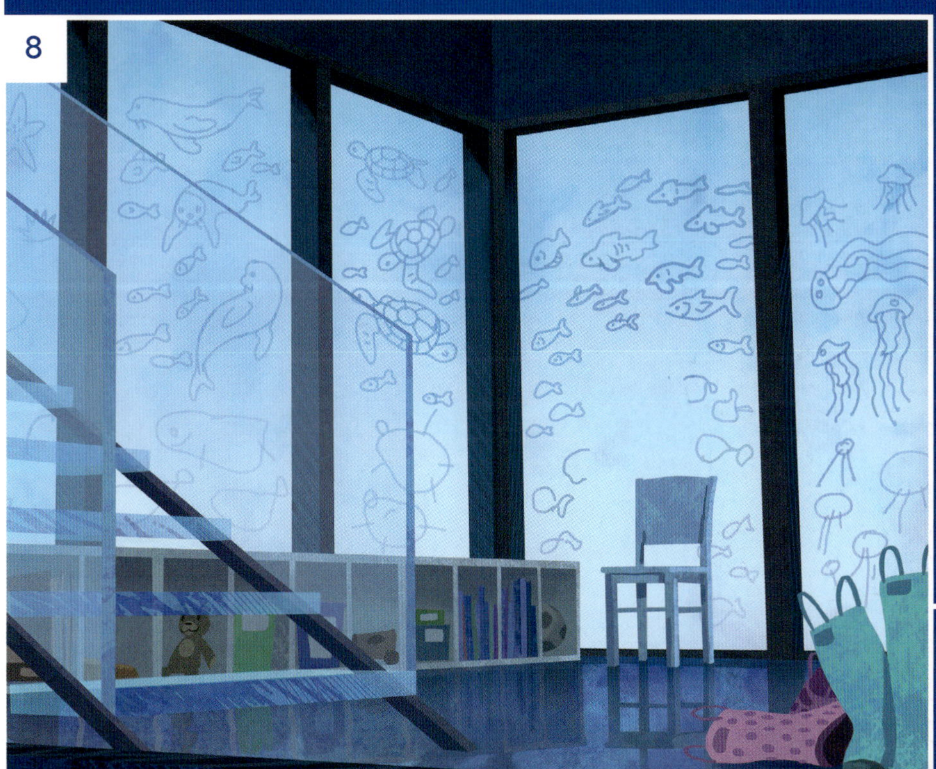

8 / WINDOW-FOG DRAWINGS

I use a subtractive method to paint the window fog – I fill the backdrop with the colors I want to see inside the drawings, then cover it with a layer of fog using various soft watercolor brushes. Next, I use a clipping mask to remove the fog in the shape of the drawings.

In the top half of the piece, I draw fully formed "adult drawings" at the height at which the adult could reach. As the child is so much shorter, even standing on a chair, I add more childlike drawings to the bottom half of the window. It now looks like the two of them have collaborated!

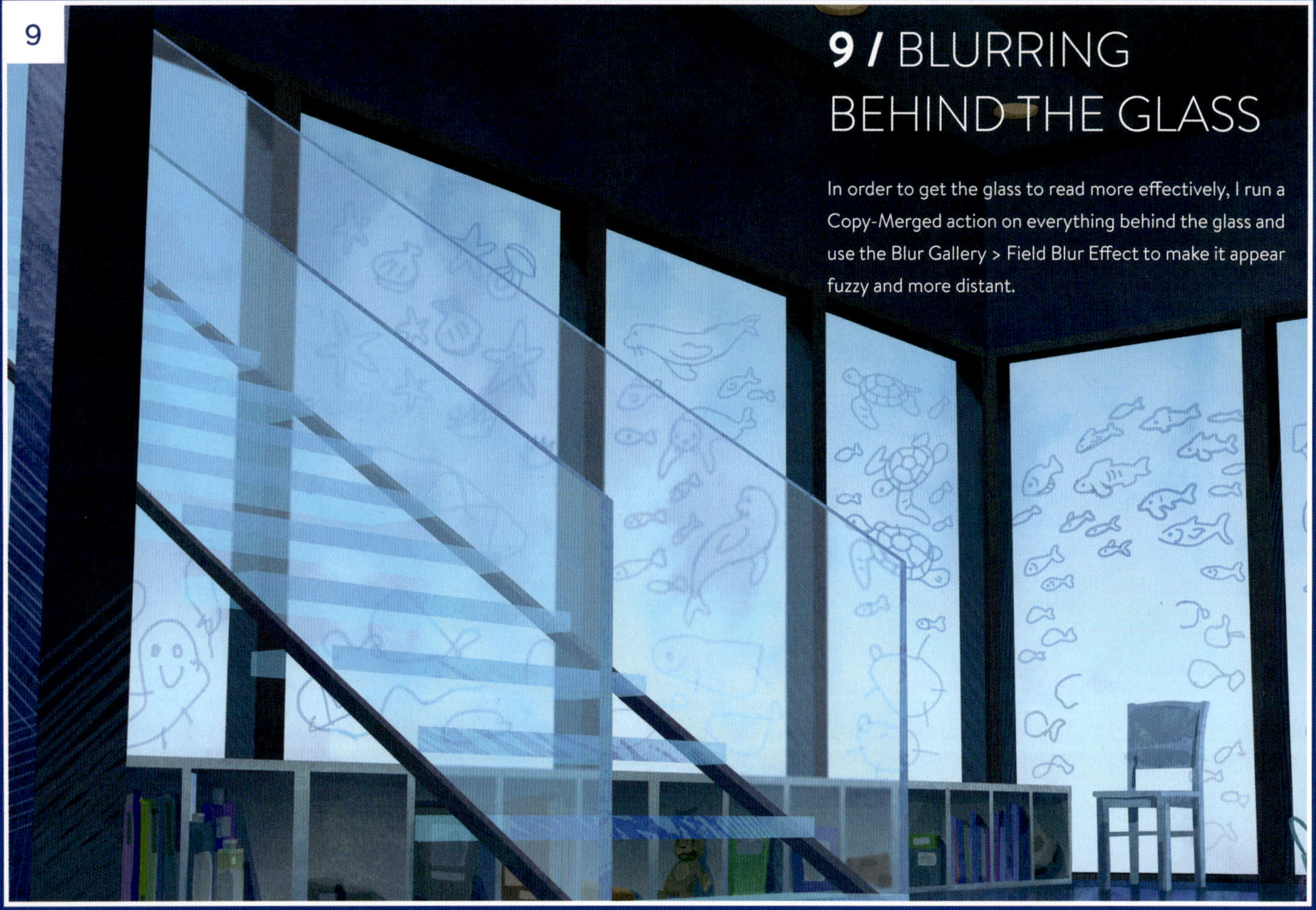

9

9 / BLURRING BEHIND THE GLASS

In order to get the glass to read more effectively, I run a Copy-Merged action on everything behind the glass and use the Blur Gallery > Field Blur Effect to make it appear fuzzy and more distant.

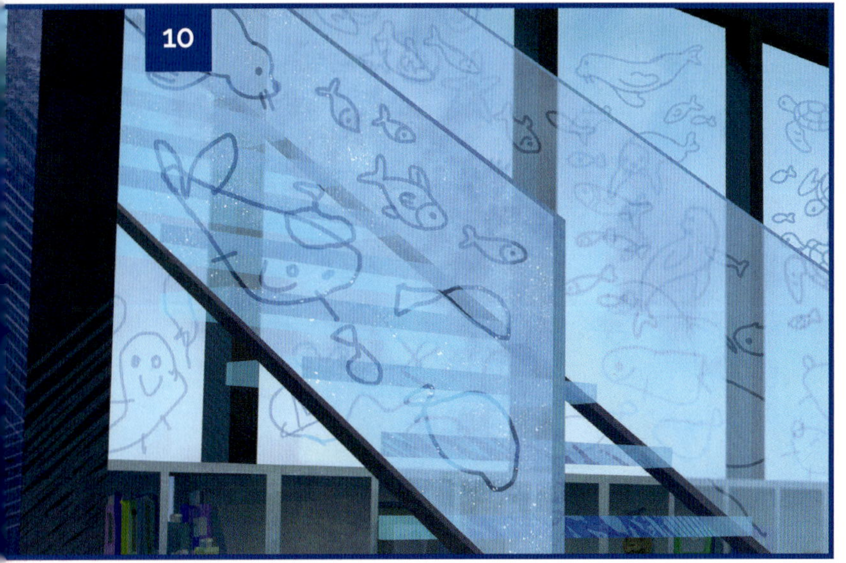

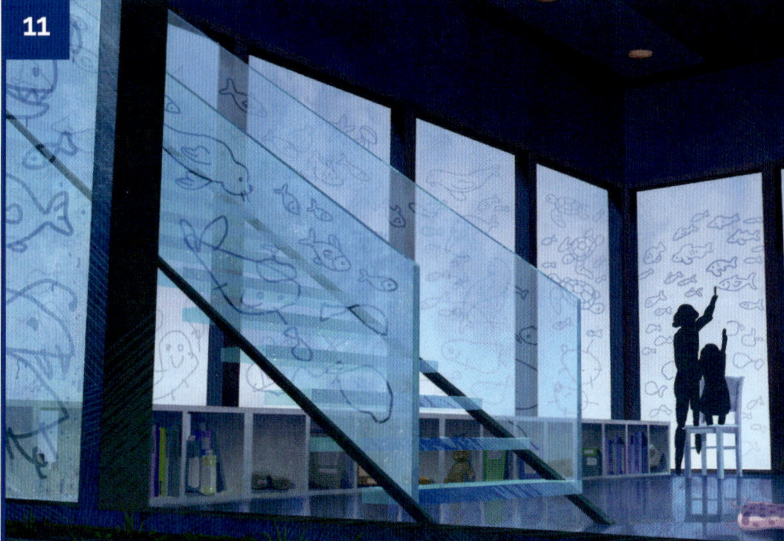

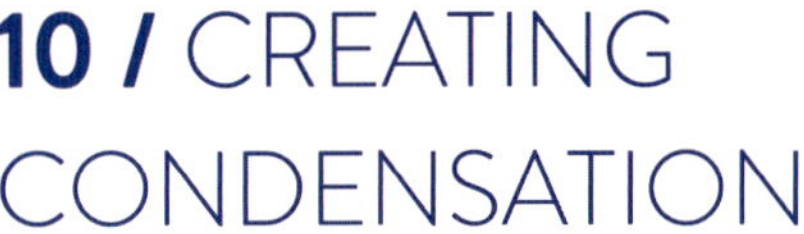

10 / CREATING CONDENSATION

I add condensation on the glass closest to the viewer to illustrate visible moisture and make sure the concept of the drawings being created in window fog is understood. I use splatter brushes to quickly brush water droplets onto the glass surface.

11 / PLACING THE CHARACTERS

Before committing to my final character poses, I block in simple silhouettes where I plan to place them in the scene. I squint at the composition to make sure I like the way everything reads.

12 / SKETCHING THE CHARACTERS

I use a hard oval brush to draw in the final sketch of my characters. In the illustration, they feature in the background, fairly far away from the viewer, so detailing is not required. I mainly just plot out the larger shapes I will Lasso in the next step.

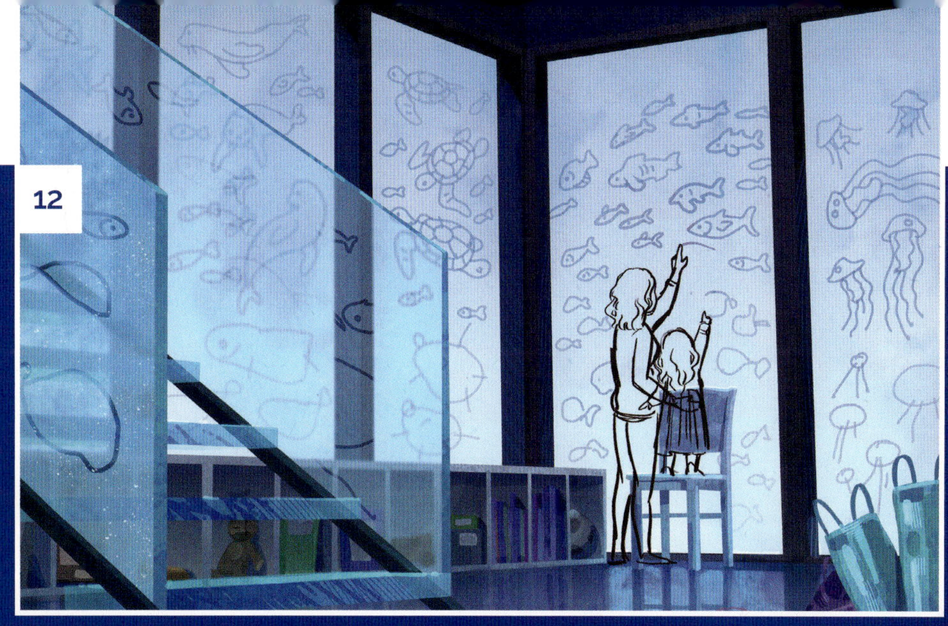

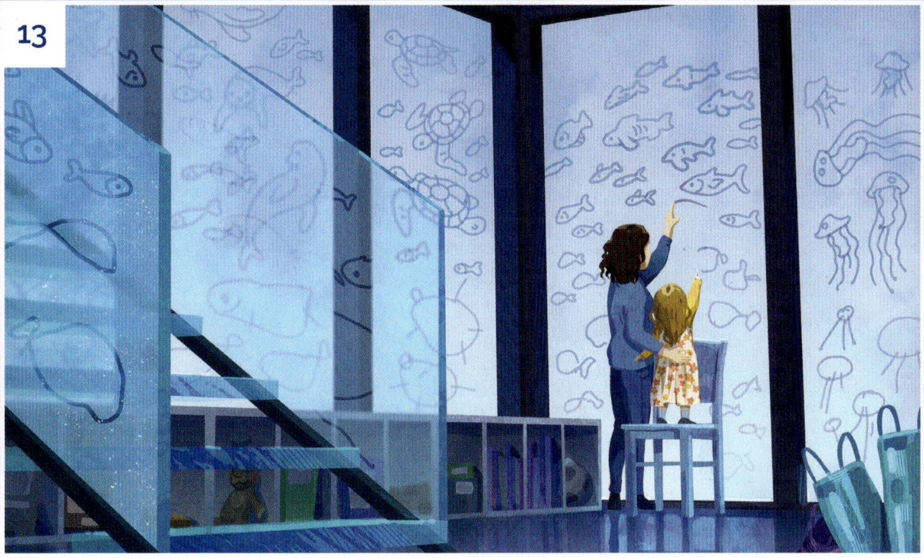

13 / LOCAL COLORS FOR THE CHARACTERS

I block in the characters' local colors using the Lasso tool along with oval brushes for smaller shapes. I create a new layer for each body part or item of clothing so I can adjust them individually at the end. I save a copy of the layered characters, then merge them down to shade and light them. I give the child a patterned dress for added visual contrast against the solid chair and adult's clothes. In addition, I add hue contrast by making her hair and clothes warmer colors such as yellow.

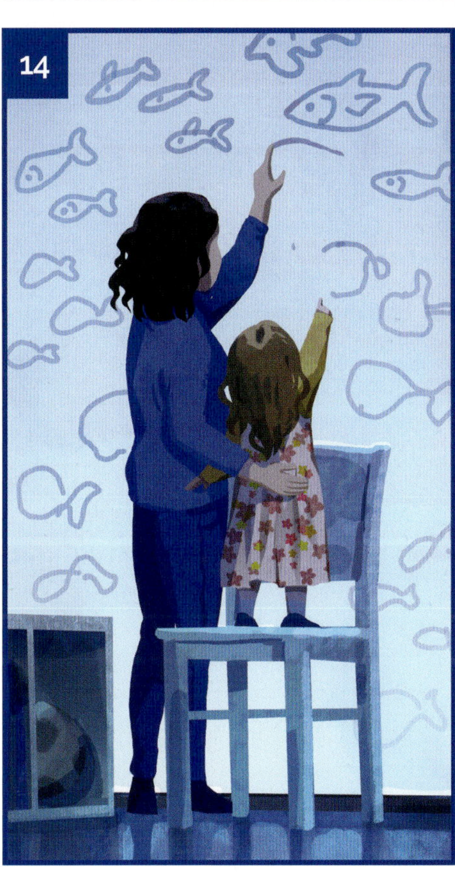

14 / UNIFYING THE CHARACTERS

After painting the characters' local colors, my next step is to unify the characters with the background using diffused lighting. Often, I'll use the Soft Light blending mode, but here I use a Multiply layer filled with a pale baby blue.

15 / SHADING AND LIGHTING THE CHARACTERS

Finally, I use Screen, Overlay, and Multiply layers to add shadows and lighting to the characters. I always try to follow the form of the characters, even at this distance, to show the viewer that they are three-dimensional, volumetric forms.

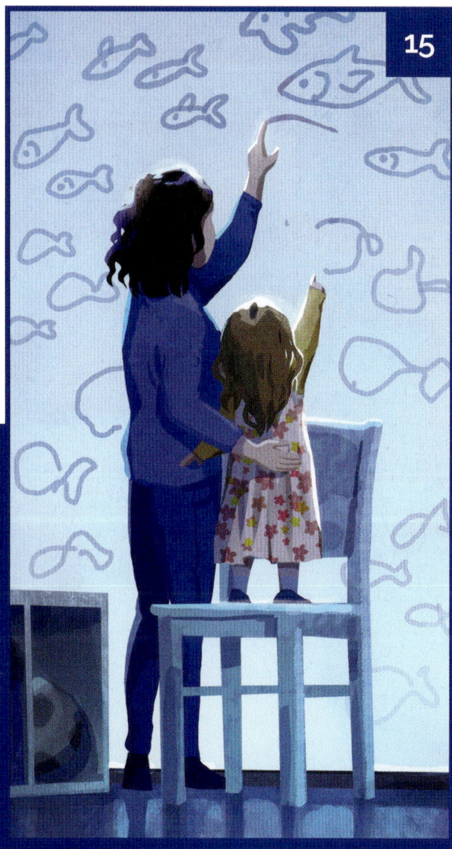

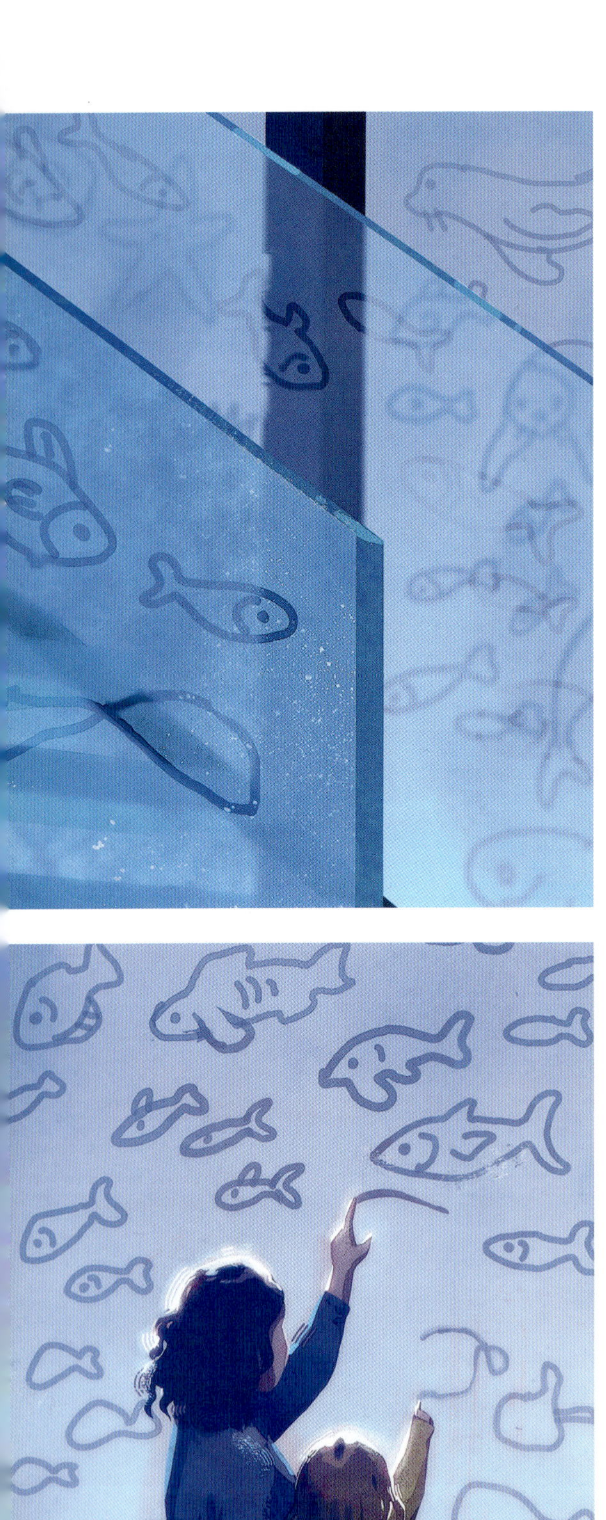

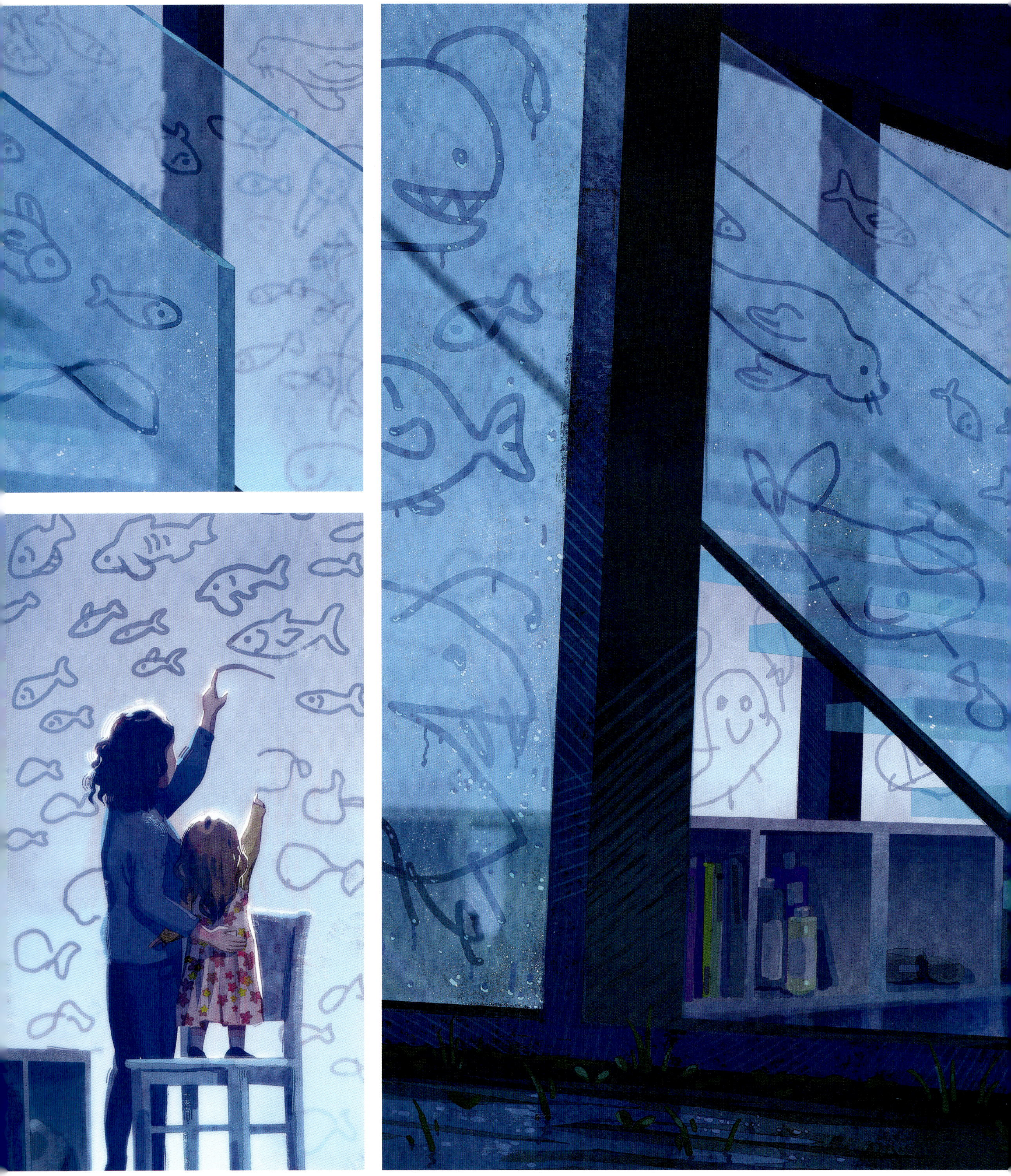

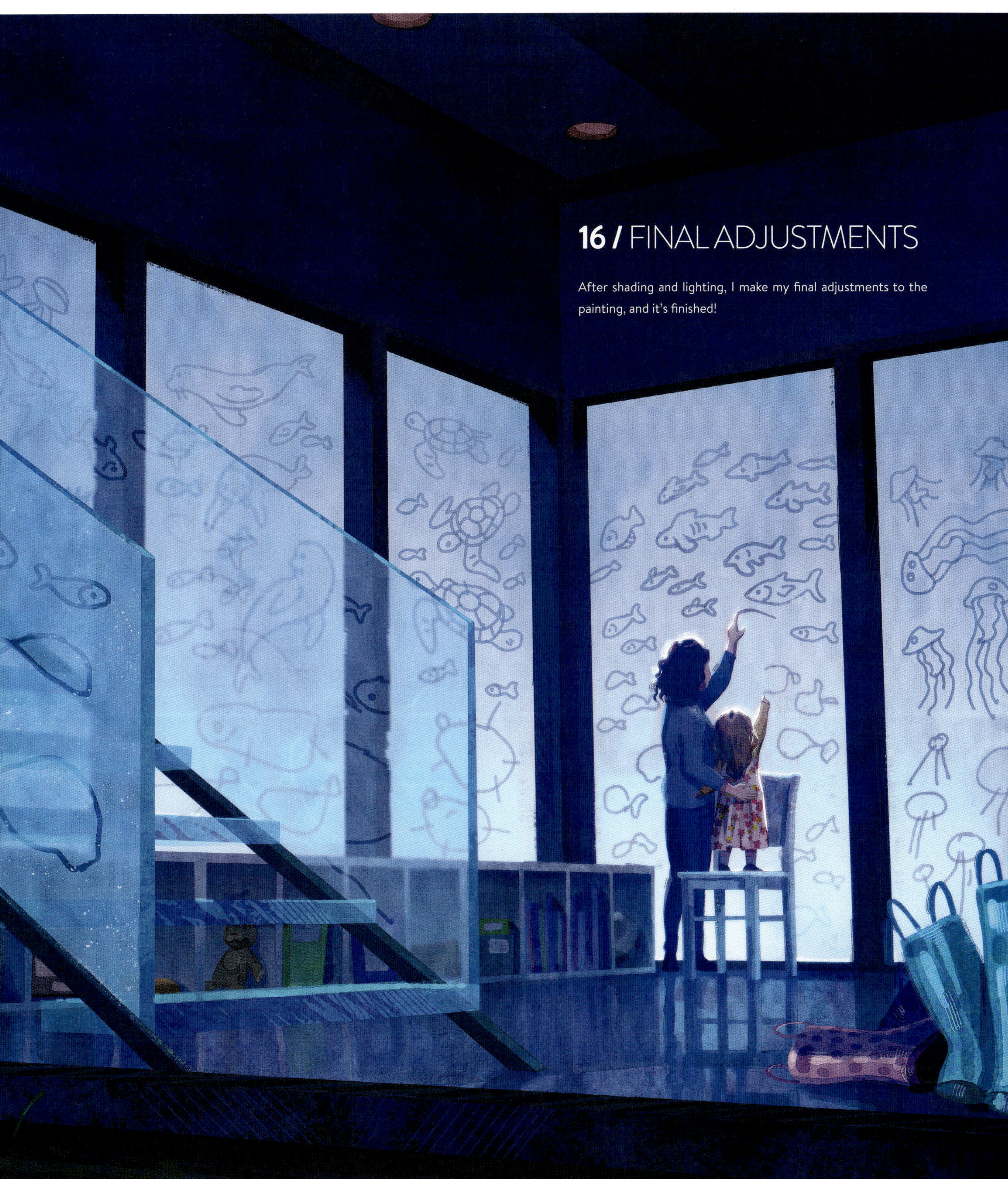

16 / FINAL ADJUSTMENTS

After shading and lighting, I make my final adjustments to the painting, and it's finished!

TUTORIAL / CRAFTING THE COVER

Sometimes, just like a cartoon "light-bulb moment," the perfect idea for a painting comes to me effortlessly. On days like those, life feels good. It's easy to pretend that I've ascended to some ludicrous new height where art won't be a struggle anymore – good ideas will flood endlessly into my mind, fully-formed and begging me to paint them. It is even quicker and easier for the illusion to shatter as I sit to paint a vitally important piece and find my mind agonizingly empty! On the following pages I'm going to detail the excruciating process of scenario number two as we chart my convoluted path toward this book's cover.

As with all of my digital work, I used my Wacom Cintiq Pro 24 to paint this piece in Photoshop CC.

1a

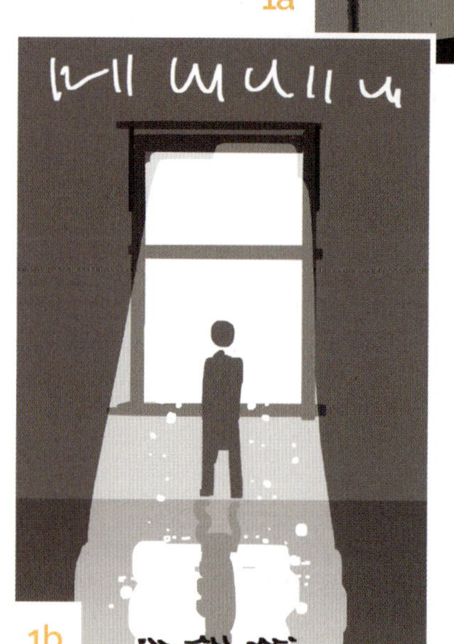

1b

1 / THUMBNAILING

Windows are a subject I find easy to paint with appealing results. Like much of what I paint, they sit firmly in my comfort zone, so creating a cover image around the theme should be easy. But, somehow, I churn through an endless slog of rejected ideas before stumbling upon anything resembling a good idea. I allow myself to get the obvious answers out of the way first. Sometimes the obvious answer actually *is* the right answer; it's obvious because it's got all the markers of being a good choice. This was not one of those moments.

Included here is only a small selection of the many ideas I scribble. Some of these ideas are valid options and have the potential to be successful paintings. But, despite being possibly interesting, something about each of them doesn't feel right for the cover. At the time, I feel they are too fantastical, or too self-important. Sitting bleary-eyed, staring at them at the end of a night of drawing, it feels like they are sneering at me and saying "You think you're very smart with these weird window metaphors, don't you?!"

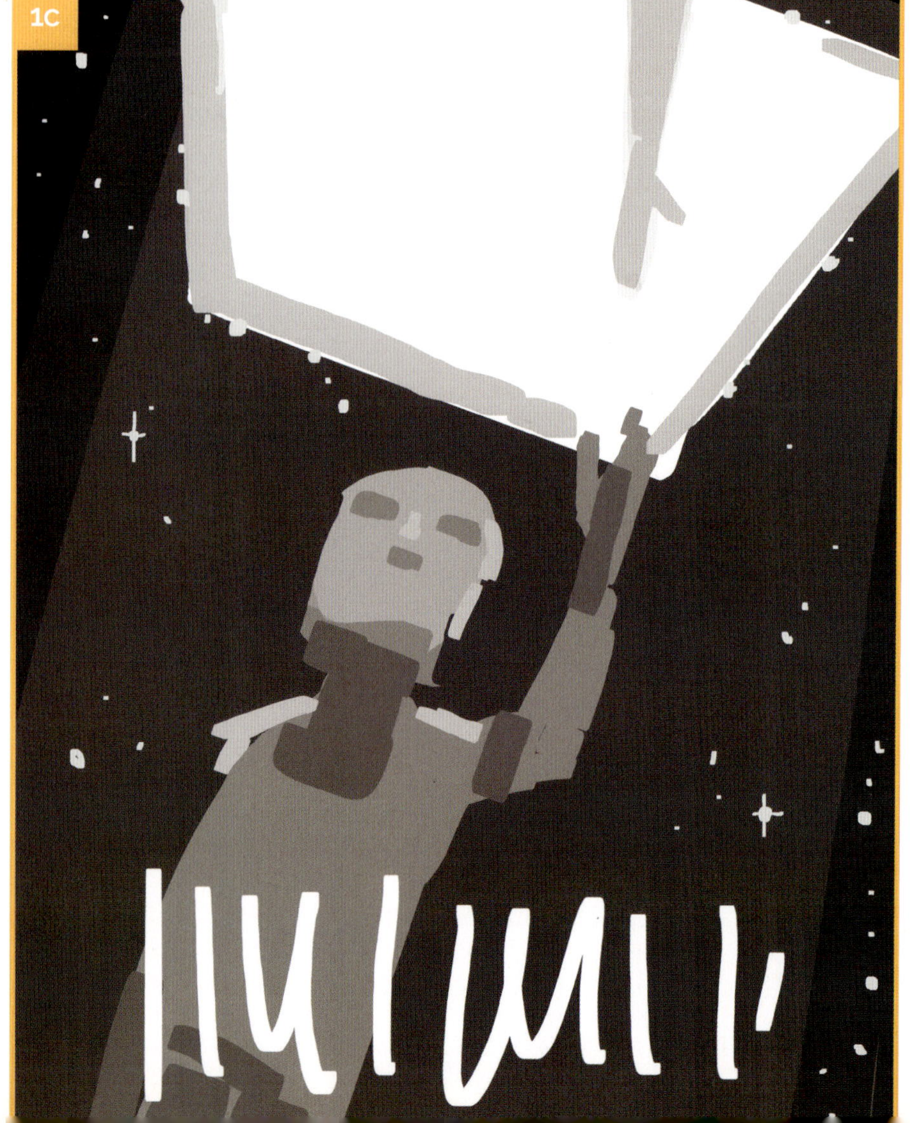

1c

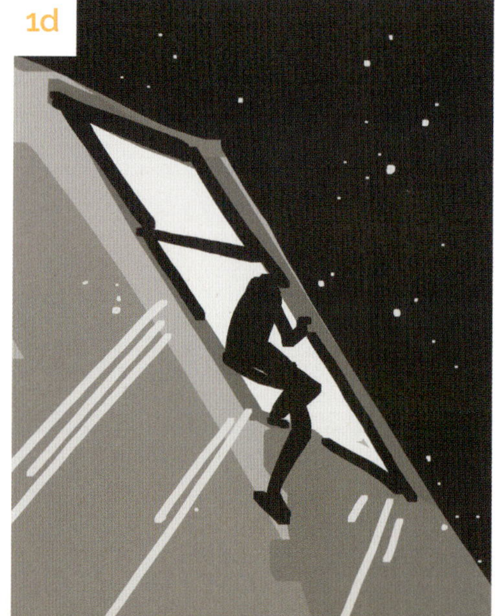

1d

WORKING THROUGH NEGATIVITY

I can be mean to myself when I'm having a difficult time with a painting. In fact, I'm being rather mean to myself again now as I write this. I wanted to allow that side of me to slip out here, to give an example of the negativity that begins to swirl around my tired mind when I try (and fail) to make something I think is good. This negativity is amplified when I work on something important. I tell myself the design is too obvious, too smug, or too pedantic. Does this negativity help? Of course not. Not even a little bit.

However, I sit and stew in this negativity for days. It really eats at me, and I don't want to sugarcoat it. When you scroll through an artist's manicured Instagram grid, it's easy to get the impression that they don't go through struggles with their art in the way that you and I do. It is possible that there are artists who really do have a head full of great ideas, who never rage-quit out of an unsaved Photoshop document and always know what to paint when they open a new canvas, but I'm definitely not one of them. In my years as a professional artist, I don't think I've met one, either.

The answer, as always, is to be kinder to myself. So, I take a day off from working on the cover, go outside, play with my dog, and complain loudly to my friends over the phone. I force myself to breathe, and to take a step back. I don't need to paint something groundbreakingly awesome and new. I don't need to recontextualize the themes of my art, or come up with the world's most clever new depiction of the window. In fact, trying to do so pulls me further and further away from what I think gives my work soul in the first place. There's one throughline that's been consistent in my art from the start: I like to paint people who feel real, experiencing something unbelievable.

"I LIKE TO PAINT PEOPLE WHO FEEL REAL, EXPERIENCING SOMETHING UNBELIEVABLE"

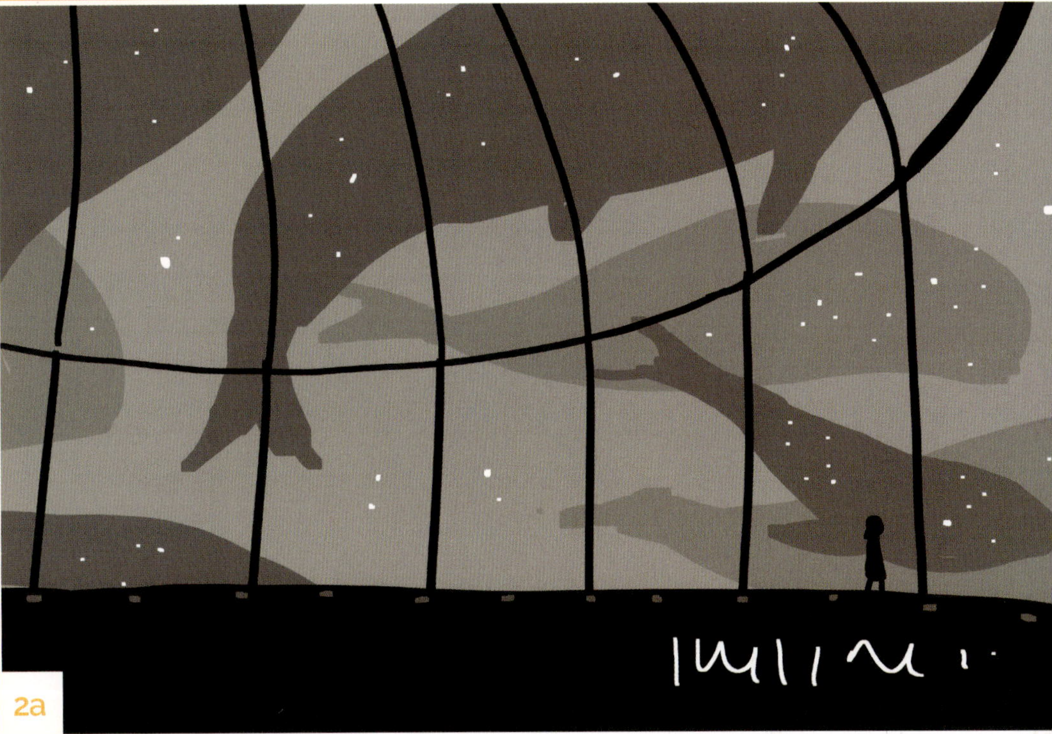

2a

2 / THUMBNAIL REFINEMENT

After revisiting my existing body of work for inspiration, I realize that I don't need to invent something new for this cover; I simply want to sum up the work inside the book. I want to represent the things I strive to represent in my work: wonder, beauty, and magic.

The thumbnail design above comes very close to capturing the feeling I am looking to achieve. But despite getting closer to my goal, the second batch is still lacking something important to me: the sense of being grounded in reality. I want to capture the feeling of standing in a place that's familiar and gazing out at something impossible. Finally, at about 10pm, with the simple and blobby thumbnail shown on the left – I land on my final design. With relief washing over me, I message my friend Elaine Ryan with a screenshot of the thumbnail and say, "I'm feeling good about this one." She simply replies, "You should be."

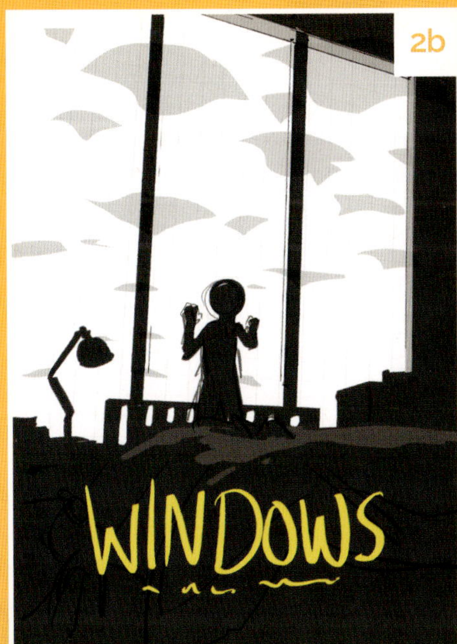

2b

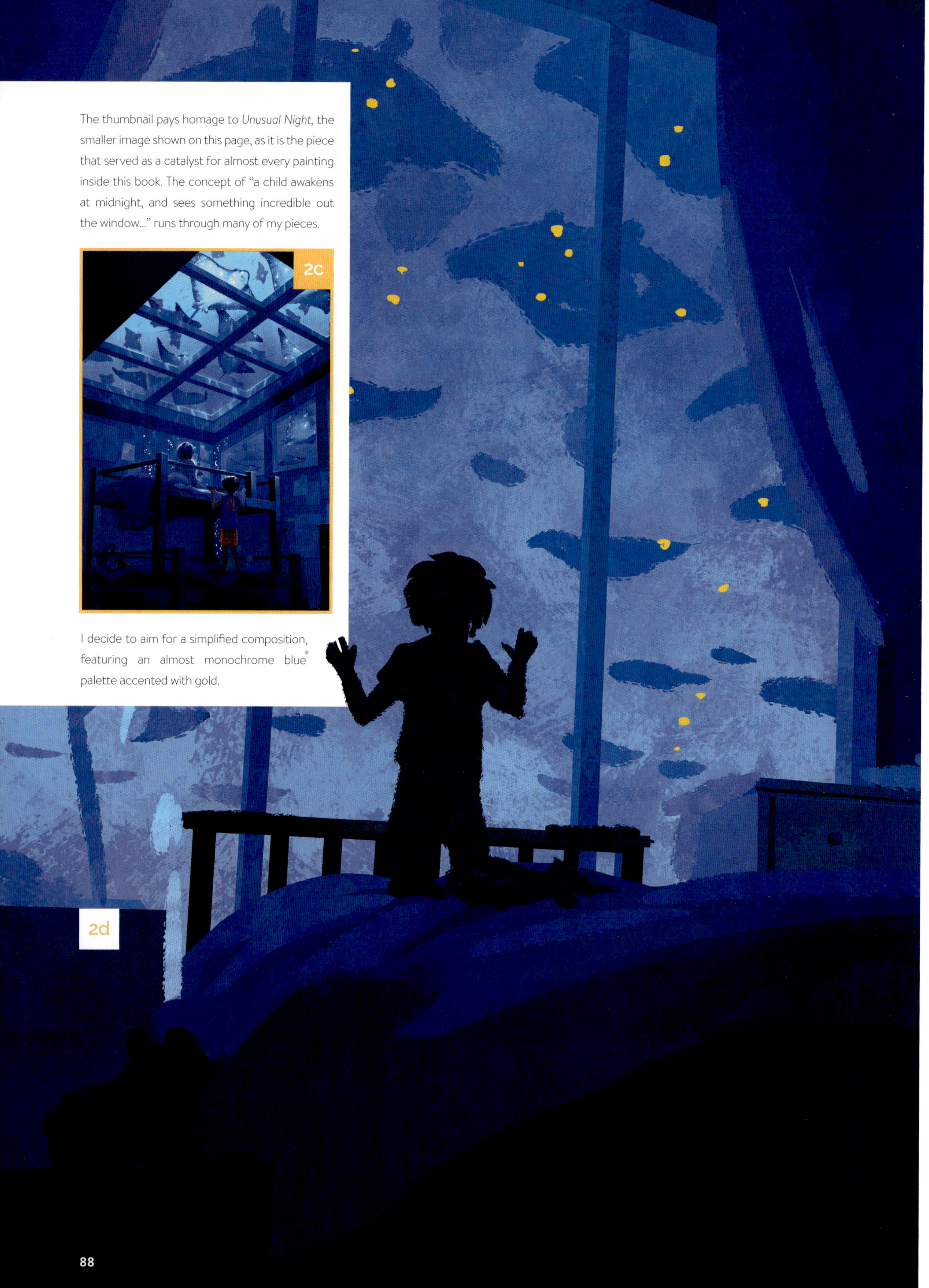

The thumbnail pays homage to *Unusual Night*, the smaller image shown on this page, as it is the piece that served as a catalyst for almost every painting inside this book. The concept of "a child awakens at midnight, and sees something incredible out the window…" runs through many of my pieces.

I decide to aim for a simplified composition, featuring an almost monochrome blue palette accented with gold.

3 / DEVELOPING THE COLOR THUMBNAIL

After some deliberation, I realize that the original color scheme feels too cold and gray. I want the cover to feel warm and inviting – magical, in the way we recall dreams from childhood. I decide to shift to a simpler and more illustrative one-point-perspective as I feel this would give the cover more balance and impact.

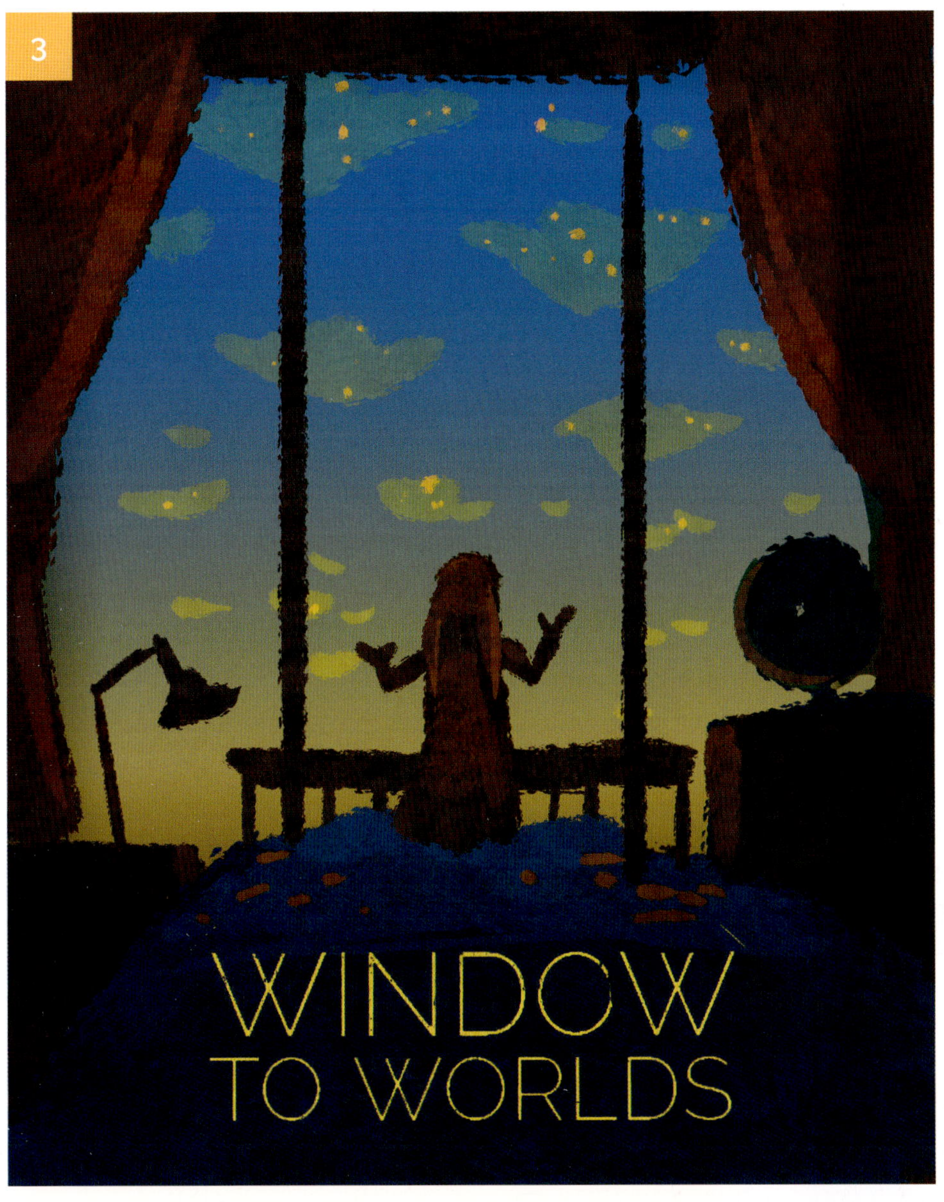

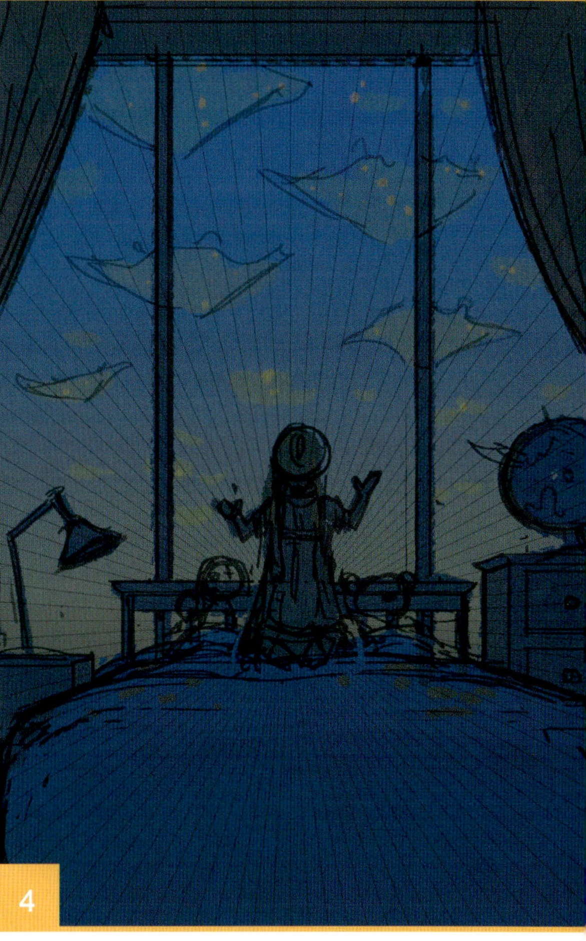

4 / PUTTING IT IN PERSPECTIVE

To adapt my initial thumbnail featuring a three-point perspective design, to a one-point perspective, I simply add the single perspective point and follow the perspective lines to construct the furniture. I also decide to add a globe to symbolize the "world" theme.

5 / BLOCKING IN THE RAYS

I use the Lasso tool to block in the silhouettes of the manta rays, then use soft painterly brushes to render the details of their bodies. I look at a large collection of references in order to accurately depict them from different angles. I try to vary the skin patterning from ray to ray so each one feels like a unique individual creature.

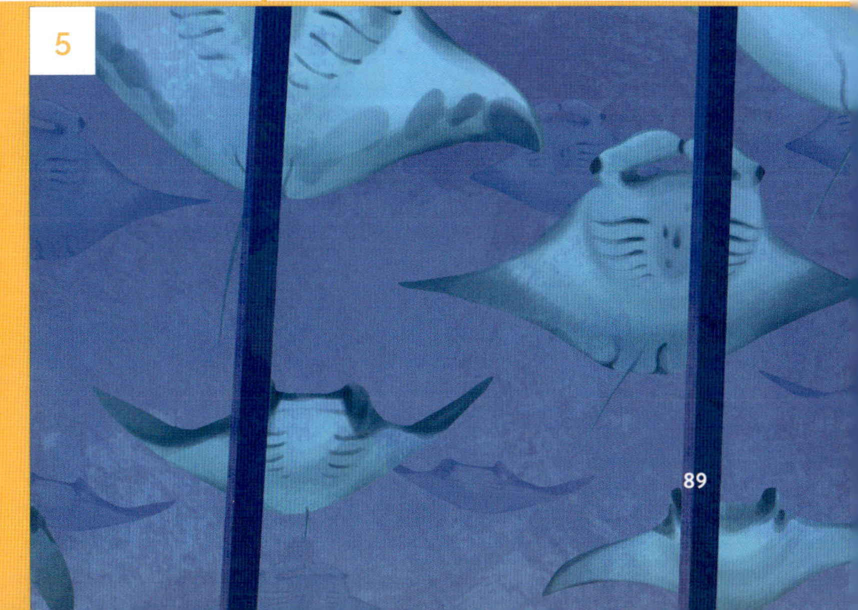

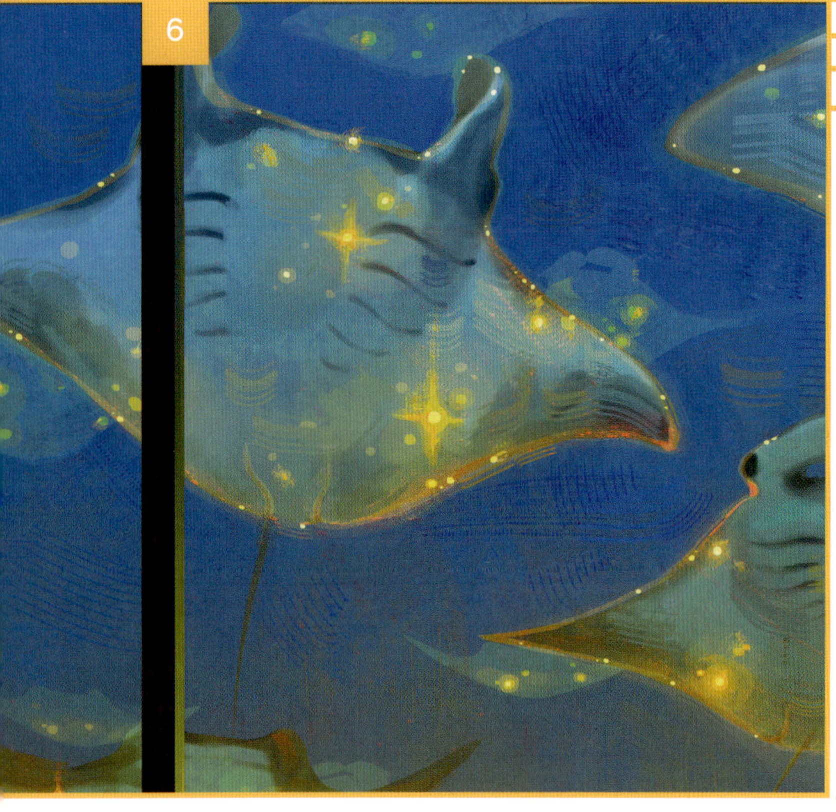

6 / PAINTING THE RAYS

I use a variety of Multiply, Overlay, Soft Light, and Color Dodge layers to add shading and lighting to the rays. I paint the stars as hard round dots first, then use soft painterly brushes on Overlay layers to paint in the cross-shaped glow. I add some watercolor-textured wash layers over the whole ocean section to create the impression of oceanic water.

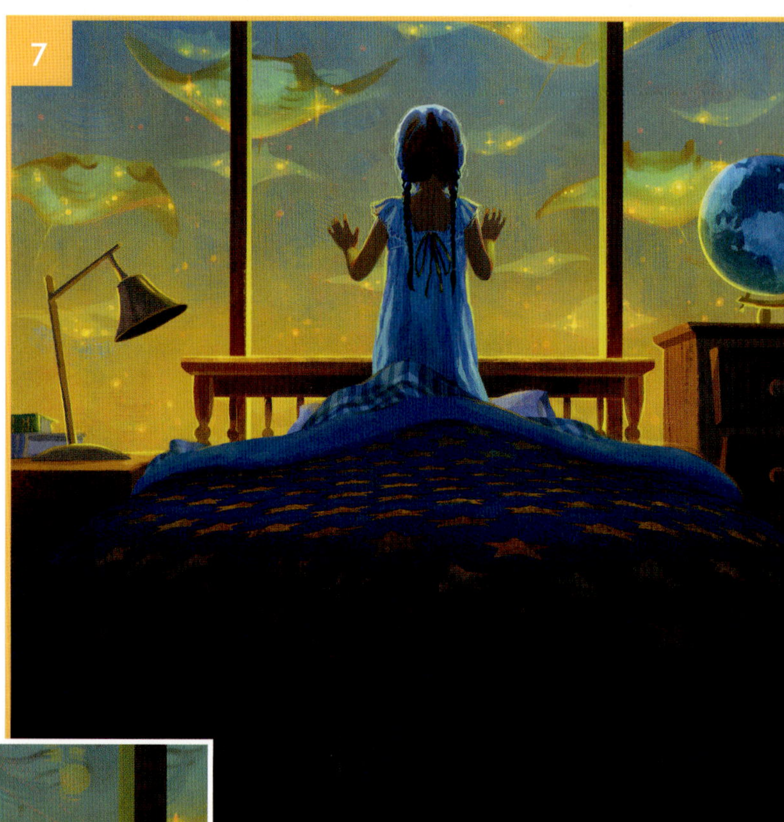

7 / APPLYING PATTERN TO THE BEDSPREAD

I realize the bed isn't reading very well in perspective, so I add a star pattern to the comforter to imply depth. This is a great way to easily show collapsed depth. First, I paint the stars as a flat pattern, then use Transform > Warp to conform them to the bedspread.

8

8 / PAINTING THE CHARACTER

I use the Lasso tool to block in the flat colors for the girl. I realize I want some tiny, noisy details to attract interest at the focal point, so I spread out her fingers and separate her hair into braids.

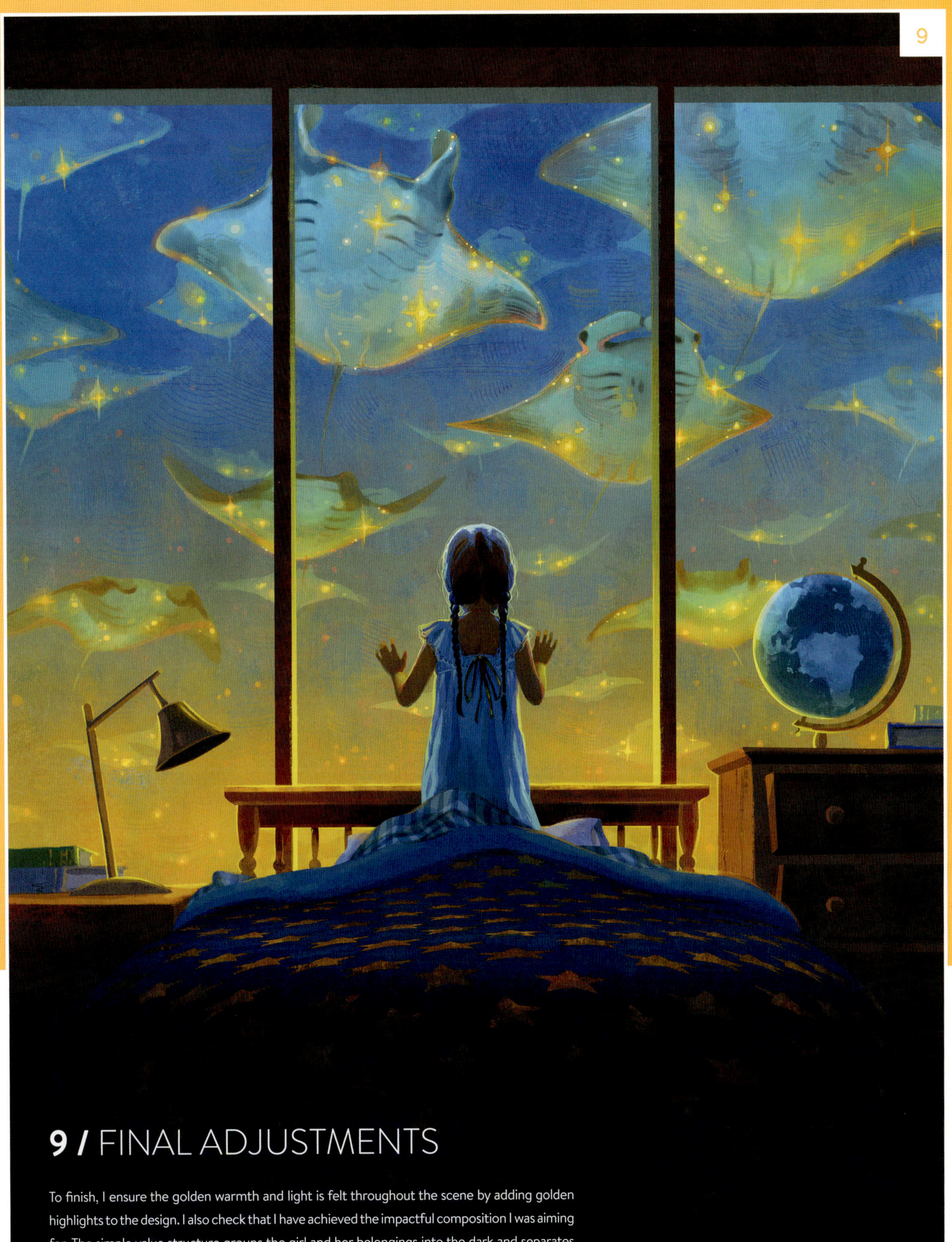

9

9 / FINAL ADJUSTMENTS

To finish, I ensure the golden warmth and light is felt throughout the scene by adding golden highlights to the design. I also check that I have achieved the impactful composition I was aiming for. The simple value structure groups the girl and her belongings into the dark and separates the ocean and the rays into the light, creating the contrast and visual interest I was hoping for!

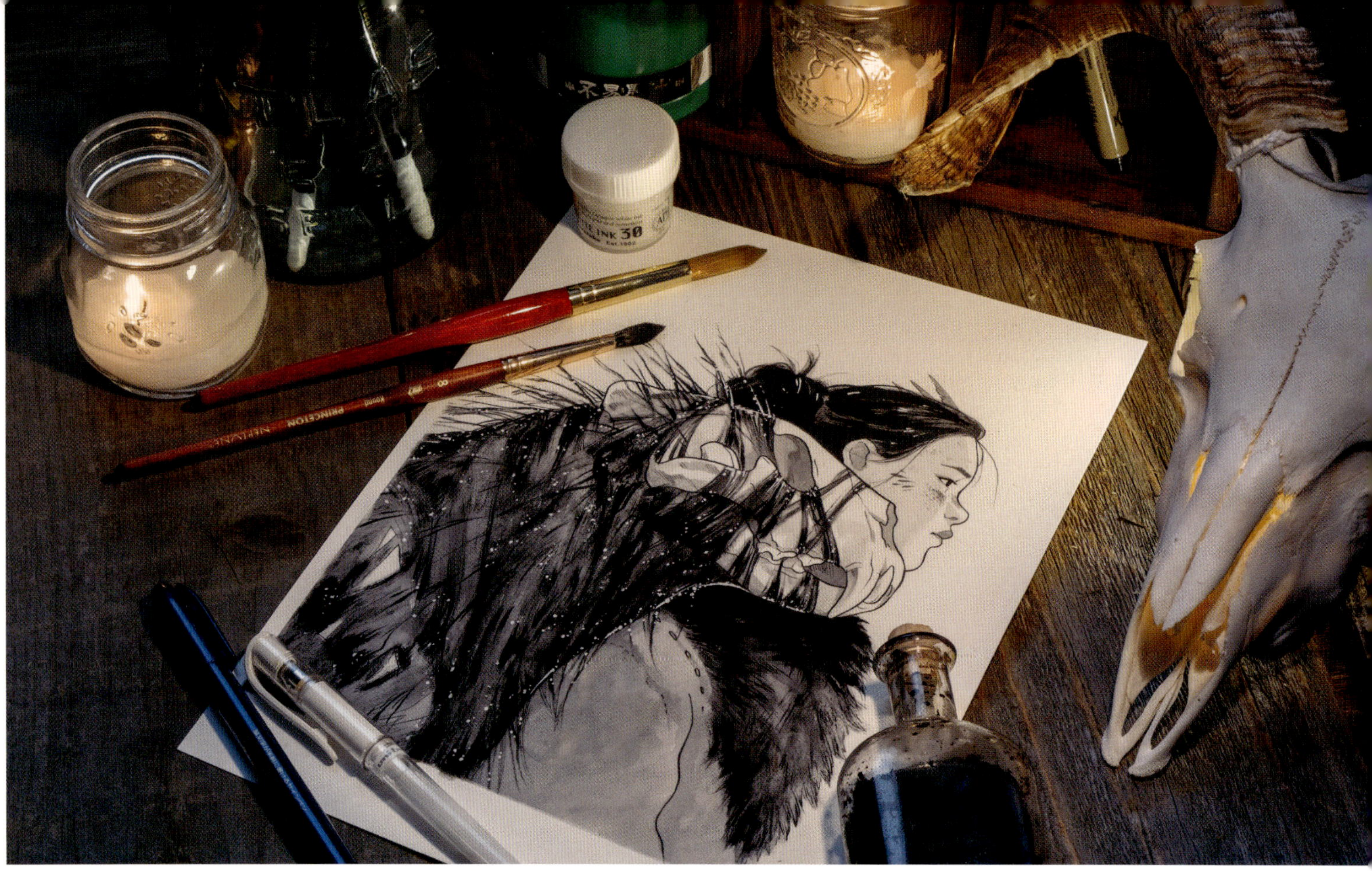

TRADITIONAL TOOLS

I find creating with traditional media to be very calming and tranquil. When I'm busy working, I use mainly digital tools, so using traditional media often feels like a vacation, an act of creation purely for myself and not for any other purpose. My favorite traditional mediums are ink and watercolor – I find their simplicity teaches me a lot about composition, value structure, and detail placement.

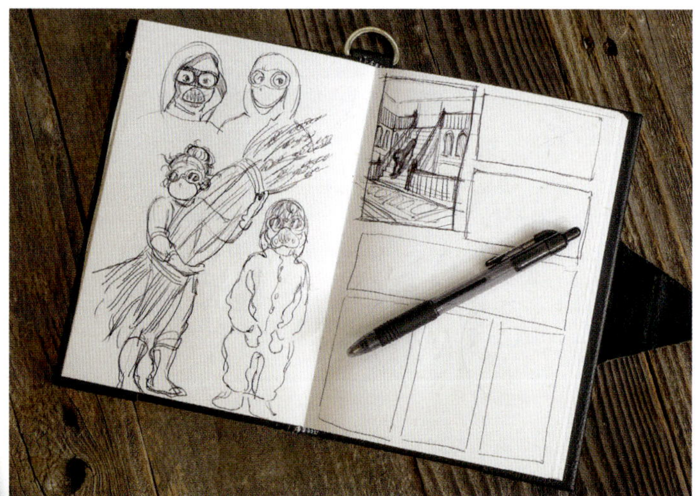

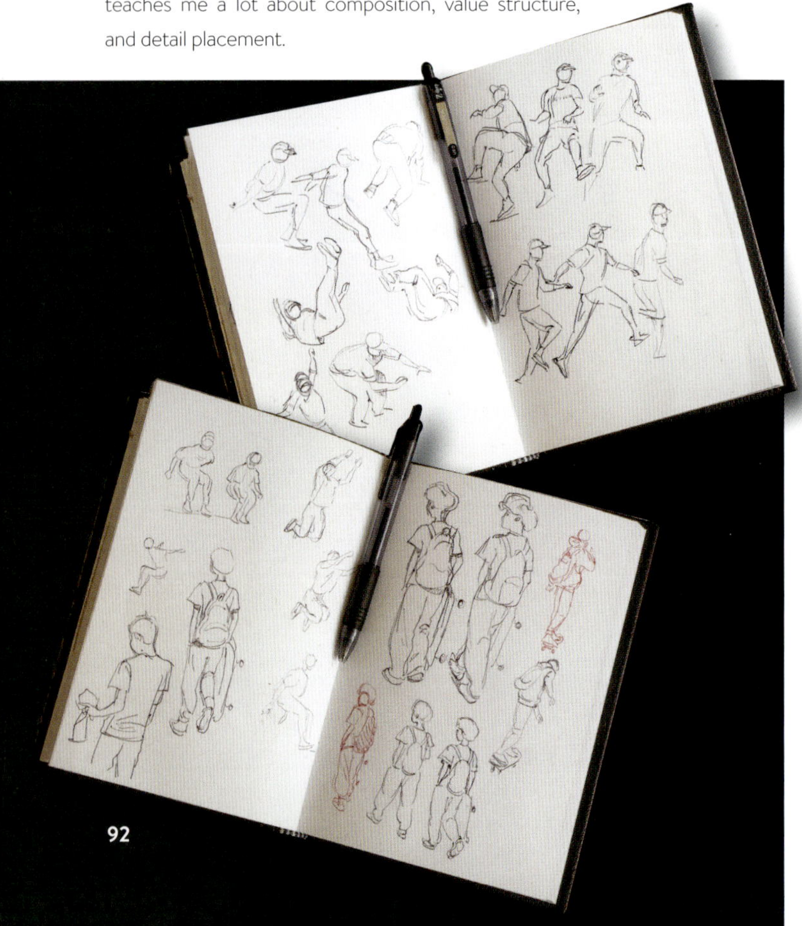

SKETCHING

I've kept physical sketchbooks for my entire life, often filling three or four a year. Very little of the art from these sketchbooks is ever seen by anyone but me, and I prefer it that way! My sketchbooks are messy, and I have no qualms about ruining a page. I like my sketchbooks to be "no-pressure zones." One page could be black-and-white thumbnails for a painting, the next could be studies from life, and the next, studies of characters from Disney films. I find a lot of value in doing tiny figure studies from life or from YouTube videos, and of people who aren't posing but are standing idly in a natural way, or interacting with the world around them.

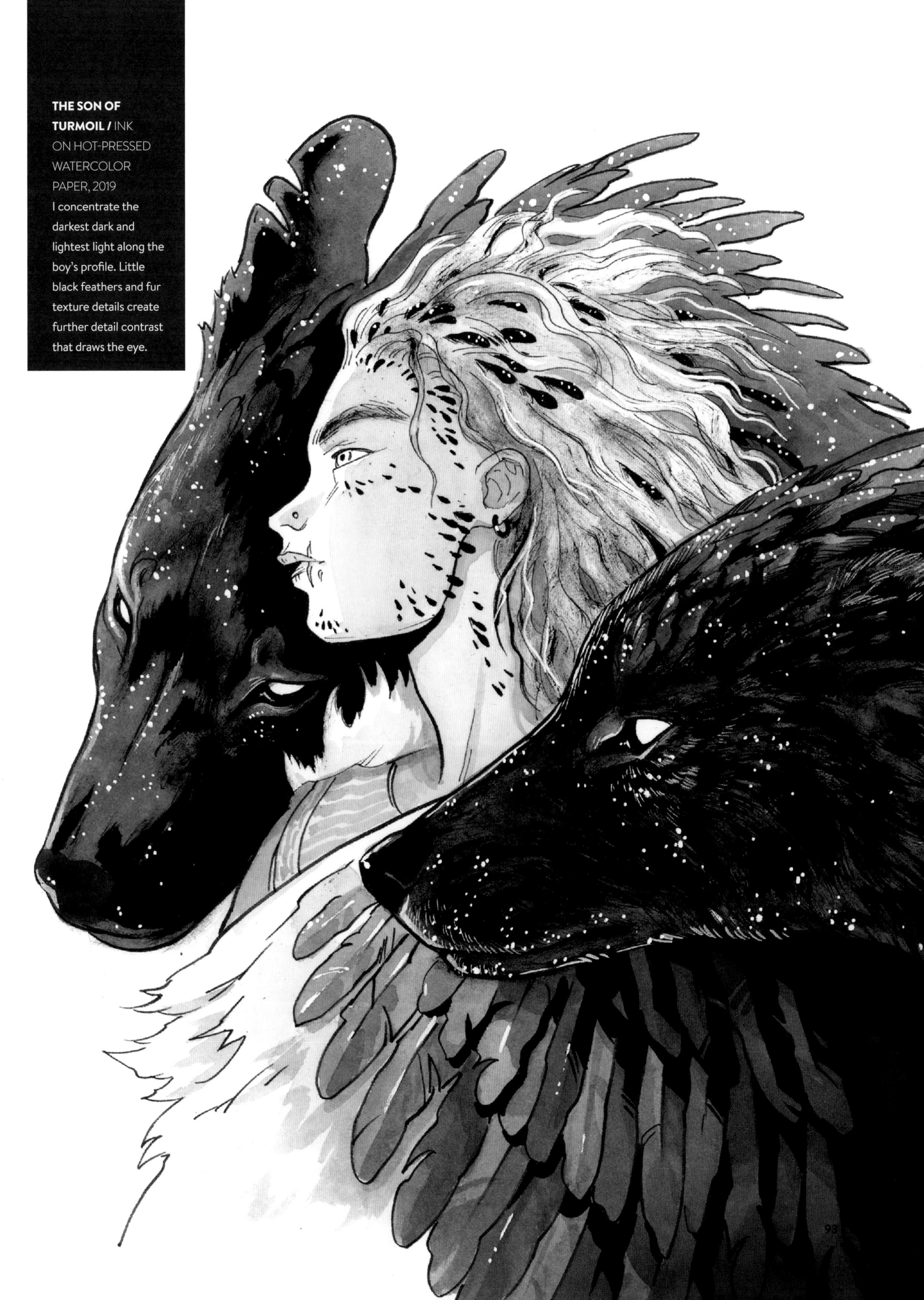

THE SON OF TURMOIL / INK ON HOT-PRESSED WATERCOLOR PAPER, 2019
I concentrate the darkest dark and lightest light along the boy's profile. Little black feathers and fur texture details create further detail contrast that draws the eye.

The ink drawings in this section are from a project I started in 2018 about a fantasy world set long in the past in a valley inspired by the Scottish Highlands. The creatures are meant to be descendants of an ancient, gigantic, kindhearted blackbird deity who still lives among them, and they grow black feathers as a physical manifestation of his power. They use his ancient magic to stitch the bones of animals back together and reanimate them with living grasses, weighted metal beads, and red twine. Their blacksmiths forge iron into lanterns, beads, and jewelry – items which they use to carry magic. I repeat these items to help build a consistent visual language throughout the series. The black-feathered wolves and lions are descendents of the blackbird god too!

THE FIRST CHILD / INK ON HOT-PRESSED WATERCOLOR PAPER, 2019

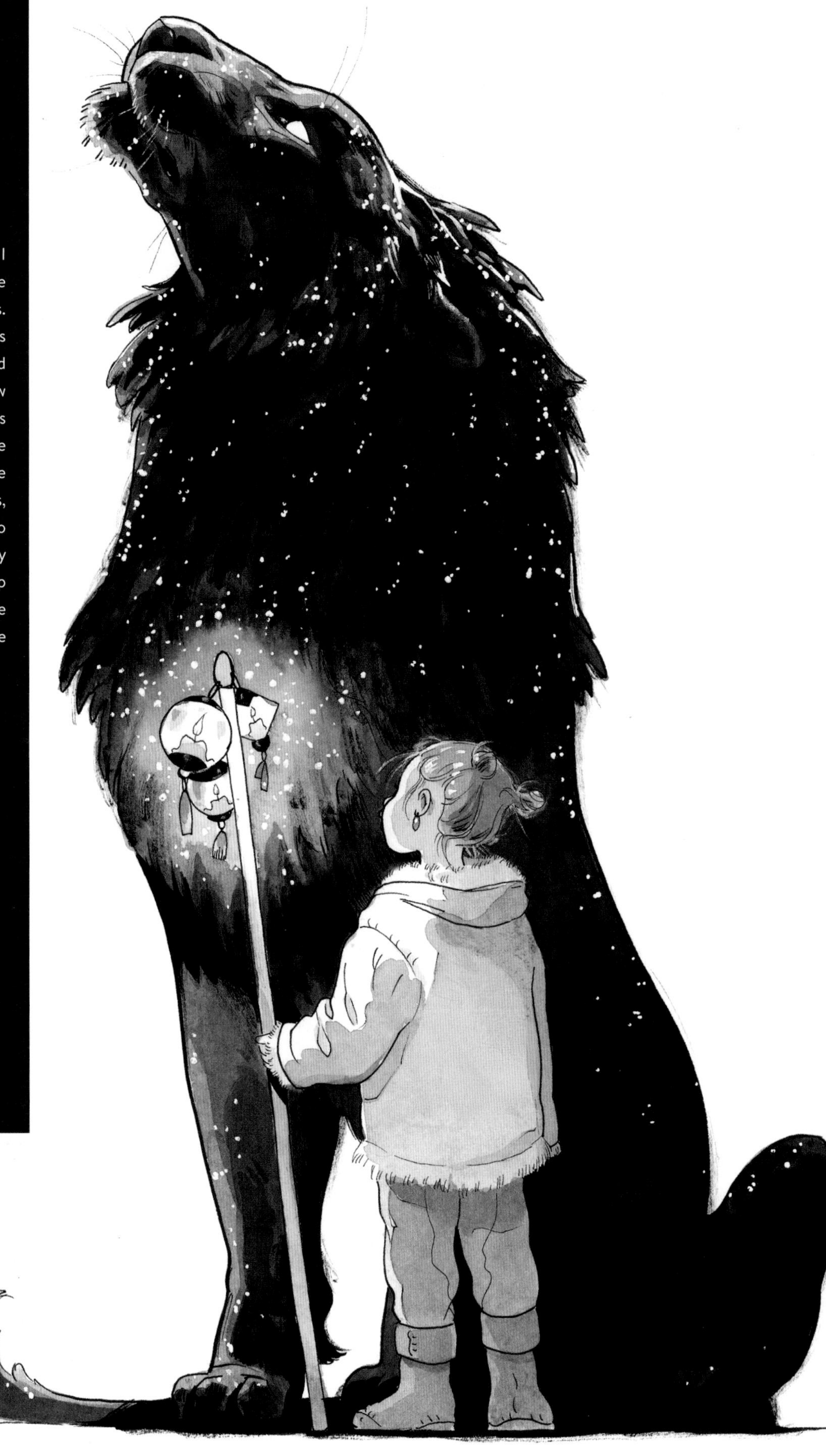

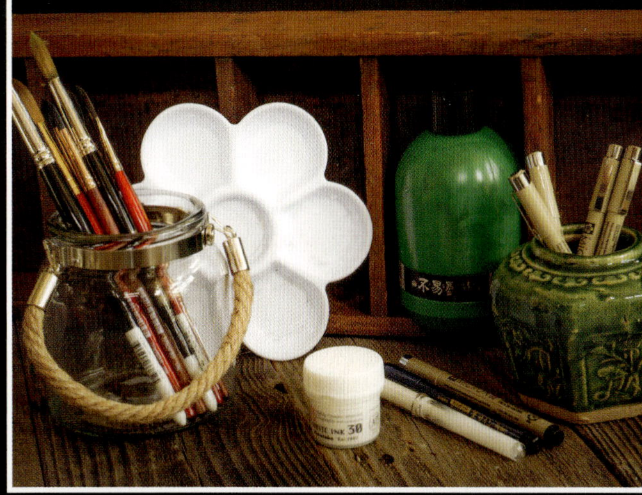

INK DRAWING

I began using ink in late 2018, and have found it both incredibly enjoyable and immensely beneficial to my creative practice. Ink is a deceptively simple medium. In its pure form, it's simply black against white. When water and texture are introduced, it encapsulates every shade of gray.

When drawing with ink, I work on smooth, hot-pressed watercolor paper. The 9-inch × 12-inch pads by Arches are my favorite because they are very high quality and don't buckle easily. For my linework, I use Zebra fine-tip brush pens along with various sizes of Sakura Pigma Micron pens for details. I use black Yasutomo Sumi ink for washes, and for white highlights I use Kuretake white ink or white Uni-ball Signo pens. I have a wide variety of brushes, many of which I have had since high school, but when I add new brushes, I usually just look for high-quality, synthetic watercolor brushes. Brushes that have been destroyed by use or accident also become an important tool in my ink toolkit, as they are excellent for applying dry-brushed ink textures.

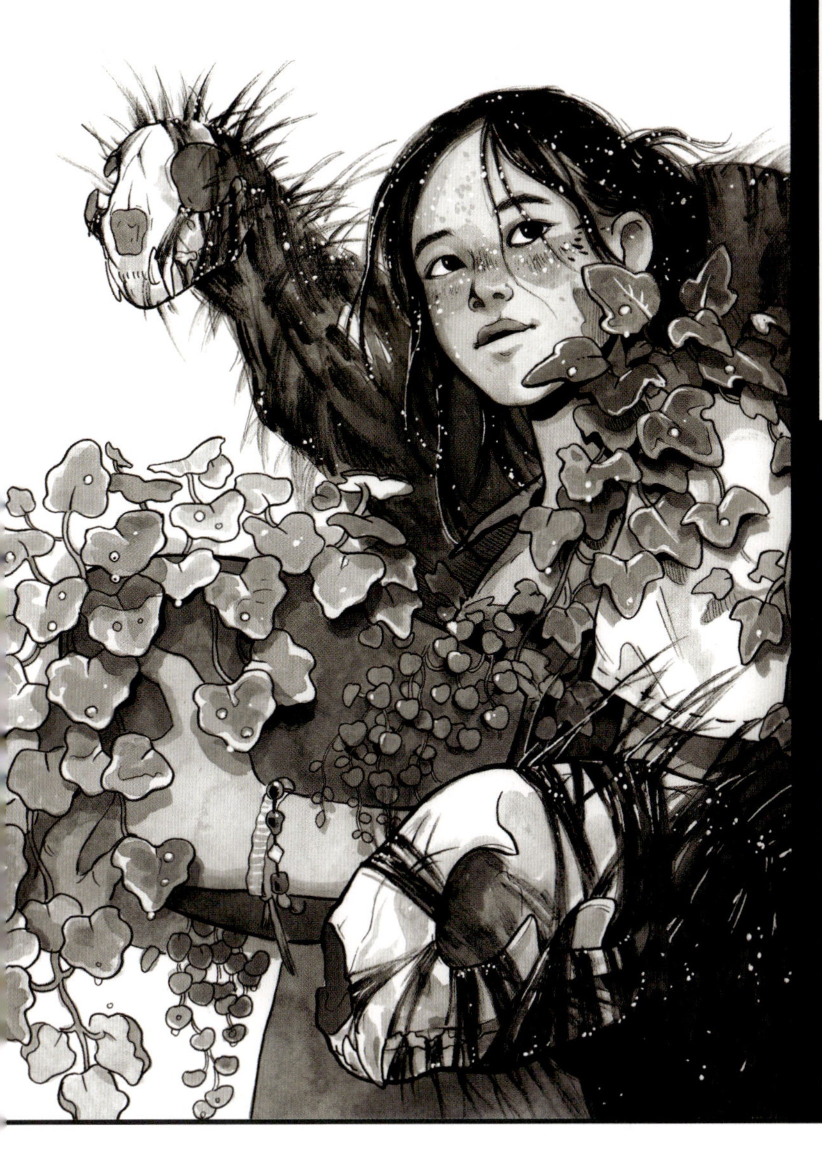

THE GREENHOUSE CATS / INK ON HOT-PRESSED WATERCOLOR PAPER, 2019

VALUE STRUCTURE

Working in ink has taught me a lot about composition and value structure. I discovered early in my adventures with ink that layering dark against light or light against dark were the best methods for achieving a clear, impactful read. Focusing the highest value contrast (usually pure black against pure white) on the focal point is an effective way to direct the viewer's focus to where I want them to look.

AILBE STORIES / INK ON HOT-PRESSED WATERCOLOR PAPER, 2019

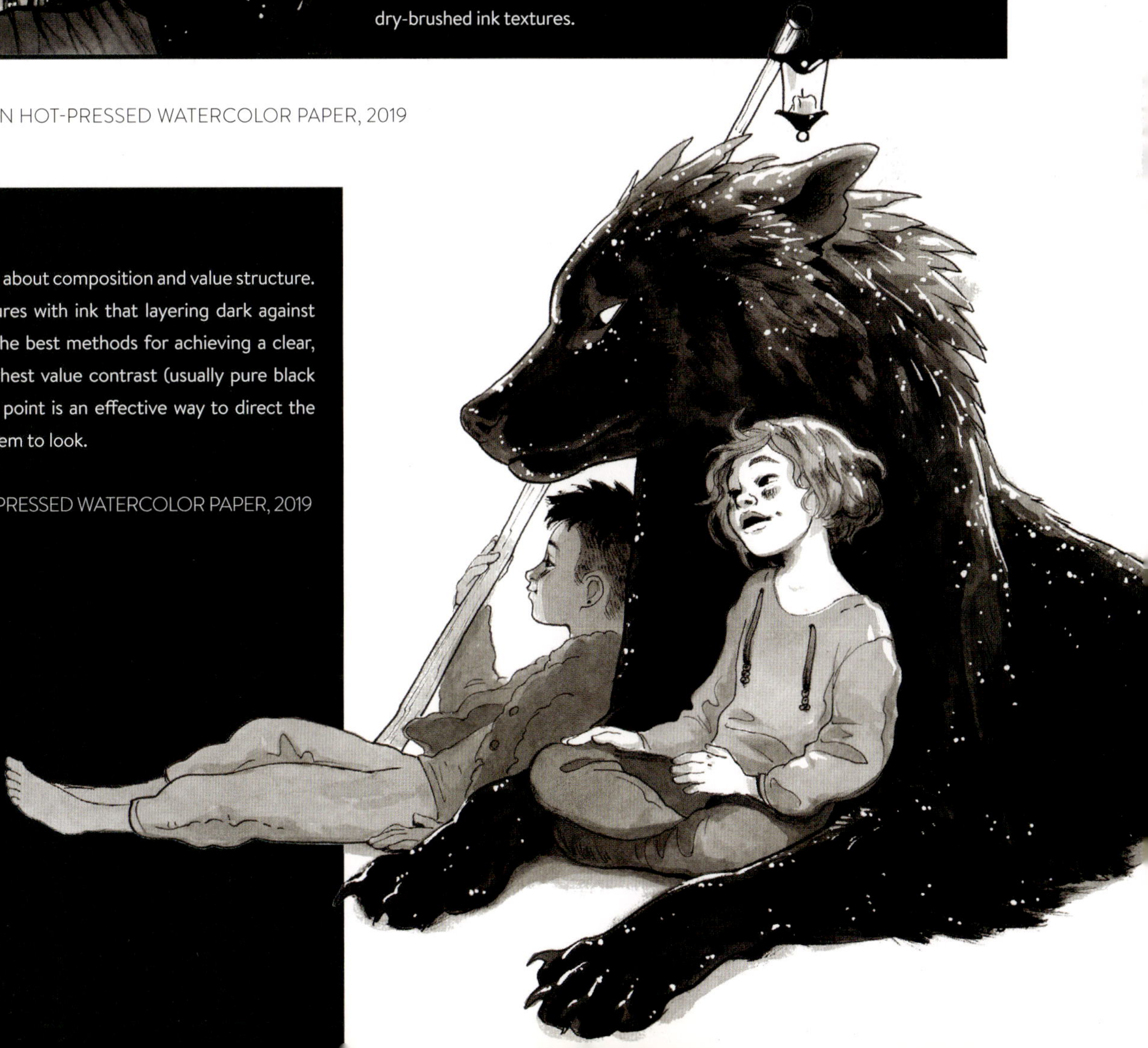

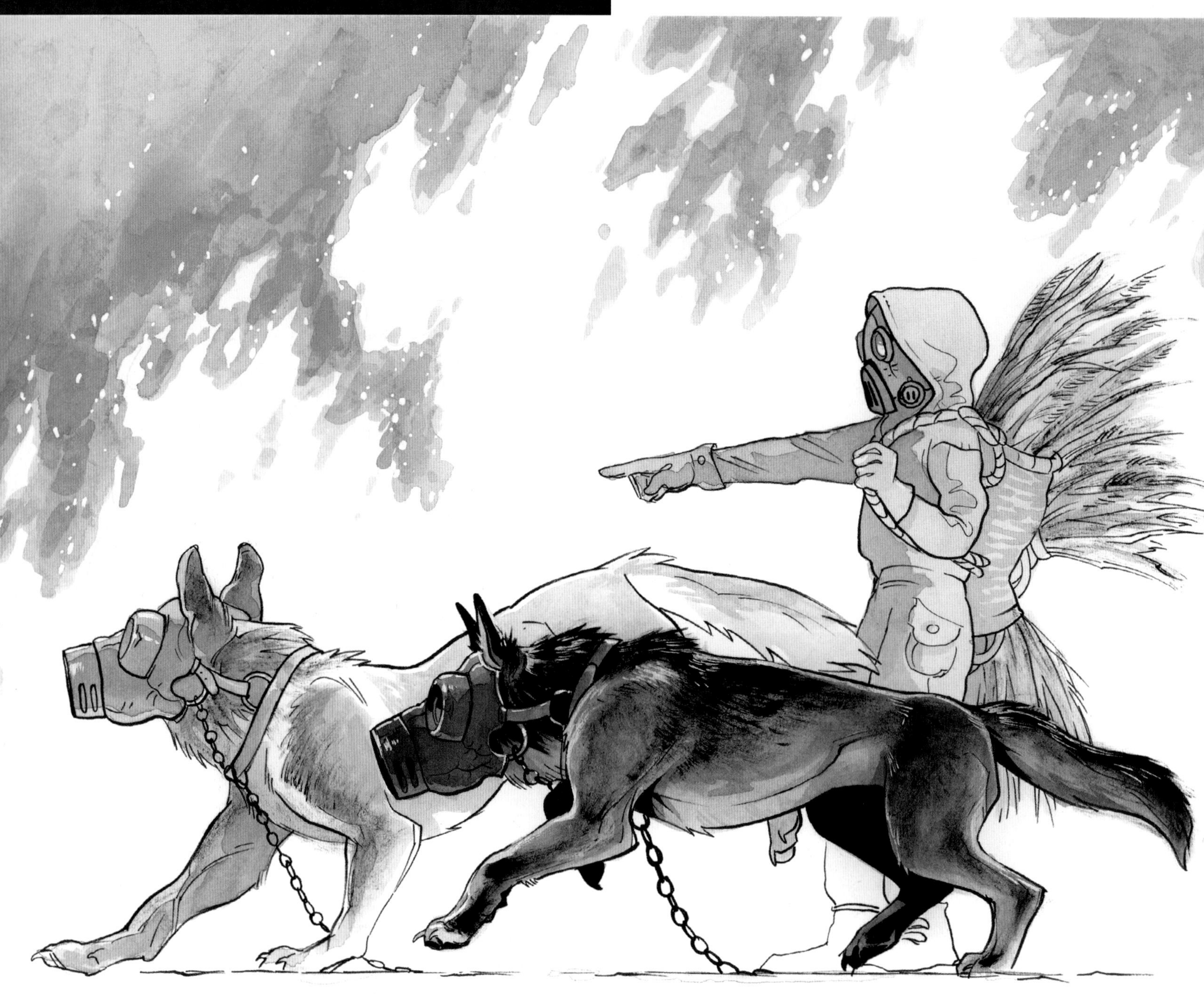

THE FIRE DOGS / INK ON HOT-PRESSED WATERCOLOR PAPER, 2019

Ink has taught me so much about how to bring elements forward and set them back in an image. The dog in the foreground pops forward because it contains a full range of values. The handler and more distant dog are compressed into a narrower, lighter value range, which sets them back behind a layer of smoke. The fire behind them is set back even further because it doesn't have hard black lines, and instead has soft, washy edges.

TEXTURE AND SILHOUETTE

When starting to work in ink, I initially used only washes to shade my drawings, but soon discovered that using dry-brush textures and cross-hatching alongside washes allows me to separate more areas of an image in a readable way. Ink can create mid-tone grays in a multitude of ways, such as in a smooth wash, a dappled wash, hatch marks, scrubbed dry brush, or stippling. Assigning a different method to each area of an image, based on the texture I want to achieve, separates areas by texture as well as value. For example, a mid-tone gray created with hatch marks will separate visually from a mid-tone gray created with a smooth wash. Working in ink also taught me the importance of silhouette. Creating impactful silhouettes offers a clear and dynamic instant read.

BACK TO FUNDAMENTALS

What I love about ink is that it forces me to use the fundamental techniques of composition in their most basic form. It has also given me the opportunity to understand them much more thoroughly as a result. Because ink is permanent and difficult to alter, it is vital that I am able to visualize or plan what I want to do before making a start. The techniques I use in ink drawings are applicable and vital to every form of art I create, but can become obscured in mediums such as digital painting, with so many tools and options available. Working in ink has helped me focus on these important building blocks and has improved the quality of my work across the board.

THE CROSSING / INK ON HOT-PRESSED WATERCOLOR PAPER, 2019

For this piece, I used a dry-brushing technique to create the grasses and reeds that hold the skeletal cat's body together, and then layered a wash on top to darken the body.

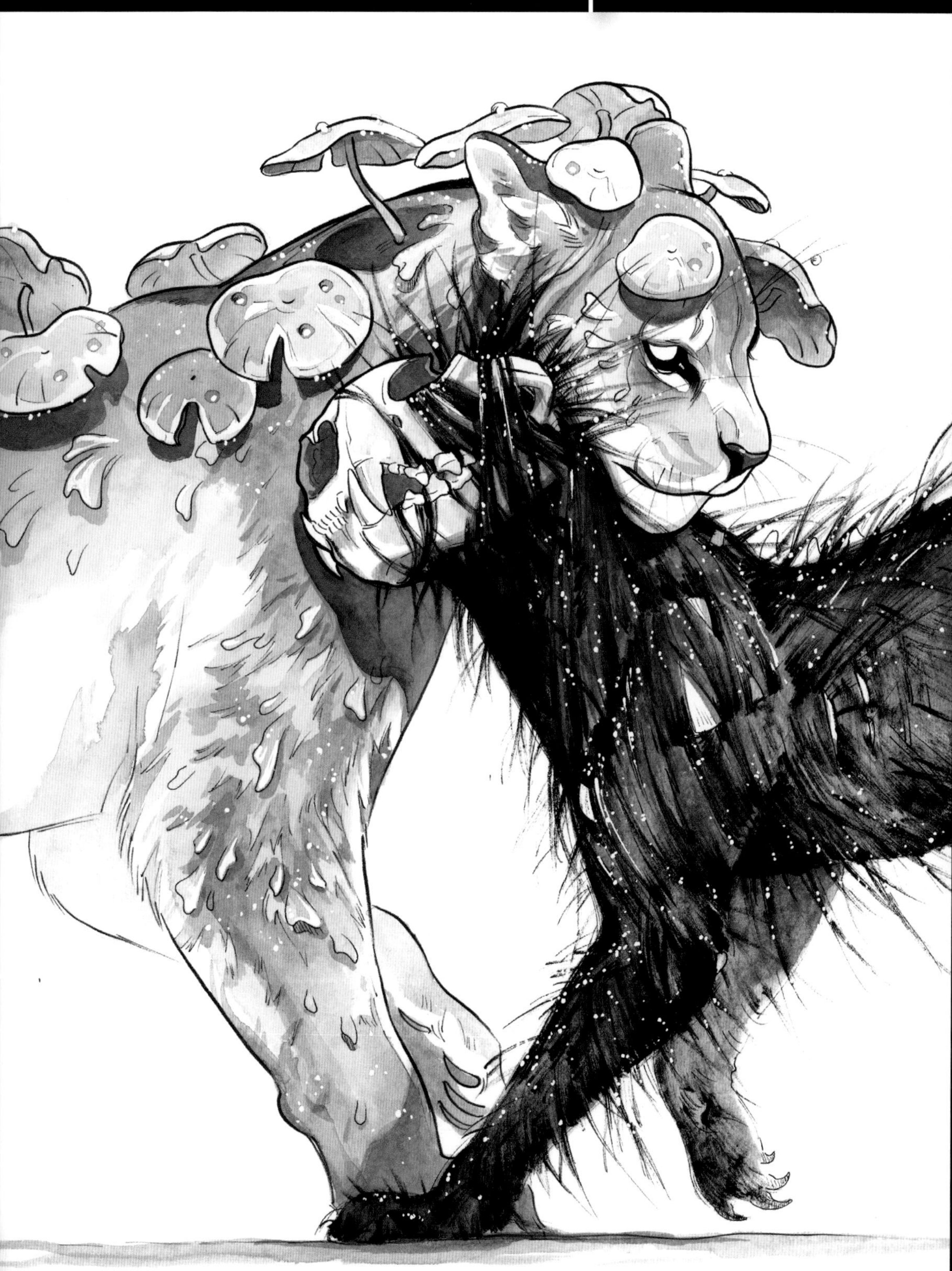

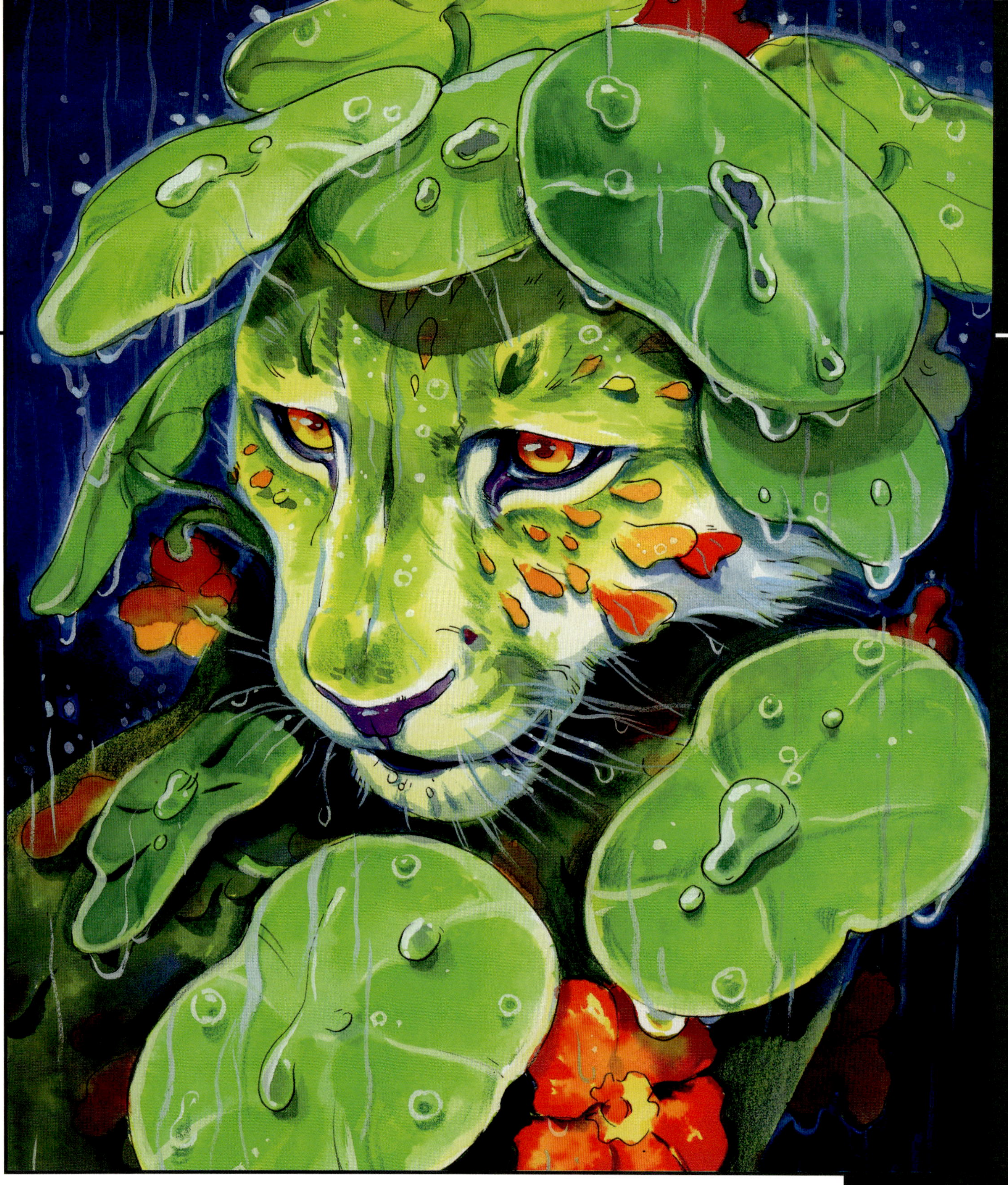

WATERCOLOR

After enjoying working with ink so much, watercolor paints seemed like the next logical direction to move in with my traditional art. My favorite watercolor paints are Dr. Ph. Martin's Hydrus watercolors. They are vibrant liquid watercolors that mix beautifully. I treat my watercolor work very similarly to how I treat my ink work, but with the introduction of color as an element to control in each composition.

Painting with watercolor has taught me a lot about color layering. I have found that watercolor builds up in layers quite similarly to Multiply layers in Photoshop, and I tend to think of it that way in my head. I usually build up colors with gradual washes and then revisit the most saturated points at the end of the painting process. I like to use Prismacolor colored pencils on top of my watercolor pieces to add extra texture and refine the rendering.

TOXIN /
WATERCOLOR ON HOT-PRESSED WATERCOLOR PAPER, 2019

FROM TRADITIONAL TO DIGITAL

I find it beneficial to translate work from traditional to digital at times. It teaches me about how my thinking can differ between the media, and about ways that I could improve my thinking by adopting pieces of the opposite mindset amid each process.

"PAINTING WITH WATERCOLOR HAS TAUGHT ME A LOT ABOUT COLOR LAYERING"

THE SOFTEST REST / WATERCOLOR ON HOT-PRESSED WATERCOLOR PAPER, 2019

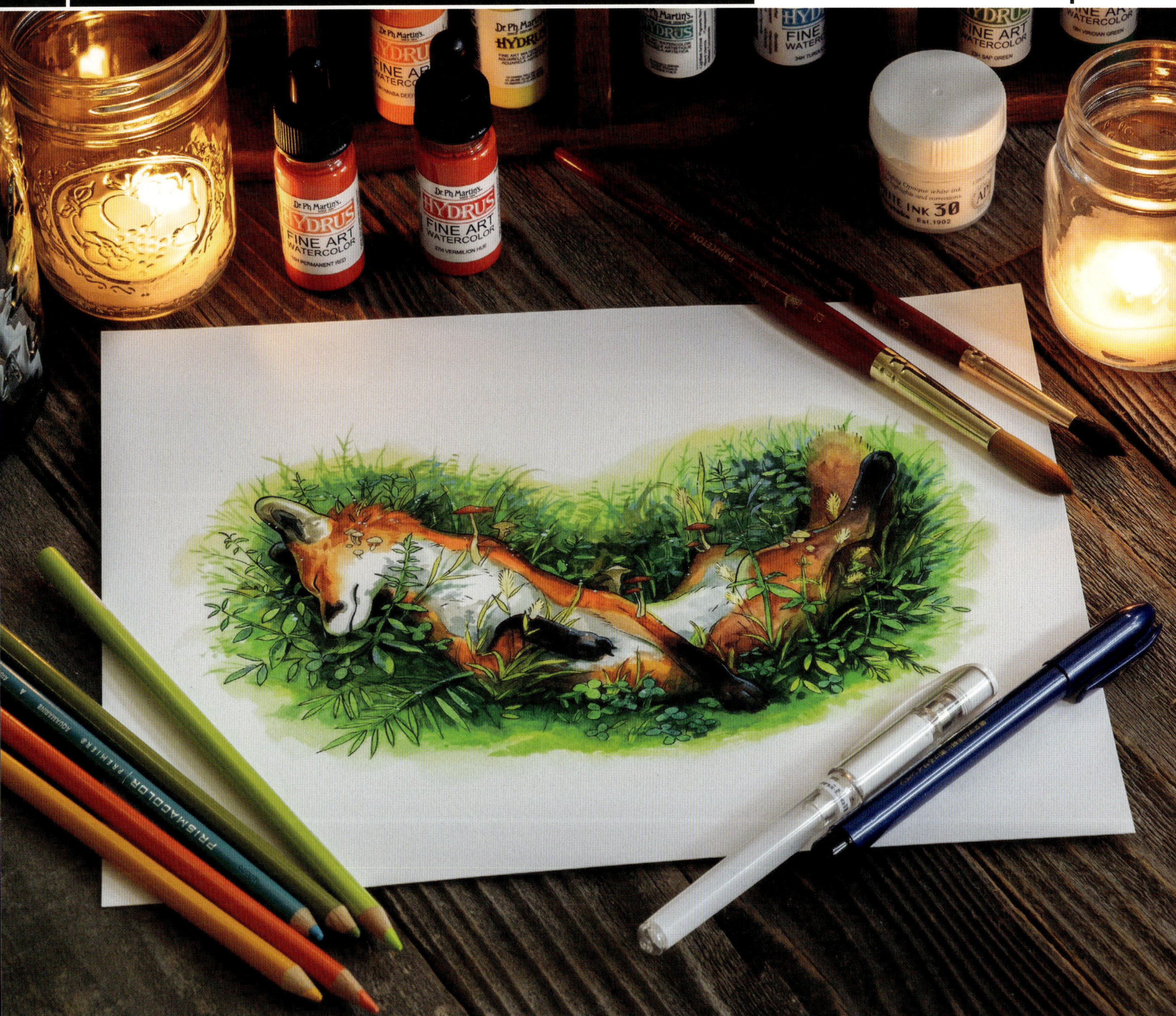

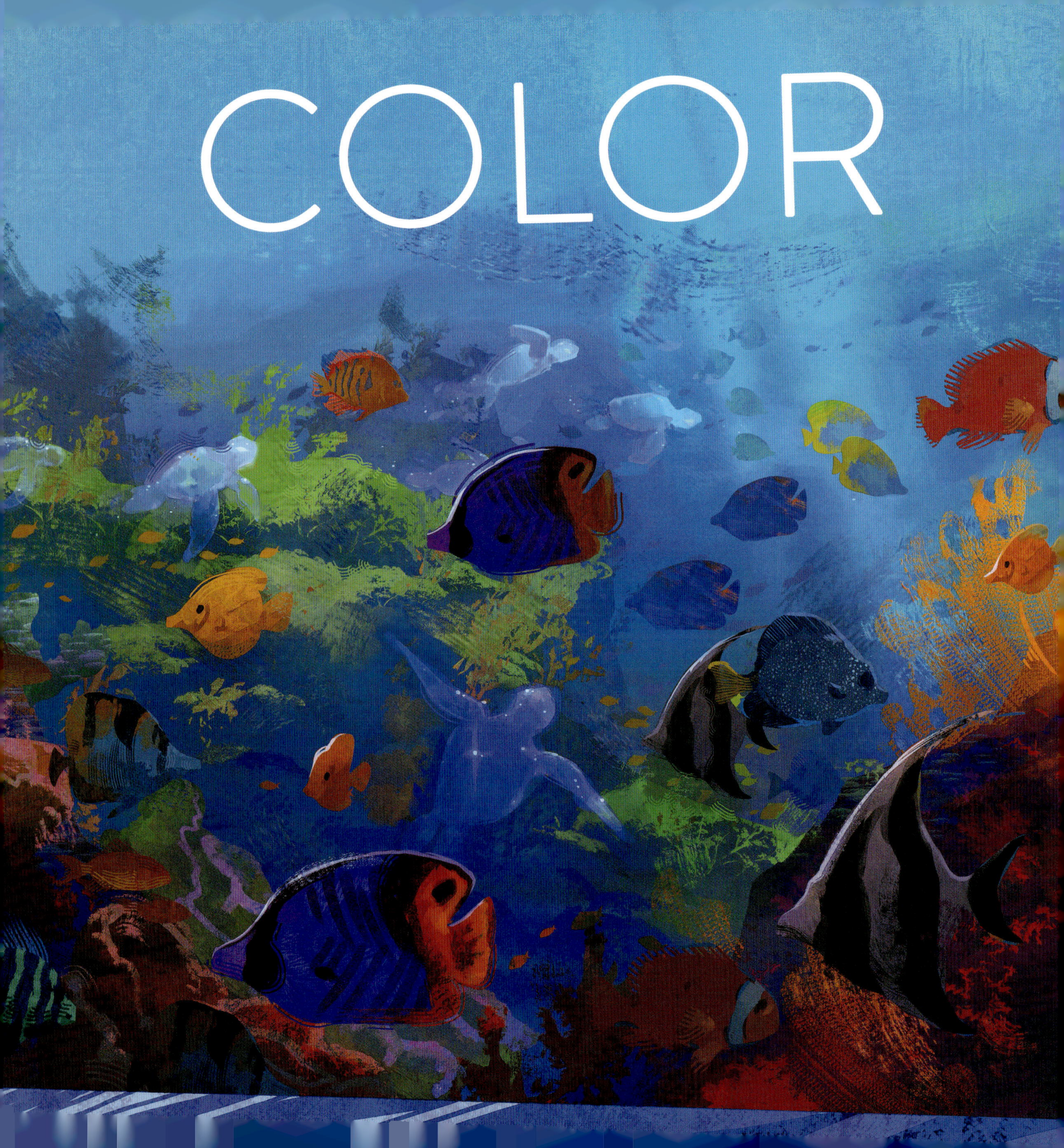
COLOR

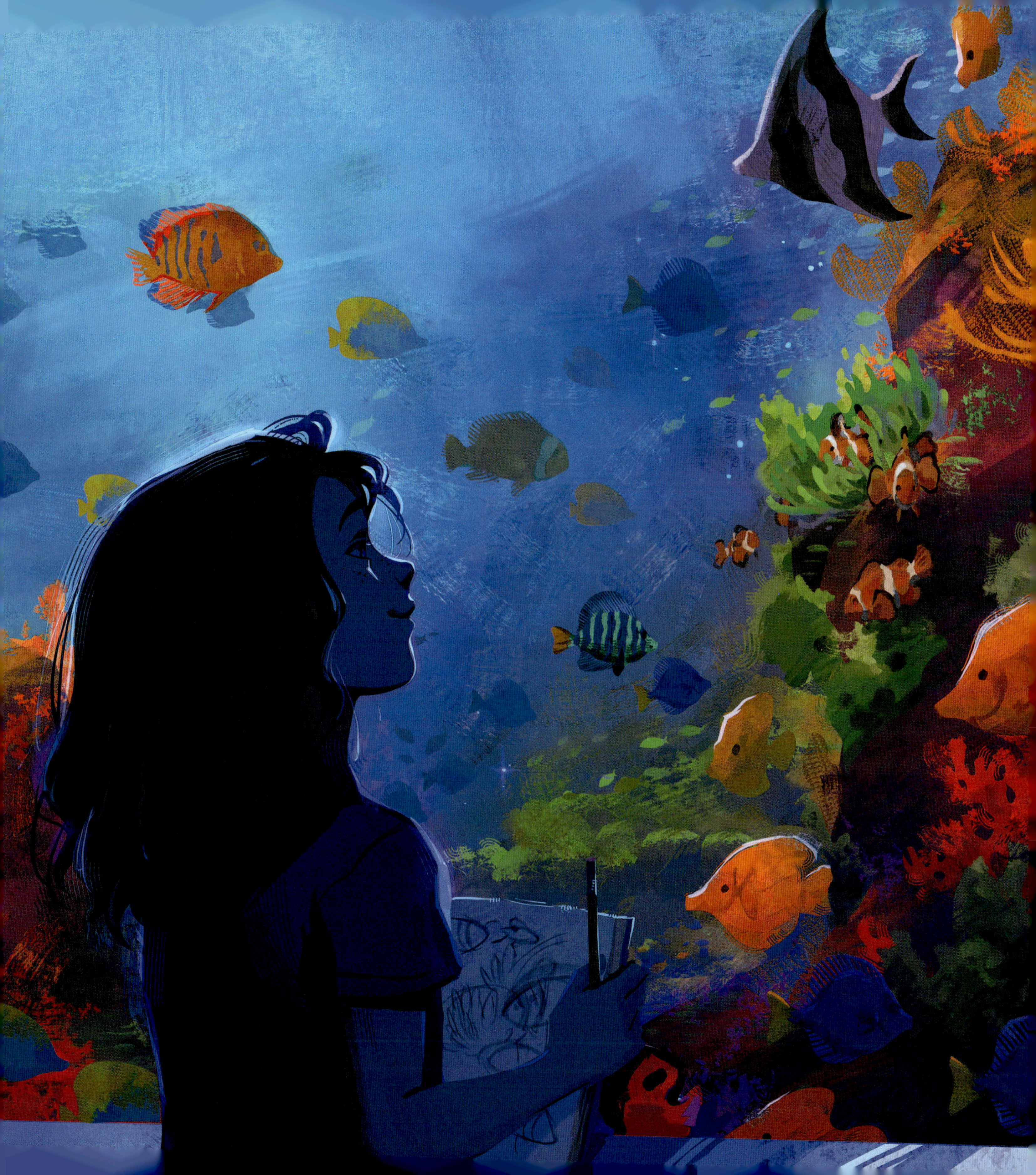

"THESE WASHY, ABSTRACT PAINTINGS WERE LIKELY MY FIRST EXPERIMENTS WITH COLOR AND COMPOSITION"

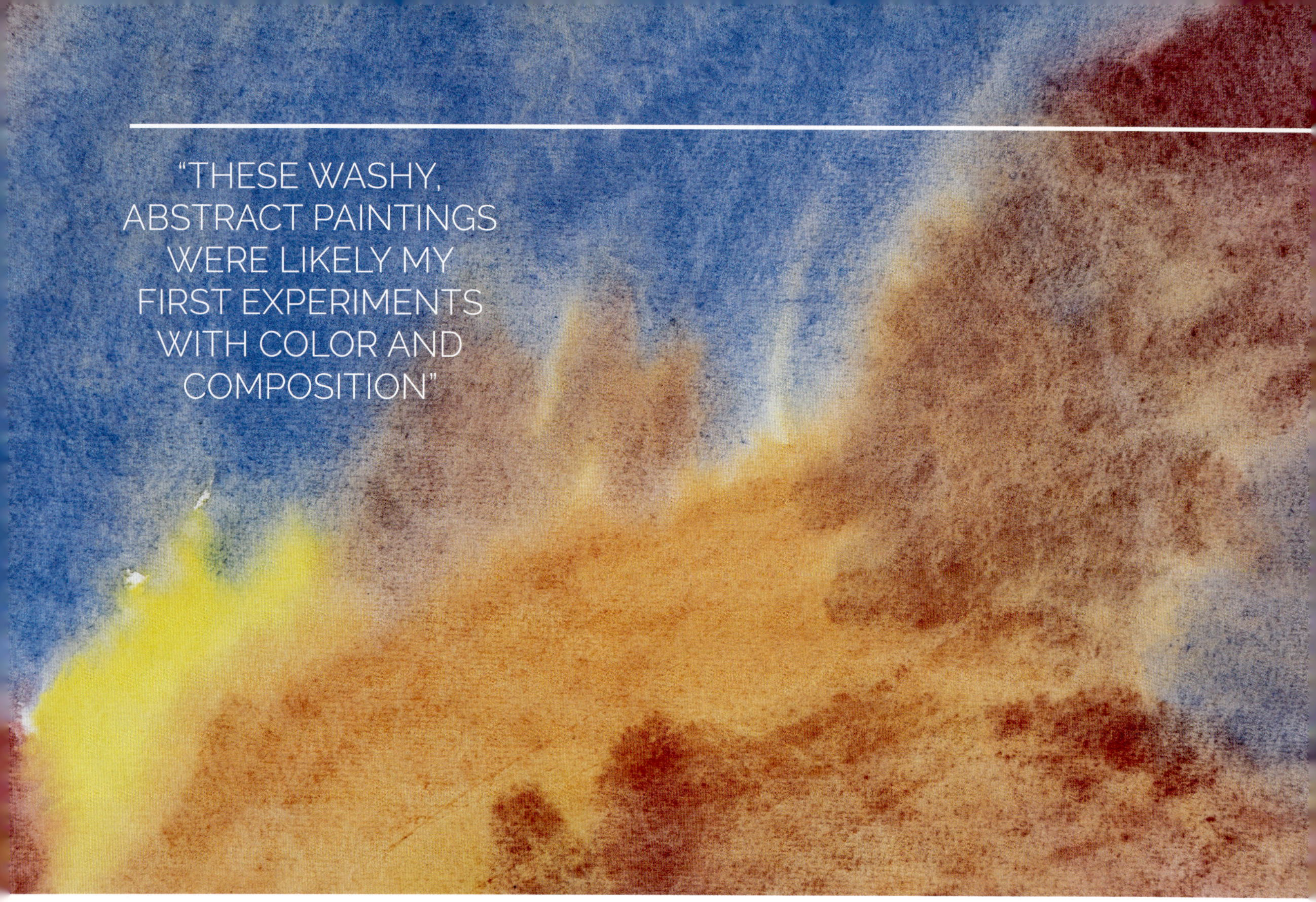

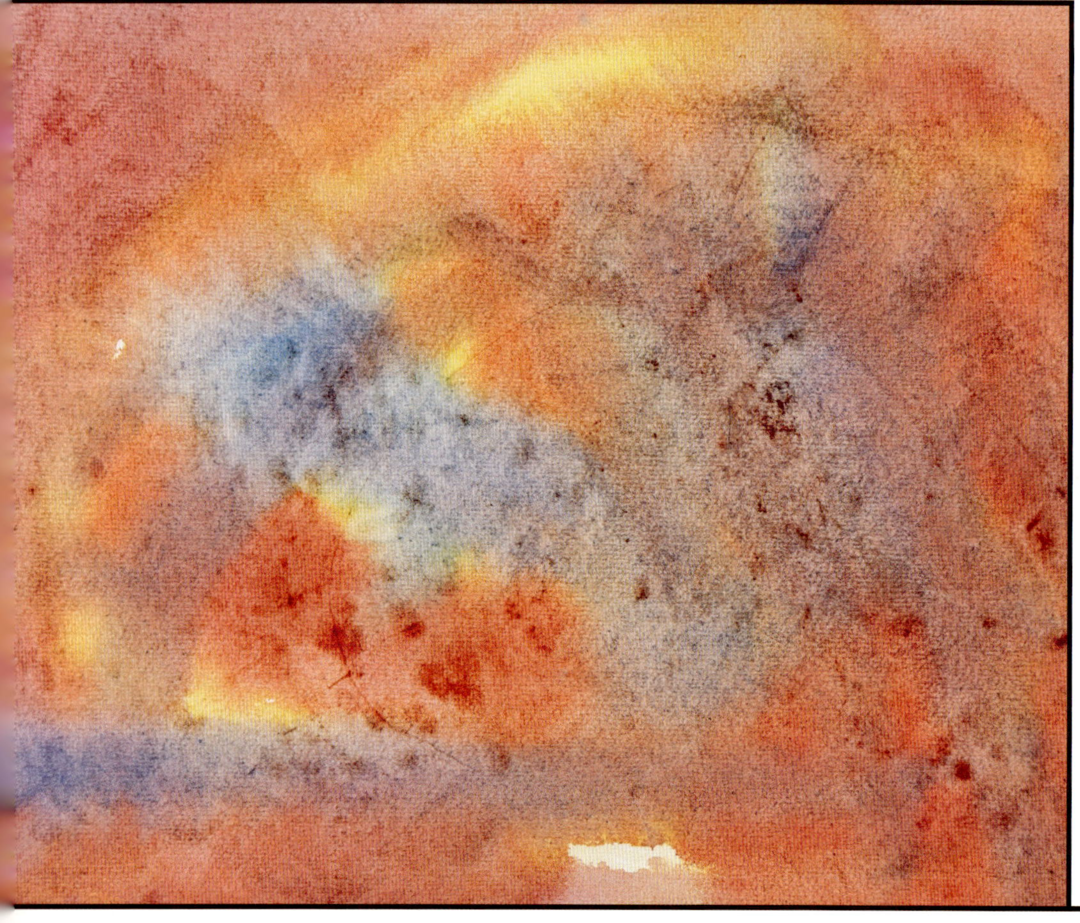

EARLY EXPERIMENTATION

I've always been fascinated by color, and the way it can affect our perception of mood and emotion in imagery. When I was two years old, I went to a playgroup called the Little Blue House twice a week. Run out of the organizer's home, it was a small daycare center that offered Waldorf-inspired activities (Waldorf education schools aim to enable students to develop through the integration of the arts in all academic disciplines) and so its approach emphasized being flexible and creative through the arts. I don't have a lot of memories of this period of time, but I do remember the classic Waldorf art activity of pushing wet watercolor paint around on a soaked sheet of cotton, round-edged watercolor paper. These washy, abstract paintings were likely my first experiments with color and composition, although it feels pretty silly to say that about something a toddler created.

WATERCOLOR PAINTINGS CREATED AS A TODDLER / 1999

STUDYING COLOR

Between the ages of eighteen and twenty, while taking online Schoolism classes to build my art education, one assignment in particular inspired me more than any other. In his Color and Light course, artist Nathan Fowkes asked his students to take a single scene and repaint it several times, using a different color and lighting scenario for each version.

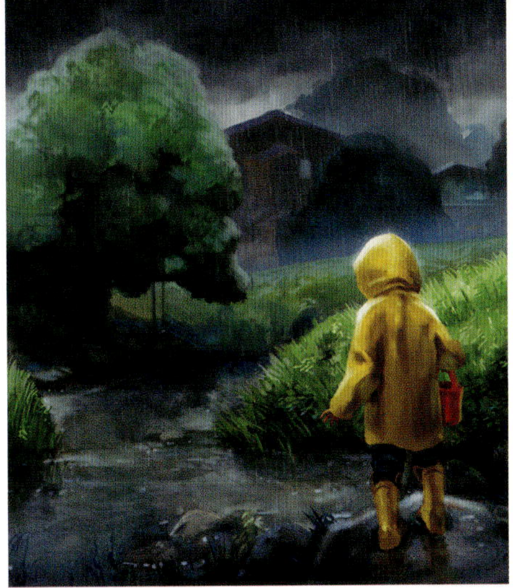

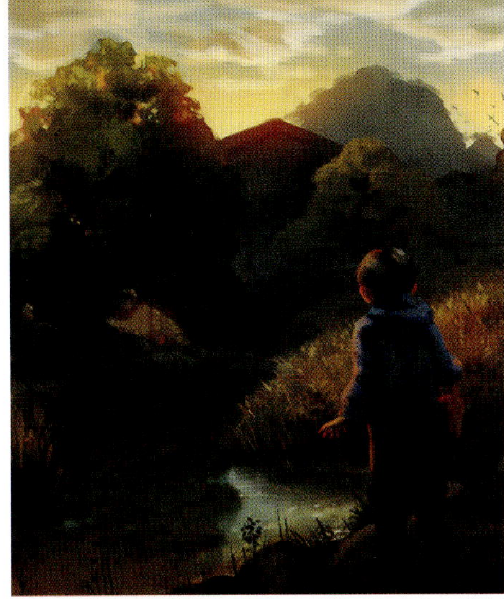

I was blown away by the variety of different scenes into which I could reconfigure a single drawing. This exercise showed me how narrowly I'd been focusing on my initial ideas for each scene I created, and how much I stood to gain from iterating on a location and imagining it at different times of day and in different months in a year.

This approach forced me to do a lot more research than I'd previously done for my paintings. For example, I didn't yet know exactly how the same tree would look at sunrise versus at night. I spent a lot of time outside, looking at objects and features around my apartment building at different times of day, pulling tidbits of information from here and there to construct each new scene. How does water react to a bright sky? What color are the shadows on afternoon snow? How does morning light affect a scene? Asking these kinds of questions encouraged me to expand my comfort zone and push the boundaries on what I was able to create.

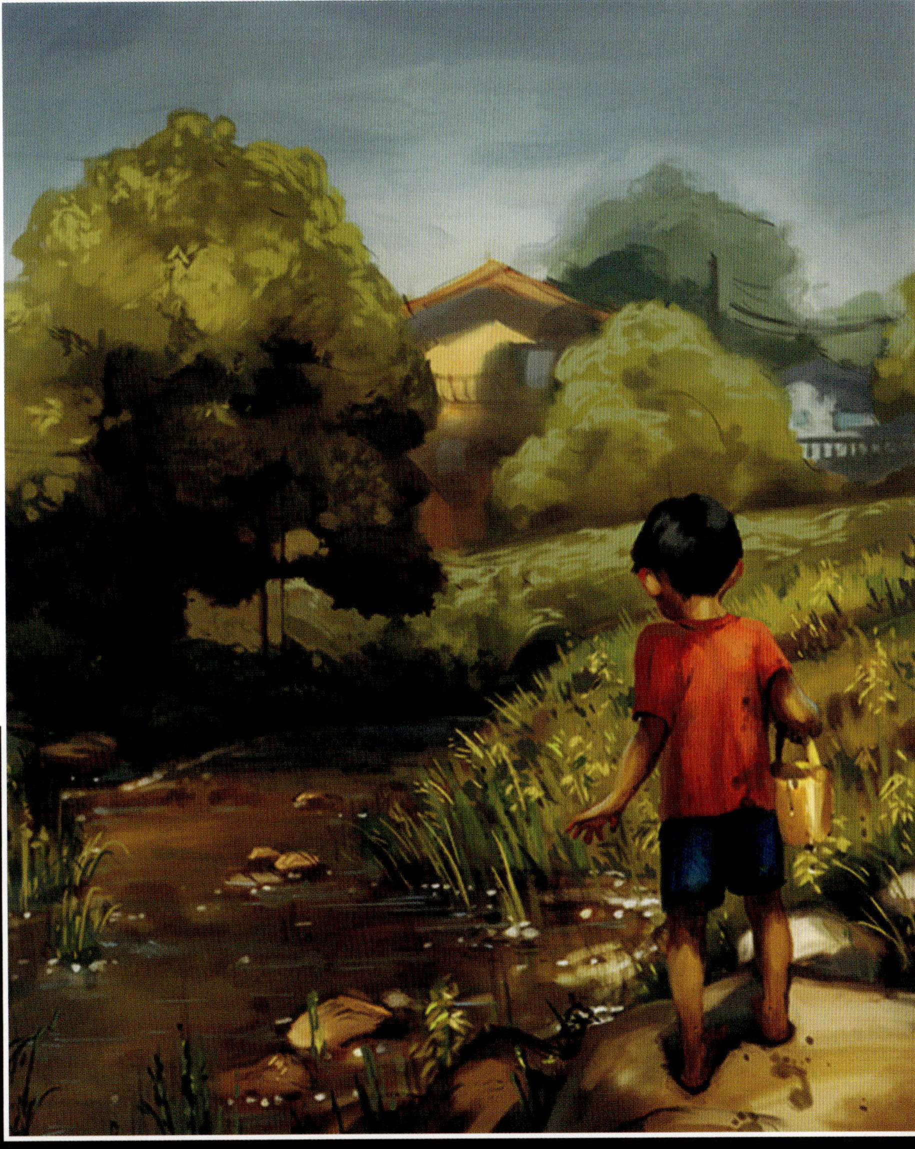

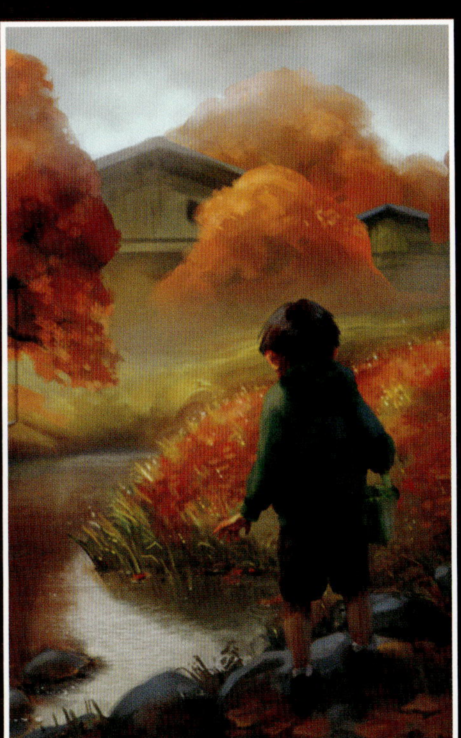

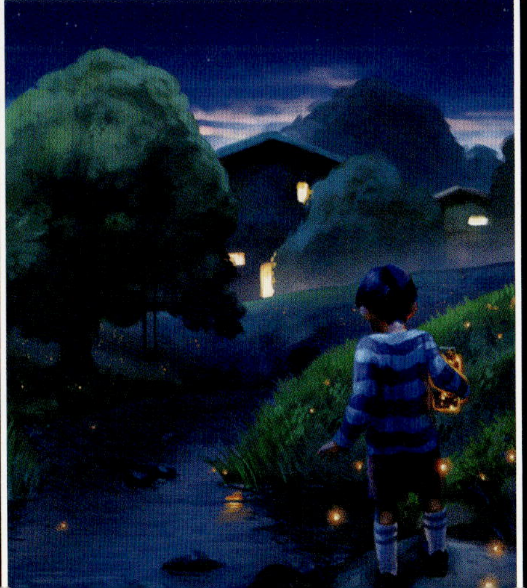

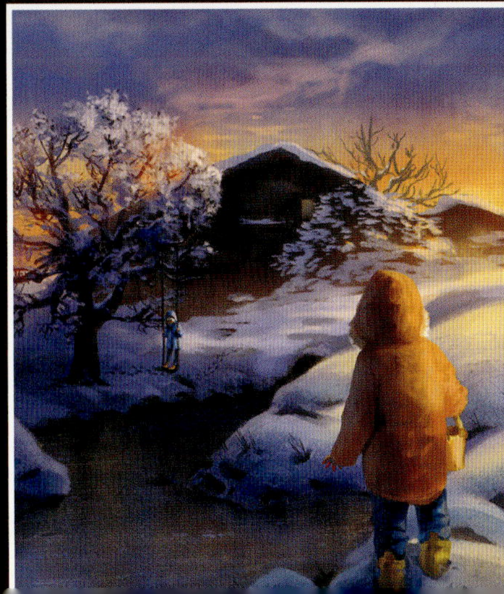

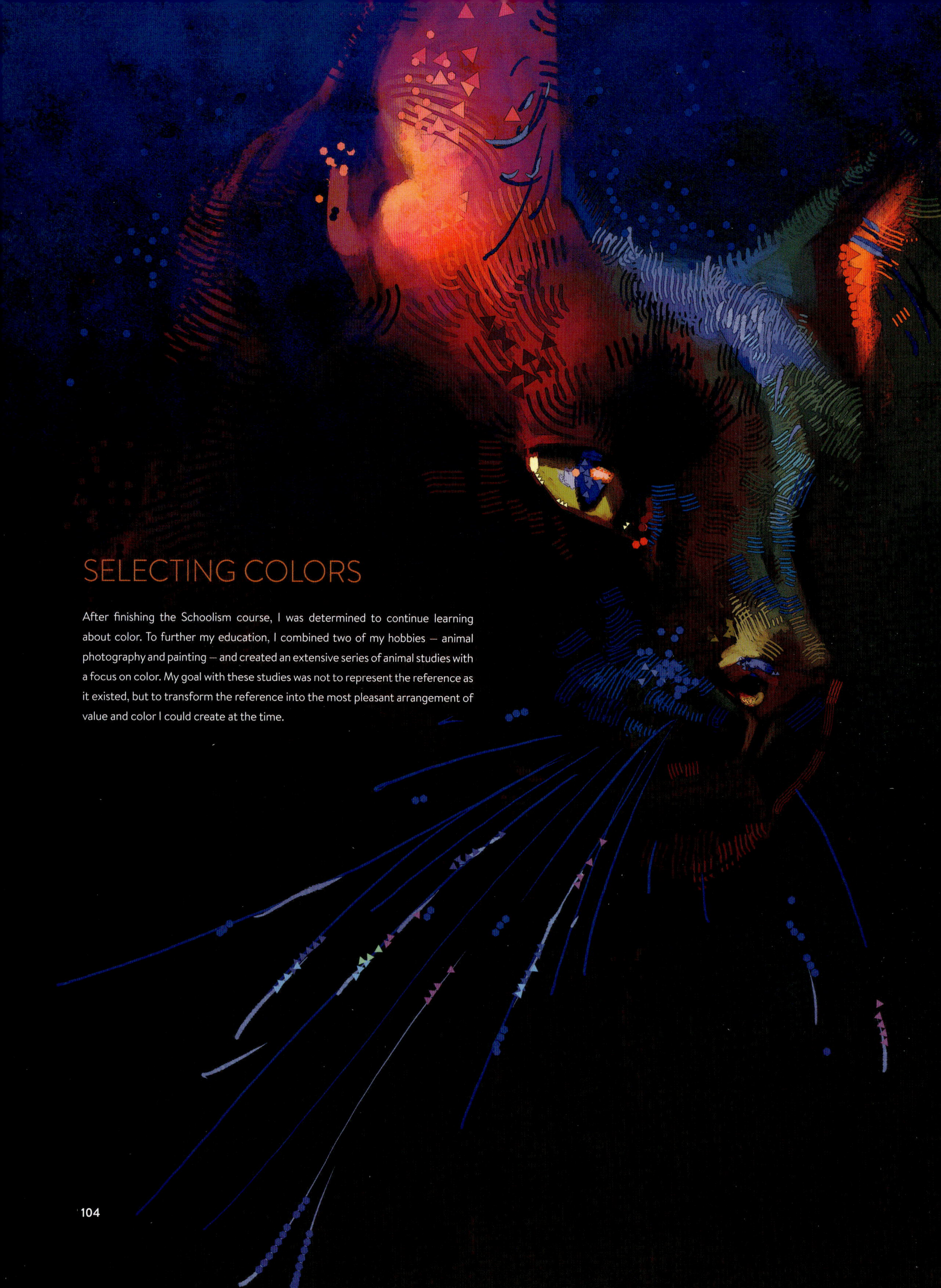

SELECTING COLORS

After finishing the Schoolism course, I was determined to continue learning about color. To further my education, I combined two of my hobbies – animal photography and painting – and created an extensive series of animal studies with a focus on color. My goal with these studies was not to represent the reference as it existed, but to transform the reference into the most pleasant arrangement of value and color I could create at the time.

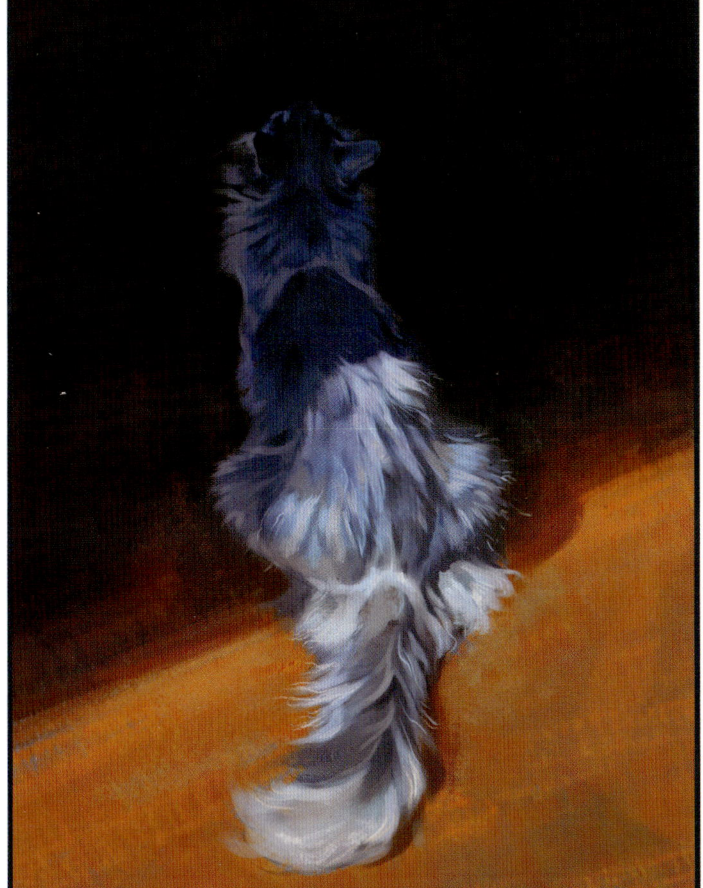

COLOR STUDY OF MY CAT, SHINJI / PHOTOSHOP, 2017

COLOR SATURATION

I quickly learned about the incredible power of color saturation. It was stunning to me how a desaturated red next to a vibrant red could look cool, or a mid-tone gray next to cyan could look warm. Although I've always liked to push saturation, I was learning that controlling saturation and being more conservative with it actually led to more pleasing, vibrant images.

THE LOOSE IMPLICATION OF A CAT / PHOTOSHOP, 2021

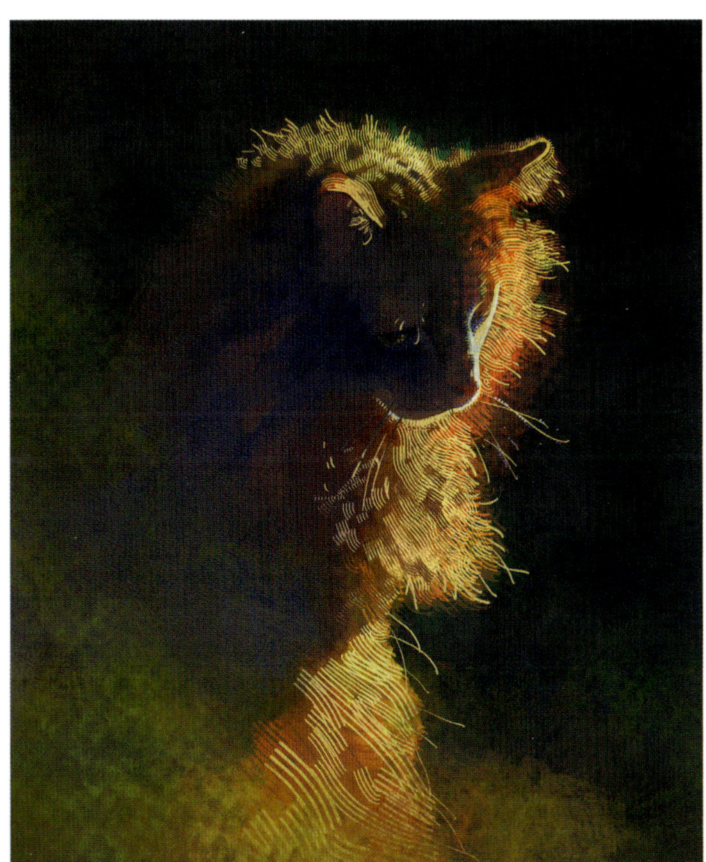

COLOR-PICKING

I am often asked if color-picking is helpful or harmful while trying to learn more about color. I believe it depends on how it is used. Using the Eyedropper tool in Photoshop to color-pick can be incredibly educational, simply by guessing a color by eye first before using it. Whenever I'm inclined to color-pick from an image, I make my best guess of what the color is first and create a swatch on my Photoshop canvas. Then, when I color-pick the color from the reference, I'll create another swatch and compare the two. The differences between the two colors often tells me a lot about the context I'm viewing the color in.

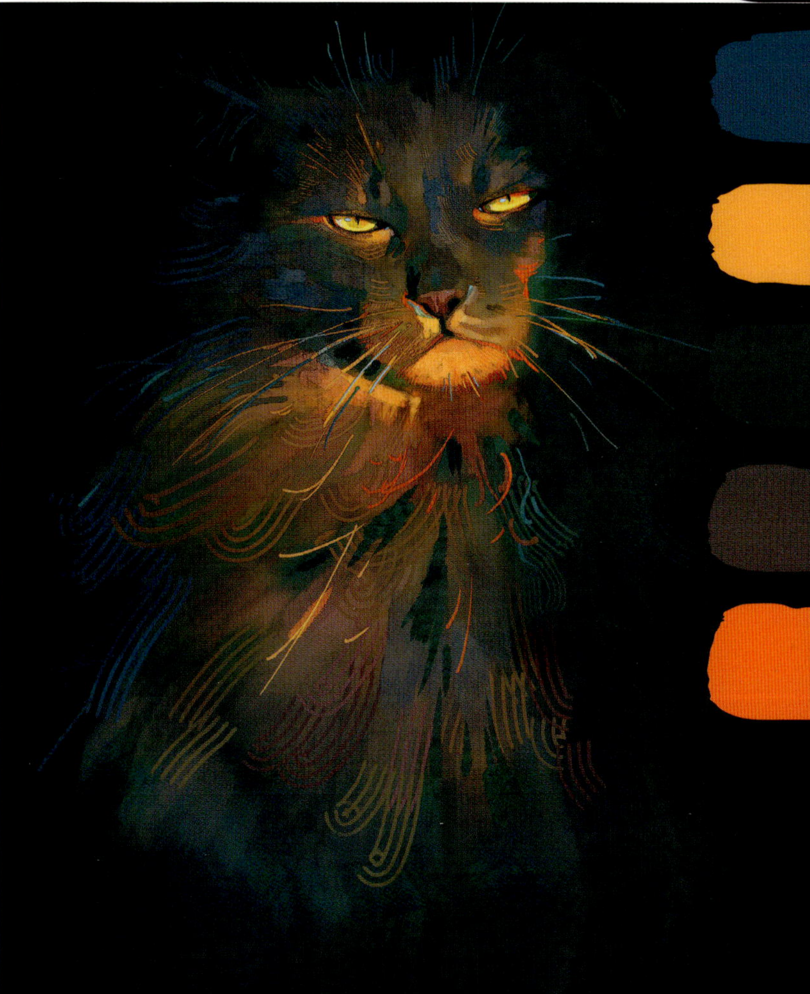

COLOR STUDY OF MY CAT, SHINJI / PHOTOSHOP, 2021

PUSHING AND PULLING COLOR

One of my favorite color exercises is to take a simple photo reference and push its colors to an extreme, to create the most interesting iteration possible. First, I look for hints of unexpected color and push them as far as possible. For example, the fur on the silver cat's face (shown above) is much sleeker and smoother than the rest of his fur, so I exaggerate these texture changes by applying glistening, cool-toned highlights on the face, and diffused, warmer highlights and chunkier texture to the longer fur of the body.

A WINDOW INTO / PUSHING COLOR

In this study of my dog, Kira, I pushed both the stylization of the drawing *and* the color. I often learn the most from finding colorful ways to represent more neutral tones such as white, cream, gray, and black. In the painting of Kira, I brought out peaches, greens, cyans, and purplish-grays all within the creamy white. The following steps demonstrate how I constructed the drawing and the decisions behind my color choices.

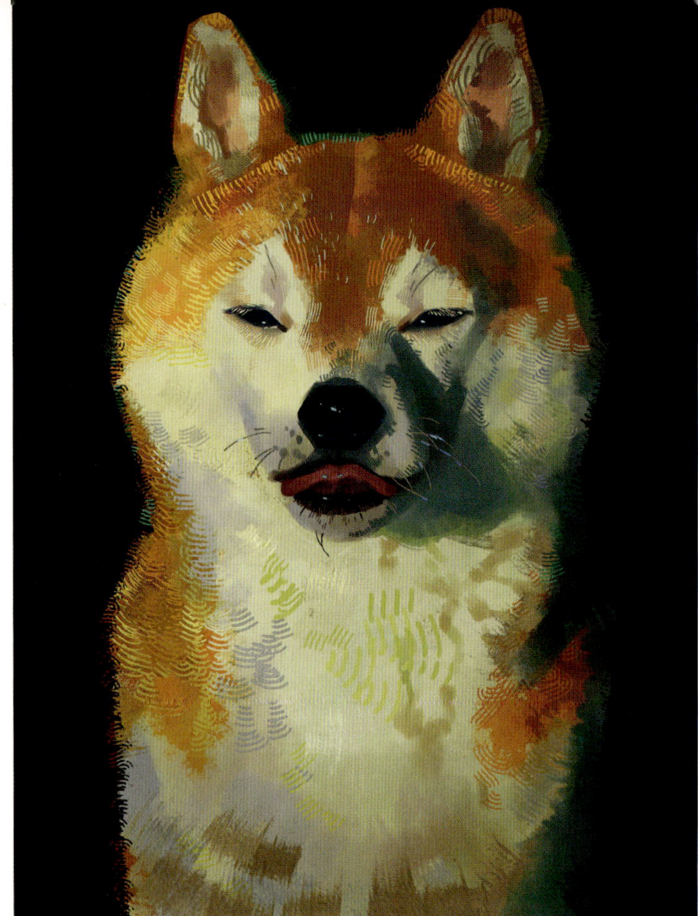

COLOR STUDIES OF KIRA / PHOTOSHOP, 2021

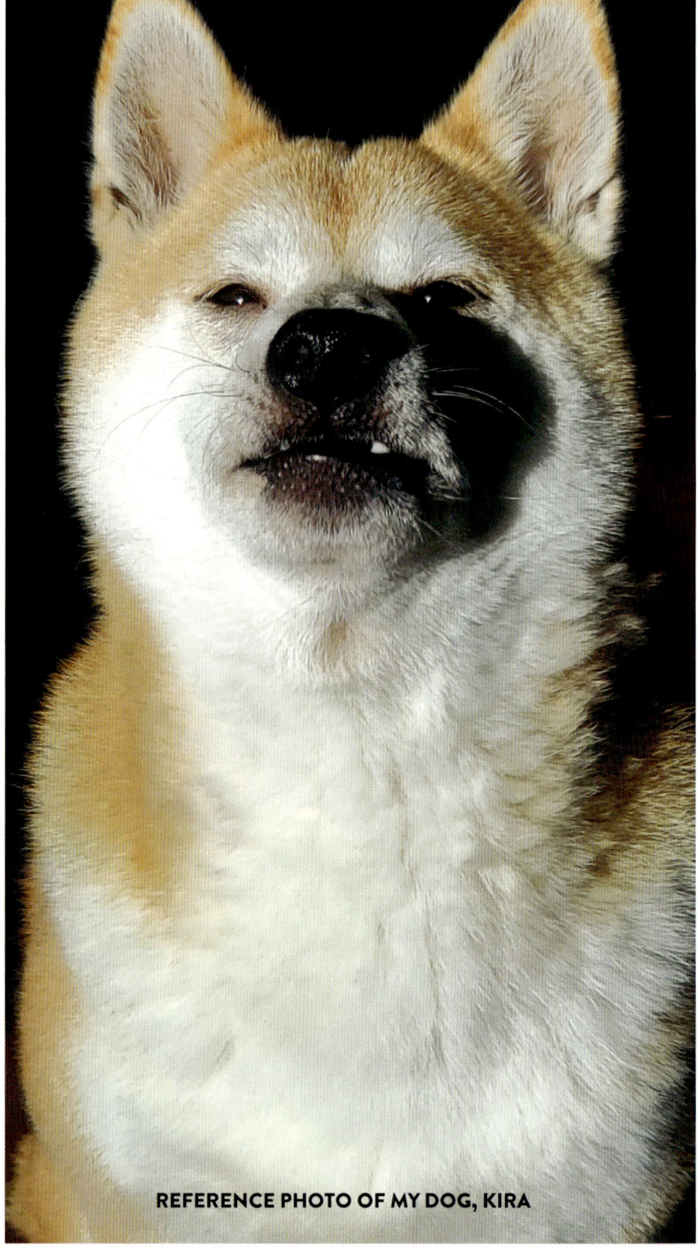

REFERENCE PHOTO OF MY DOG, KIRA

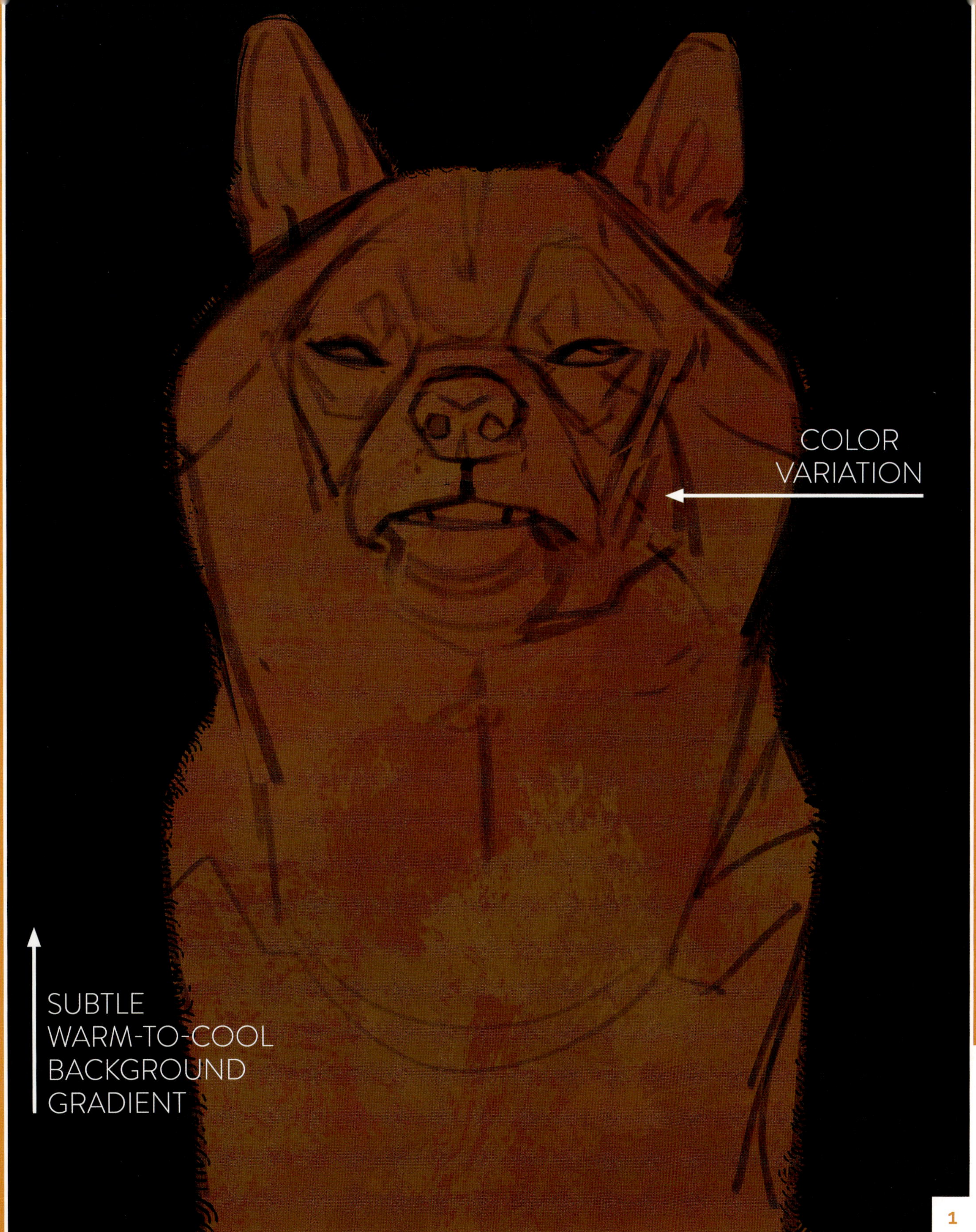

"I OFTEN LEARN THE MOST FROM FINDING COLORFUL WAYS TO REPRESENT MORE NEUTRAL TONES"

1 / SKETCH

During the sketch phase, I aim to define as much structure as I can. This allows me to focus solely on color choice as a vehicle for form portrayal once I move into painting. I prefer not to start with flat color, so set up my base layer with some color variation. The Color Jitter in the warm hues starts to mimic the color range that can be seen in real fur, and the subtle warm-to-cool gradient in the background keeps it from looking too flat.

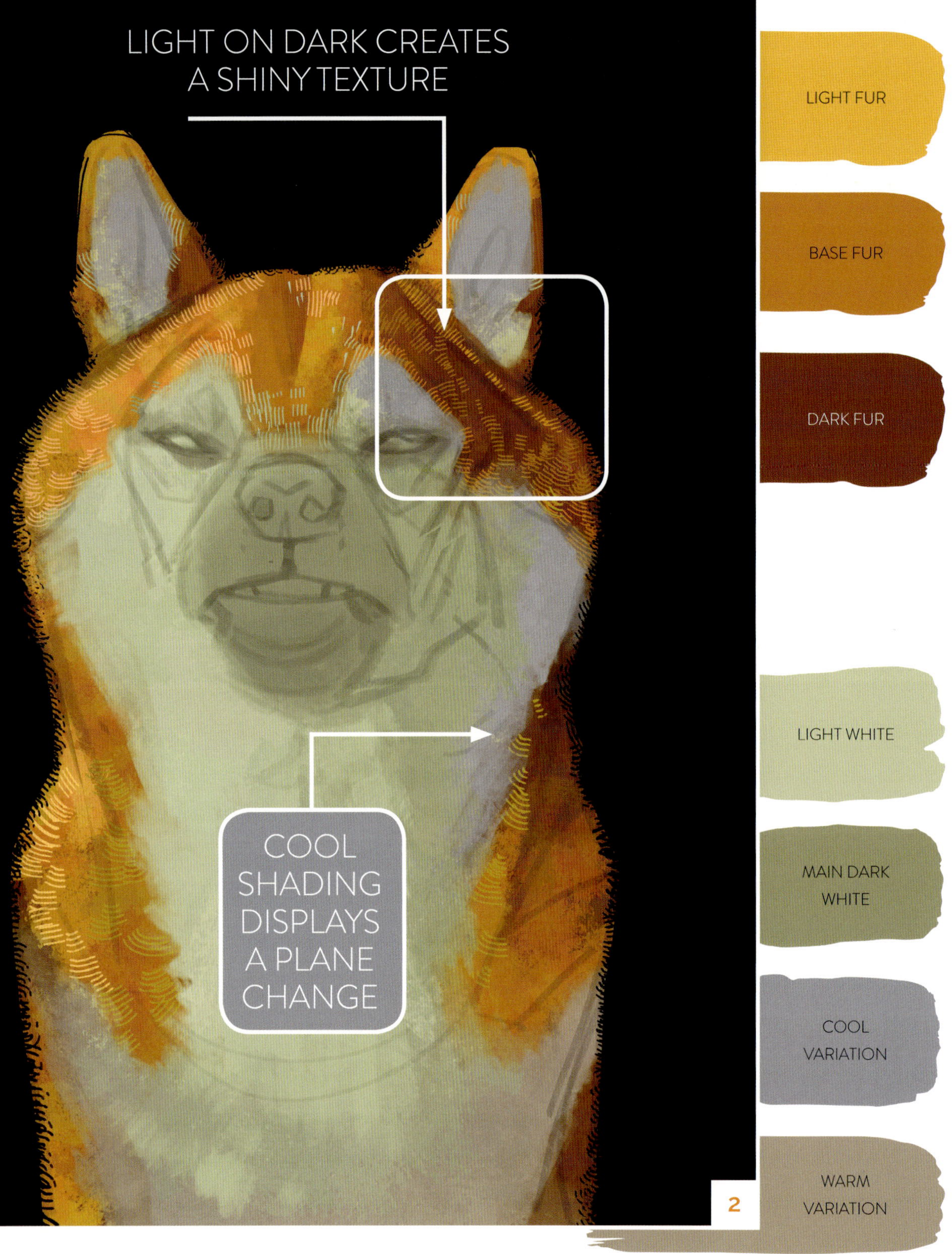

2 / PAINTING BASE FUR

I paint the orange fur with three main shades of peachy gold. I push the original neutral tan tones of the fur into a more saturated orange-gold color range, but maintain the structure of light and shadow visible in the reference photo. I notice how the flecks of light fur against the warm shadows show the sleek texture of the fur, and so accentuate that in my painting.

I divide the dog's white underbelly into color zones to build the tones within the pale fur. I select an off-white for the lighter areas, including the side of the body. A darker version of the off-white is used for the primary shadows and I choose a cool and warm variation of the shadow color to demonstrate plane changes and add energy to the shadows.

3 / FUR HIGHLIGHTS

I push the highlights into neon cyans and magentas to indicate bright shine without needing to use white. Often, I find the best way to illustrate shine is by adding small strokes of neon color, either in place of white or as a border around white.

I notice subtle hints of green in the reference and decide to push the shadow sides toward a green and cool palette. I border the green shadows with a more typical orange-brown to bridge the gap. To unify the palette, I introduce olive greens into the light side.

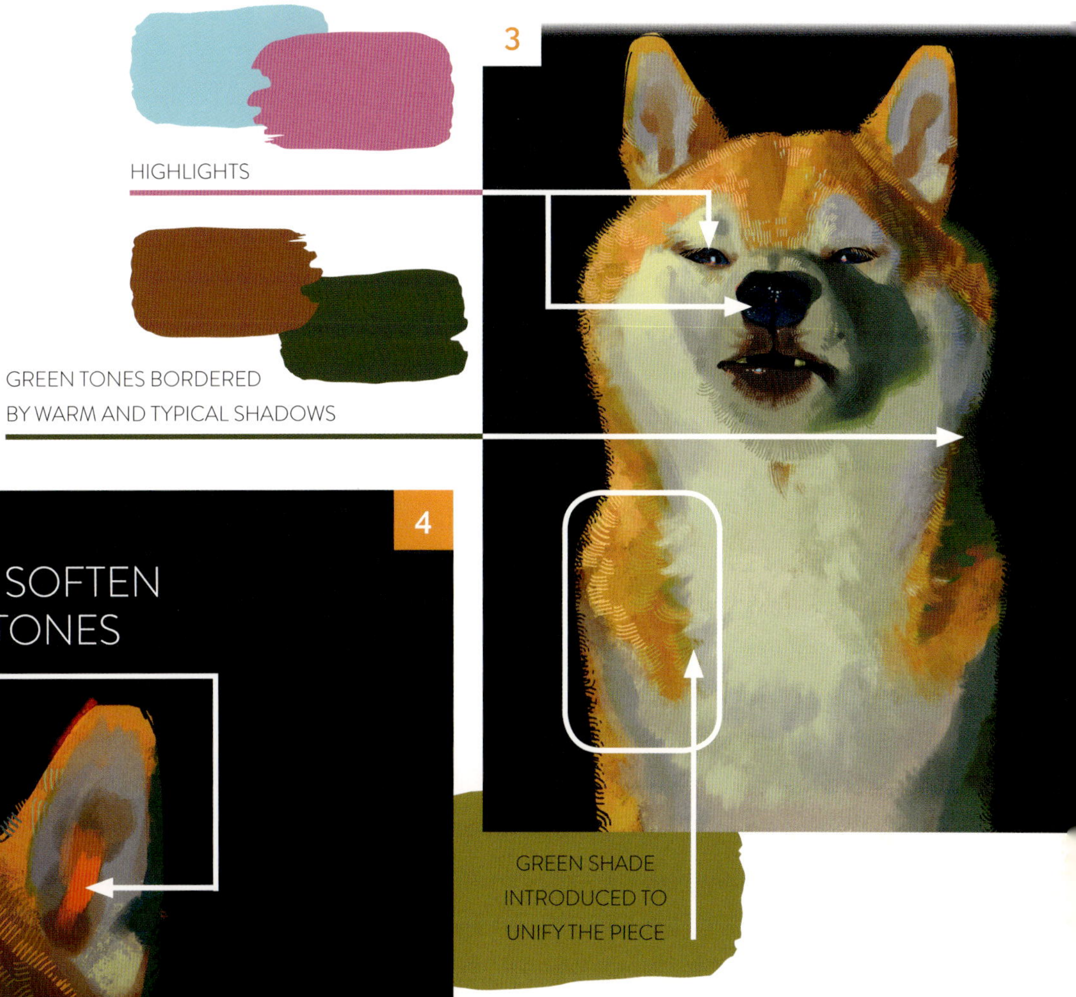

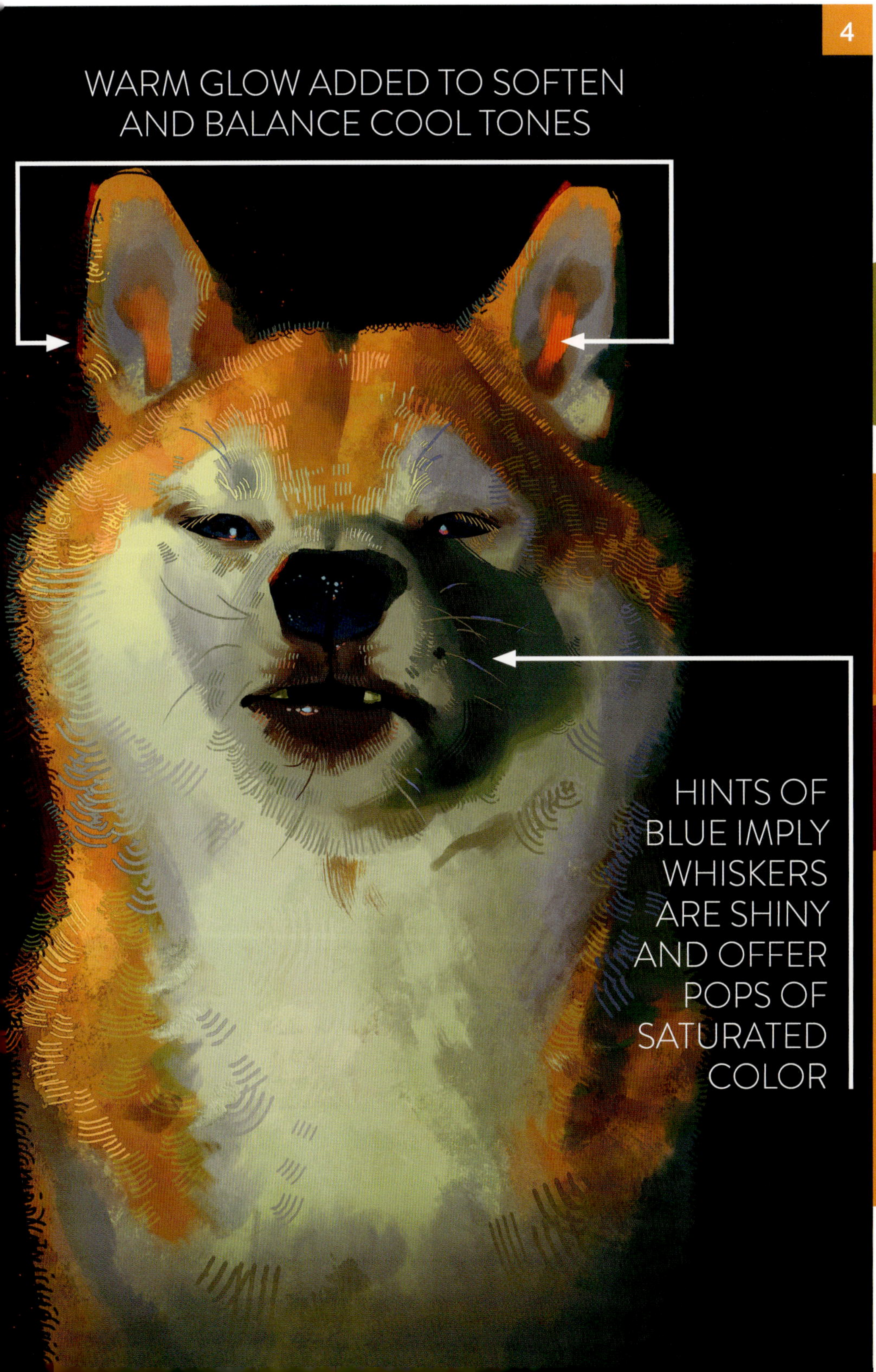

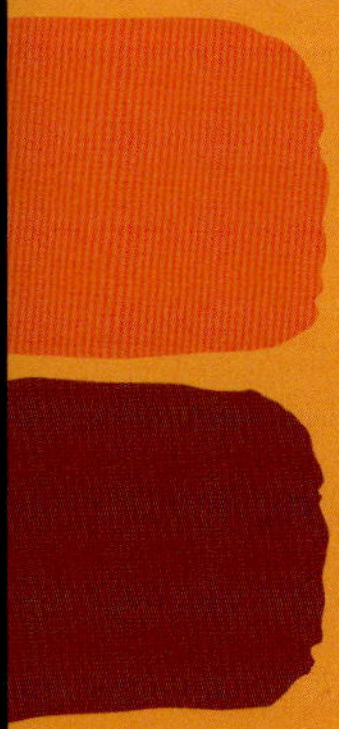

4 / LIGHT TOUCHES

I add a warm light bloom on the lighter side of the body to soften the edge and balance against the cools. The pops of subsurface scattering in the ears also help the balance. I then add a blue glint to the whiskers to show how reflective and finely textured they are. Just as with the shine on the eye and nose, I choose to introduce a pop of unusual saturation to demonstrate the shine rather than push the white.

COLOR IN CONTEXT

Finding colors to push within an image often involves looking very hard at the image – I use existing color knowledge to make educated guesses about the discreet undertones present in the colors I see. If I paint an object or scene under a blue sky, I know I can expect to find blue hidden within the shadows. The blue comes from the sky above, but it only comes through when it isn't being overpowered by the much stronger primary light source – the sun. Because the harsh sun dramatically overpowers the diffused sky light, hints of blue are only picked up in the shadows.

In this painting, the light from the blue sky is competing with warm bounce light in the shadows. This bounce light is caused by sunlight reflecting off both the water and the swan's back into the dark. The things I learn about the world through these exercises are incredibly useful later on when I'm working on paintings that are closer to reality. I have a backlog of color knowledge I can pull from to add interesting and vibrant hints of color variation throughout my paintings.

COLOR STUDY OF A SWAN /
PHOTOSHOP, 2017

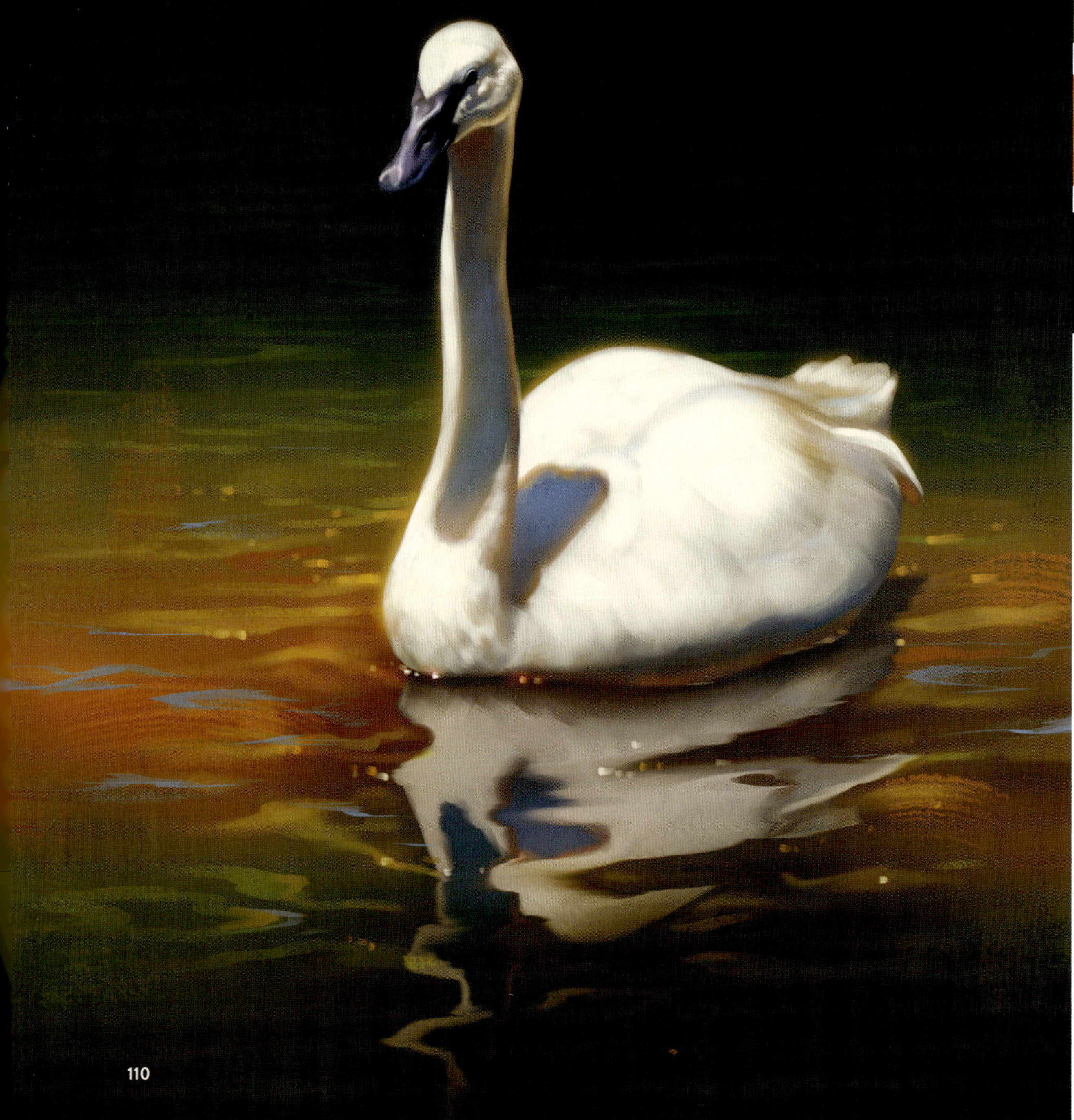

The way we perceive a color is based entirely on the context in which it features. In the same way that a gray can look warm or cool based on the colors around it, vibrant, unusual colors can look believable in the right context. This cheetah is painted with various shades of pinks and purples – not realistic colors for a big cat. However, because the background is an even more intense purple, the color reads as a warm neutral in this context. This makes the unusual color of the normally warm orange cheetah more believable in its context.

COLOR STUDY OF A CHEETAH / PHOTOSHOP, 2017

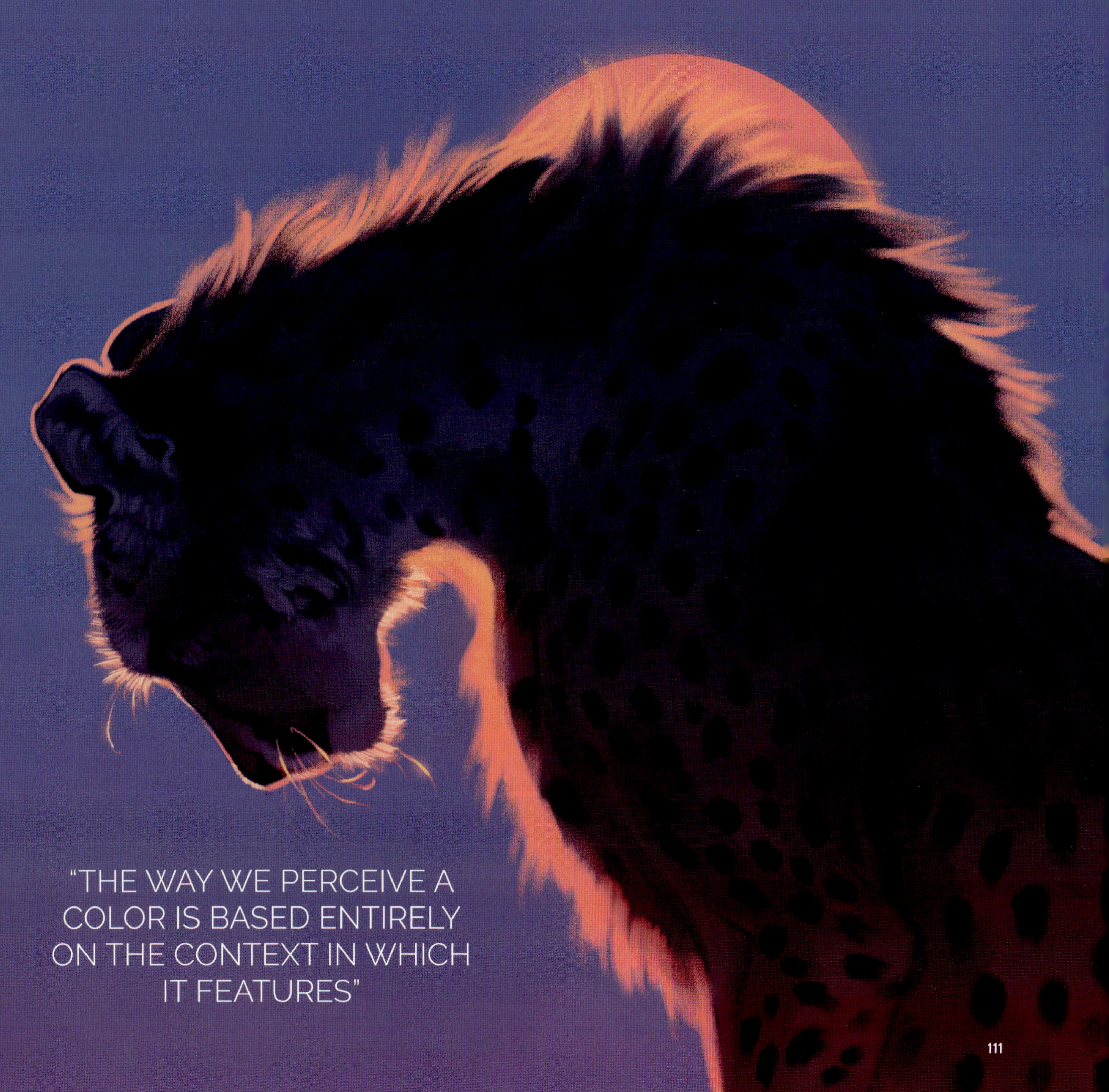

"THE WAY WE PERCEIVE A COLOR IS BASED ENTIRELY ON THE CONTEXT IN WHICH IT FEATURES"

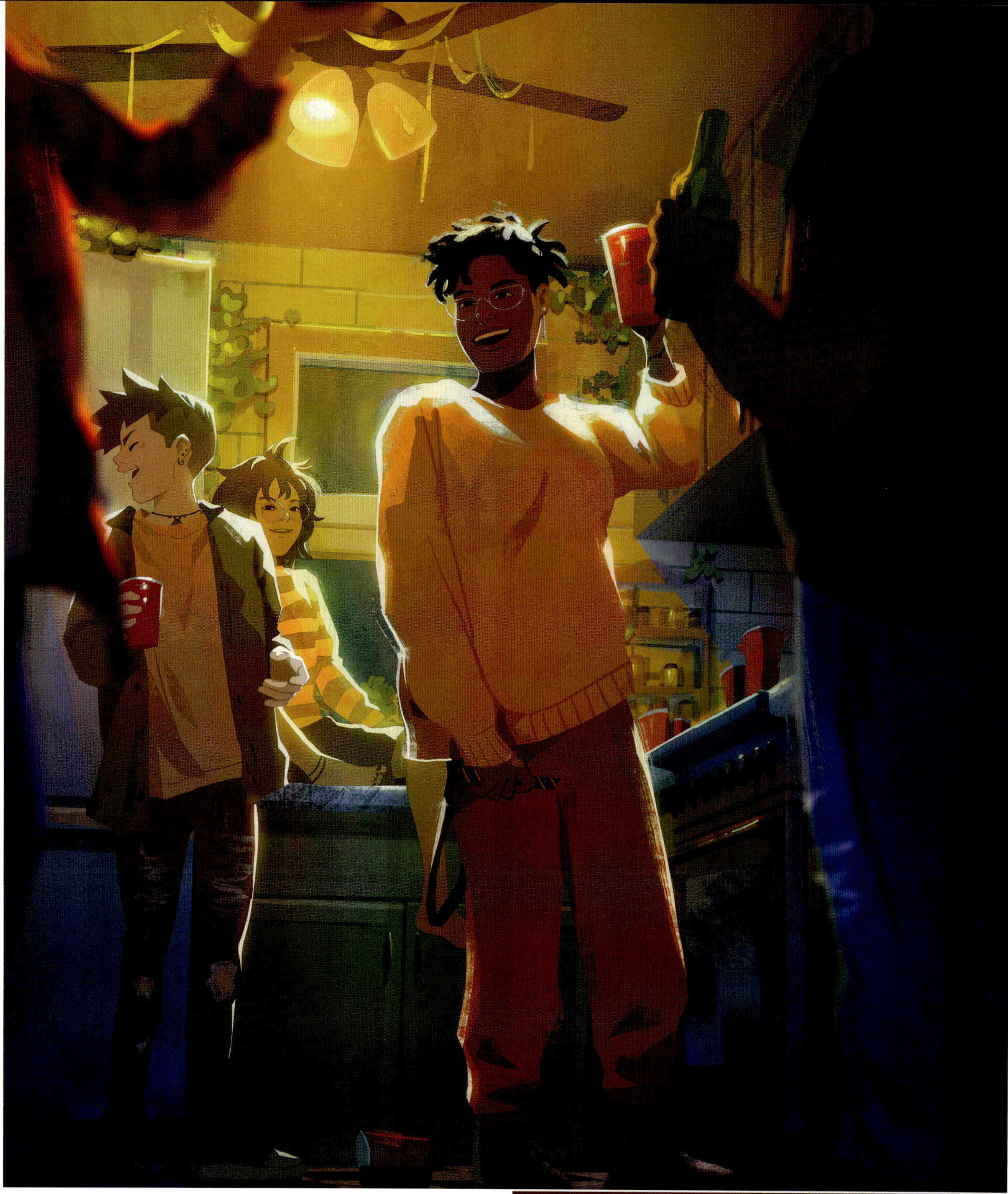

COLOR AND MOOD

Color has strong ties to our emotional perception of imagery. I created the images on these pages to represent the stark difference in mood before and during the global pandemic, Covid-19. In these two pieces, I used a hue shift to give emotional weight to the loneliness I hoped to portray in the New Year's Eve 2020/2021 image. In the New Year's Eve 2019/2020 piece however, I used oranges, reds, and yellows to give the image a sense of coziness and warmth, punctuated by pops of greens and blues to give the painting a busy and energetic feeling. To encourage a mood shift and apply a sense of emptiness to the New Year's Eve 2021 image, I replaced the golden warmth with a cool and eerie cyan glow.

ABOVE / NEW YEAR'S EVE 2019/2020

These paintings were created on the last day of 2020. In addition to the carefully considered color palettes, I created a wallflower-type character to appear in each. They sit in the background of the glowing past, happy to hang around the edge and bask in the warmth. I contrasted that with cold desolation in the 2020/2021 New Year piece.

PRESS PAUSE

One of my favorite ways to study color and emotion is by pausing my favorite films and deconstructing the colors that are used at emotional moments. During the pre-production of animated movies, artists create color scripts and story beats (a structural element used to mark a shift in tone in a narrative) to explore the emotional ups and downs of the film. In TV, we generally don't have time in the schedule to plan that thoroughly, but we always refer to the story for guidance on how we should paint each location.

BELOW / NEW YEAR'S EVE 2020/2021

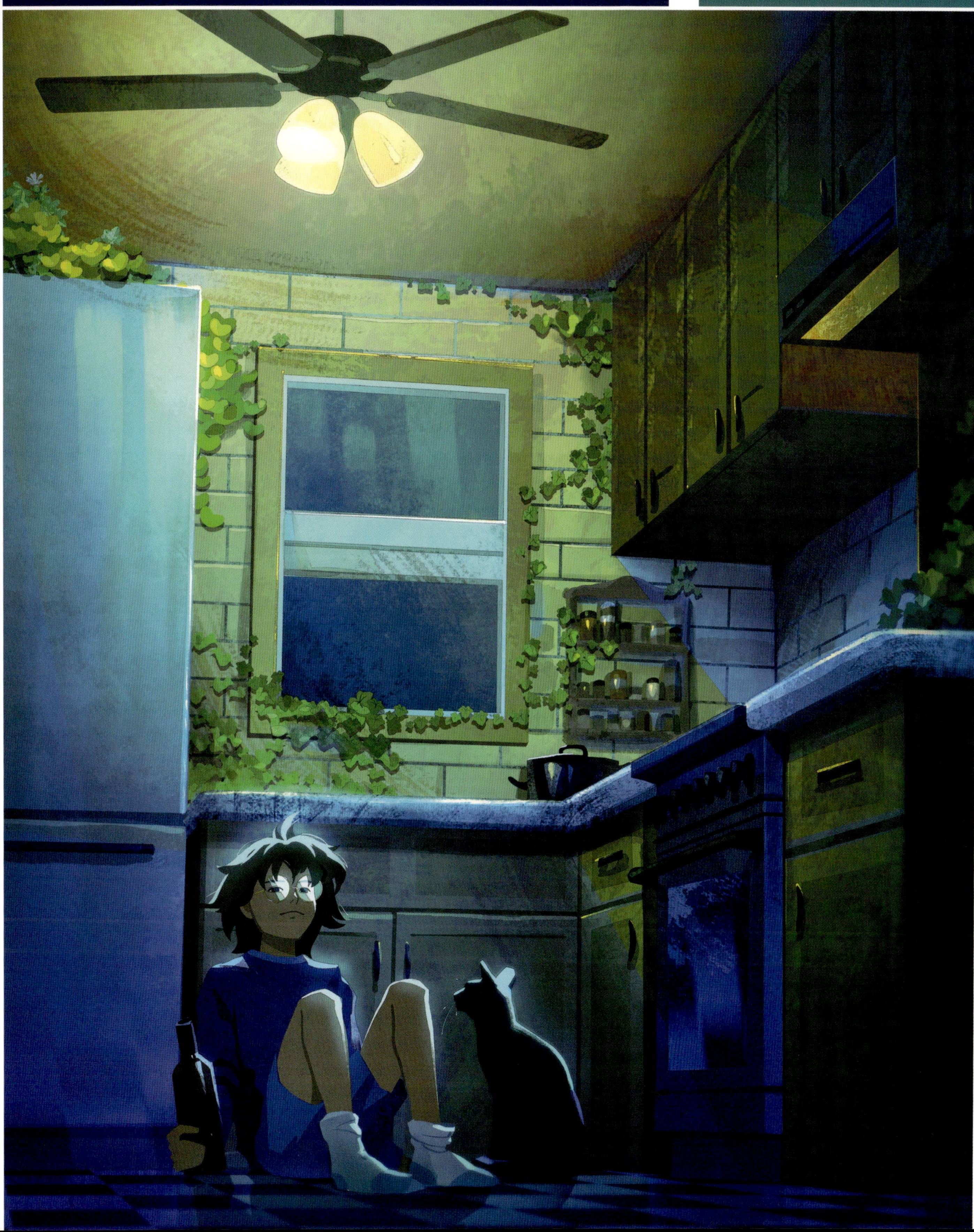

ABSTRACTION EXERCISE

Here's an exercise I use to help develop my color skillset. Choose a unique emotion, then find images that represent it. Examples of interesting complex emotions include "the moment you realize the true impact of your actions and how much pain they've caused" or "the moment you return to your childhood home after you've moved away and realize you don't know what 'home' means anymore." Use Pinterest to identify eight to ten images that reflect the feelings generated by those circumstances.

The catch? You can't use imagery that is related to the subject matter of the prompt. The chosen emotion must be expressed *solely* through other means, mainly color, in an abstract way. I find this exercise is similar to creating an emotional playlist, but using art or photography instead of music. In both cases, we can study the fundamentals of why a particular creation makes us feel a certain way, such as major versus minor chords, or cool versus warm colors. However, nothing compares to figuring out what appeals to your particular sensibilities. This exercise also helps to avoid falling into patterns of repeating the same color schemes. The more bizarre the prompts you set out to fulfill, the more you are forced to push the boundaries to identify colors you might attribute to more general emotions such as "sad" or "angry."

Once you feel more comfortable assigning abstract colors and shapes to distinct emotions, the next step is to push yourself to create your own thumbnails that represent the prompts.

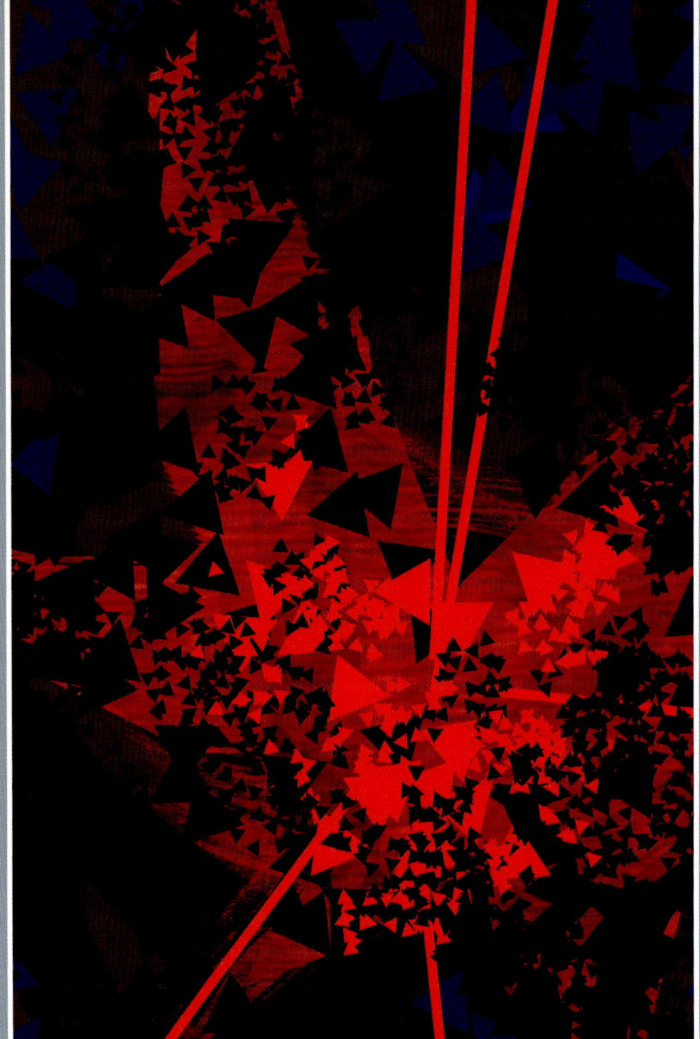

This design is inspired by the prompt: "A high-school senior with dreams of becoming a professional basketball player breaks her ankle before the championship match. She broke it because of a mistake she was warned not to make."

This design is inspired by the prompt: "A man is talking about helping his mother in the kitchen as a child. He is on the podium at her funeral."

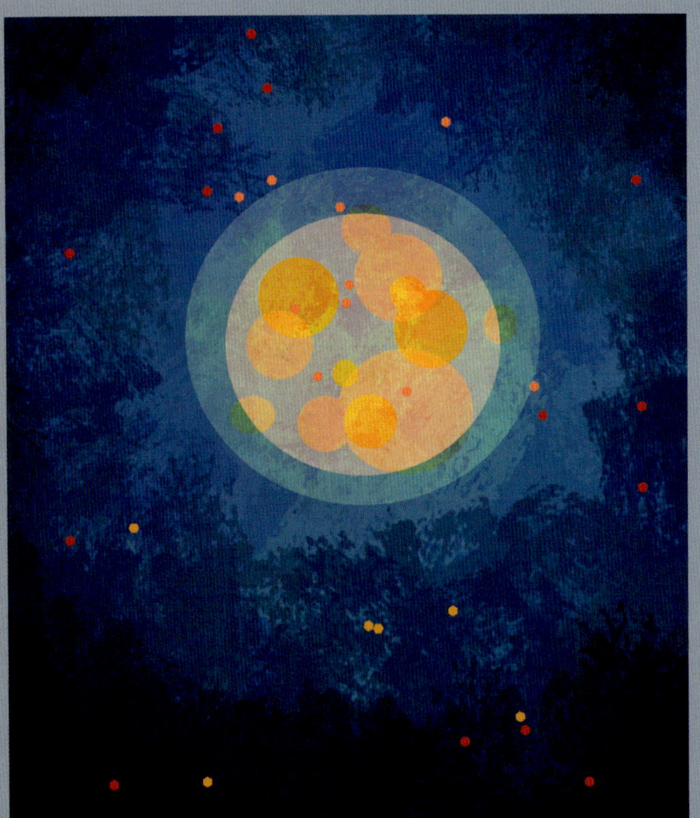

SAMPLE PROMPTS

Here are some prompts you can try yourself. Try to represent these complex emotional prompts through abstract color and shape alone:

- A father hears his daughter singing in her room and listens in the hallway.
- While on social media, an estranged mother sees a photo of a grandchild she's never met.
- A family spends one last day with their fourteen-year-old dog before he is put to sleep.
- A young man discovers his younger brother is cancer-free and breathes a sigh of relief more deeply than he has in years.

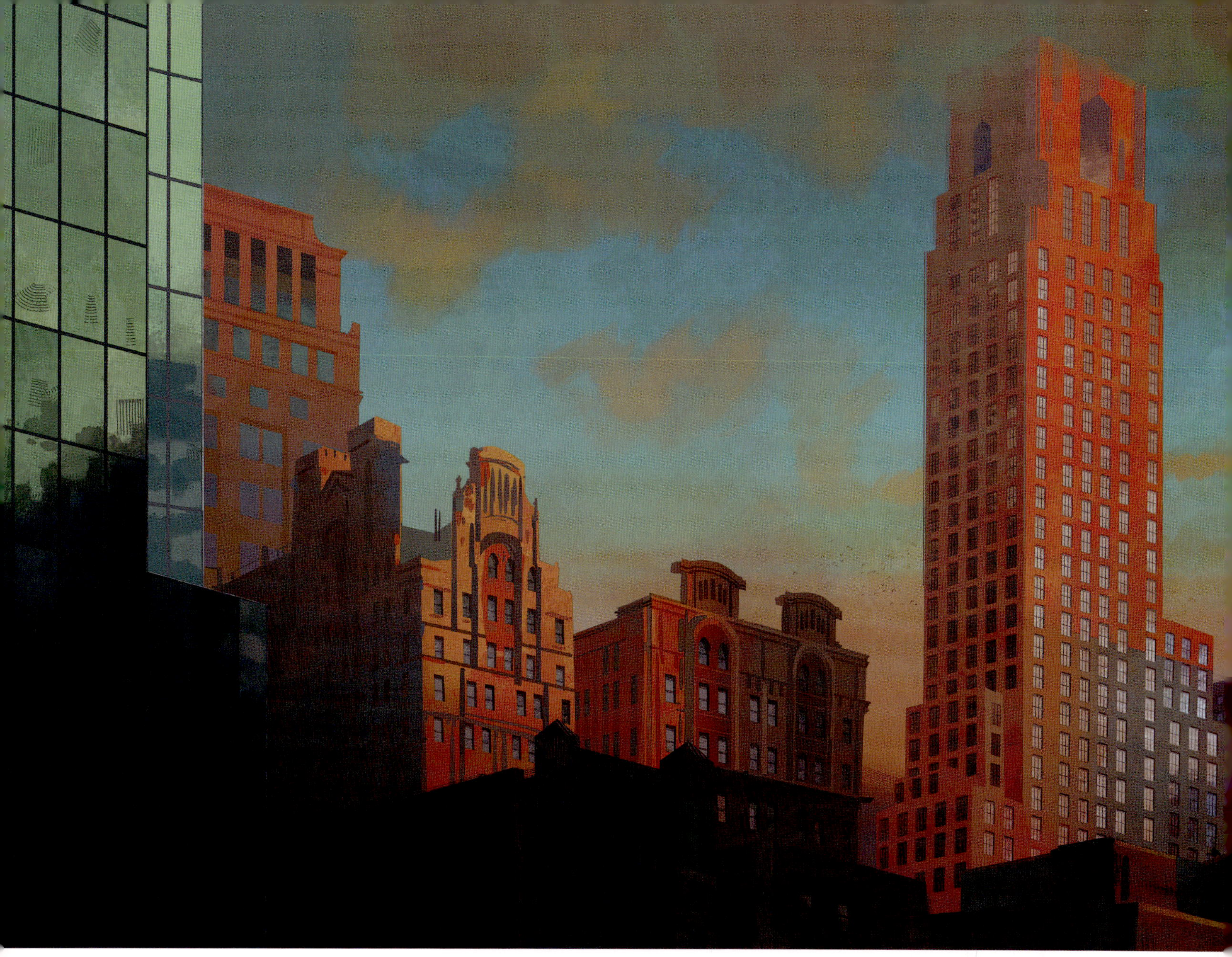

CRAFTING A UNIFIED PALETTE

When pushing and pulling colors in studies created from photographs or real life, it's important to keep any newly introduced colors balanced with the rest of the palette. In the study above, which is of a photo taken by my dad, Steve Kurtz, I felt that introducing greens would help bring out the peachy warm tones and make for a fun combination of colors. However, introducing green only to the building on the left would have looked a bit out of place, so I unified the palette with that green by introducing hints of greens and neutral yellows in other areas of the painting, such as in the sky and in the shadows.

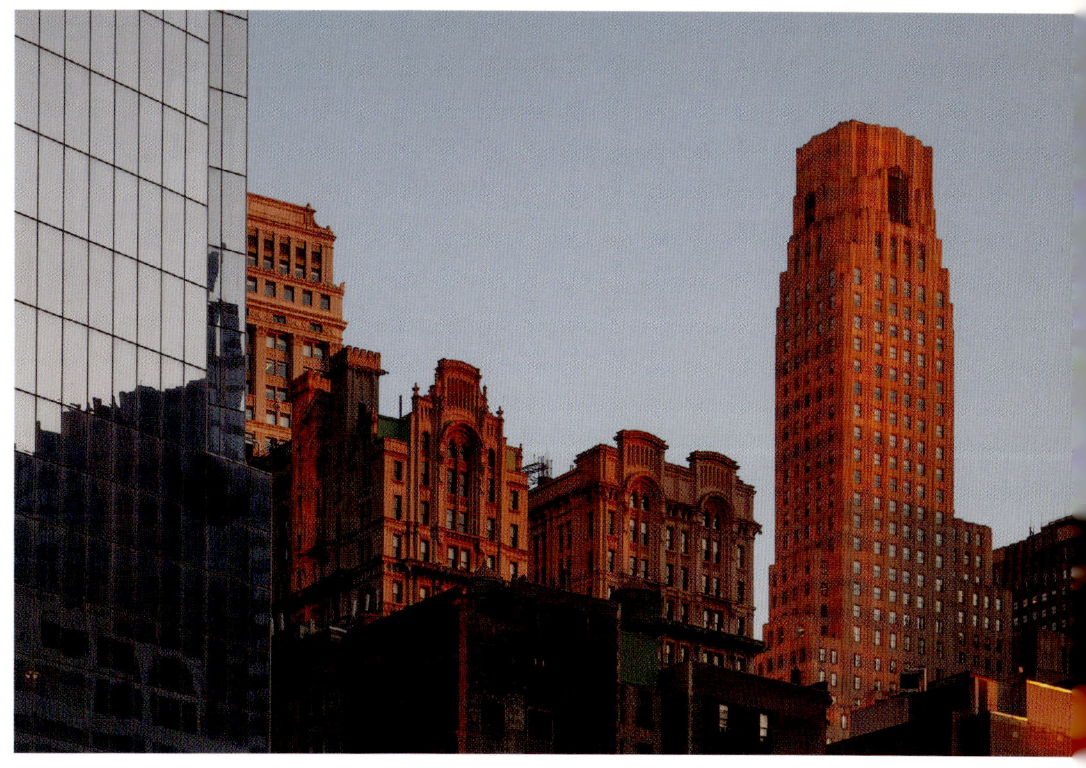

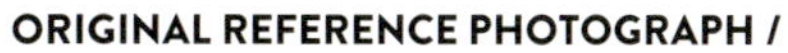

ORIGINAL REFERENCE PHOTOGRAPH /
TAKEN BY MY FATHER, STEVE KURTZ

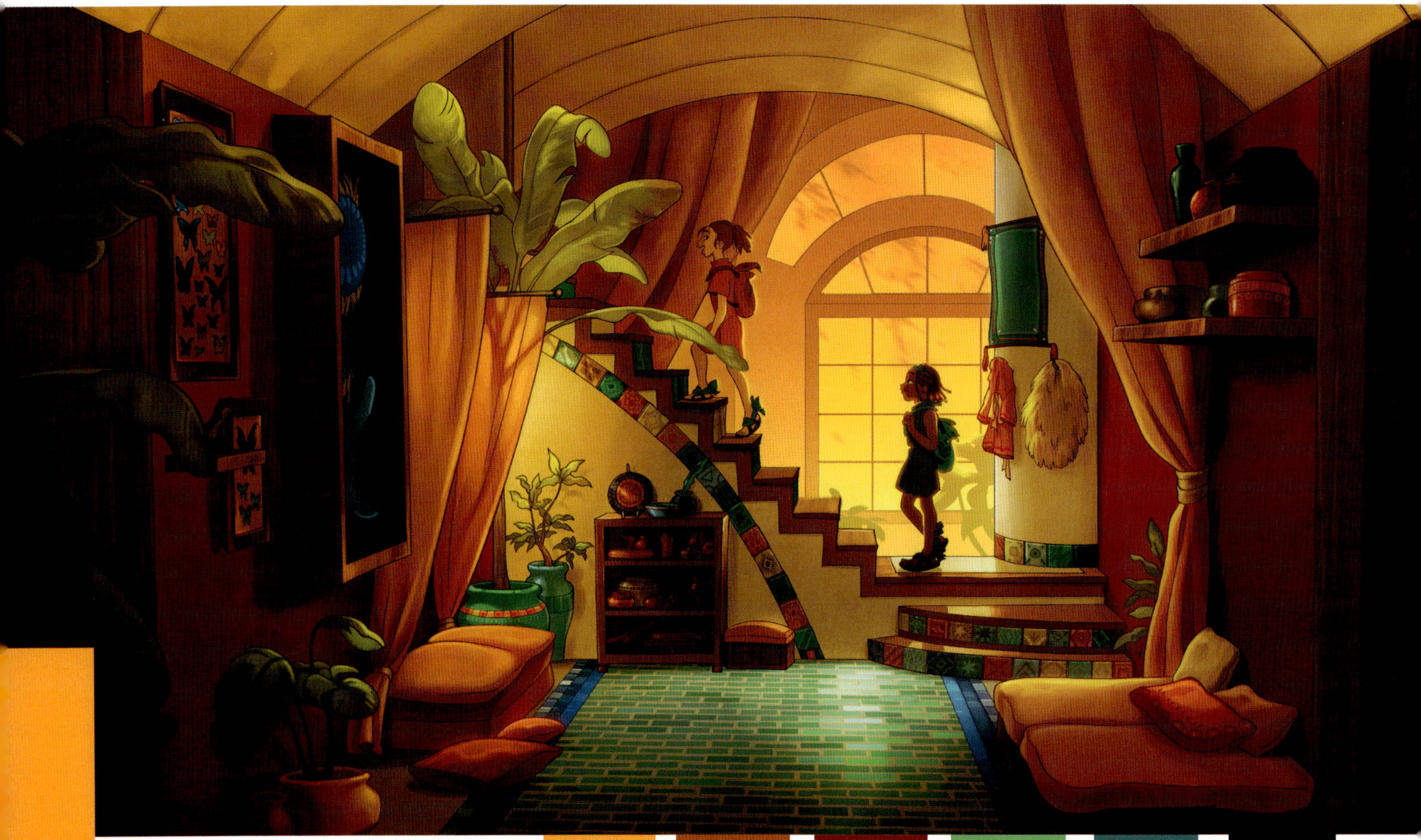

DEVELOPING A COLOR SCHEME FOR A PROJECT

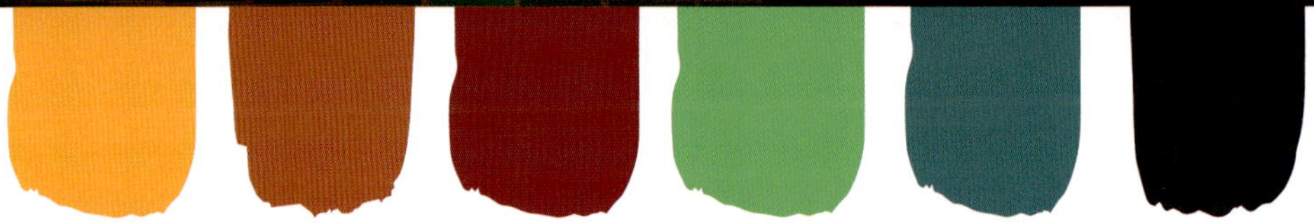

When I start a new project, whether it's a graphic novel, a location design for a TV show, or a series of illustrations, I begin by establishing a cohesive color palette to tie the subsequent images together. Creating cohesive color palettes that maintain interest and feel consistent is often a multi-step process. First, I push colors close enough together so that they feel unified. Then, I pull each one away slowly, just a bit at a time, until the palette is unique and varied enough to be interesting.

RUA AND MIA HEADING OUT FOR SCHOOL /
PHOTOSHOP, 2019
This palette consists of earthy greens, reds, golds, and browns with pops of saturated blue. In each design within the series, I allowed a different color from the palette to take center stage, while maintaining an overall cohesion. Here, gold warmth spreads from floor to ceiling.

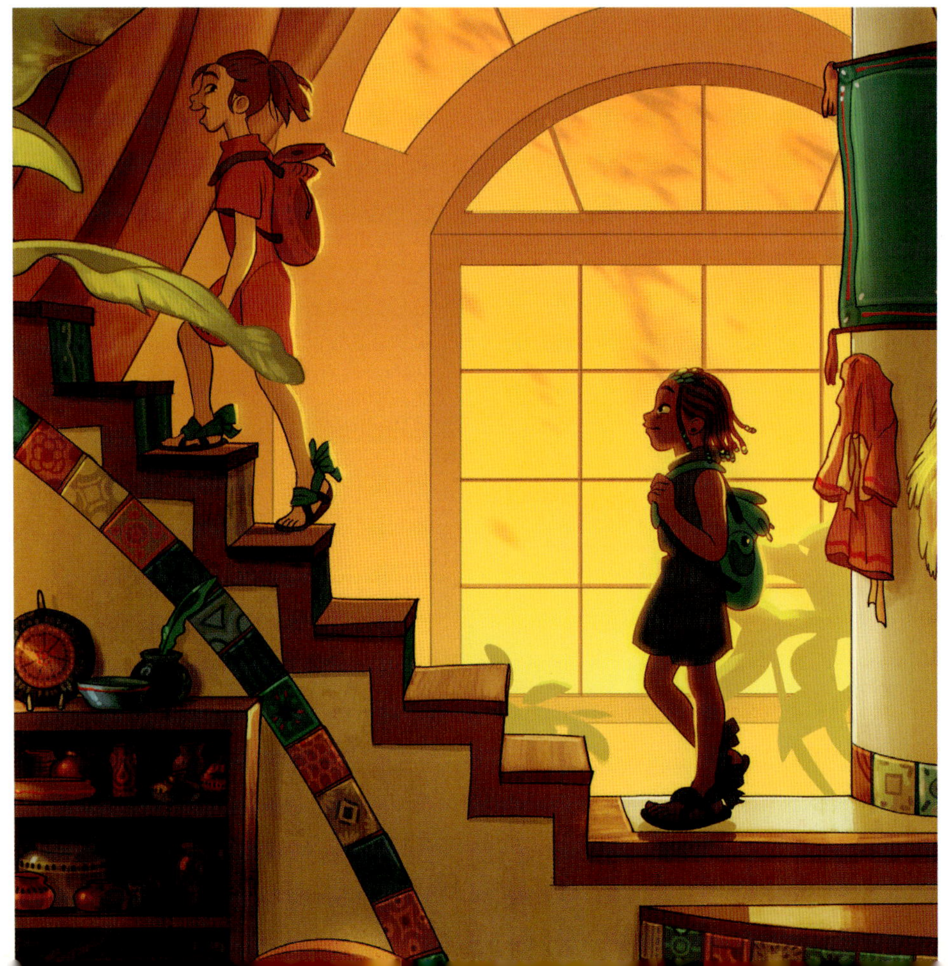

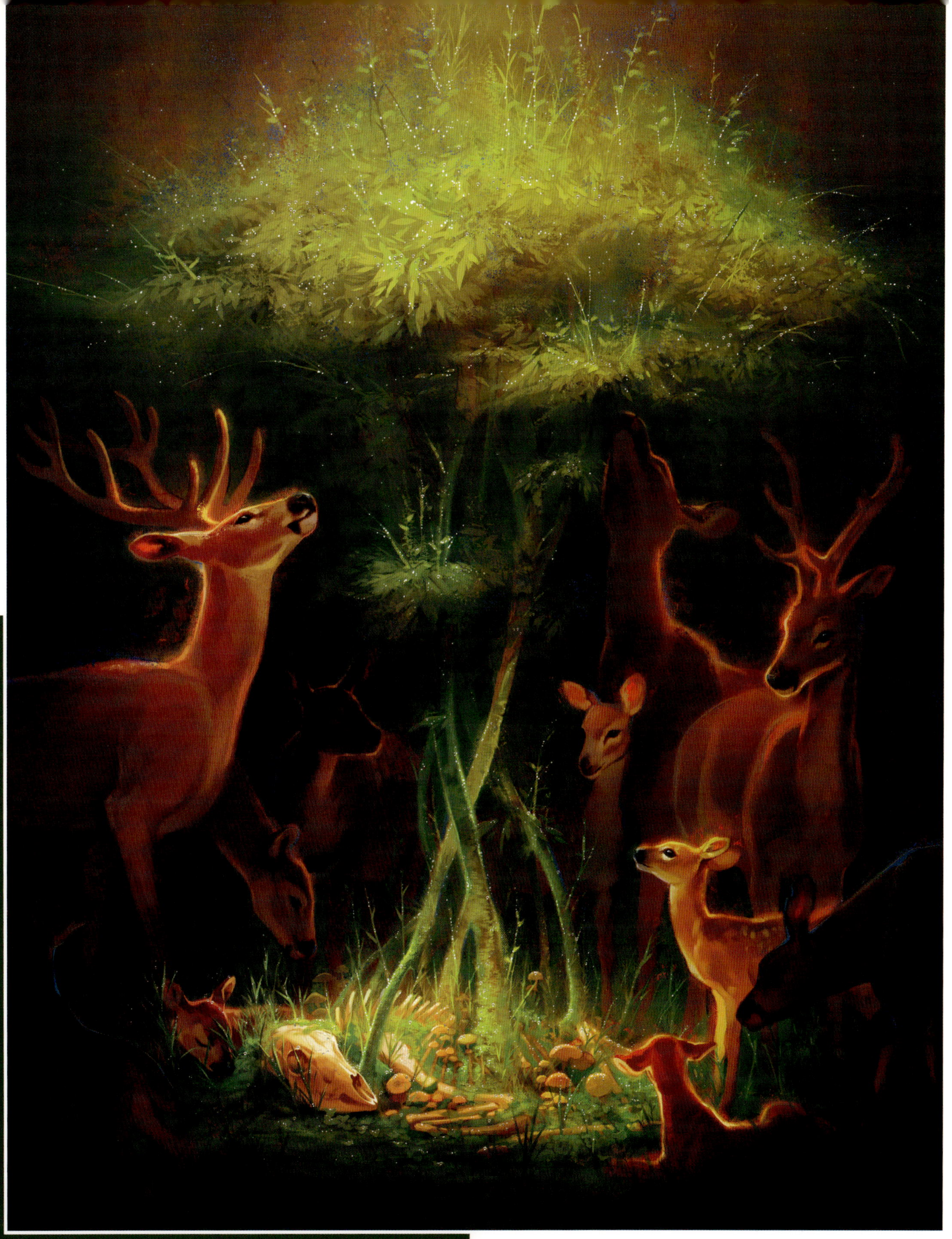

MATRIARCH / PHOTOSHOP, 2020

Adding contrast to small details with pops of bright colors prevents the image becoming stale and repetitive. Greens are used heavily here and balanced with warm brown, while yellow functions as an accent to highlight the bones. This color statement can be seen in all images created as part of this project, including *Restoration* on page 22 as well as *Reunion* and *Reclamation* on page 37.

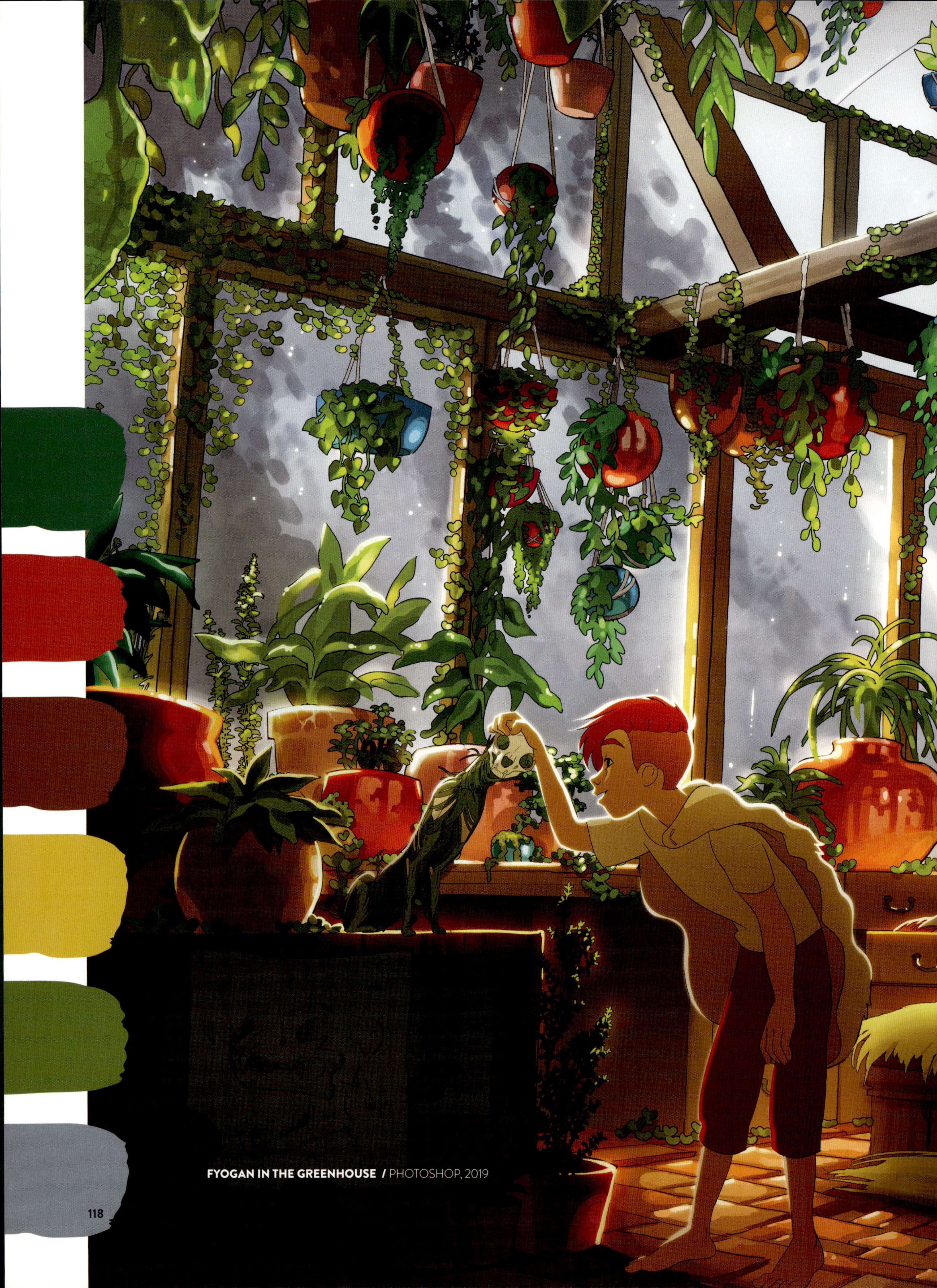

FYOGAN IN THE GREENHOUSE / PHOTOSHOP, 2019

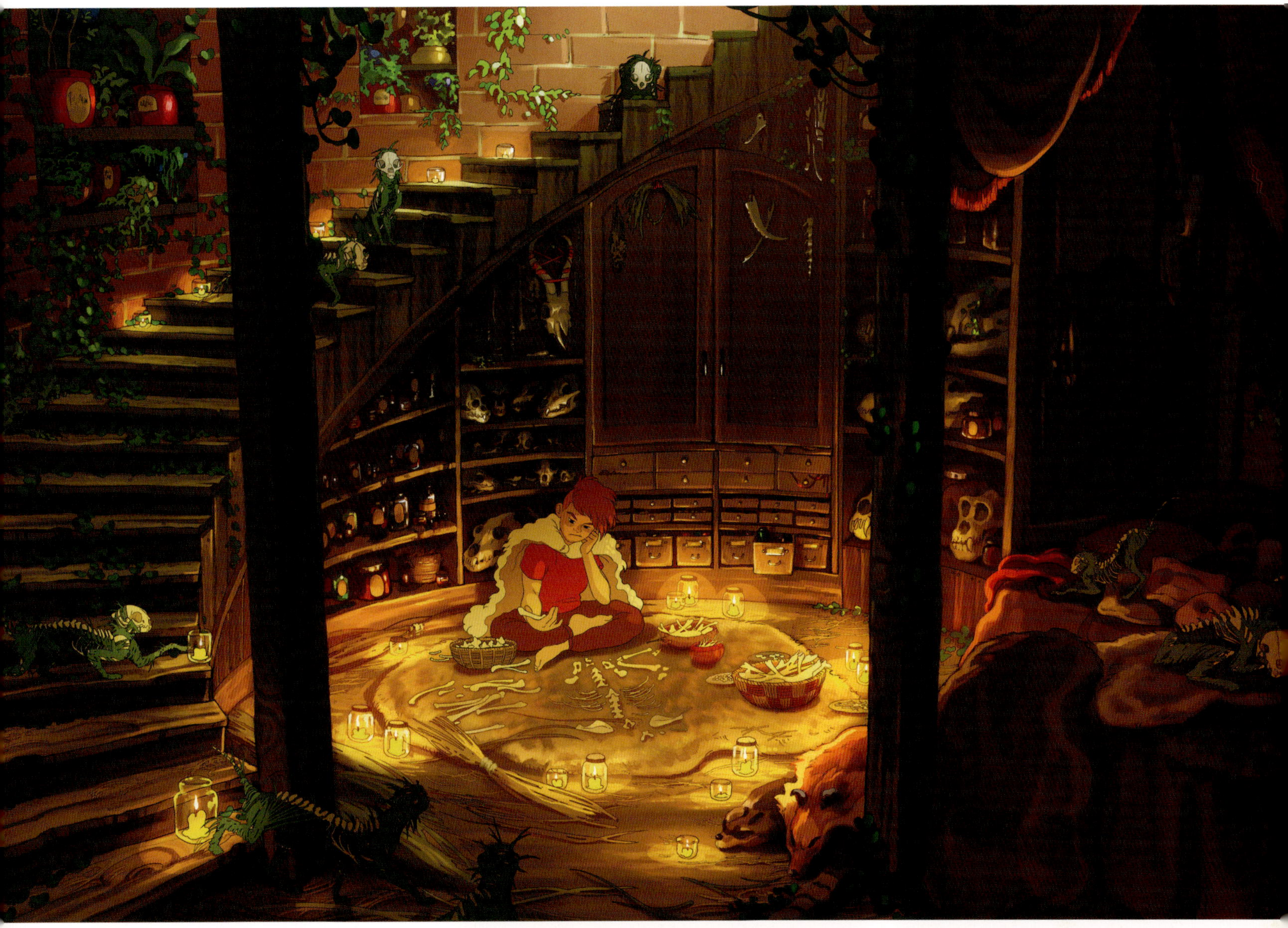

FYOGAN'S WORKSHOP / PHOTOSHOP, 2019

I always establish the local colors for the biggest elements in an environment first, then color the smaller details. I keep each major element on its own layer. This layering structure allows me to block in color without agonizing over each decision. Once everything is filled with color and the overall tone is established, I adjust each color individually until I'm happy with the overall composition.

I often use adjustment layers in Photoshop, such as Selective Color or Color Balance, to adjust colors globally. I then clip the adjustment layer to each major object to maintain the layer structure of the piece. When painting small decorative details, I often select the area and apply a Hue/Saturation adjustment layer, then slide the hue scale around wildly to see if there are any potentially fun pops of color I might be missing!

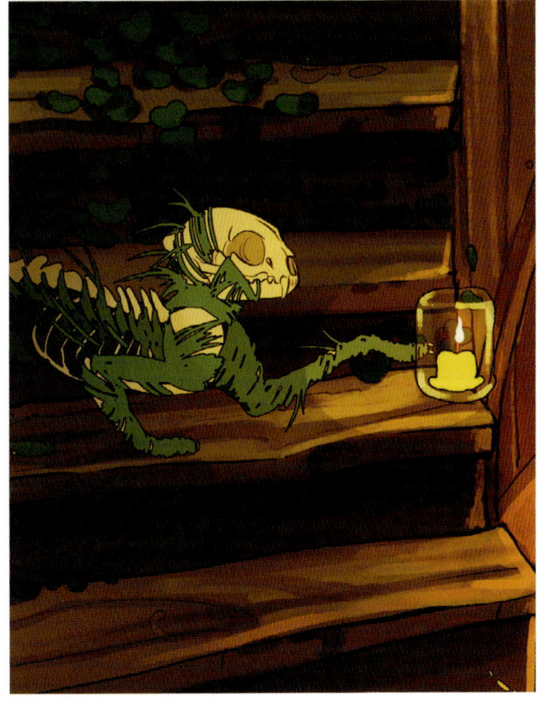

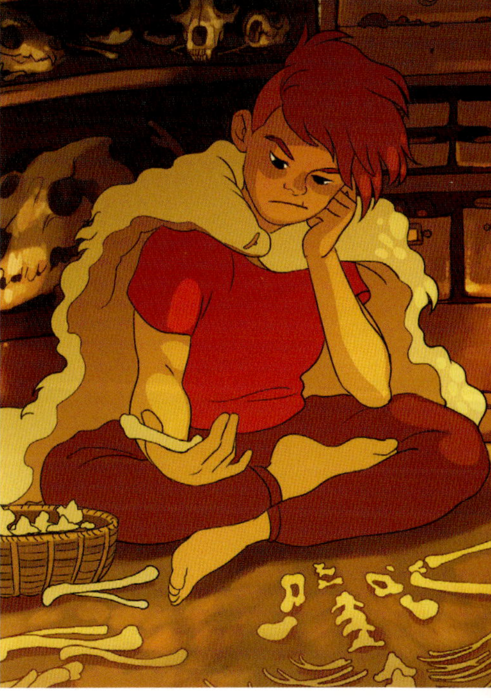

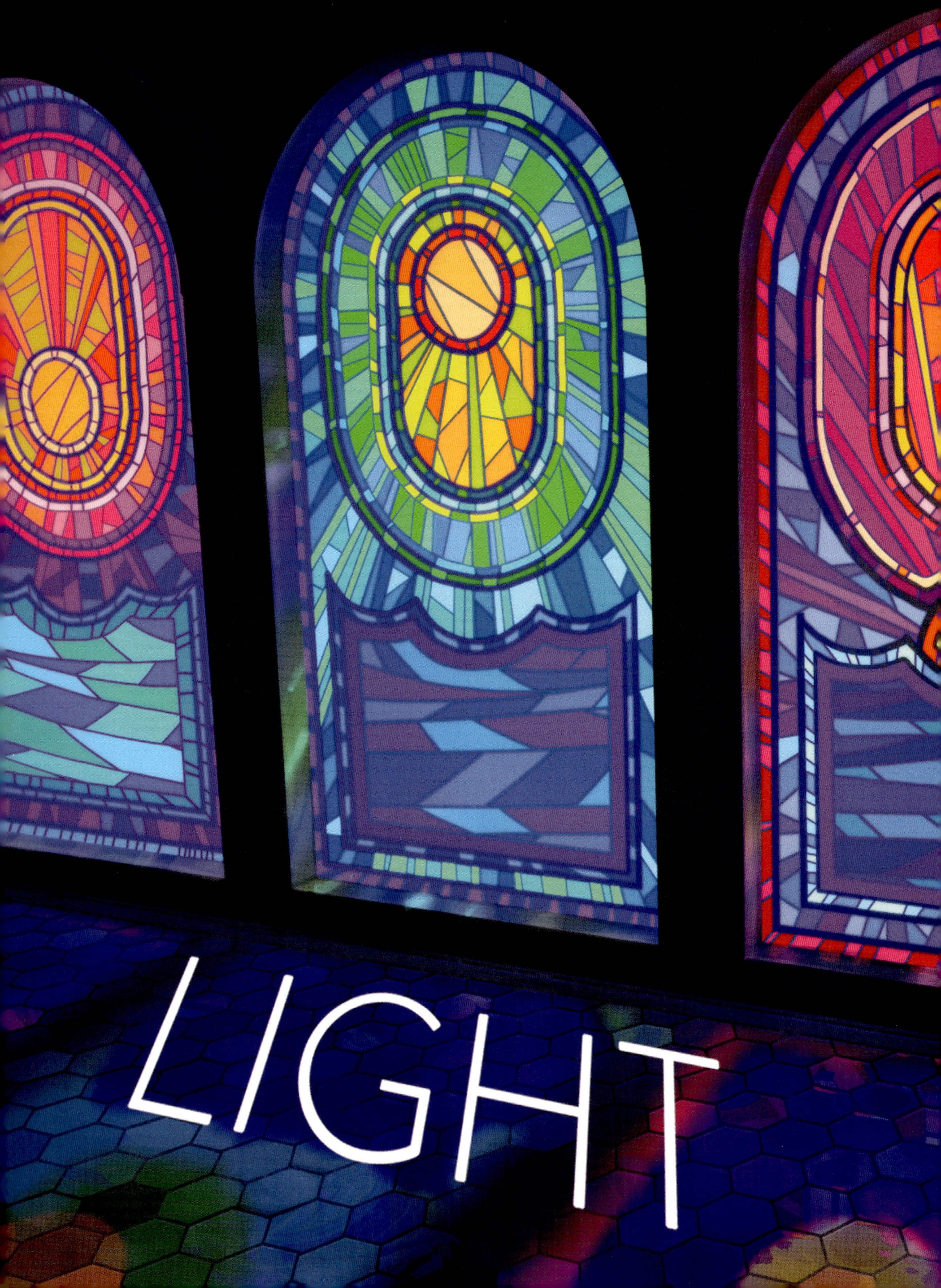
LIGHT

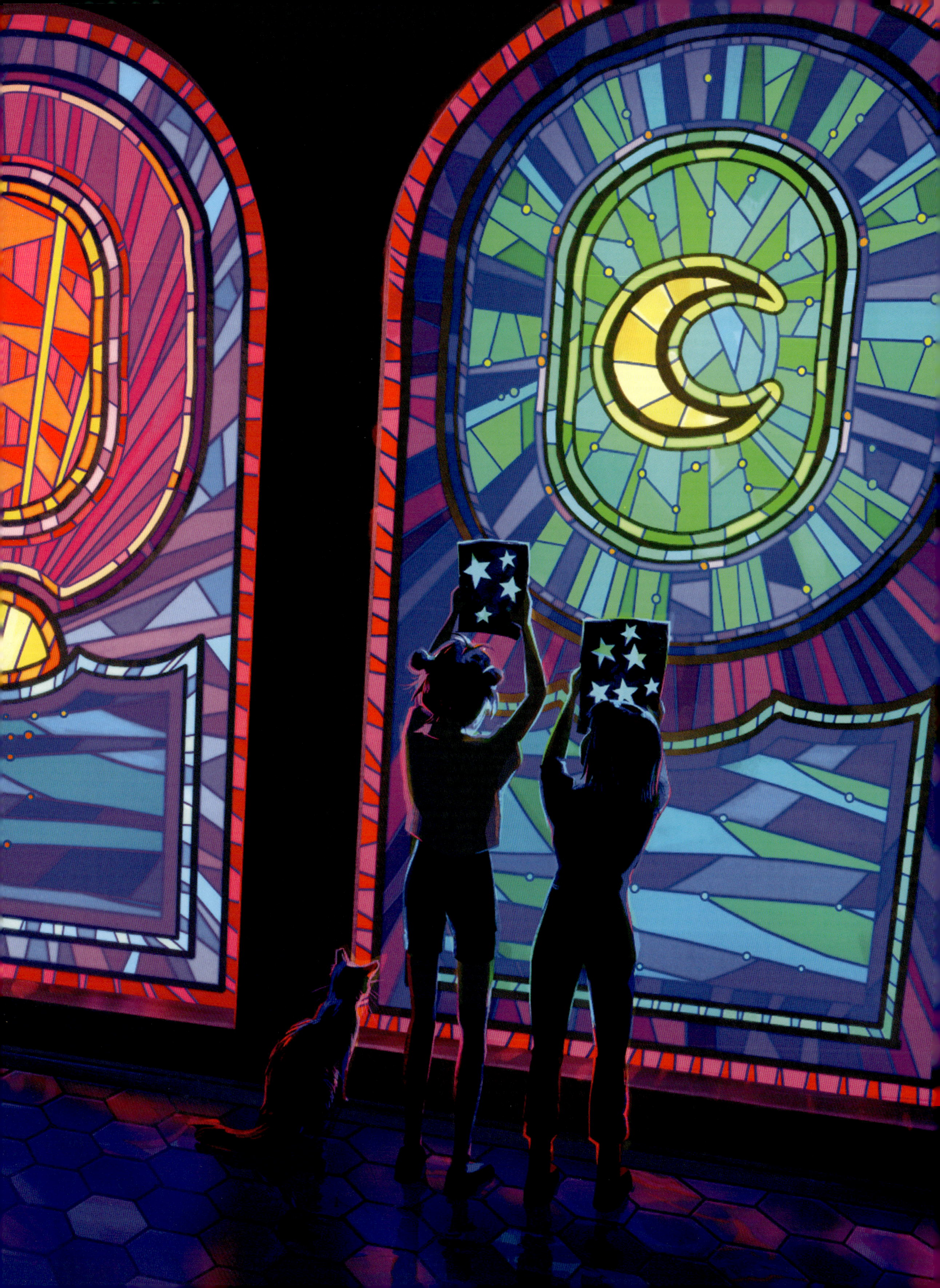

INITIAL EXPLORATION

During the same time period that I spent studying color, I also studied light. The two are tied to one another inextricably. In the total absence of light, neither form nor color can be seen. Through light, form and volume can be depicted using color applied to the canvas.

Growing up, I always did my best to color and light my images in a believable way, but often fell short because I was relying on uninformed guesses. I didn't understand the physics of how light works. I spent too much time over-rendering in search of the right combination of hues and tones that would read as an accurately shaded form. What I was doing was more akin to memorizing multiplication tables, instead of learning how to multiply in the first place.

A turning point for me was when I learned, through my high-school art teacher, that I could test light and shadow out myself, at any time, using materials from around my house. I had this breakthrough around the age of fifteen, and promptly spent an entire weekend playing with flashlights, lamps, and cereal boxes. I didn't know the technical terms for anything I was discovering, but have since put more technical names to this intuited knowledge.

My discoveries came to me in the following order:

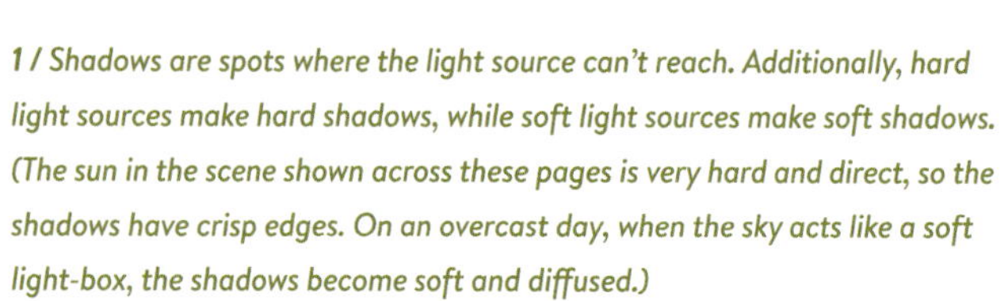

1 / Shadows are spots where the light source can't reach. Additionally, hard light sources make hard shadows, while soft light sources make soft shadows. (The sun in the scene shown across these pages is very hard and direct, so the shadows have crisp edges. On an overcast day, when the sky acts like a soft light-box, the shadows become soft and diffused.)

2 / Unless it is nighttime, there are always secondary light sources.

3 / Light bounces off surfaces and onto surrounding objects; as it does this, it picks up the color of the surface it has bounced off.

4 / Certain types of materials are more reflective than others, and smooth surfaces tend to reflect brighter, harder highlights than rough surfaces.

5 / Light enters semi-translucent forms, bounces around inside, and creates a saturated glow called "subsurface scattering."

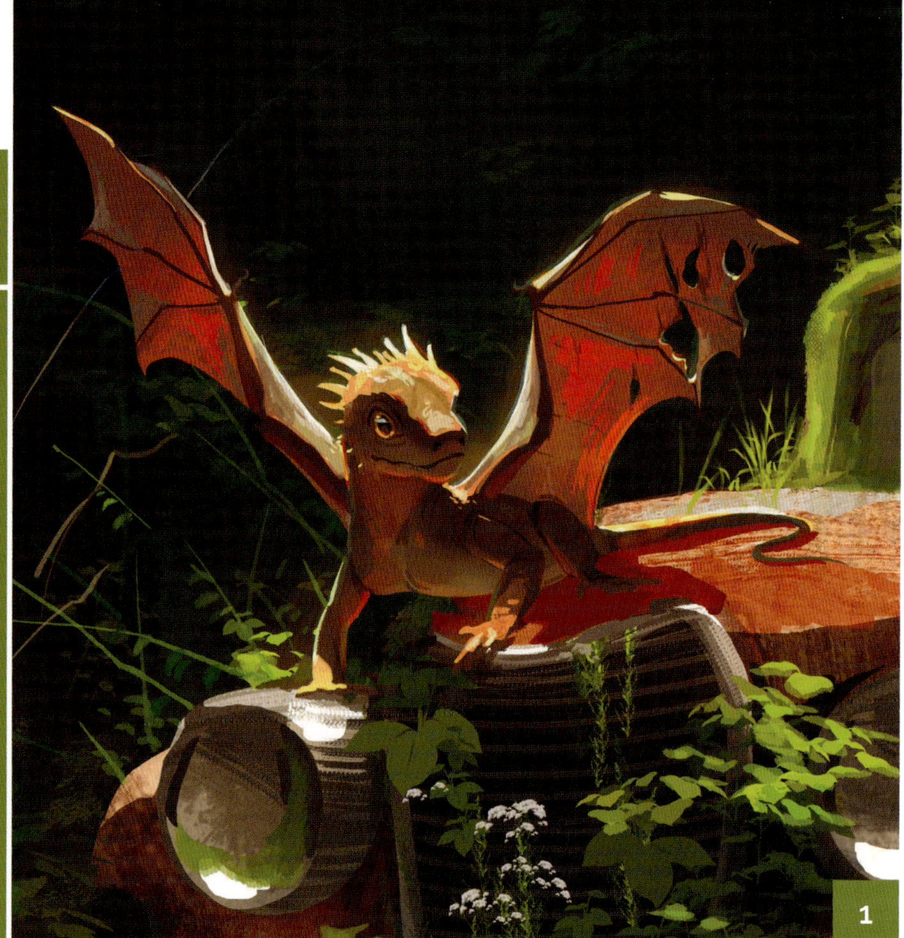

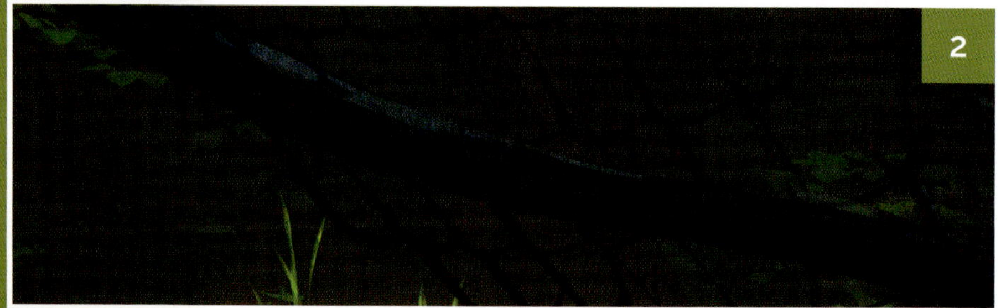

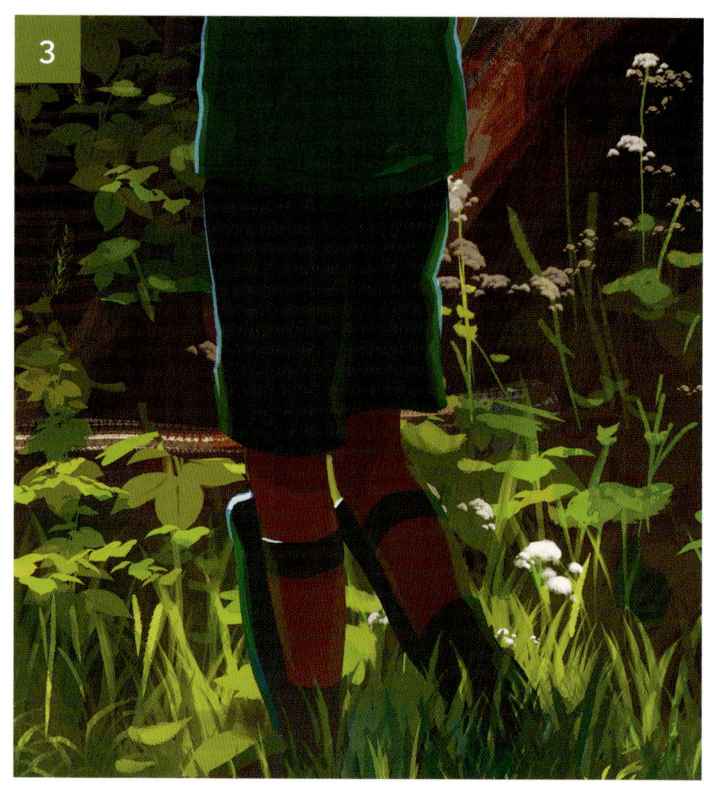

The five bitesize pieces of information described on the previous page form the basic equations for how I decode the world around me and do "light math" to reasonably guess how imaginary scenes would look in reality. I started calling the process "light math" back in high school and the term stuck with me because it's exactly how it feels.

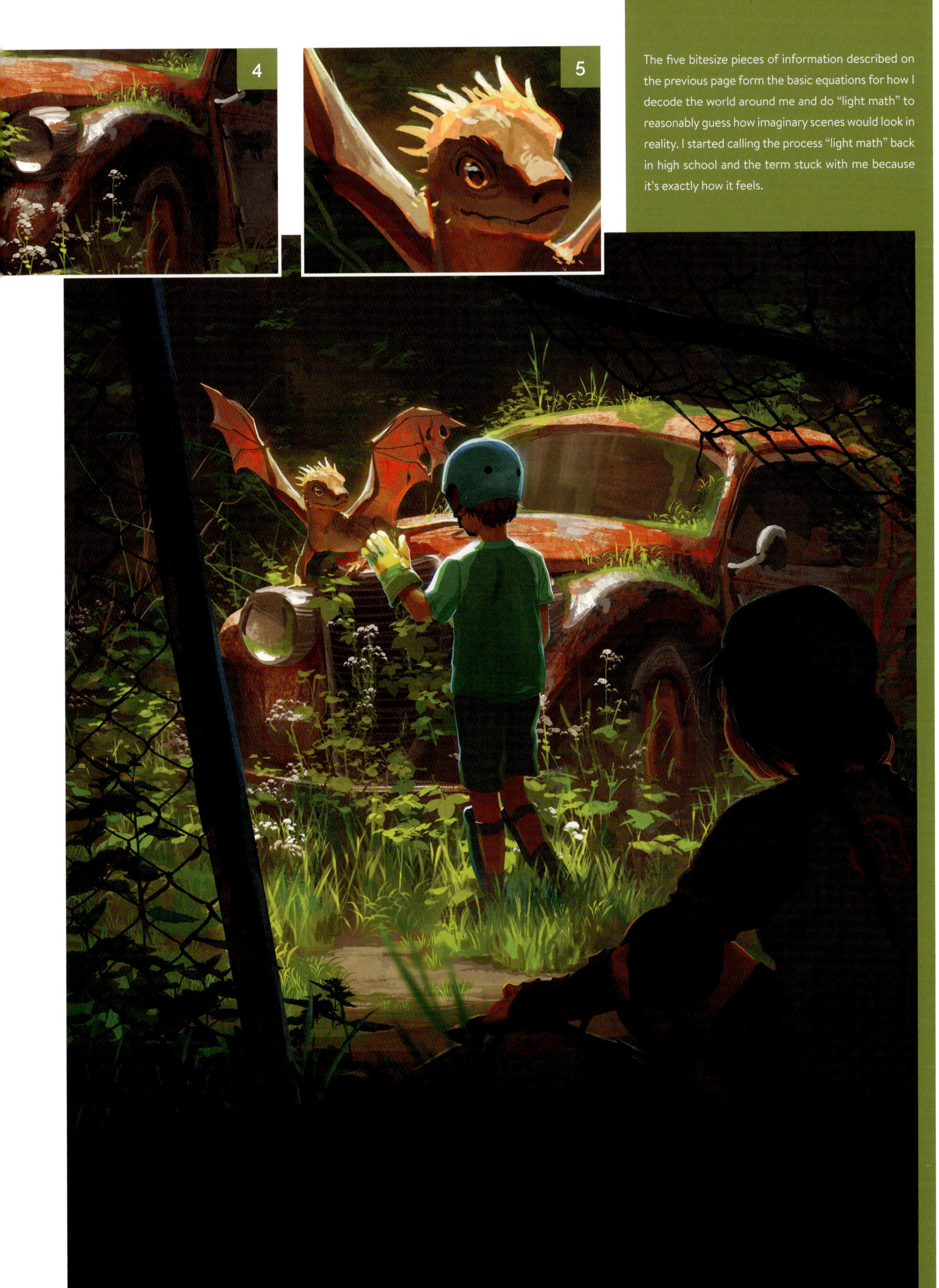

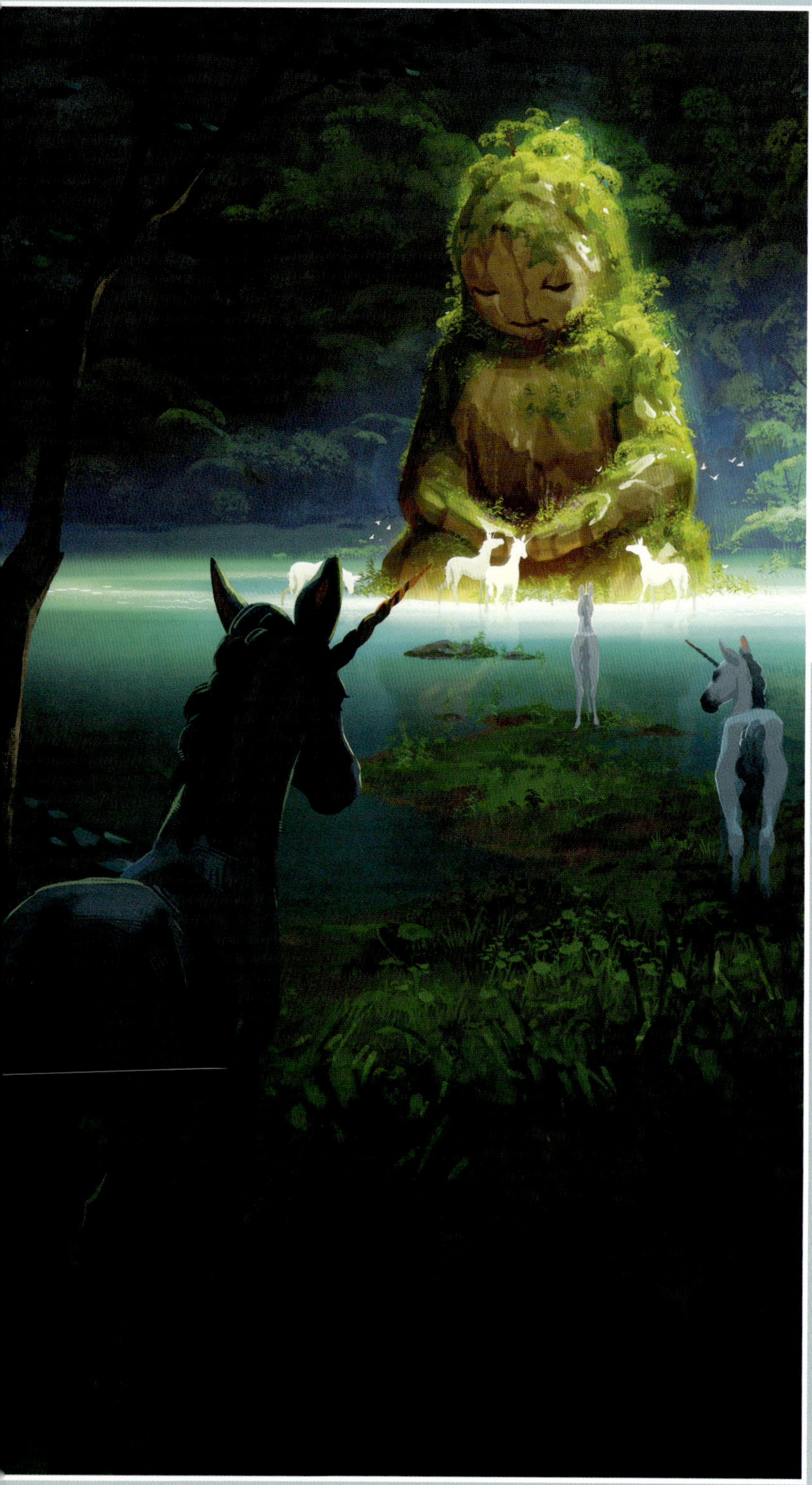

LIGHT MATH

The following equations aren't scientifically accurate; they are only intended to be used as a guide to what goes into the lighting of a complex scene. Understanding the physics of lighting helps build believability in the pursuit of better illustrations. Here, I use percentages to describe the levels of brightness in each scene.

EQUATION A

The equation I follow for the piece on the left is 80% direct white sunlight at a three-quarter angle + 10% diffused blue sky light + 20% diffused warm bounce light. The image features a strong band of neutral sunlight at 80% brightness falling across three-quarters of the giant. The sunlight bounces off the reflective water surface and diffuses in the process, bouncing a soft 20% bounce light up into the underside of the giant's hand. A cool, diffused sky light at about 10% brightness can also be seen, which, coupled with bounce light, defines everything seen in the shadows.

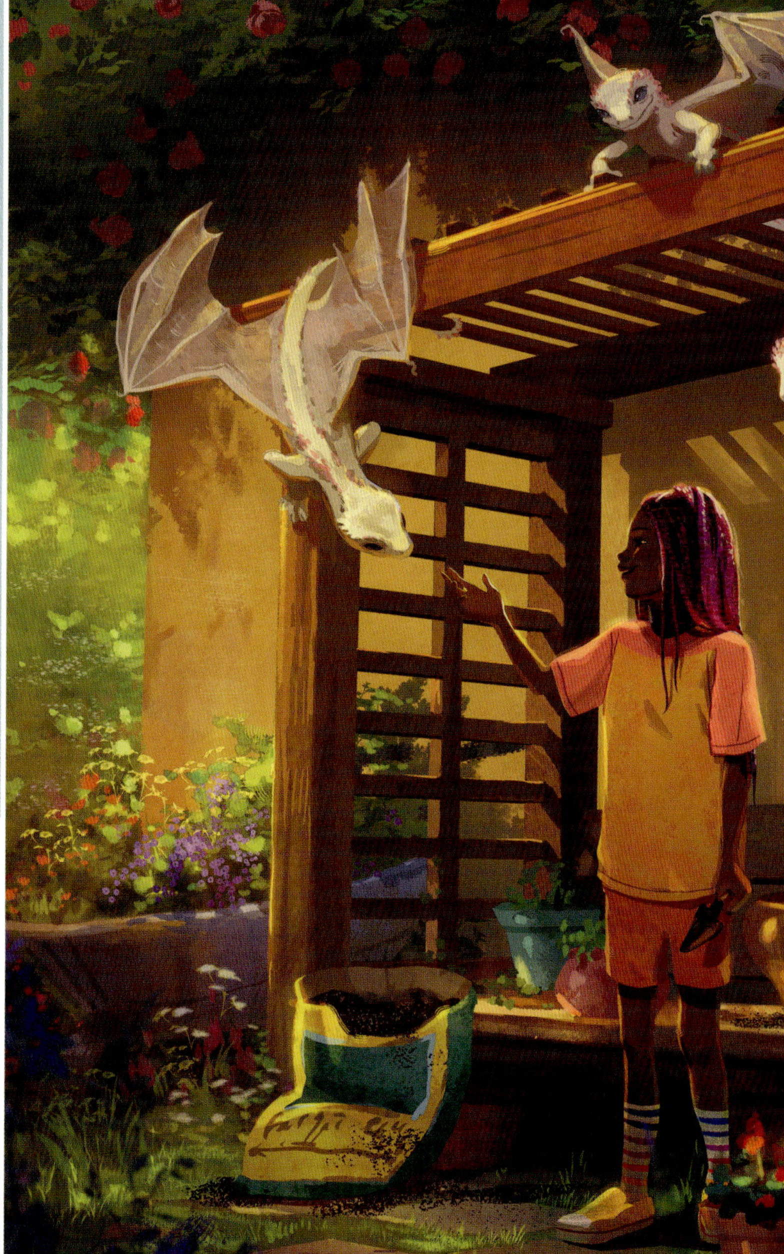

EQUATION B

The equation I use here is 60% warm sunlight at a three-quarter angle + warm bounce light at around 15%. In this middle image the warm afternoon sunlight at about 60% brightness creates cast shadows in a diagonal to the right. The girl's hair reflects a bright rim light along with the pots and the bag of soil. Bounce light can be seen picking up the pink from the girl's shirt onto the underside of her braids, as well as from the bench onto the underside of the pots, both at around 15% brightness.

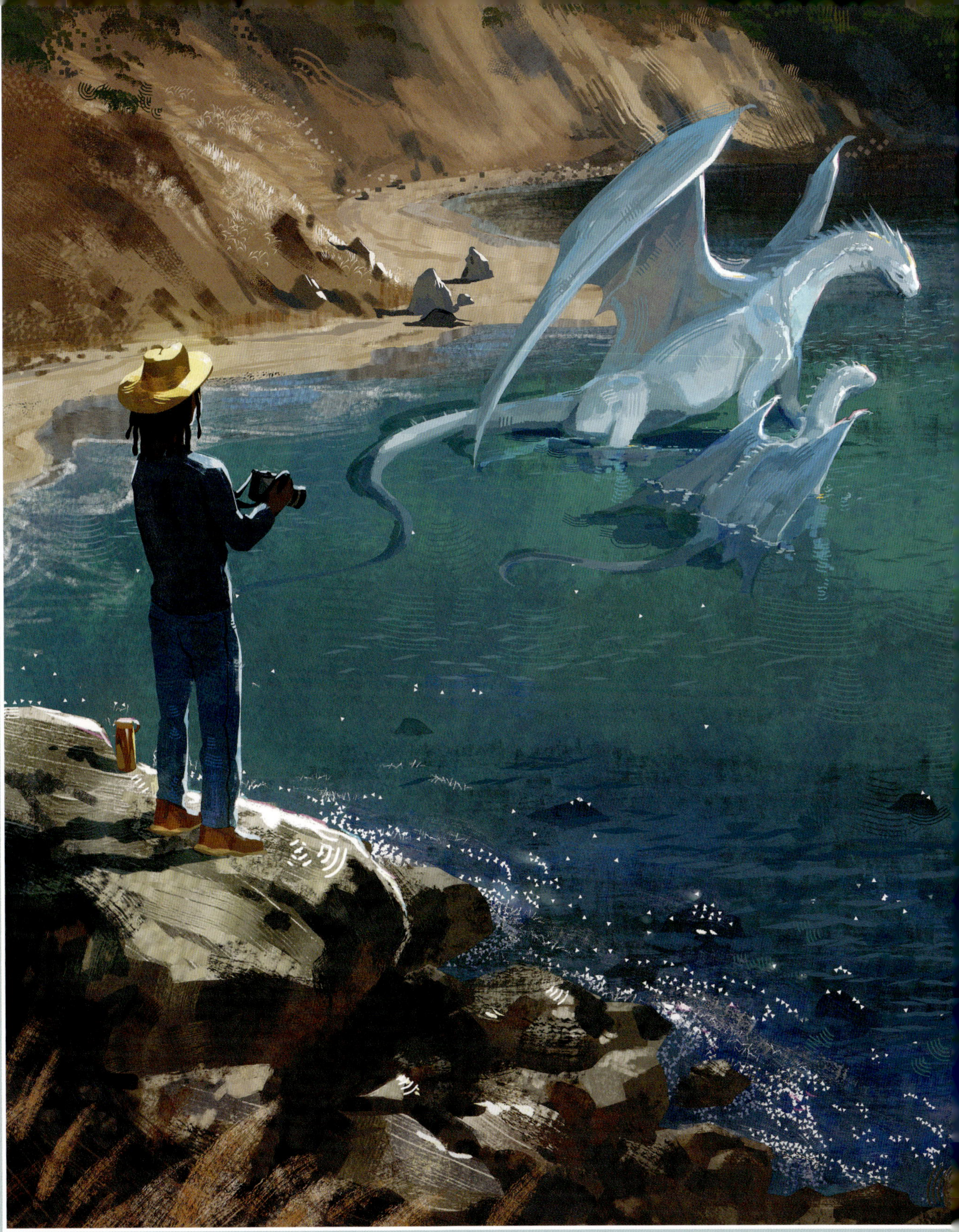

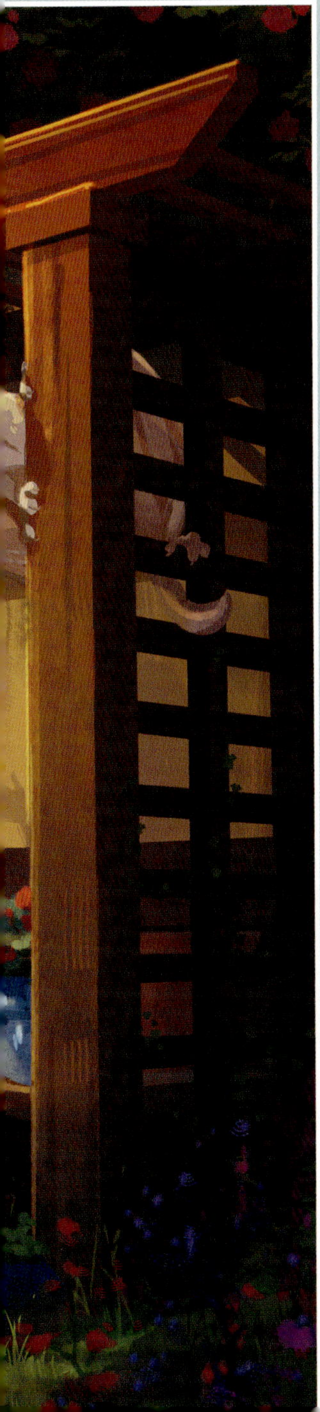

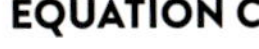

EQUATION C

My equation for this setting is 90% direct neutral sunlight at a high angle + 20% warm bounce light + 15% diffused blue sky light . The painting above features a bright 90% noon light coming down from high in the sky at a very slight angle, at perhaps a 1pm position in the sky. The bright light creates a glow on the rocks, and bounces at 20% brightness off them onto the underside of surrounding rocks as well as the man's body. The hard light on the brim of the hat also causes bounce light to reflect onto the sides. The influence of a 15% cool sky light can be seen in the cool cast shadow formed by the man's legs.

A WINDOW INTO / CAPTURING LIGHT

In 2017, I spent a lot of time at the San Diego Zoo and Wild Animal Park watching the lions bask in the Southern California sun. I watched how their manes picked up bright rims of golden light as the sun dipped lower on the horizon. I noticed how I struggled to focus my eyes on their blinding sunlit backs during high noon. I did a lot of lion paintings during this time period, trying to capture some of what I was observing as I watched them.

1 / FILLING THE DARKS

I like to start my light studies by filling in my darkest darks first, using whatever my equivalent of black is going to be in the image. I usually steer clear of introducing a true black in this type of painting, as my focus is often on illumination. If I have a readable silhouette and composition at this stage, I take it as a good sign for the success of the painting.

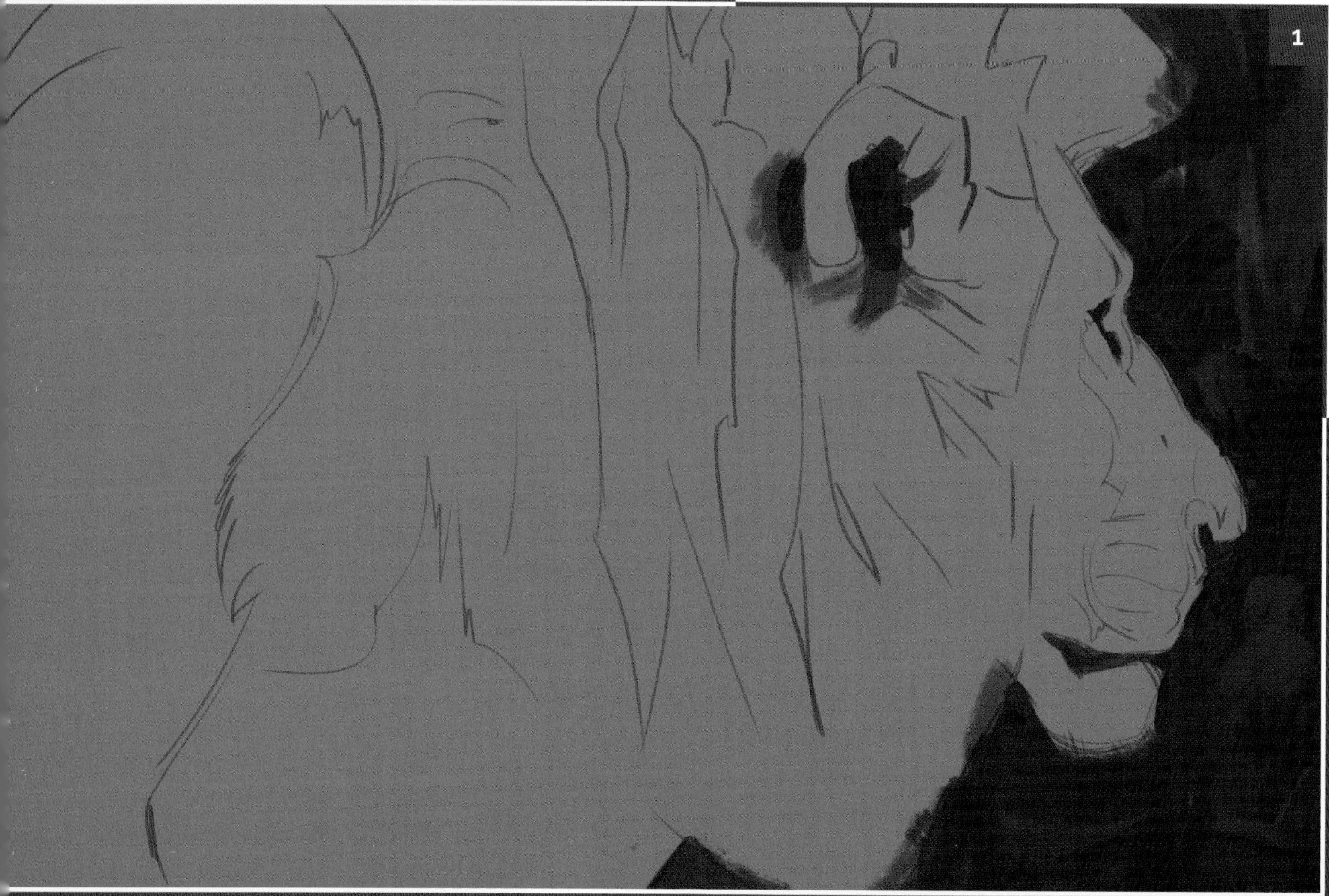

1

2 / PAINTERLY SHADOWS

I tend to render my shadow areas using soft painterly brushes. I like to have hard-edged highlights and soft, washy shadows. I try to introduce a lot of variation in tone and hue at this stage, because the brightest highlights will be fairly monotone and compressed. I leave the highlight zones blank at this point.

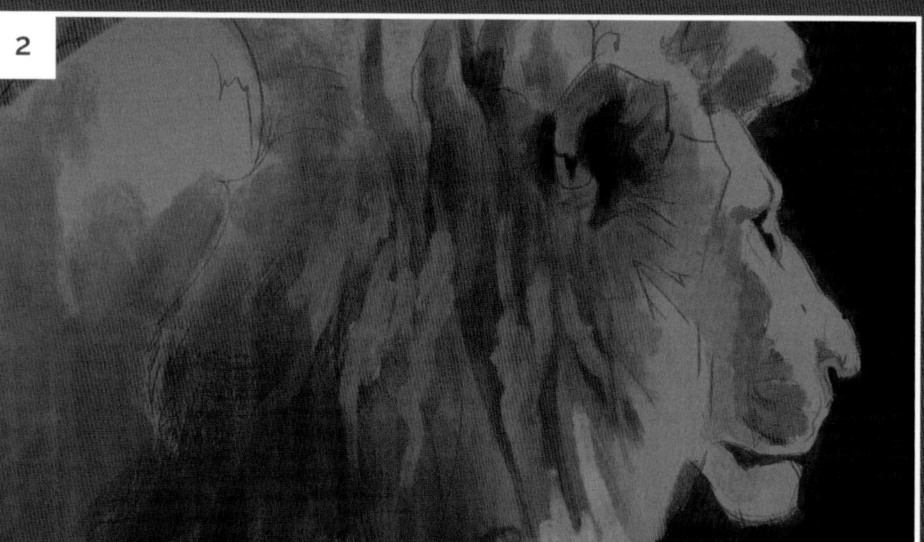
2

3 / HIGHLIGHTS

The next step is to add highlights. This step makes the most dramatic change in the painting. It's hard to believe that all that has been added between steps 2 and 3 is a single layer of opaque yellow highlight. Because I use essentially a single color here, I focus all of my attention on capturing texture and volume. This narrow focus allows me to study how light interacts with each surface in an attentive way.

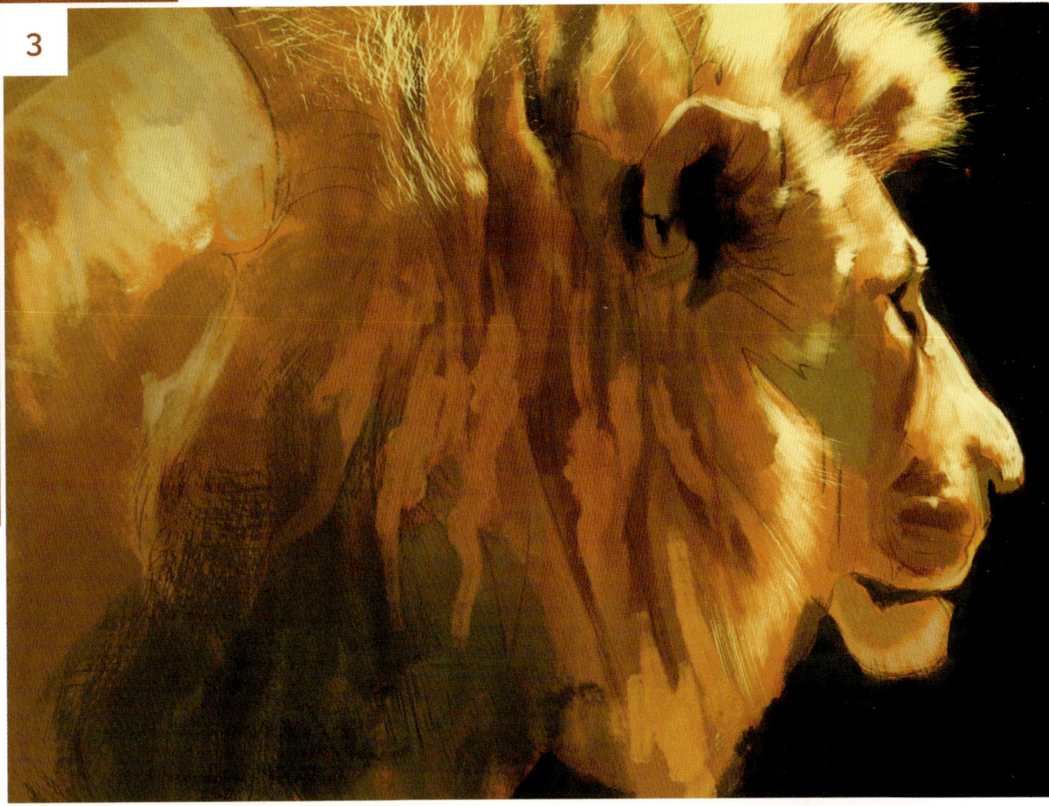

4 / FINAL TOUCHES

During the final rendering pass, I add little details such as hairs catching light, specular highlights, and little glowing light bloom effects (more on this later) on shiny elements such as whiskers. This step is the final polish, but you can see the work is largely accomplished during step 3.

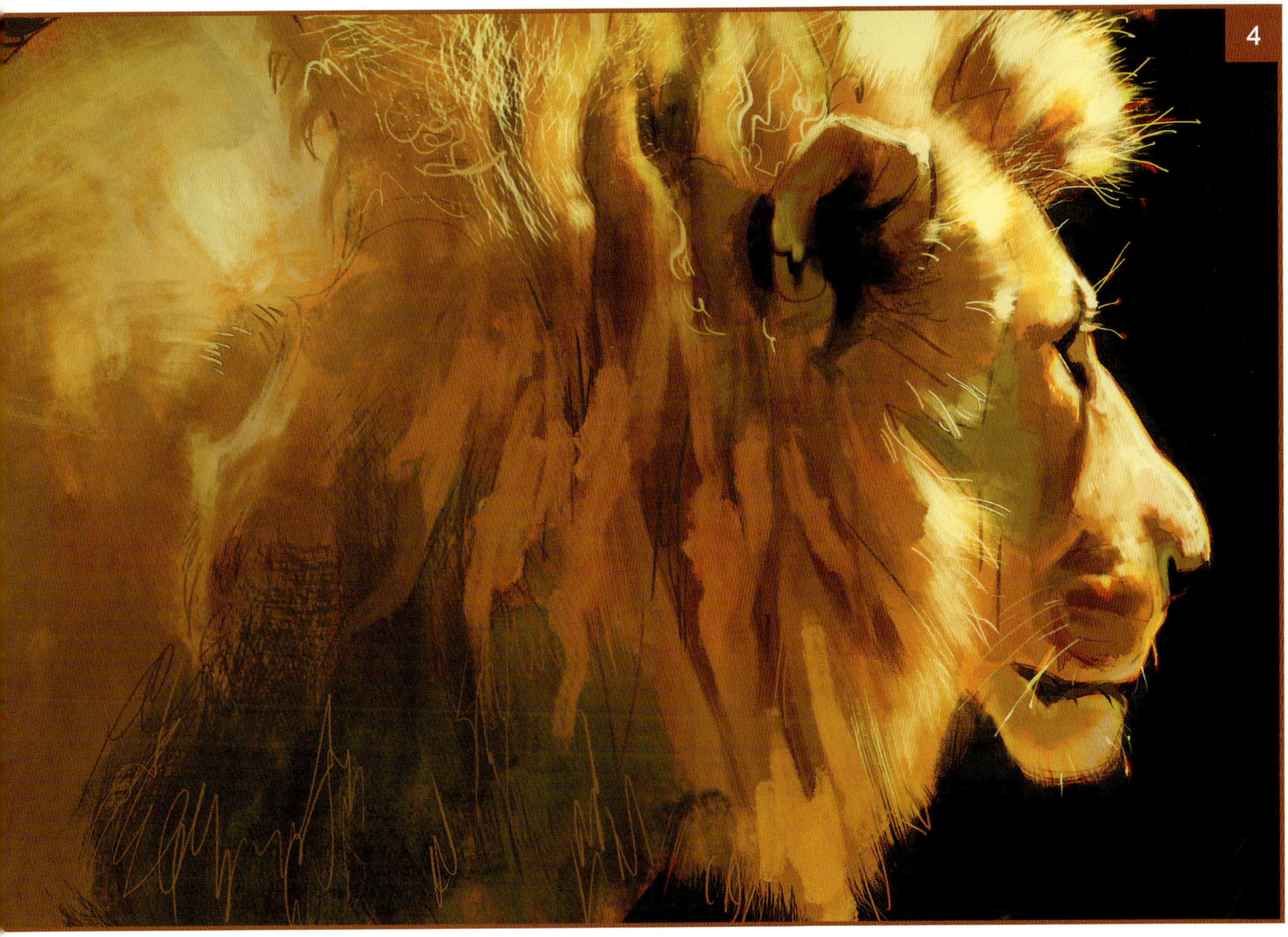

4

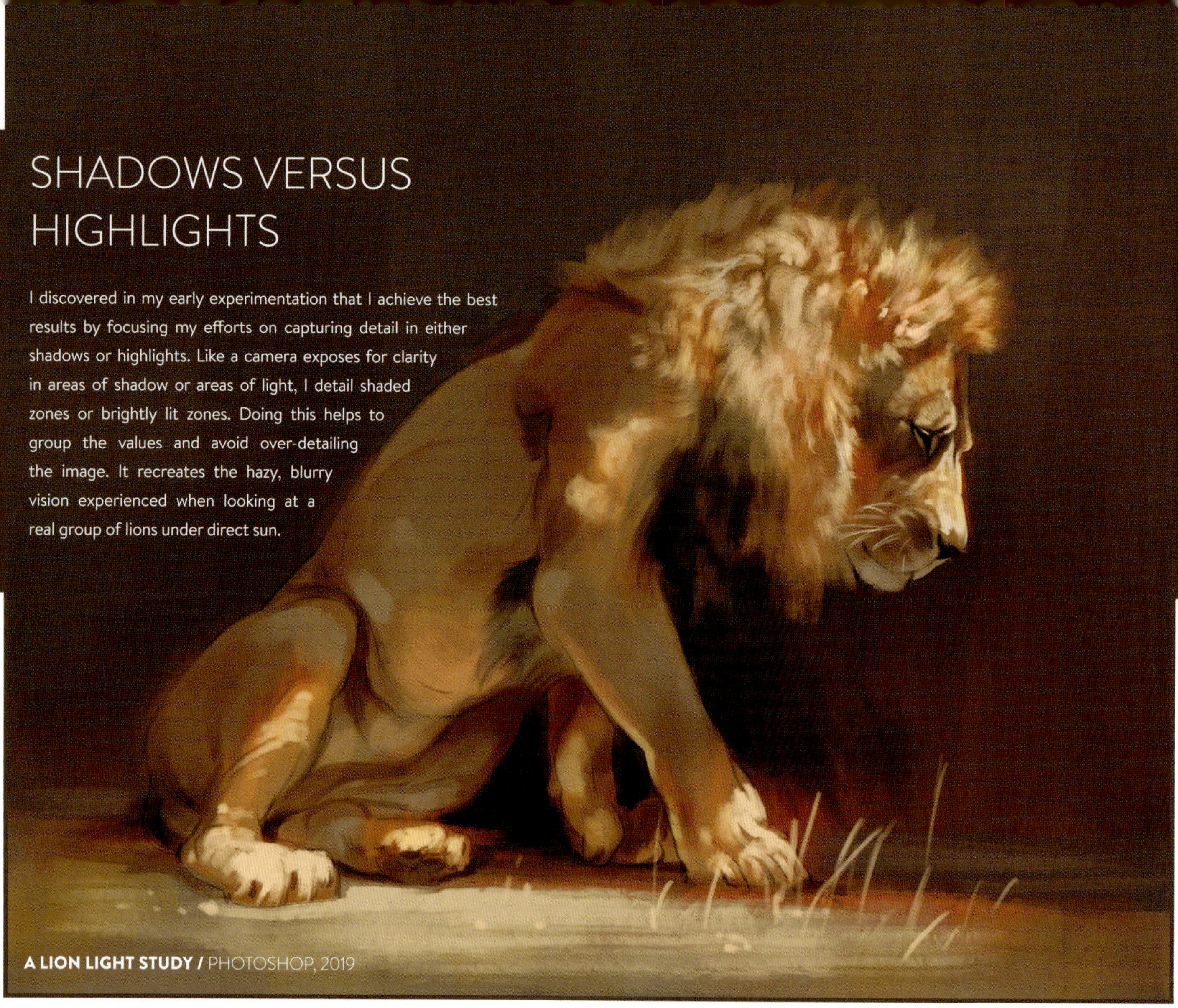

SHADOWS VERSUS HIGHLIGHTS

I discovered in my early experimentation that I achieve the best results by focusing my efforts on capturing detail in either shadows or highlights. Like a camera exposes for clarity in areas of shadow or areas of light, I detail shaded zones or brightly lit zones. Doing this helps to group the values and avoid over-detailing the image. It recreates the hazy, blurry vision experienced when looking at a real group of lions under direct sun.

A LION LIGHT STUDY / PHOTOSHOP, 2019

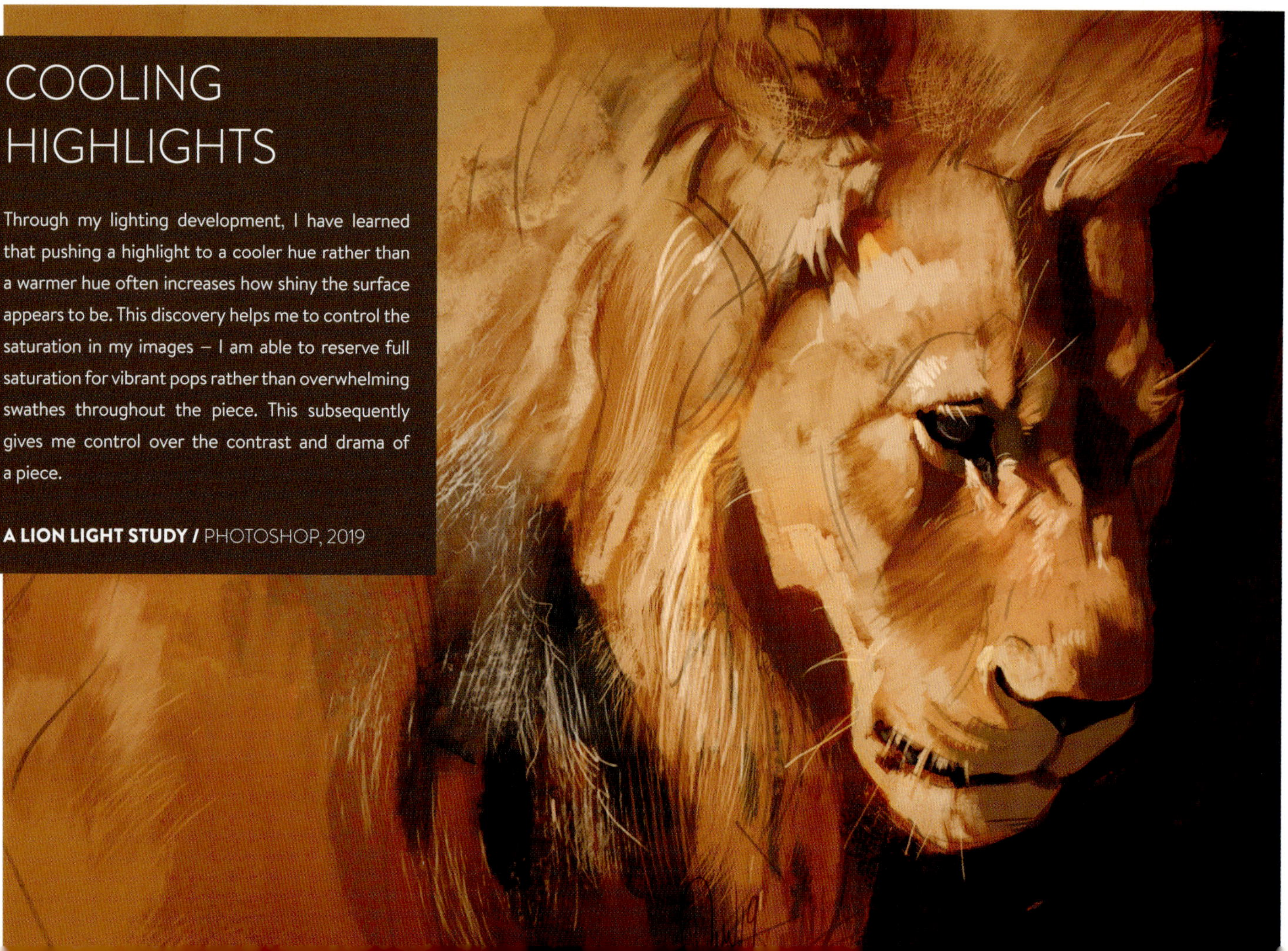

COOLING HIGHLIGHTS

Through my lighting development, I have learned that pushing a highlight to a cooler hue rather than a warmer hue often increases how shiny the surface appears to be. This discovery helps me to control the saturation in my images – I am able to reserve full saturation for vibrant pops rather than overwhelming swathes throughout the piece. This subsequently gives me control over the contrast and drama of a piece.

A LION LIGHT STUDY / PHOTOSHOP, 2019

LIGHT BLOOM

Another lighting technique I discovered is a phenomenon sometimes referred to as "light bloom." I like this term and think it is quite descriptive, as light bloom is the glow-like effect created when areas of a scene are very brightly lit. I create light bloom by painting a soft and vibrant halo of saturated color outside the edge of a brightly lit form. This helps the highlight appear even brighter, and helps to ease the transition into whatever is behind the object.

This effect creates a blown-out look, as if our eyes or a camera can't depict the sheer brightness of a surface without bleeding that light into the surrounding space. This effect becomes even more potent when the particles in an atmosphere are increased – think of car headlights or a traffic light illuminating fog.

A SWAN LIGHT STUDY / PHOTOSHOP, 2017

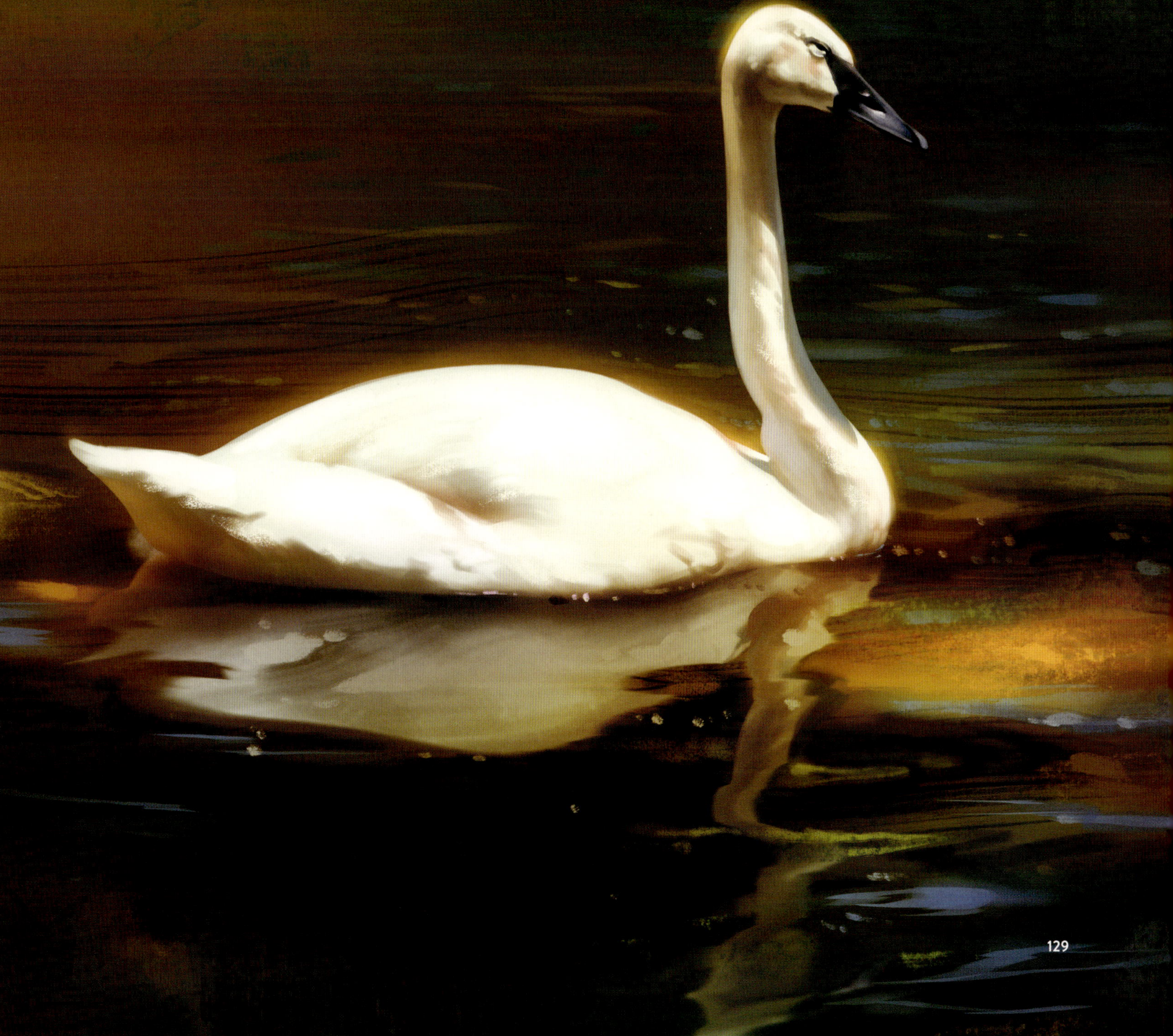

RIM LIGHTING

When a light shines brightly from behind a subject, an outline of light, also known as rim light or back light, can be seen. This effect is perfect for creating contrast and interest around the silhouette of a character or object. Often, drawing the eye toward the silhouette of a character is a primary concern in my compositions. Rim lighting is an easy and impactful way to achieve this, and it is quite beautiful to look at. When it is illuminating hair or fur through subsurface scattering, rim lighting offers an especially dazzling effect.

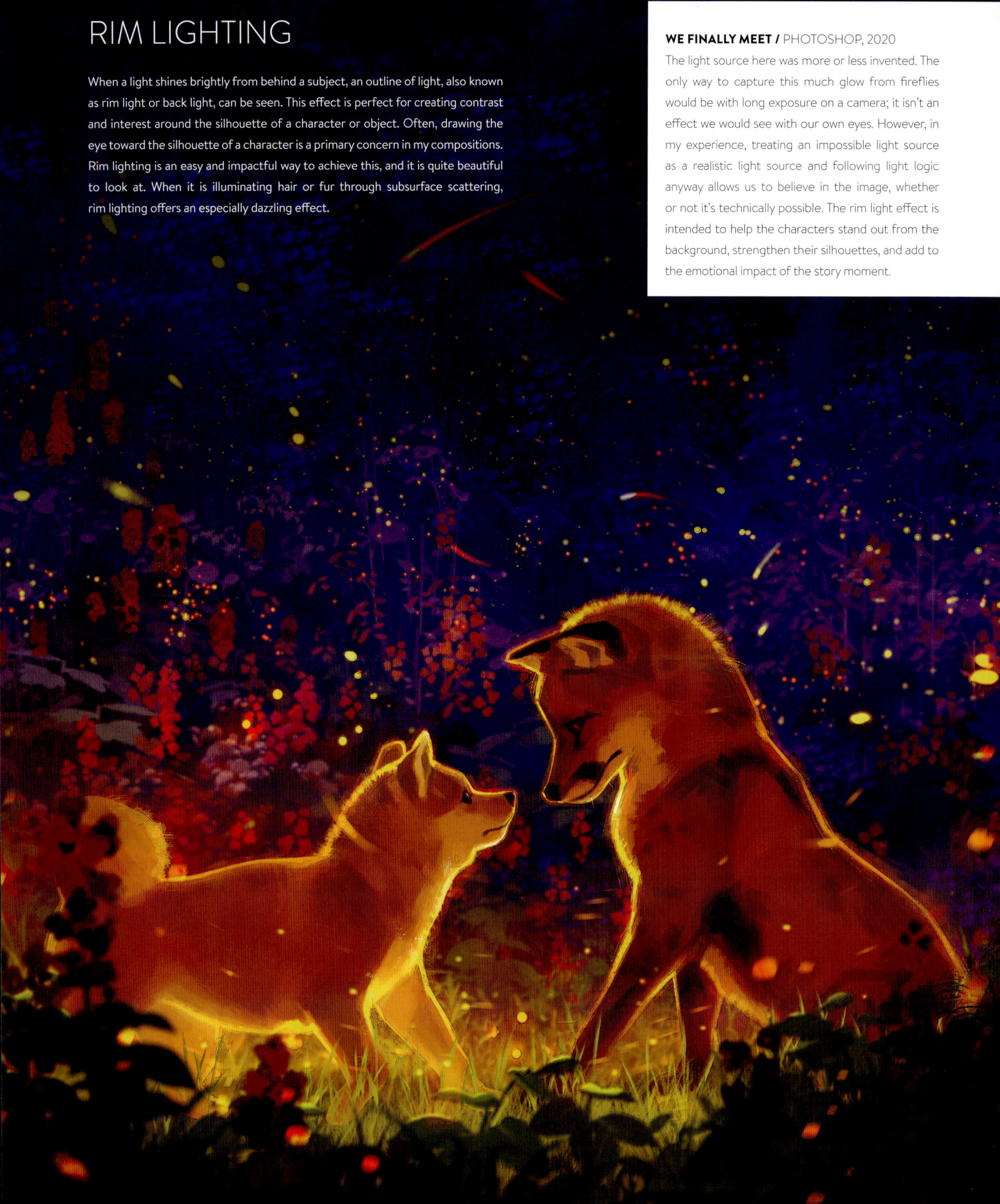

WE FINALLY MEET / PHOTOSHOP, 2020

The light source here was more or less invented. The only way to capture this much glow from fireflies would be with long exposure on a camera; it isn't an effect we would see with our own eyes. However, in my experience, treating an impossible light source as a realistic light source and following light logic anyway allows us to believe in the image, whether or not it's technically possible. The rim light effect is intended to help the characters stand out from the background, strengthen their silhouettes, and add to the emotional impact of the story moment.

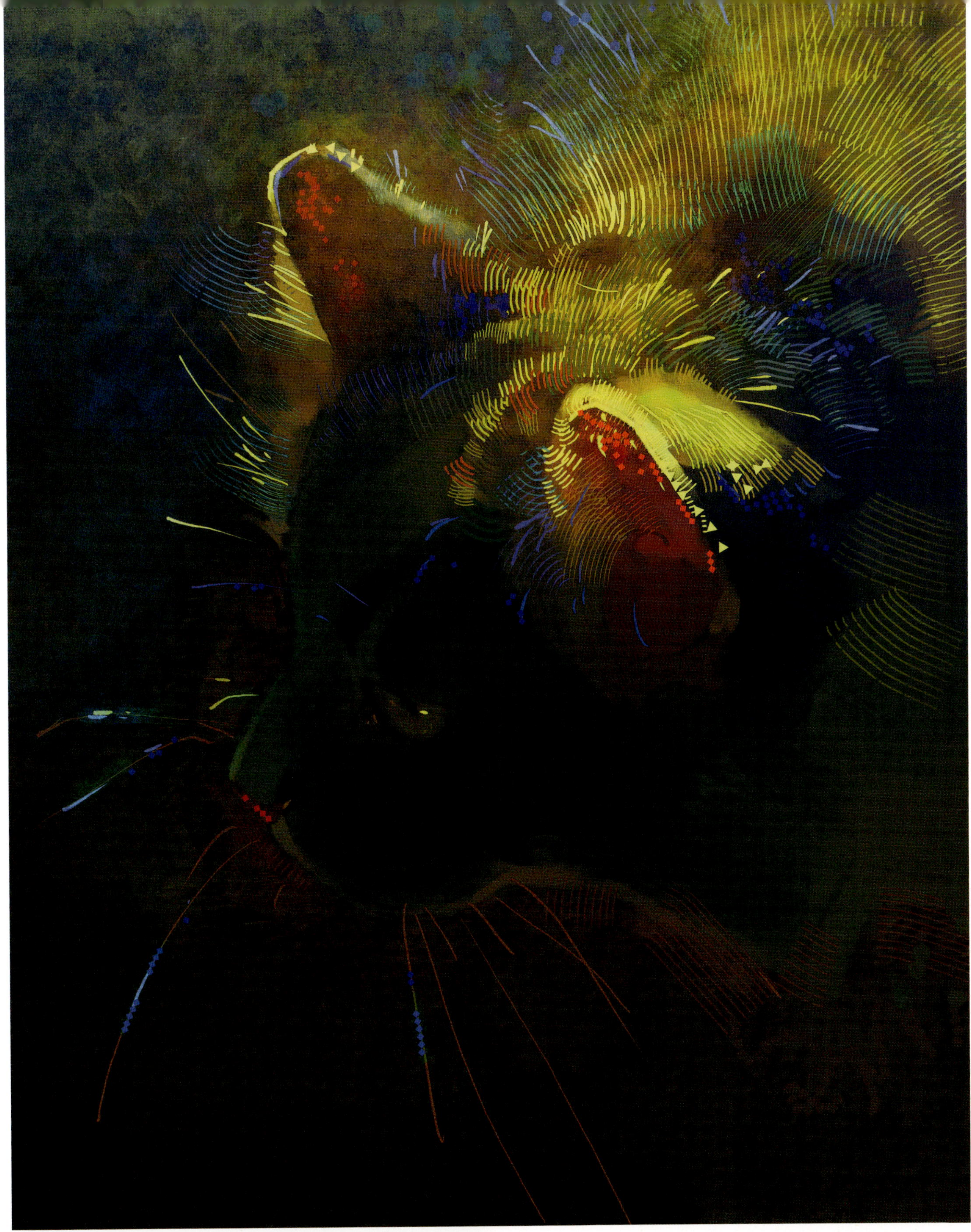

THE LOOSE IMPLICATION OF A CAT 2 / PHOTOSHOP, 2021
I wanted a bright pop of warm red color to triangulate with the primary yellow and hints of blue; subsurface scattering inside the ears was the perfect opportunity. This is an easy trick for saturated color in any cat or dog painting, and I rely on it often in compositions featuring animals.

SUBSURFACE SCATTERING

In semi-translucent forms such as ears, fingers, or leaves, light is able to somewhat pass through and ends up bouncing around wildly to create bright, vibrant colors. You can see this effect for yourself by putting your fingers or a leaf in front of a flashlight. This phenomenon can provide wonderful opportunities for bright pops of color.

BOUNCE LIGHT

When a strong, direct light source hits an object, that light can bounce from the object onto anything facing it in the surrounding area. In the process, the bounced light picks up the color of the object it bounces off. In *Waiting by the Window*, bright sunlight hits the warm surface of the table and bounces up into the shadows of the books and the side of the dog's face. A distinct temperature shift can be seen in the shadows directly above the table compared to the shadows further down the dog's body.

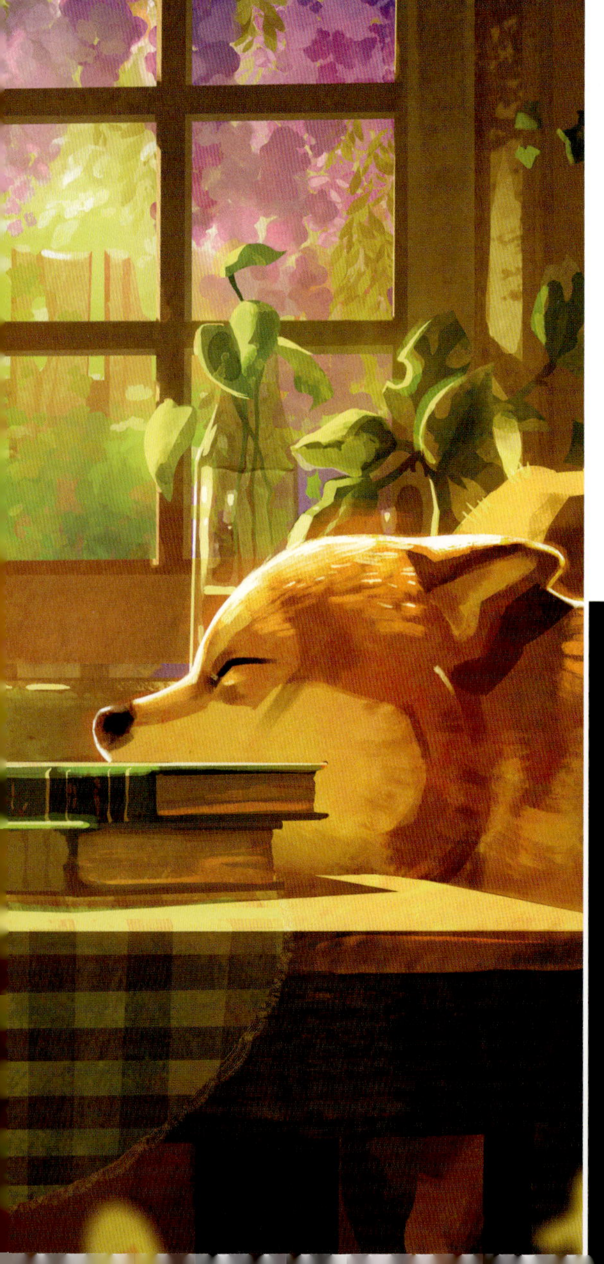

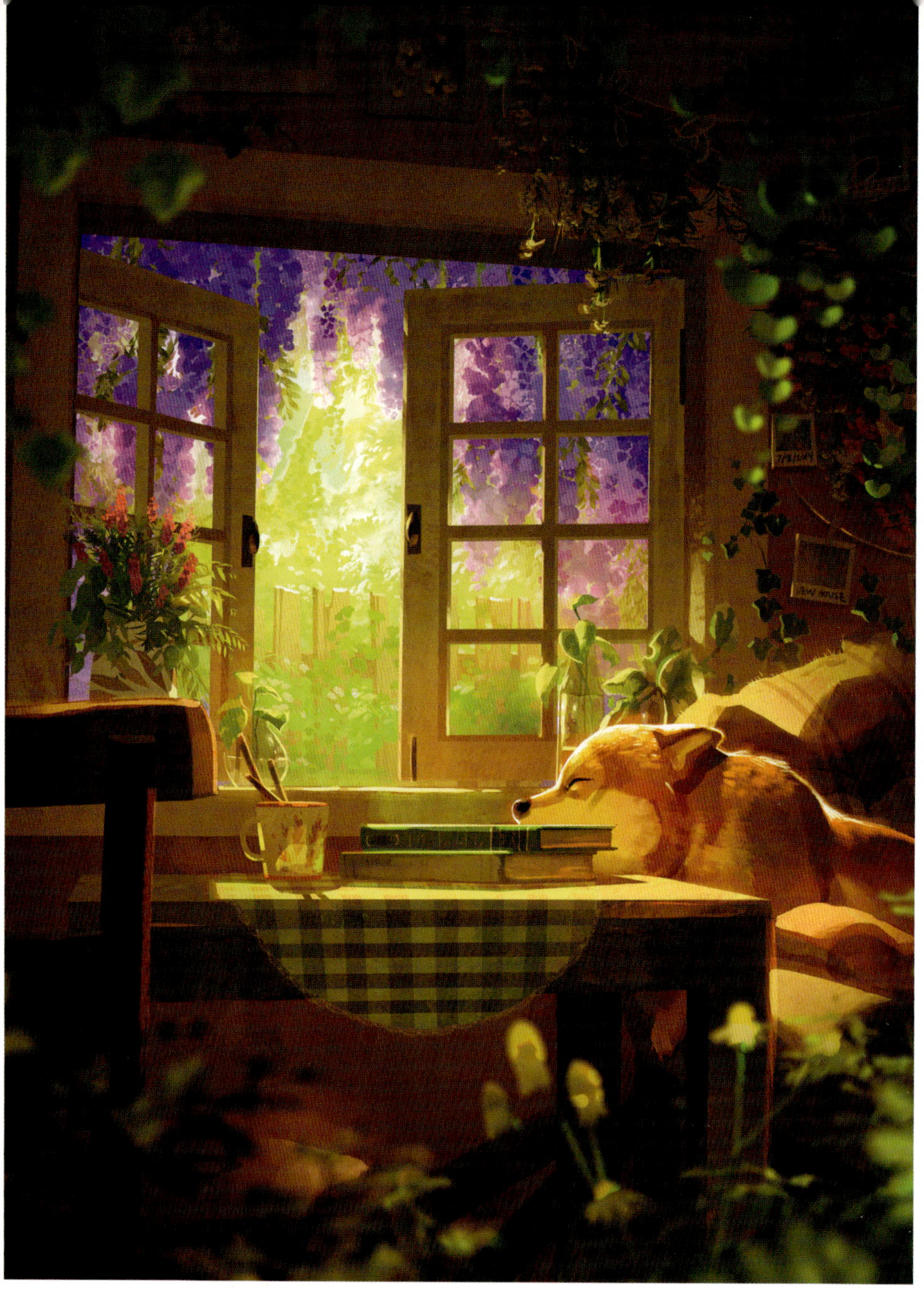

WAITING BY THE WINDOW / PHOTOSHOP, 2020

MULTIPLE LIGHT SOURCES

In *I Knew You'd Come*, the fox is illuminated by two separate light sources: the direct, warm light source coming from the left, and the diffused blue glow of the moonlight outside. Balancing multiple light sources in a single image can be tricky, especially when they are on opposite ends of the warm-cool spectrum. It's easy for the colors to become confusing and unreadable.

To prevent confusion and creating "muddiness" with multiple strong light sources, I'd recommend building them up individually using layer blending modes such as Soft Light, Screen, and Overlay. When beginning with a more neutral-toned base of local colors, build up light and shadow in stages; each light source can be considered individually, one after another, rather than trying to balance them all at once. I usually begin with the most direct light source and build up additional light sources from there.

After practicing this process, it will become clear that there is often more than one light source in any given lighting scenario. Less prominent light sources such as bounce light or ambient glow from the sky aren't as easy to identify, but when the eye is trained to pay attention and search for them, light sources reveal themselves. Adding them into paintings helps bring a higher level of believability and three-dimensionality.

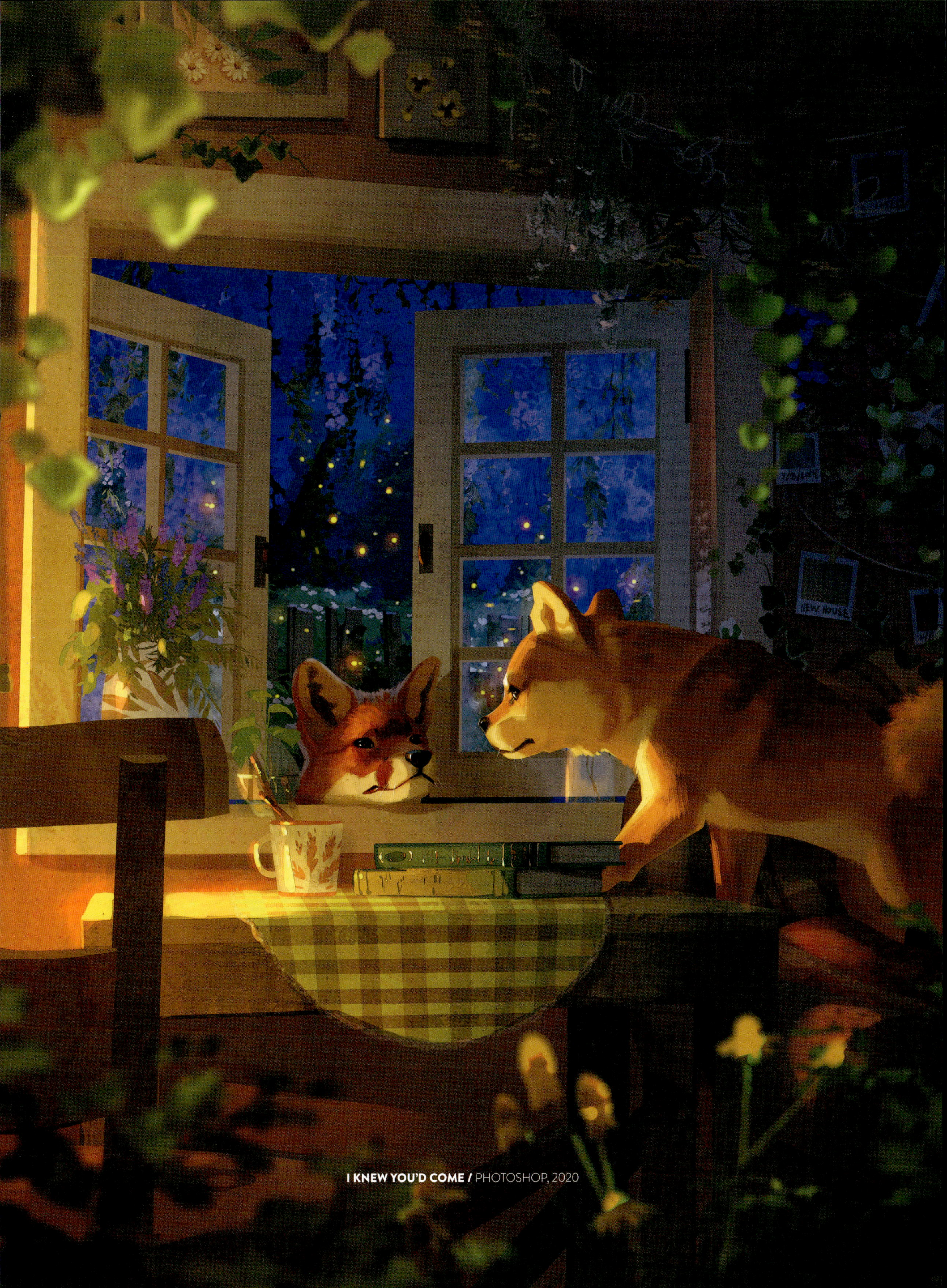

I KNEW YOU'D COME / PHOTOSHOP, 2020

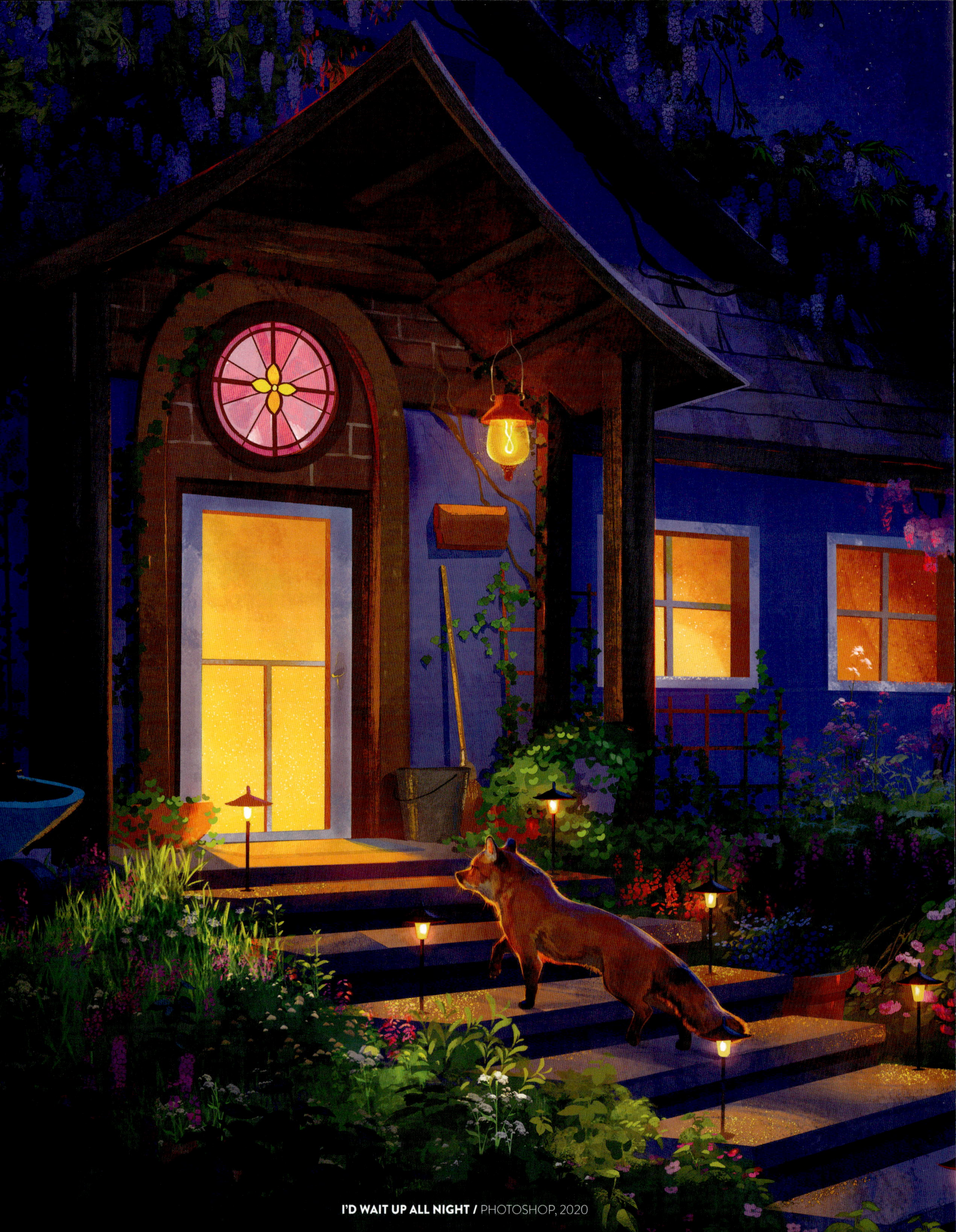

I'D WAIT UP ALL NIGHT / PHOTOSHOP, 2020

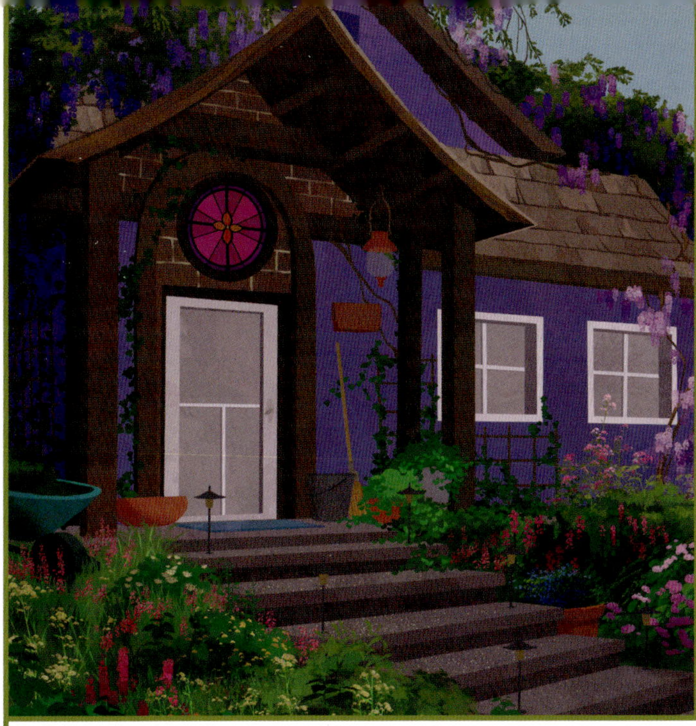

Base design for *I'd Wait All Night* and *I'd Wait Until Morning*

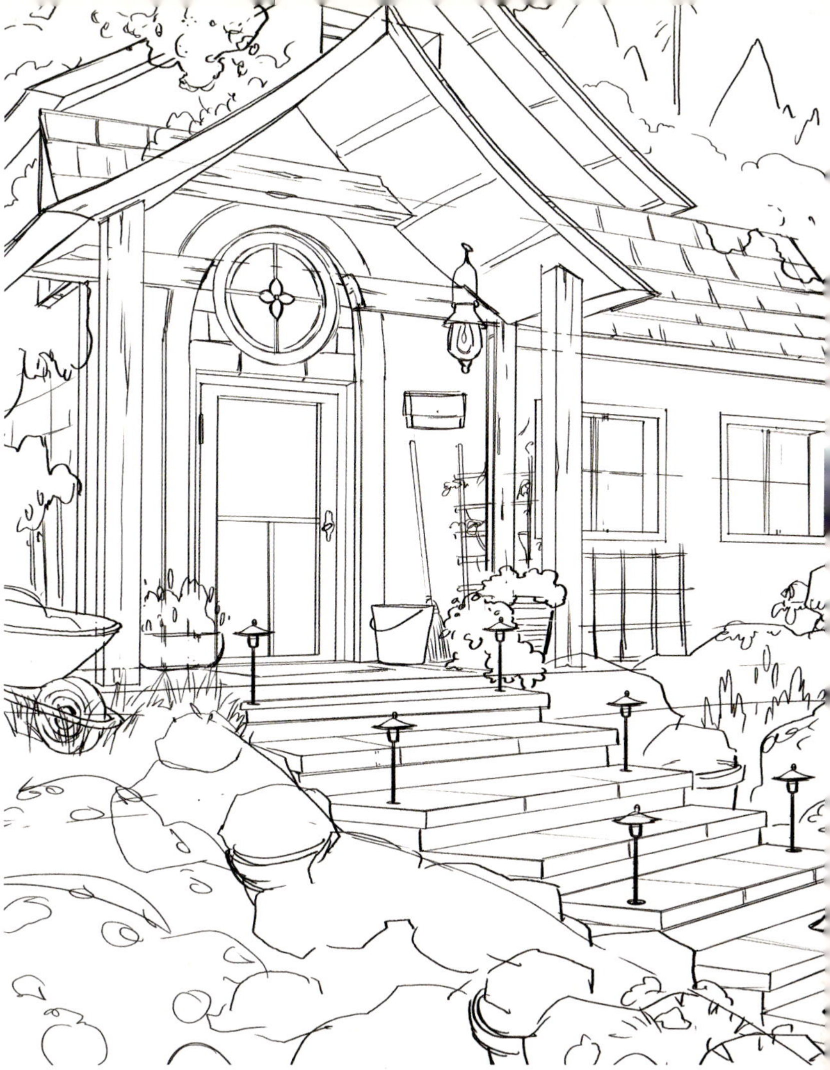

TIME-OF-DAY CHANGES

Depicting a single location at multiple times of day is one of my favorite ways to tell a story using limited resources. Using the same drawing multiple times allows me to get more use out of it, and crafting a narrative in two images is a wonderful exercise in storytelling. I've done a lot of time-changes during my years as an animation background painter, and I employ a lot of the tricks I use in my day job to speed up and streamline the process.

When I paint multiple times of day, I first create a neutral base with desaturated local colors and occlusion shadows only. Local colors are the colors of an object when it isn't being affected by any strong light or shadow; the best real-world example of this is an overcast day. When the clouds obscure the sky completely, very soft white light is emitted evenly across the world beneath it. Shadows are very soft and diffused, mainly concentrated in crevices. These shadows in cracks and crevices are called occlusion shadows.

I paint my entire base image in neutralized versions of the local colors of objects. I keep everything as layered as I can. I always label my layers clearly and group them as much as possible so I can find them easily. I then save out two copies of this neutral base, one for each time of day, and then use a combination of adjustment layers, blending layers, and direct painting to transform each one into a fully realized time of day. I use blending modes such as Multiply and Darken for my shadows, and Overlay, Screen, Hard Light, and Color Dodge for my highlights. I use my carefully organized layers to easily select areas to add shadow and light. I try to keep every major object on its own layer, and many of the smaller objects get their own layers as well. I try to find a balance between how much time I invest in early organizing and how much time that organization saves me during the final painting phases.

I like to change the light source when doing time-of-day changes; it's the primary tool at my disposal for making radical changes to a single location. I often build light sources such as lanterns or other artificial lights into my scenes so I can turn them off and on as the time of day changes. I really like how much control it gives me over my compositions in each image.

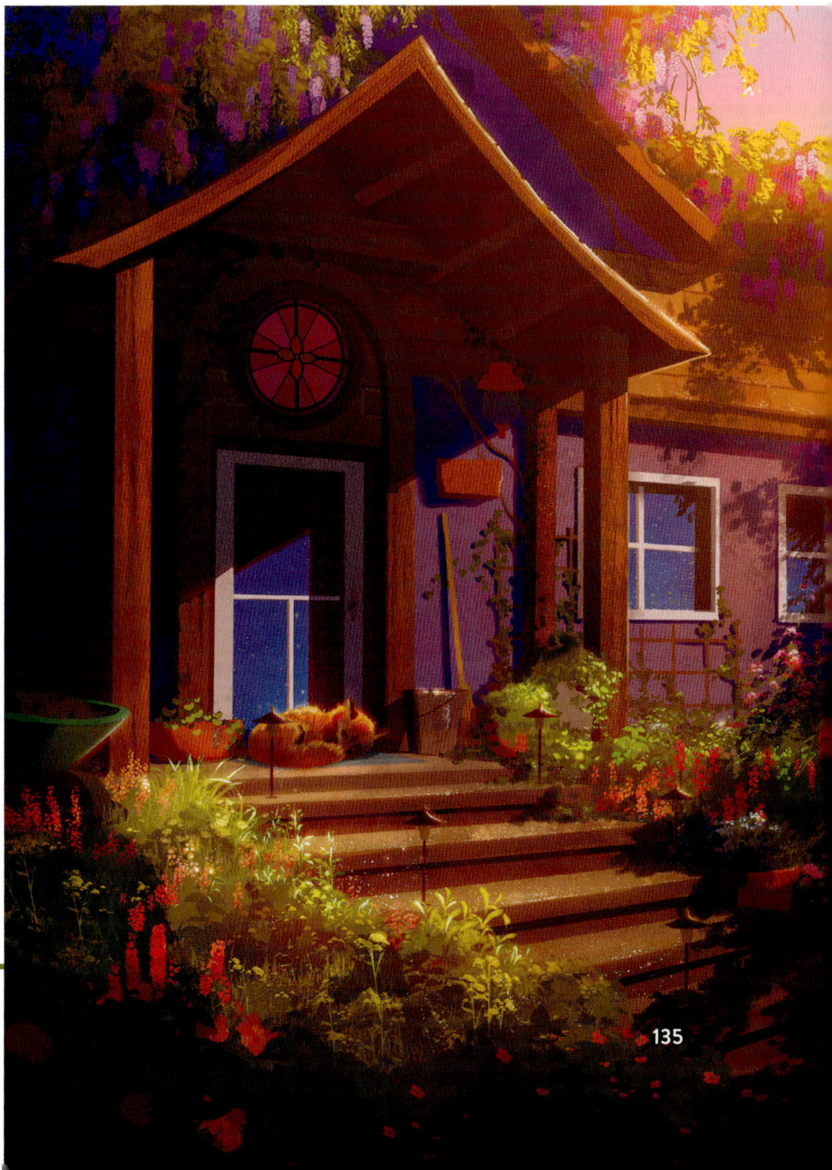

I'D WAIT UNTIL MORNING / PHOTOSHOP, 2020

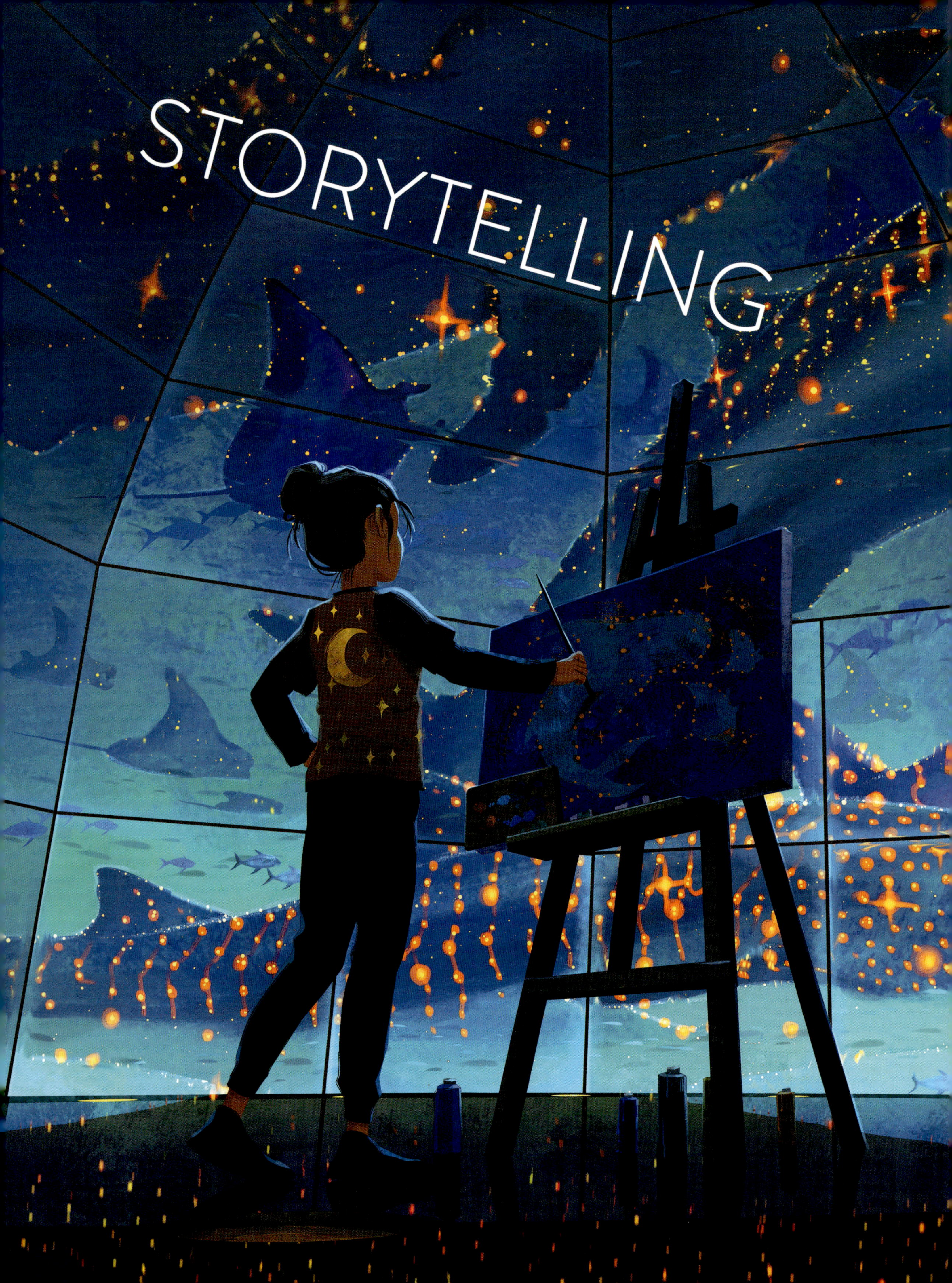
STORYTELLING

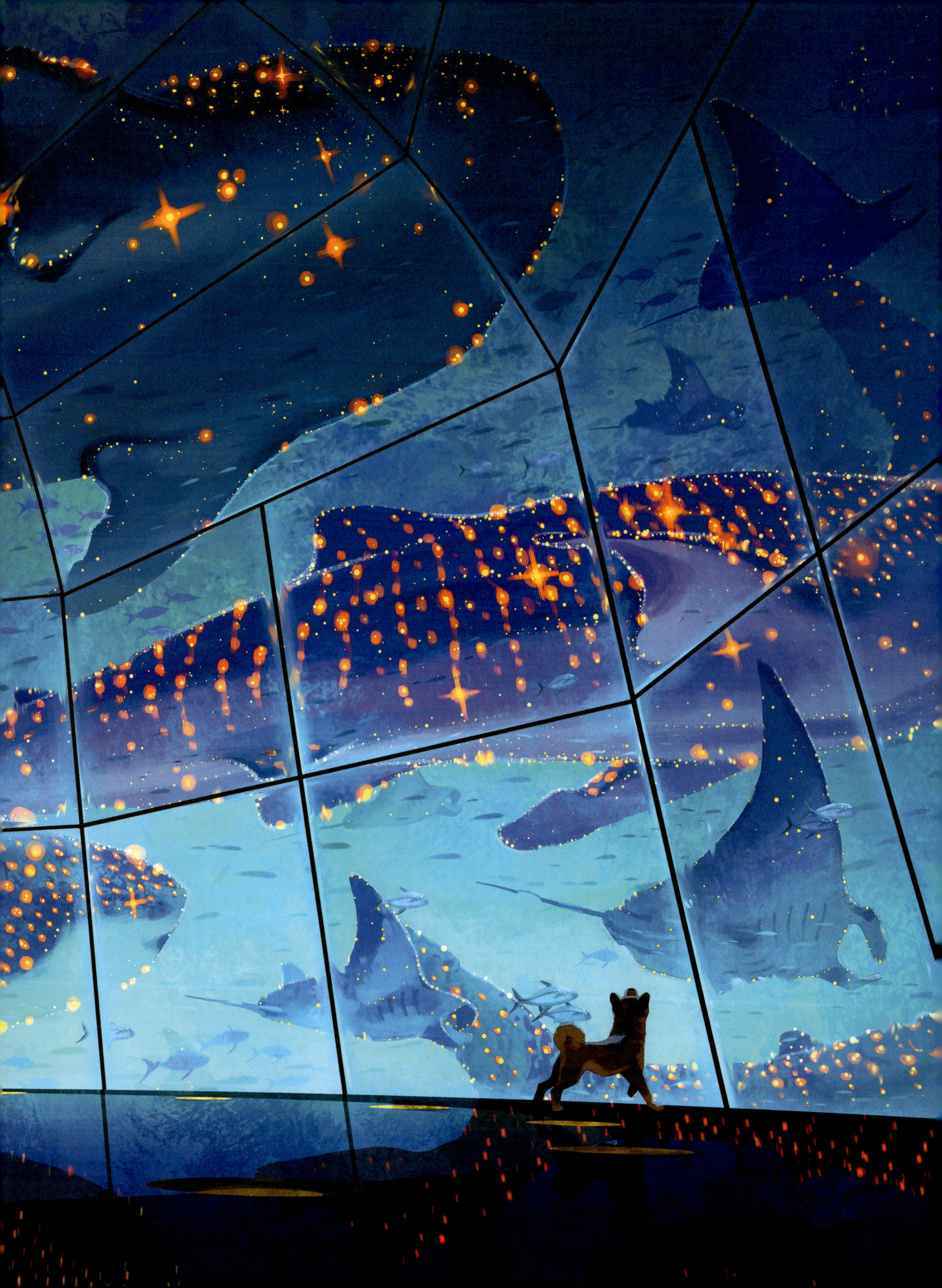

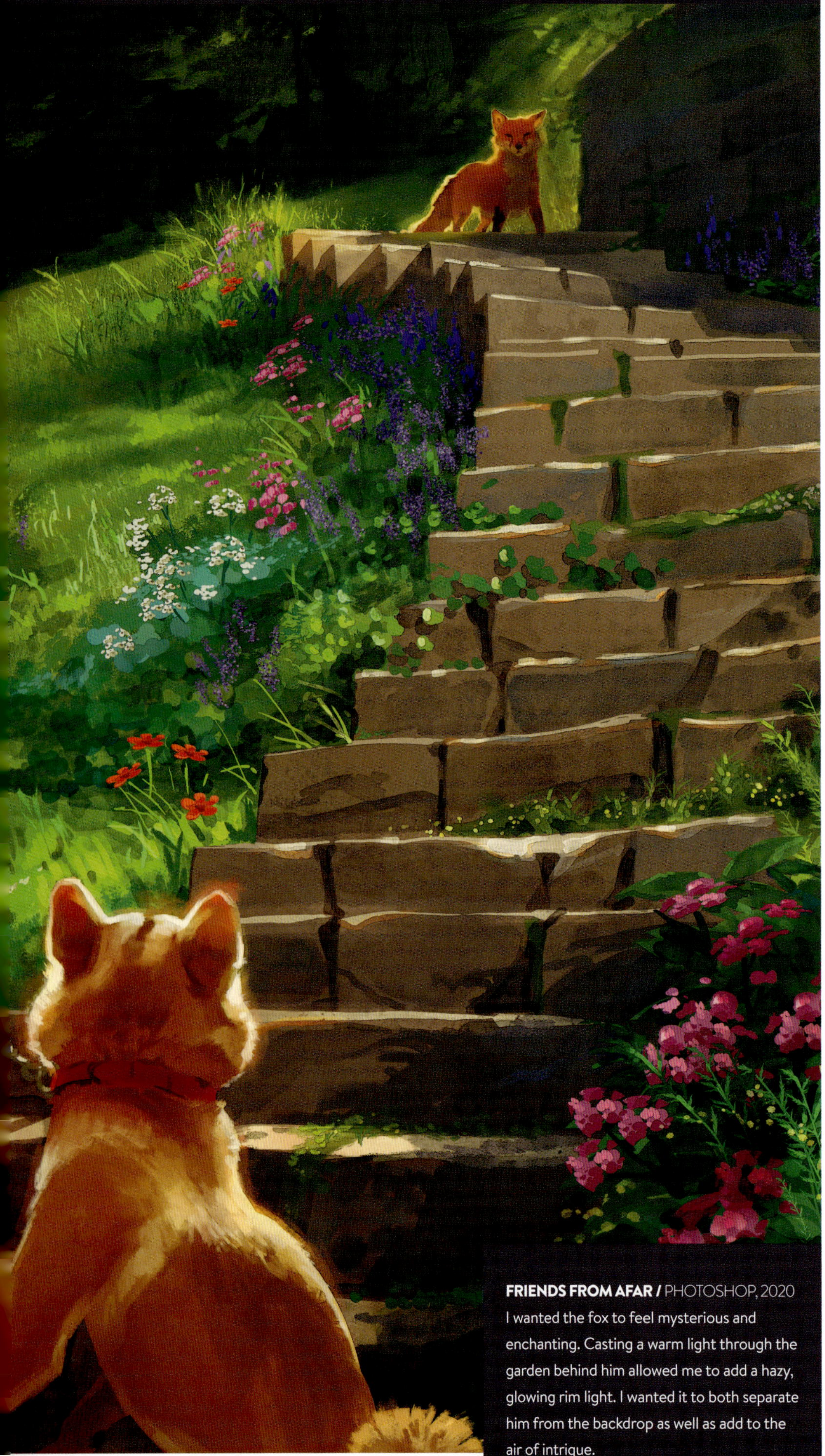

COMPOSITIONAL STORYTELLING

Storytelling and composition are very closely interwoven subjects. A story can be lost if the visual cues meant to portray it aren't given clarity and importance in an image. We can bring attention to the storytelling cues through contrast, implied lines, and prominence in the composition. The ability to communicate information visually is key to telling a story through a single image. My goal is to guide the viewer's eye to each storytelling cue, and have the cues work in conjunction with one another to visually communicate the message or situation I'm hoping to describe. Clarity is key – finding concise ways to visually communicate complex emotions and information is a skill that can be actively practiced and improved.

One of the best ways to dissect visual storytelling and learn elements to apply to our own work is to look at story-based art that we enjoy to figure out exactly how it communicates the story to us. What cues do we pick up on? In which order did we notice those cues? How did the artist bring attention to cues to ensure we would see them? Even if an artist doesn't consider themself a storyteller, the truth is that we are all storytellers. Every design decision we make adds to the story of an image. As people, the clothes we choose, the way we decorate our home, and even the activities we participate in, tell a story about who we are. This is true for characters and locations in drawings and paintings as well.

Just before the holidays at the end of 2020, I was struck by a burning need to represent the history I was living through in a painting (image shown on the right). So many of us spent our holidays away from loved ones, for both their protection and ours. Staying home and seeing loved ones only through a computer screen brought about a kind of resolute, aching sadness that I wanted to capture. As I painted, though, and as I talked to my own loved ones through video calls, the unusual warmth of the moment began creeping into the image. Seeing friends and family from afar was sorrowful, but also magical; the connection that technology permitted us during the pandemic saved me and many people that I know from so much additional heartache. Being able to talk to distant people via live video may seem commonplace now, but described to someone half a century ago, it would sound like pure make-believe. I wanted to capture both the sadness and the warmth of this strange moment in time.

FRIENDS FROM AFAR / PHOTOSHOP, 2020
I wanted the fox to feel mysterious and enchanting. Casting a warm light through the garden behind him allowed me to add a hazy, glowing rim light. I wanted it to both separate him from the backdrop as well as add to the air of intrigue.

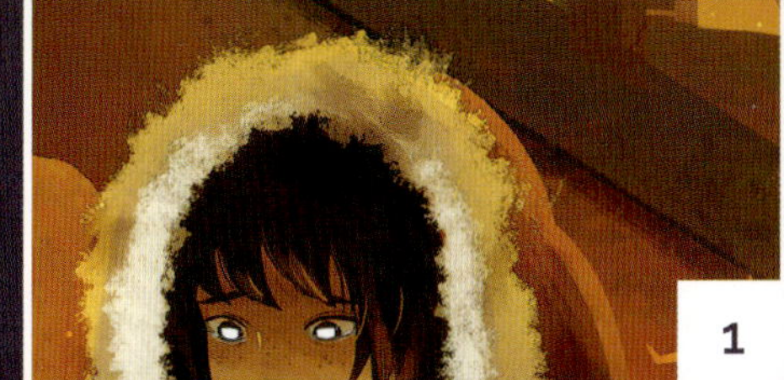

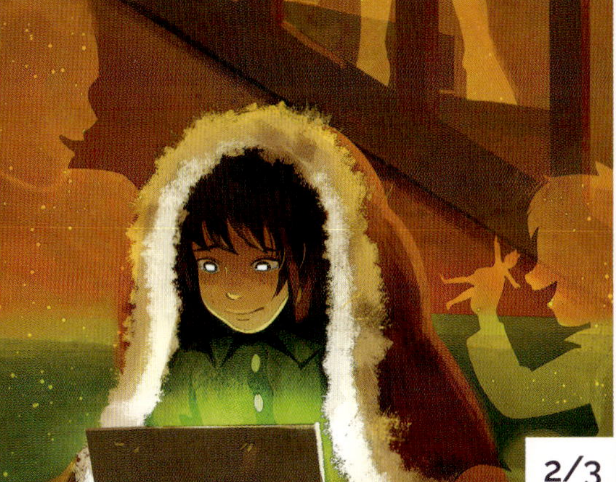

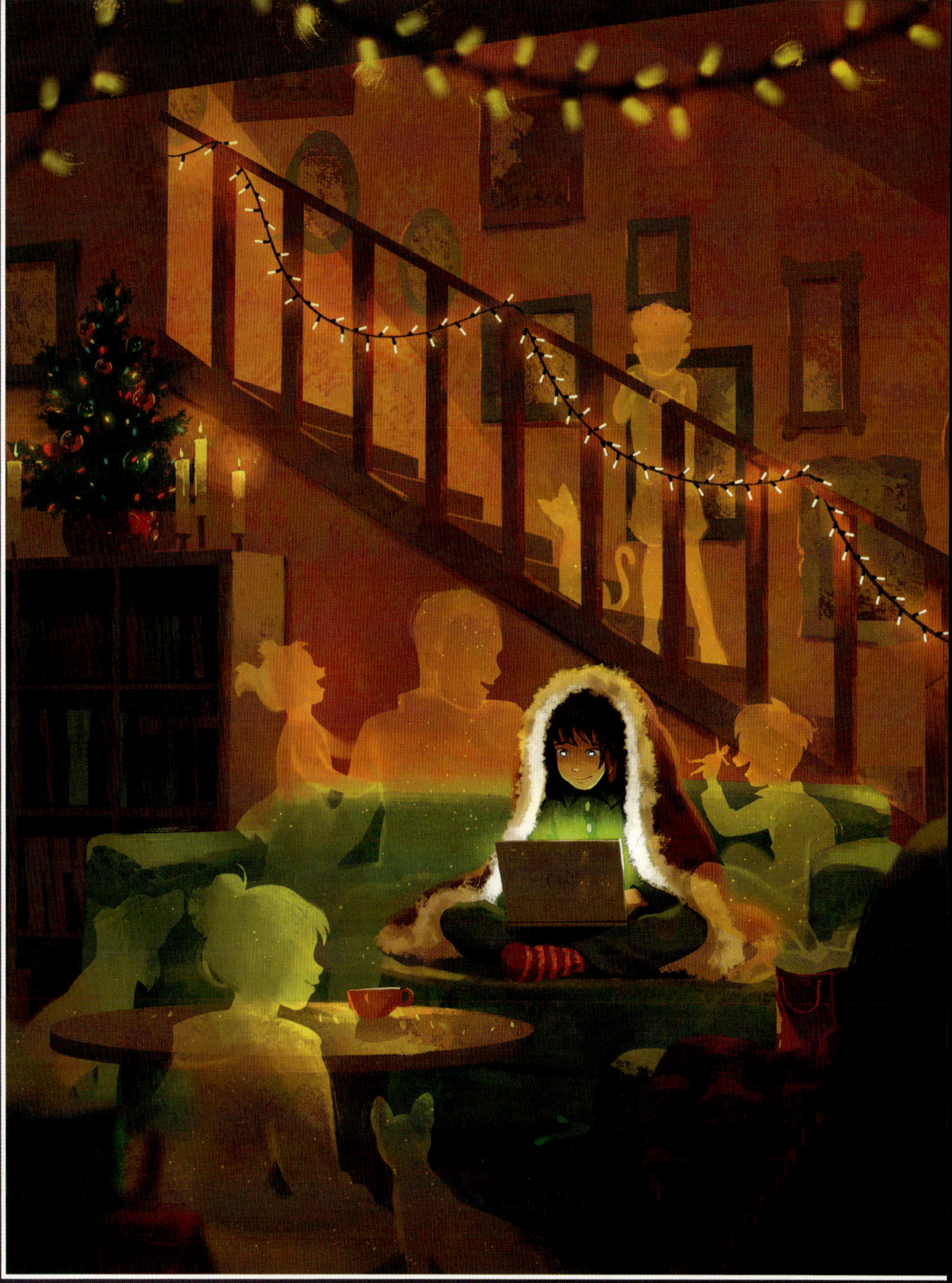

IN SPIRIT / DIGITAL, 2020

In this painting, the first cues I wanted the viewer to notice were those of the main character sitting on the couch. I used value contrast and reflected light to draw the viewer's gaze to her eyes, and remind them of the meaning of the computer. These elements together are intended to spark the connection that the ghostly figures are the people she's seeing on her computer screen.

The blanket over her head functions both to emphasize her visually and to let us know that she may be feeling the need to wrap herself up in something physically, a thing I do often when I don't want to feel alone. It's unlikely that every person who glances at this image would pick up everything, but my hope is just that each person who sees it is able to pick up on enough cues to get a general understanding of the story being told.

1 / Contrasting her dark hair with the white edging of the blanket emphasizes her face. Focusing on that area of the painting brings attention to her teary eyes.

2 / Her face is lit both by a glowing computer screen and the glowing figures in the room.

3 / The screen light reflected in her eyes draws attention to that feature, reminding us of the meaning of the computer.

4 / Candles, Christmas tree, and fairy lights dot the background to reinforce the time of year. Wrapped presents in the foreground also help.

5 / The framed photos along the staircase let viewers know that she's a sentimental person.

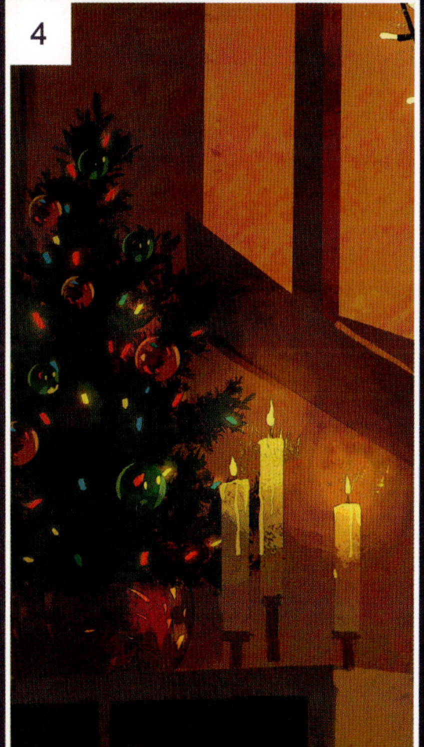

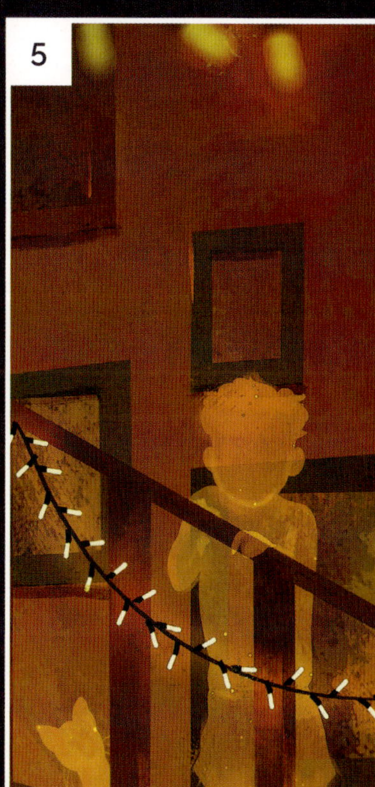

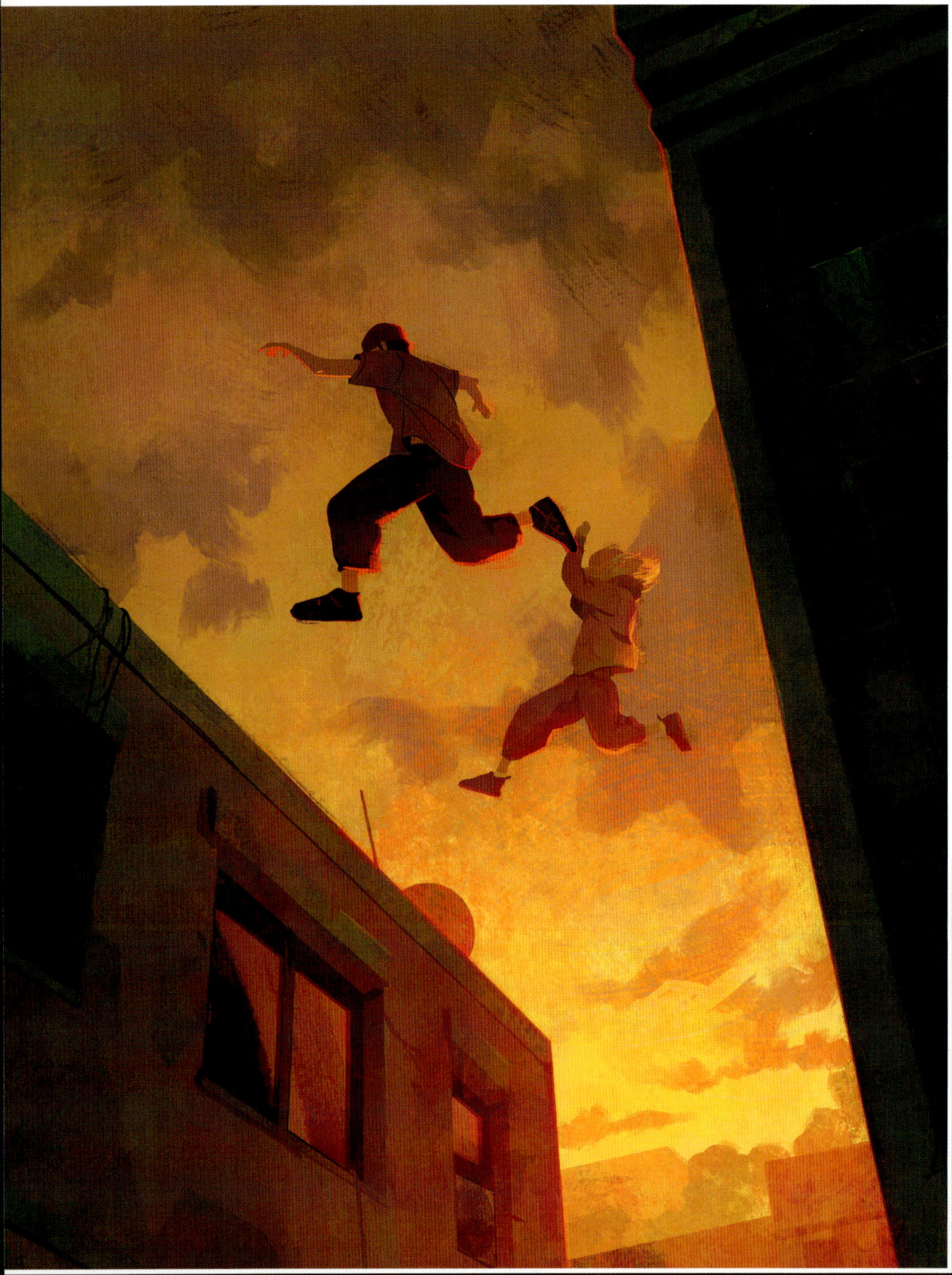

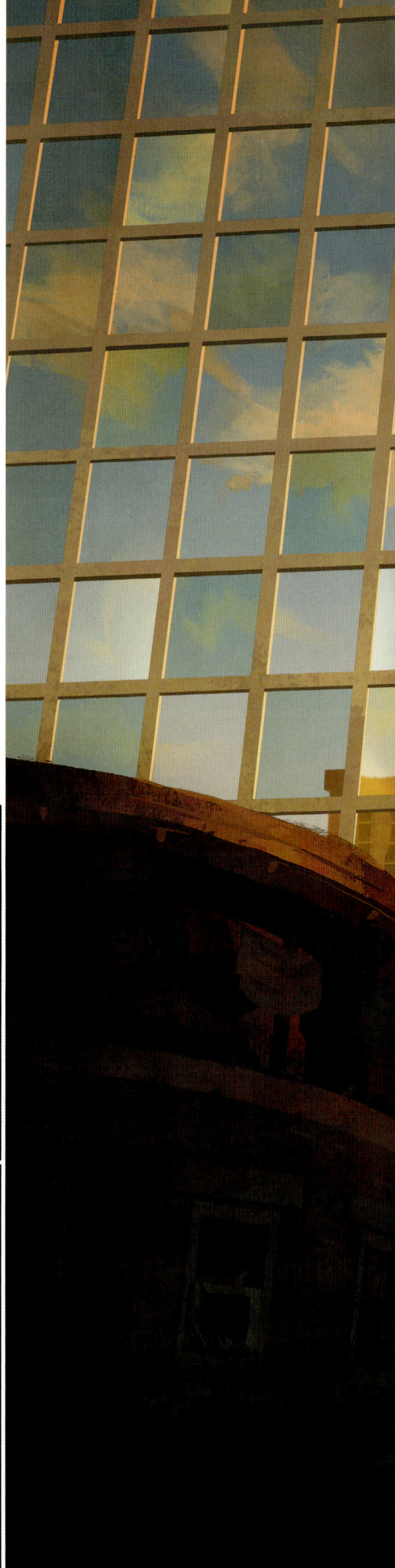

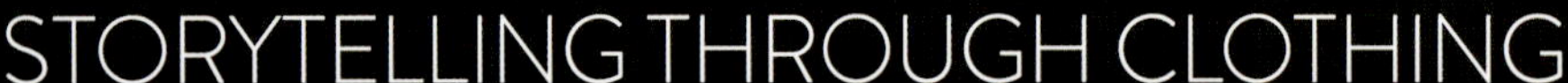

STORYTELLING THROUGH CLOTHING

In the parkour (free running) painting above, I wanted the characters to look experienced and self-assured. I knew that someone experienced in parkour would be wearing clothing and shoes well suited to the activity, so I spent some time researching parkour experts and observing what they wore. I found that loose, lightweight clothing was most common. The clothing needed to allow for flexibility and full range of movement. The shoes were also highly important; thin, flexible black shoes seemed to be most common. Undertaking detailed clothing research may seem tedious, but it adds tremendously to the visual experience of a painting.

LEAP INTO SUNSET /
DIGITAL, 2021

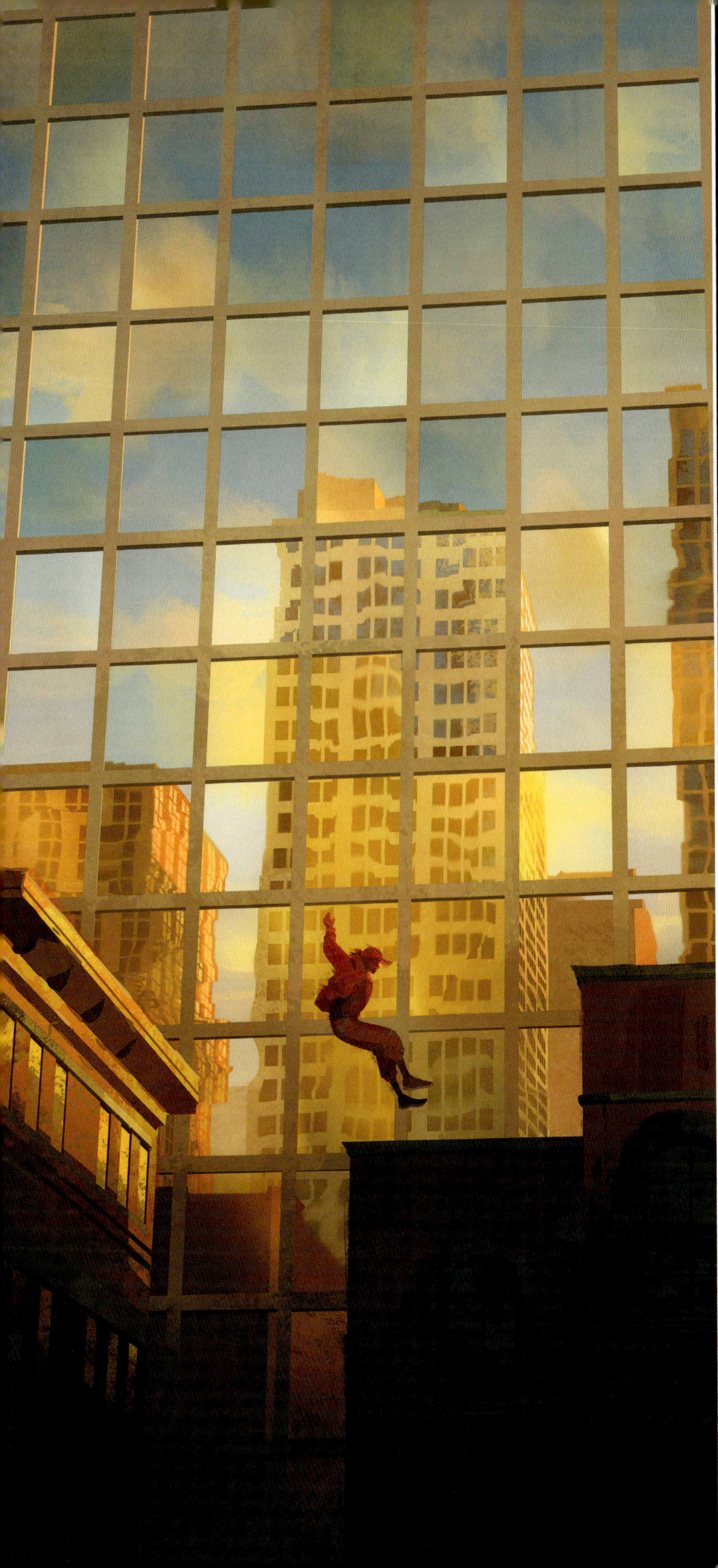

"DETAILS BASED IN REALITY MAKE AN IMAGE FEEL MORE BELIEVABLE, AS IF DEPICTING A PLACE IT MIGHT BE POSSIBLE TO VISIT"

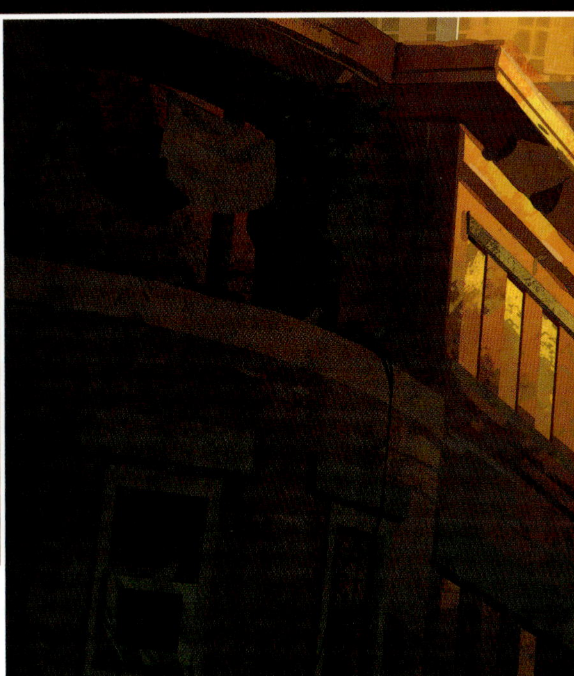

ENVIRONMENTAL STORYTELLING

In the same way that clothes can tell us the story of a character, set decoration in an environment tells a story of a location. In this second parkour painting, I aim to show a clash between older, smaller architecture and towering, modern skyscrapers. I want the rounded, intricate architecture of the lower buildings to tell the viewer of their history and how they are cast physically and metaphorically into shadow by the huge buildings around them. In a residential building, adding details such as air-conditioning units, power cords, plants, and clothes-lines tells a story about the people who live there. Weathering and stains hint at the building's history and age. Details based in reality make an image feel more believable, as if depicting a place it might be possible to visit.

REFLECTED CITY / DIGITAL, 2021

COMMUNICATING EMOTIONS

Sometimes rather than telling a literal story, art can communicate emotional experiences. It is often easier for me to communicate a feeling through art than through words. In *Fatigue* I wanted to communicate the resigned acceptance of true exhaustion. One might think that the more specific an emotion is, the less relatable an artistic depiction it might be. Yet I often find that the most personal and unique emotional experiences I have painted are the ones that resonate most deeply with an audience. The experience of having an innermost struggle be understood and represented by someone else can be profound. I often find that writing in metaphor first is a good entry point to portraying complex emotions through imagery.

Sharing deeply personal artwork often brings on a complicated array of emotions — both positive and negative. It can be emotionally turbulent to expose intimate truths about our experiences or who we are as people, and I think doing so needs to come from a genuine desire to share and not a feeling of obligation.

I don't believe we owe it to the world in any way to share that type of work if we don't wish to. I also don't believe that art needs to be deep or intimately personal if we don't want it to be; the value of it doesn't have to do with the emotional weight it carries. However, when I do choose to share that type of work with my community, I've often found the connection and camaraderie I receive is worth the mortification of being seen and known. Recognizing shared experiences is a powerful force in strengthening communal ties. I've often found sharing artwork that carries inner turmoil has been deeply gratifying and has led to important connections with both strangers and people around me.

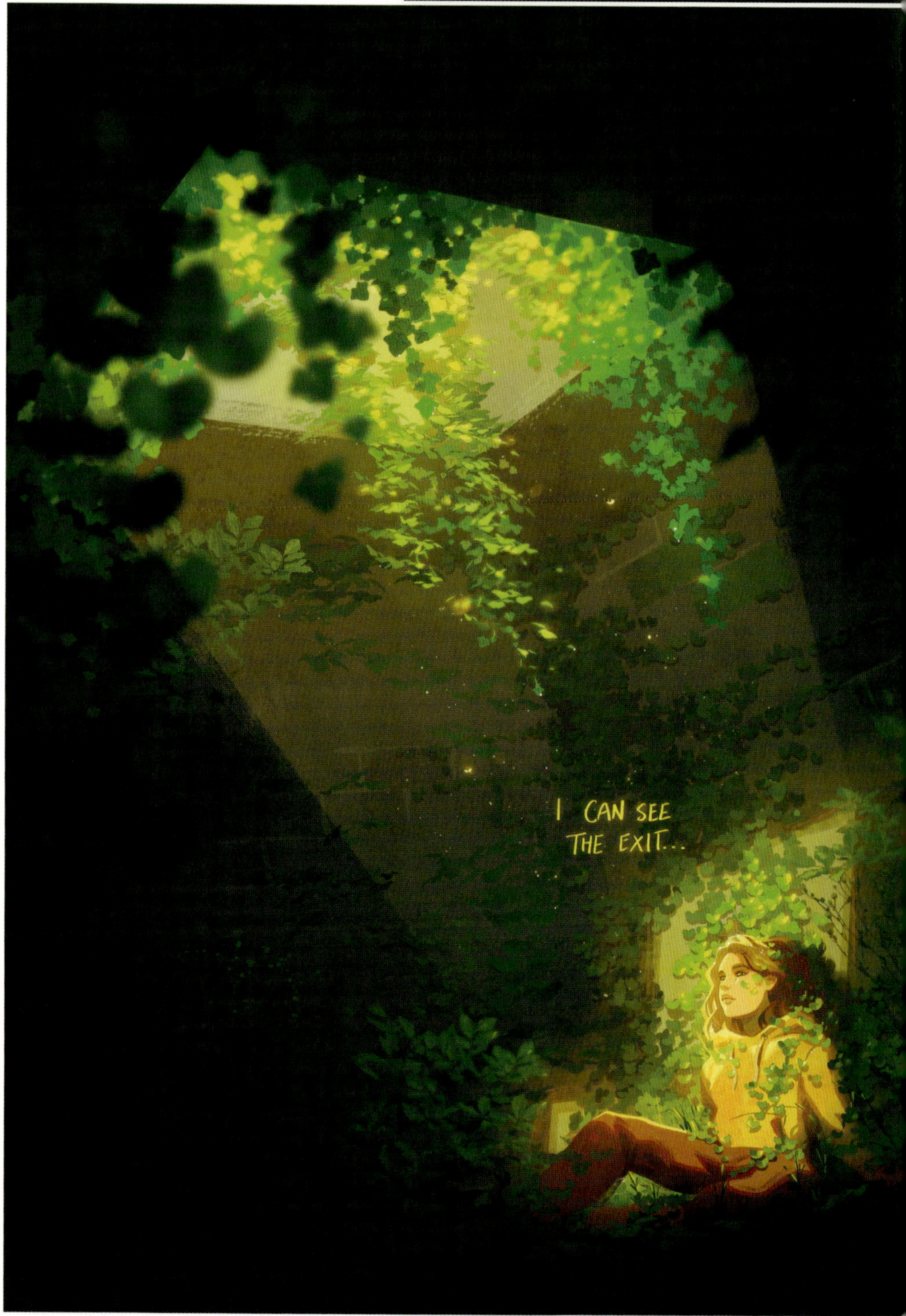

FATIGUE / DIGITAL, 2020

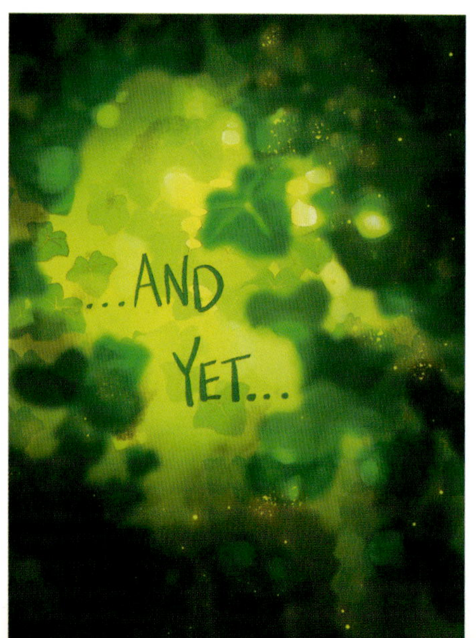

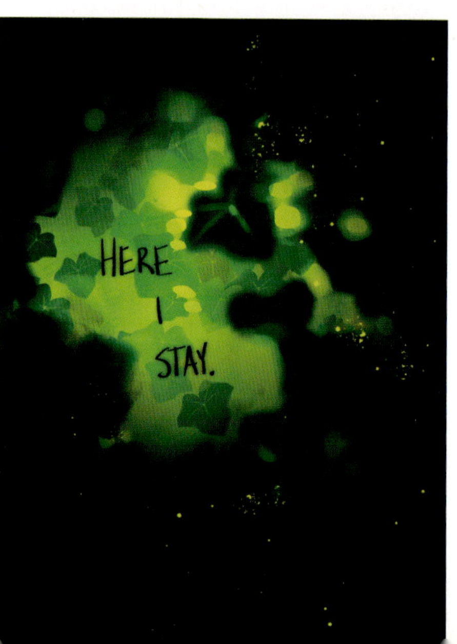

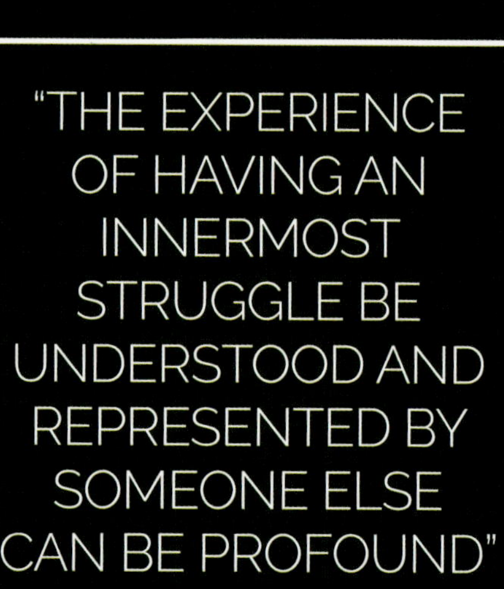

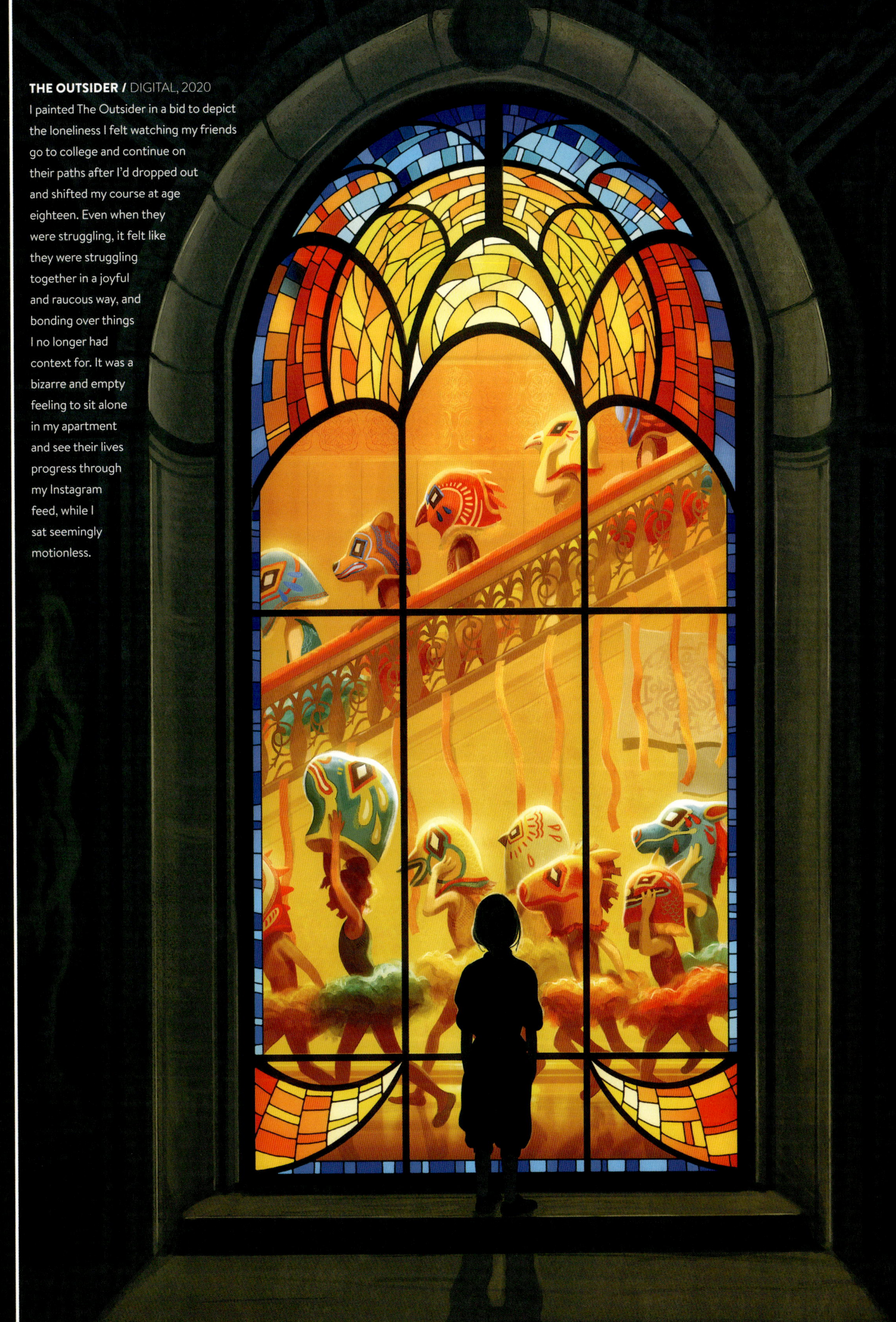

THE OUTSIDER / DIGITAL, 2020

I painted The Outsider in a bid to depict the loneliness I felt watching my friends go to college and continue on their paths after I'd dropped out and shifted my course at age eighteen. Even when they were struggling, it felt like they were struggling together in a joyful and raucous way, and bonding over things I no longer had context for. It was a bizarre and empty feeling to sit alone in my apartment and see their lives progress through my Instagram feed, while I sat seemingly motionless.

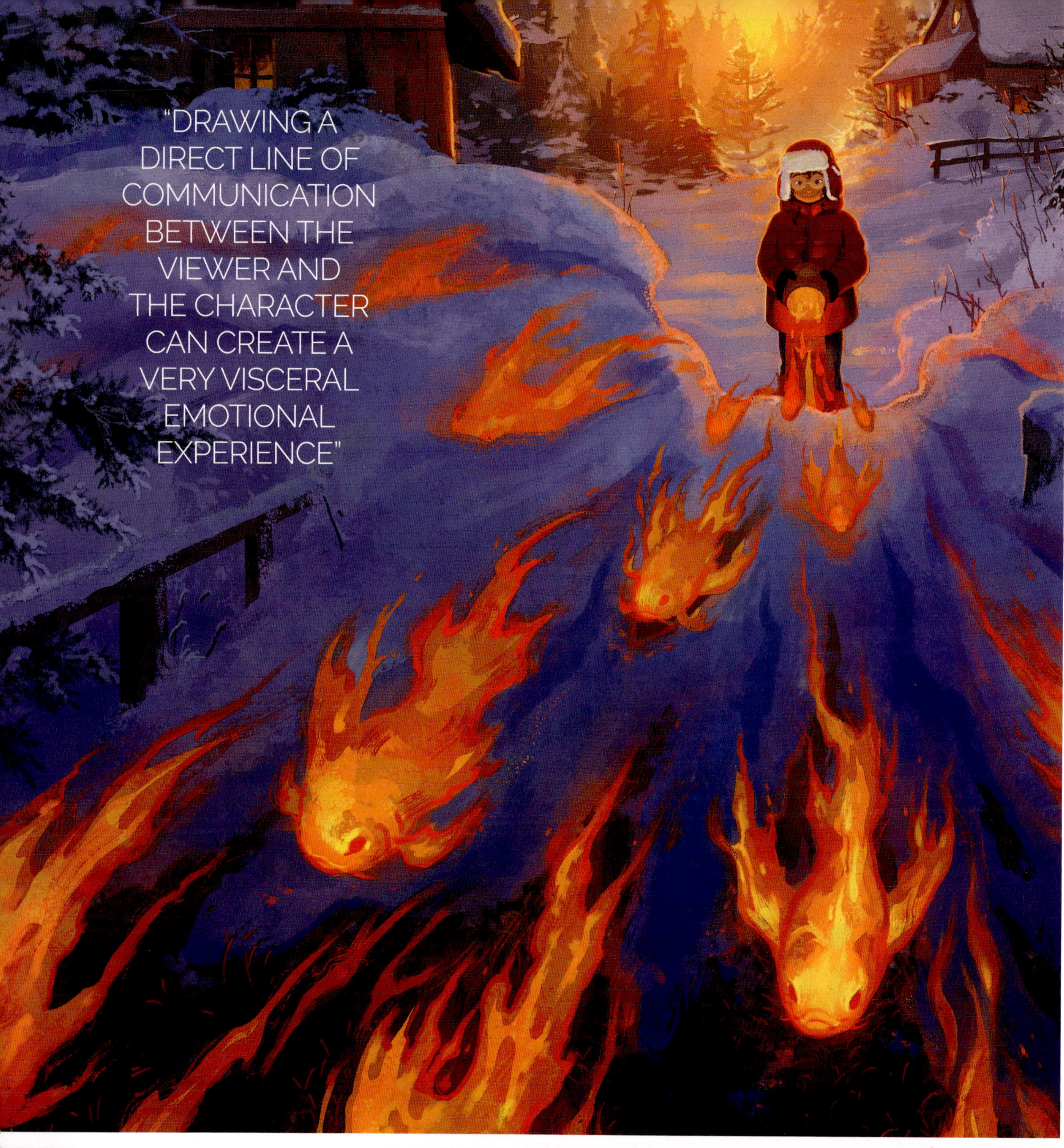

FIRE FISH / COMMISSIONED BY DEVIANTART/WIX, DIGITAL, 2020

I painted *Fire Fish* as a commission for the DeviantArt Magic Week. I have had the opportunity to work with DeviantArt many times since 2016, and have made genuine friendships along the way. It feels like just yesterday that I was posting my middle-school anime fan art there!

IMMERSIVE INTERACTION

A piece can feel very intimate and interactive when meeting the direct gaze of a character, almost as if the viewer is a participant in the events taking place. Drawing a direct line of communication between the viewer and the character can create a very visceral emotional experience – it automatically introduces a tension between the two. The connection invites the viewer to occupy the world the character exists in, and to experience the feelings that might be felt while there beside them. I sometimes find it hard to tear my eyes away from a powerful look from a painted character!

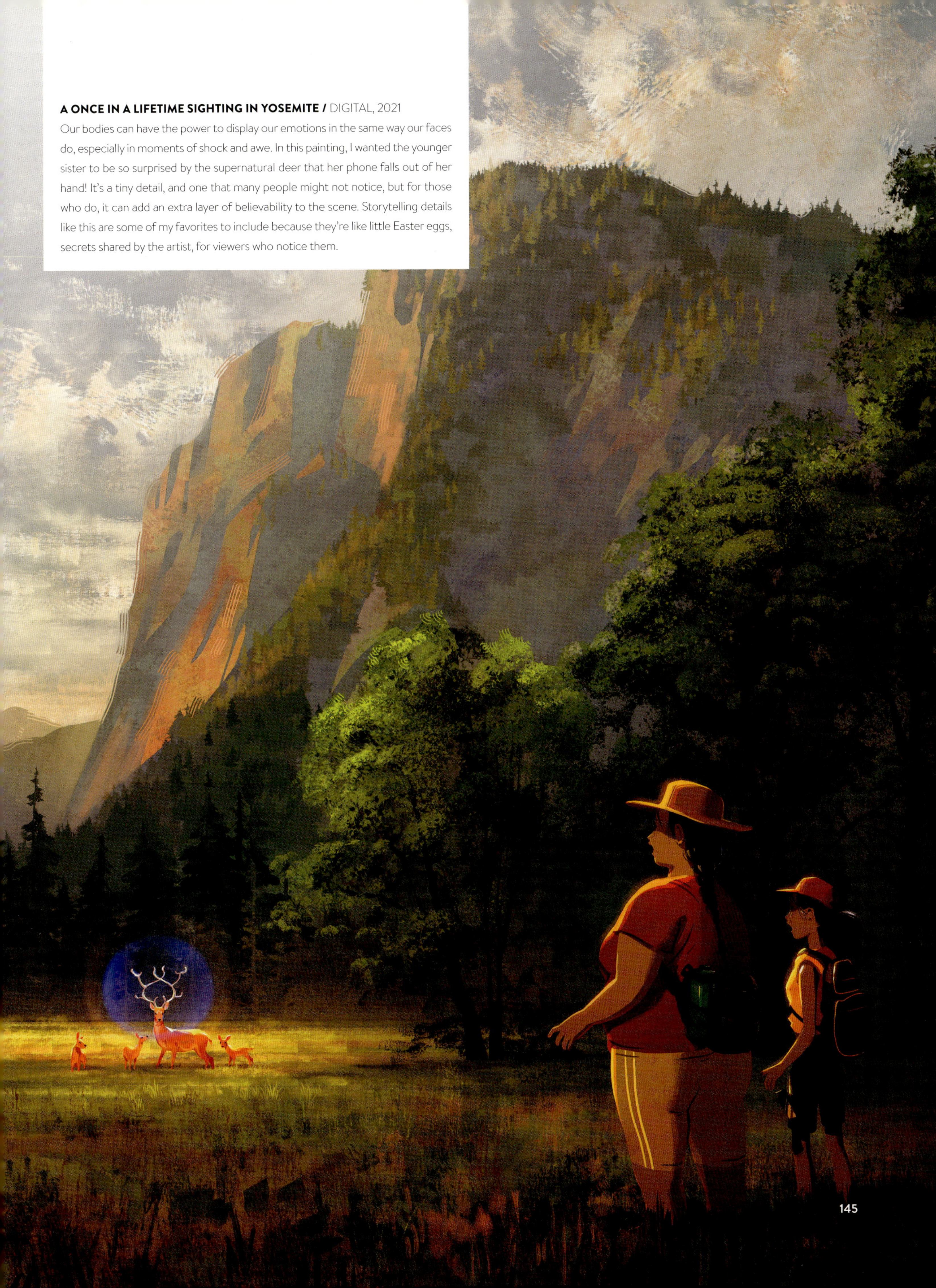

A ONCE IN A LIFETIME SIGHTING IN YOSEMITE / DIGITAL, 2021

Our bodies can have the power to display our emotions in the same way our faces do, especially in moments of shock and awe. In this painting, I wanted the younger sister to be so surprised by the supernatural deer that her phone falls out of her hand! It's a tiny detail, and one that many people might not notice, but for those who do, it can add an extra layer of believability to the scene. Storytelling details like this are some of my favorites to include because they're like little Easter eggs, secrets shared by the artist, for viewers who notice them.

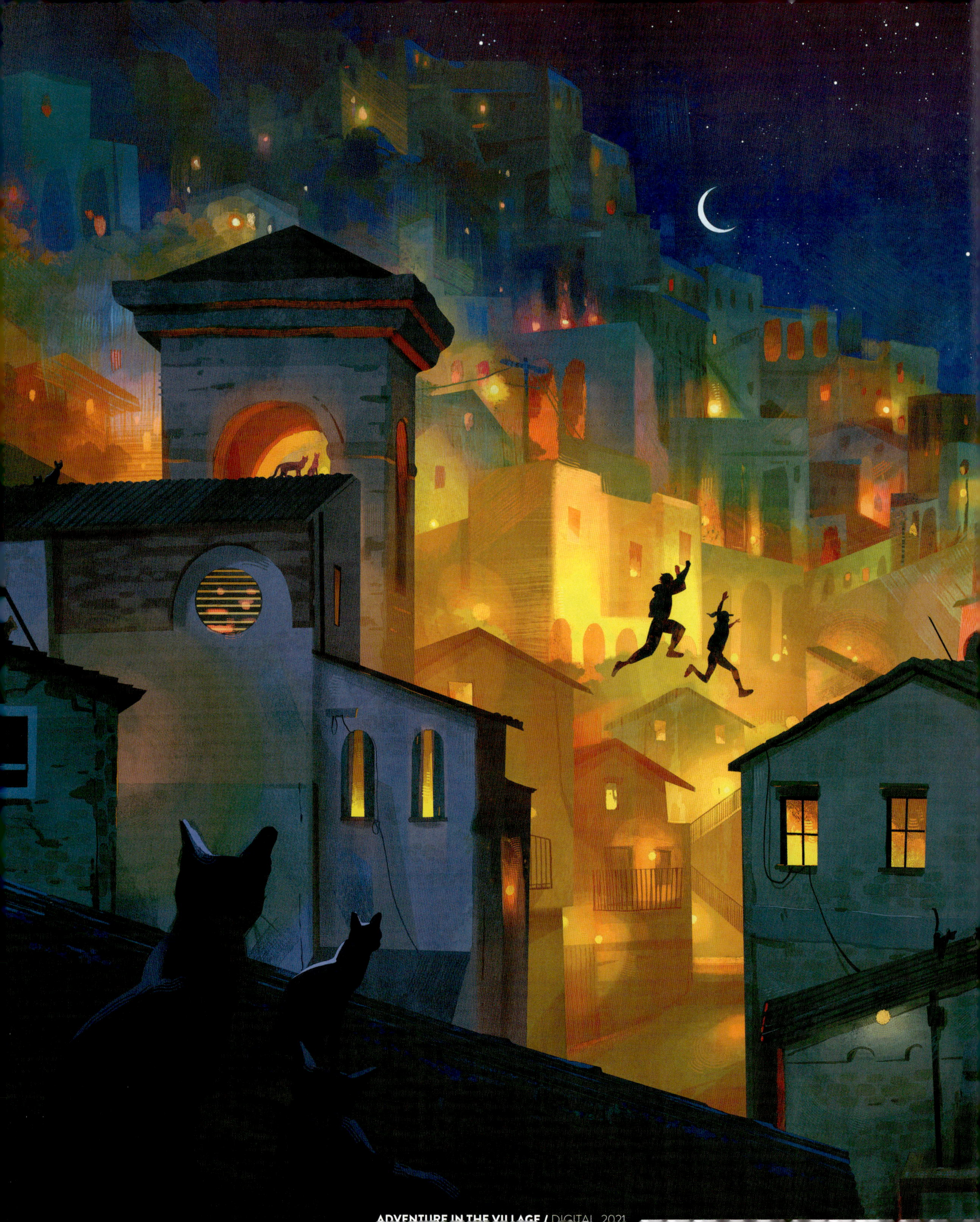

ADVENTURE IN THE VILLAGE / DIGITAL, 2021

BREAKFAST IN THE VILLAGE / DIGITAL, 2021

BEAUTY IN THE MUNDANE

I enjoy depicting quiet moments between characters just as much as I like painting dazzling action scenes. While otherworldly moments often speak to our inner child and dreams, intimate, mundane scenes of everyday life have the power to create incredibly resonant connections to the activities we participate in on a daily basis. The ritualistic experiences we share as humans, such as sleeping, eating, resting, talking, and sitting in comfortable silence with one another, hold a universal power and magic. I think it's important to recognize both the beauty of human imagination and the beauty of our daily lives and activities.

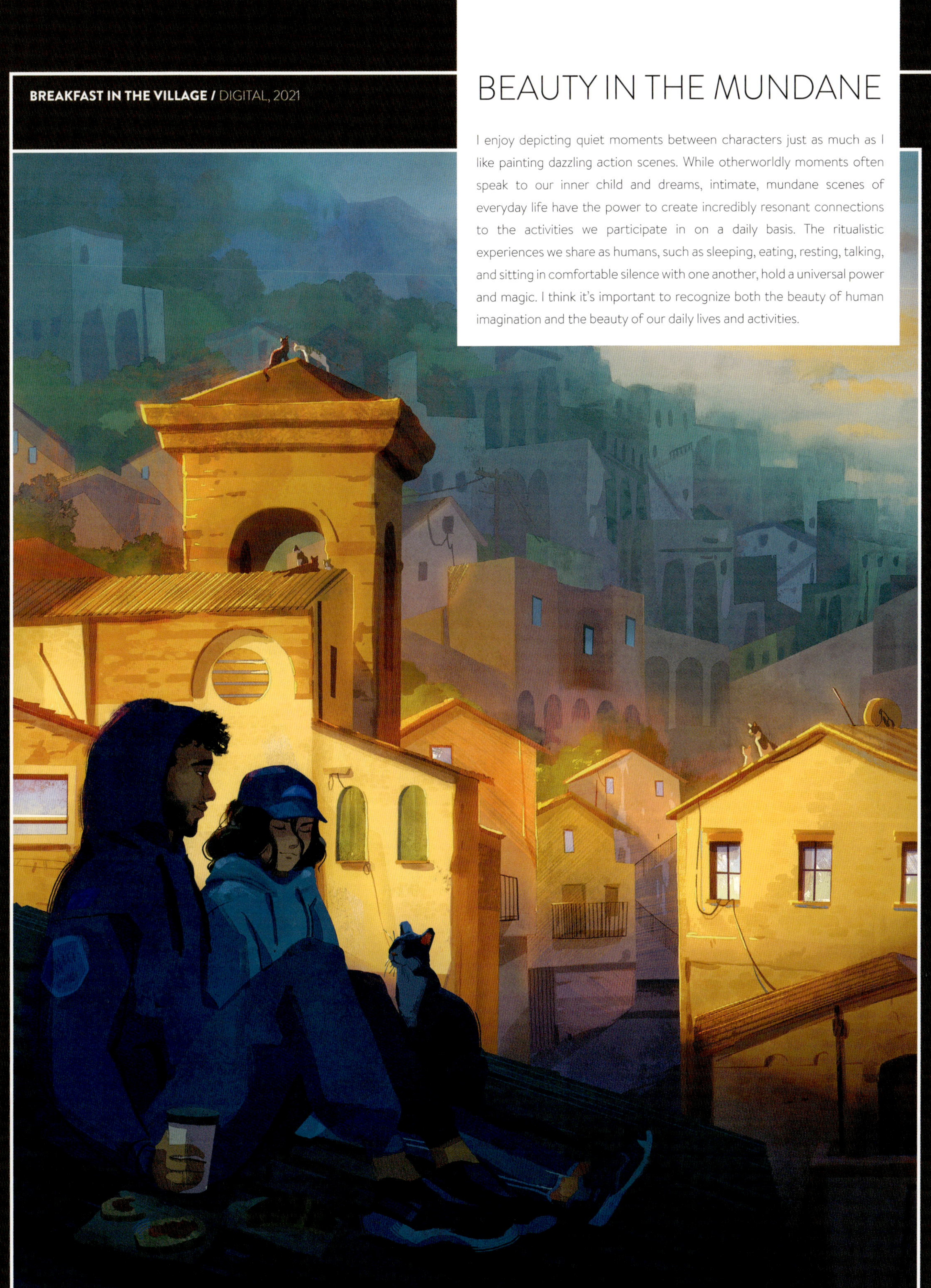

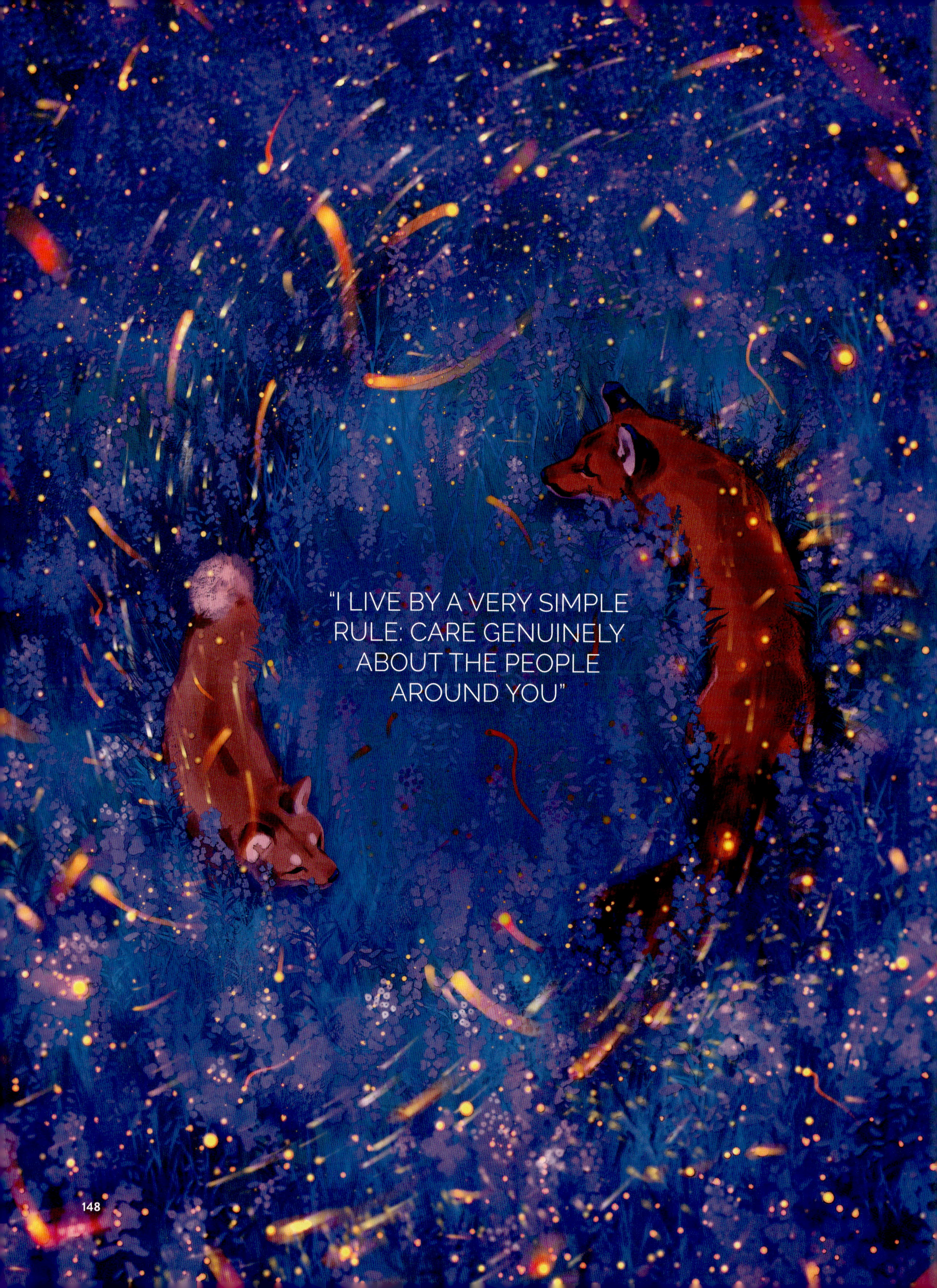
"I LIVE BY A VERY SIMPLE RULE: CARE GENUINELY ABOUT THE PEOPLE AROUND YOU"

TELLING MY STORY AND ENRICHING THE STORIES OF OTHERS

As I find myself with an oversized microphone and on relatively stable footing, it has felt increasingly vital to use my platform to assist others in reaching the same position. Alongside creating emotional ties with the community around me, I've always found it deeply important to give back in whatever way I can. As I've grown older, it has become more apparent how much I owe every ounce of my success to the people around me. Nothing I have accomplished in life would have been possible if it weren't for the people in my life who have supported and cared for me, both in person and online. Especially as I find myself on more stable ground, finding ways to pull as many people as I can up onto that stable shoreline with me has amplified in importance.

I see it as a responsibility, but also as an incredible privilege, to have the means and resources available to organize giveaways for tablets, raise money for fundraisers, and devote time and energy toward creating free and accessible resources and educational content. I believe that if my platform continues to grow in this industry, my responsibility to use it wisely and generously will continue to grow as well. The possibilities of what I could do in the future excite me, and I could not be more thankful to every single person who supports me along the way. I live by a very simple rule: care genuinely about the people around you. It's a pretty basic motto, but applying it to my life hasn't let me down yet.

One of the simplest ways I've aimed to do so is by sharing more about my chronic illness and the way it has impacted my life and career. It is only recently that I have felt secure enough, financially and mentally, to reckon with the pitfalls of broadcasting my unpredictable health on platforms potential employers and clients can access. I hope that doing so will allow other artists with chronic illnesses and disabilities to feel like there is someone like them out there in the world. As a kid I never heard about artists with illnesses like mine finding success in the world. There are many people like me, whether they're able to be public about it or not, and I am hoping desperately for a better, kinder art industry in the future: one that is safer for everybody, including people with chronic illnesses and disabilities, and all people who belong to marginalized communities.

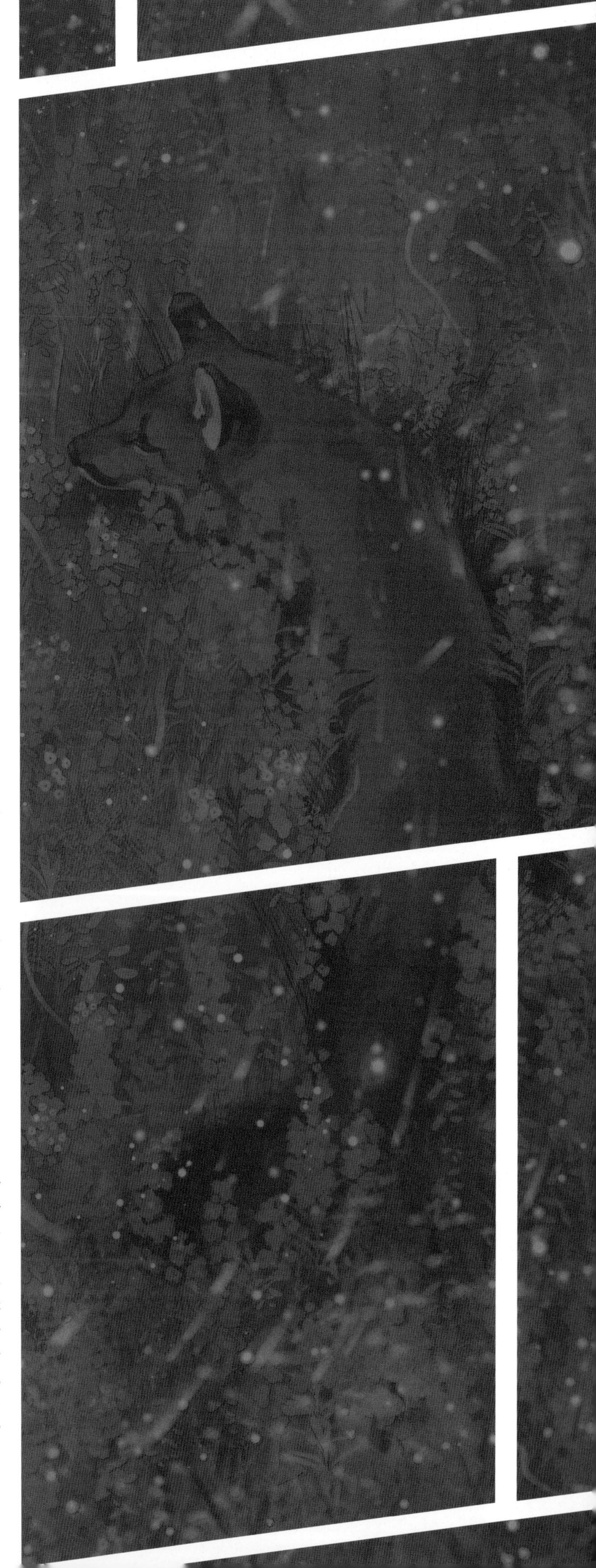

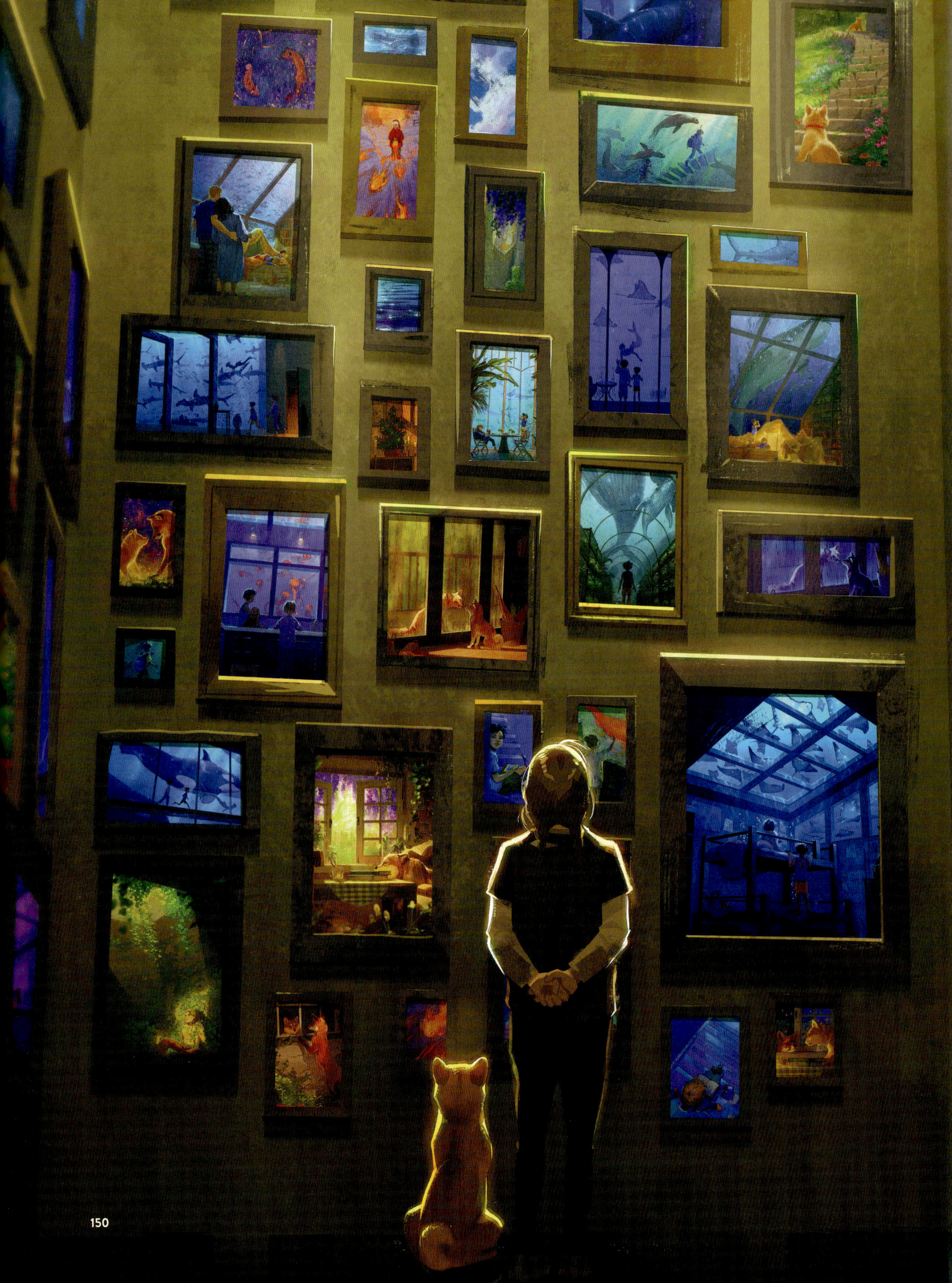

THANK YOU

I couldn't have completed this project without the support and encouragement of my parents, Susan and Steve Kurtz, who were with me every step of the way. Thank you to Chloe for making me laugh every day, and quite literally mailing me food to ensure I don't forget to eat! Thank you to John and Eevee for listening to my every complaint, no matter how incoherent, and supporting me through all the ups and downs. Thanks to Elaine and Xander for helping me sort through the unbelievable amount of art I produced as an embarrassing pre-teen, and for being a miniature focus group for almost everything I paint. A huge thank you to my editor, Sophie, the lead designer, Fiona and the entire team at 3dtotal.

Last but definitely not least, thank you to every single person who has supported me online and off for my entire life as an artist. That support is the only reason you're holding this book right now. There will never be a day in my life that I'm not grateful to each and every one of you! Thank you for allowing me to pursue my dreams and spend my life doing what I love. You've given me the greatest gift imaginable.

Although I still think I am quite young and certain of very little, I'm going to leave you with some parting advice. Be kind to yourself, and care about the people around you. Remember to take care of yourself, not just for the "you" of today but for the "you" of the future as well. Remember that your value as a person has nothing to do with your productivity, the work you do, or the things you make. You are valuable just for being. Remember that creating art is opening a window for the world to see inside your imagination; that alone is a worthy cause for creation.

Devin

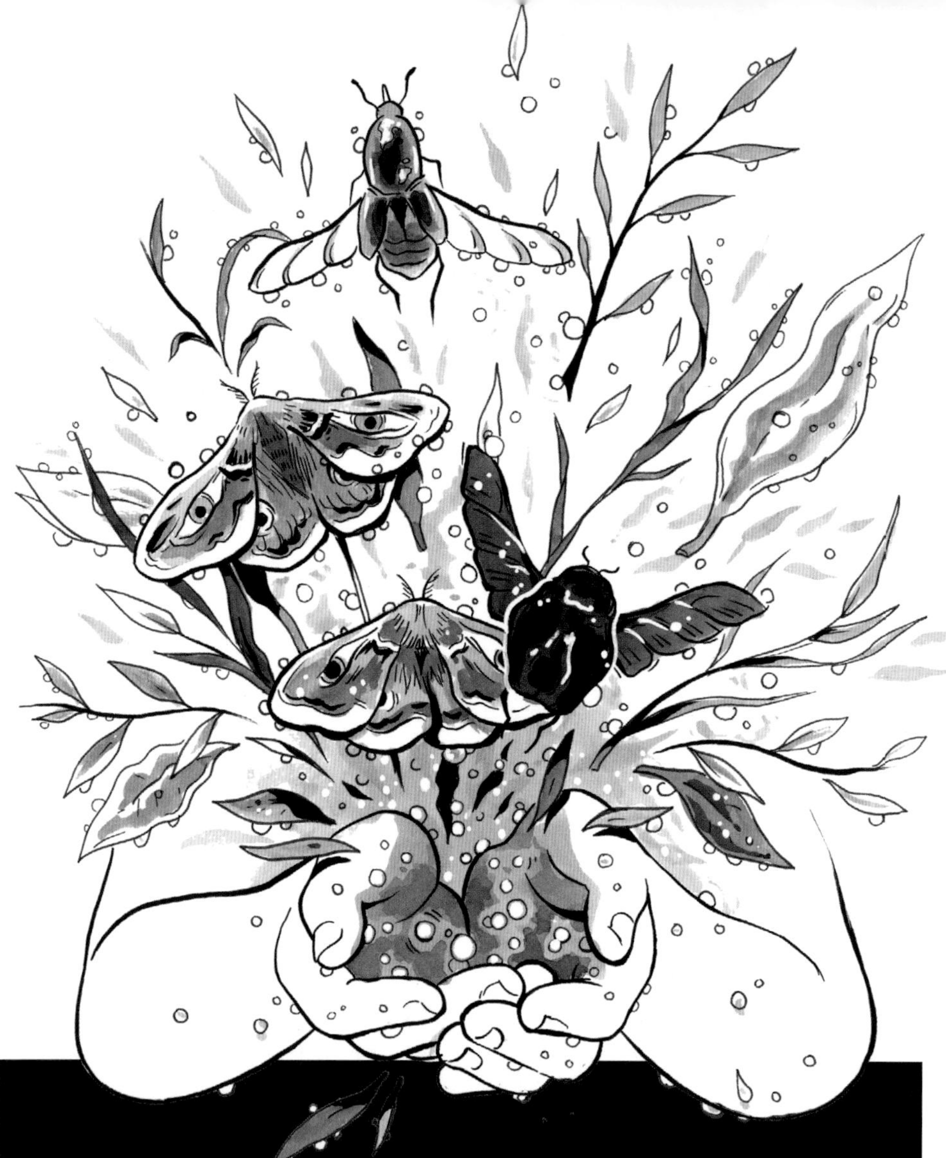

ABOUT 3DTOTAL

3dtotal Publishing is a trailblazing, creative publisher specializing in inspirational and educational resources for artists.

Our titles feature top industry professionals from around the globe who share their experience in skillfully written step-by-step tutorials and fascinating, detailed guides. Illustrated throughout with stunning artwork, these best-selling publications offer creative insight, expert advice, and essential motivation. Fans of digital art will enjoy our comprehensive volumes covering Adobe Photoshop, Procreate, and Blender, as well as our superb titles based around character design, including *Fundamentals of Character Design* and *Creating Characters for the Entertainment Industry*. The dedicated, high-quality blend of instruction and inspiration also extends to traditional art. Titles covering a range of techniques, genres, and abilities allow your creativity to flourish while building essential skills.

Well-established within the industry, we now offer over 100 titles and counting, many of which have been translated into multiple languages around the world. With something for every artist, we are proud to say that our books offer the 3dtotal package:

LEARN | CREATE | SHARE

Visit us at 3dtotalpublishing.com

3dtotal Publishing is part of 3dtotal.com, a leading website for CG artists founded by Tom Greenway in 1999.